Rebuilding
the
ROYAL NAVY

Rebuilding the ROYAL NAVY

WARSHIP DESIGN SINCE 1945

D K BROWN RCNC & GEORGE MOORE
Line Drawings by JOHN ROBERTS

Seaforth
PUBLISHING

Frontispiece
The Batch III Type 42 destroyer *Manchester* in heavy seas off Australia. Since 1945
British warships have established an enviable reputation for their seakeeping. (MoD)

This edition first published in Great Britain in 2012 by
Seaforth Publishing,
Pen & Sword Books Ltd,
47 Church Street,
Barnsley S70 2AS

First published by Chatham Publishing 2003
Reprinted 2012

www.seaforthpublishing.com

British Library Cataloguing in Publication Data
A catalogue record for this book is available from the British Library

ISBN 978 1 84832 150 2

Typeset and designed by Roger Daniels
Printed and bound in China by 1010 International, Limited

Contents

Foreword and Acknowledgements

D K Brown

In some ways, this is the sequel to my series of four books dealing with British warship design from 1800 to the end of the Second World War. It is similar in that it concentrates on naval architecture and marine engineering, with developments in weapons, electronics etc, mentioned only in so far as they affect the design of the ship. For much of the period, this distinction governed design, enshrined in the separation of DG Ships and DG Weapons.

However, this book differs from its predecessors in several important aspects. The 'Thirty Year Rule' means that official documents are not available for the whole period, though much information is given at an earlier stage than in the past. Nor can I pretend to be unbiased, as I was party to many of the decisions made. On the other hand, I can give an insider's view which some later historian may use in less biased form. This is my excuse for intruding my memories into George Moore's chapters! Rather than attempting to impose a uniform style, we have chosen a lead author for each chapter (George Moore for Chapters 1-5, and David Brown for the remainder); but each chapter has been vetted by both authors, who may have inserted their views.

This was a period of great change: in particular, the RN was no longer the biggest and, in some aspects, not even the best navy in the world, but it was a long time before the government, the Navy itself and the general public realised and accepted this fact. Technically, armour and (except in nuclear submarines) steam engines disappeared, and guns lost their predominance. Electronics dominated the topside layout and had a major impact inside. Everyone expected vastly better living conditions. At the same time, many ship classes were severely cost-limited.

Nuclear weapons influenced building policy as well as the design of ships, while submarines turned to nuclear power (it was also considered for surface ships). Considerable space has been devoted to designs that were not built, as often these form the missing link between classes that were put into service, and they are inherently fascinating as so little is known about them.

And now a word from my co-author.

George Moore

The reader may wonder just why a second author is involved in the compilation of this work. The answer lies in the expanse of time and the sheer complexity of the subject in an period lasting more than 50 years.

The chapters for which I take prime responsibility are set in the first two decades covered by the book. The evolution of each warship design is chronicled by the use of original documents to ensure that the history is accurate. However, as a general rule only some 1 per cent of the paper produced by government departments survives in archives, which inevitably means that there are gaps in the detail. Another problem faced is that some records are restricted for far longer than the stipulated 30 years for either security or practical reasons. Some warships do, after all, have very long lives, and policies, particularly in the nuclear area, have sensitive security considerations. It is, however, feasible to compile an outline history of each class from conception to birth, and this has been this author's aim. The political and financial aspects are not neglected.

The first two decades of the post-war era, although not encompassing major hostilities, were some of the most dramatic, technically and economically, in the long history of the Royal Navy. The battleship died, the cruiser and destroyer were effectively merging, the desirable aircraft carrier proved unaffordable, whilst the submarine grew into one of the world's most formidable weapons. It is a fascinating story.

Any views expressed are those of the authors and do not necessarily represent those of the Ministry of Defence.

Acknowledgements

As usual, this book would not be possible without the help of many friends.

First come former colleagues who contributed so much to the design of the ships described in this book and then put their memories on paper: Messrs Alan Bull, Martin Cawte, (Dr) David Chalmers, (Dr) John Coates, Alan Creighton, Keith Foulger, Geoff Fuller, Norman Gundry, Arthur Honnor, Jim Lawrence, Peter Lover, Dennis O'Neill, Doug Pattison, Ken Purvis, Jack Revans, Eric Tupper, (Dr) Peter Usher, Alfred Vosper, Brian Wall, Fred Yearling, all RCNC, also Miss Mcnair, the HTP specialist, and Les Savage. Also Nick Pattison and John Sadden, shipbuilders, and Ian Johnston.

Then the keepers of historical records and librarians: John Shears (*Journal of Naval Engineering*); Ms Jenny Wraight (Admiralty Librarian); the late J David Brown and his successor at Naval Historical Branch, Chris Page; Bob Todd and his staff (National Maritime Museum, Brass Foundry); the Cambridge University Library (Vickers Archive); the Public Record Office; the Chairman of the World Ship Society, Dr Richard Osborne.

The Chief Executive, Royal Institution of Naval Architects is thanked for permission to quote from RINA papers. The Crown Copyright Administrator is also thanked. Some illustrations are © Crown Copyright MoD, reproduced with the permission of Her Majesty's Stationary Office – and individually identified as MoD.

We are particularly grateful to John Roberts, who has not only drawn many illustrations but has also cast an informed and critical eye over the text. Other drawings are by Len Crockford. BAE SYSTEMS, the World Ship Society, Walter Cloots and Mike Lennon are thanked for permission to use their photographs.

Introduction

[1] See works by Eric Grove, Desmond Wettern, Norman Friedman and others listed in the Bibliography.

[2] Hurried programmes led to problems for the overloaded design staff and hence to errors in almost all classes. See, for example, the 'Ham' and 'Ford' classes in Chapter 10.

Economics and Political Commitments

The political and economic background to the Royal Navy over half a century is far too complicated to cover in part of a chapter, let alone when linked to the events of the Cold War.[1] However, many key events greatly affected the size and shape of the Navy and a brief note seems necessary. In 1945 the RN was the second biggest navy in the world with the navy in third place a very long way behind. On the other hand, most of its ships were of pre-war design, obsolescent and worn out from years of wartime steaming.

The first priority was to demobilise the wartime conscripts, whose departure revealed vast gaps in key technical areas, particularly those in the new field of electronic warfare. It proved increasingly difficult to recruit long-service volunteers, whilst conscripts took so long to train that it was doubtful if they were of overall value. Initially the Admiralty hoped for a large fleet, with a distribution very similar to pre-war days. The battleship was still seen as essential, and it was even hoped to complete at least two new ones. A large force of aircraft carriers was also required, but British naval aircraft were inferior and US planes could not be afforded.

The county's economy was in dire straits and there was no money for a big navy. Steel was in short supply, so there was great pressure to scrap as many ships as possible, and

certainly not to build more than a very few new ones, while ships already started were delayed again and again. The civilian labour force was needed to earn foreign exchange and could not be used on warship building.

The Admiralty appears to have thought that these were short-term problems and was slow to recognise economic reality. It was not fully appreciated that the equipment, attitudes and management skills of the UK's industrial base were out of date. On the other hand, Britain was still responsible for the security of large areas of the world, the remains of empire. The potential threat from the Soviet Union became increasingly apparent, whilst minor wars and police actions stretched the Navy to the limit.

In consequence, there was a series of Defence Reviews aimed at reconciling commitments with available funding, which always ended in a smaller navy. Increasingly, the Defence budget was treated as a single entity, leading to bitter inter-service feuding. Sudden increases in the temperature of the Cold War, such as the Korean War, led to additional funding and new building programmes.[2]

Defence Reviews

In the context of this book it is possible only to give a brief outline of the way in which successive Defence Reviews affected the size and shape of the Navy and the design of specific classes. In 1945 the UK economy was in such a parlous state that it was almost impossible to think of new construction for the next five years. The Royal Navy was over-endowed with ships, though many, particularly the bigger ships, were of obsolescent design, and even the more modern escorts were of limited capability against the new, fast submarines. The new cruiser was ultimately abandoned, and the carriers of the late war programmes proceeded slowly, if at all.

The Government and the Admiralty Board gave some priority to research, since its demand from industry was small and the need for counters to the new threats was clear. The most conspicuous outcome was the Sea Slug surface-to-air missile. Less obvious was the work that went into the reduction of underwater noise from machinery, flow and propeller cavitation. This was paralleled by the development of new sonars – very large by the standards of the day – and ASW weapons. The design of prototype frigates to operate these systems proceeded slowly, and took into account the lessons from the Ship Target Trials programme.

The outbreak of war in Korea in 1950 provided the stimulus for rearmament with a modest frigate programme and a very large MCMV programme. However, by the

Creators of the early post-war fleet. Directors of Naval Construction: Sir Stanley Goodall (second left) 1936-44; Sir Charles Lillicrap (second right) 1944-51; Sir Victor Shepheard (left) 1952-58; Director General Ships, Sir Alfred Sims (right) 1958-67. (*D K Brown collection*)

mid-1950s there were further financial problems, which led to the 'Radical Review', and post-Suez problems, which ended the guided missile cruiser programme and caused several frigates to be cancelled. On the other hand, the destroyer programme and that of the Sea Slug came together in the 'County' class. Limited resources were made available to start the nuclear submarine programme.

The next major review came in 1965/66 with the cancellation of the carrier CVA-01, all but one of the Type 82 destroyers, the fifth SSBN, and the Type 19 cheap frigate. The aircraft carrier had been progressed by the Admiralty, in the teeth of Treasury and RAF opposition, and with only lukewarm government support. Any such support died when the Labour Party came to power. Dennis Healey, the new Minister of Defence, rightly pointed out that he would not approve one carrier and that a case had to be made for the three in the long-term plan. This review led to a total rethink of the structure of the RN without the traditional fleet carrier. The 'East of Suez' role was to be abandoned, except for occasional cruises. On the design side a 'Future Fleet Working Party' was set up, which proposed a number of options, most of which led to actual ships.

The new fleet had three 'Through Deck Cruisers' (the *Invincible* class) as its core and, once RAF opposition had been overcome and Sea Harrier VSTOL aircraft were embarked, the fleet had some effective air defence. The Type 42 destroyer was smaller and cheaper than the Type 82 and could be built in some numbers. This was supported by the cheap Type 21 frigate until the more capable Type 22 AS frigate entered service. A considerable number of 'Hunt' class MCMVs were built. All these classes

gave excellent service and were a credit to the Working Party. Further reviews came in 1974 and 1976 because of the effects of raging inflation on the economy. Building programmes were reduced, but the only new design to be cancelled was a commando carrier to replace *Bulwark* and *Hermes*. Little work had been done on the design and the cancellation did not cause the upset of the 1966 cuts.

Defence Minister John Nott's review of 1981 cancelled the Type 44 destroyer with Mark II Sea Dart;[3] it was also intended to scrap the amphibious assault ships *Fearless* and *Intrepid* and to sell the carrier *Invincible* to Australia.[4] However, most of the cuts were cancelled on the outbreak of the Falklands War in 1982 and the Type 23 frigate was enhanced – it was allowed to have a main engine on <u>both</u> shafts! The Trident SSBN programme of four boats was not affected (see later discussion on 'Weapon-Platform Ratio').

The end of the Cold War in the 1990s brought a succession of reviews aimed at reducing defence spending – the so-called 'Peace Dividend'. As a result there were fewer orders for new ships and older ships which still had many years of effective life were sold or scrapped. The most serious loss of capability was the abandonment of the diesel-electric submarine, with the four *Upholder* class leased to Canada and follow-on boats cancelled.

However, at the time of writing (2002) the future seems bright, with the commando carrier *Ocean* in service and the landing ships *Albion* and *Bulwark* nearing completion; other amphibious force ships are in hand. Two new aircraft carriers are being designed to operate the Joint Strike Fighter and six Type 45 destroyers have been ordered. Three *Astute* class attack submarines are in hand.

This aerial view of *Cleopatra* in 1967 shows the lines of the *Leander* class frigate to advantage. The class was designed by Ken Purvis. (*MoD*)

[3] Most of the features of the Mark II Sea Dart were eventually retrofitted in the Mark I.

[4] The main corridor of design headquarters was decorated with ships' badges. The day after the Nott review was published, *Invincible*'s badge had a 'SOLD' label over it.

[5] See Appendix 1.

Other Factors

The atom bomb that brought an end to the Second World War, and the post-war Bikini trials, showed that fundamental changes were needed in the way that the sea war was fought and ships were designed. The later test of a hydrogen bomb brought a sudden end for schemes of shipbuilding after a war had broken out and to the large reserve fleet, as no-one believed that there would be long wars any more.

The NATO alliance recognised that the UK could not meet a major threat alone but needed allies. It introduced the need for inter-operability, and also led to a number of information exchange projects (IEP) in which ideas were traded on aspects of ship design (and other topics), and some joint research and production programmes were started.

Cost, Inflation and Budgets

During the period covered in this book the value of Sterling fell and fell, making comparisons very difficult both of the cost of individual ships and of the total value of the 'Navy Estimates'.[5] For nearly 20 years, 1956 to 1972, the cost of the Type 12 frigates (*Whitby*, *Rothesay* and *Leander*) formed a convenient reference point. The technical content did increase between classes, particularly with the introduction of the *Leander* class, but the cost, corrected to a common value of money (1984 £ in the table, right), was fairly constant.

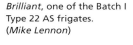

Brilliant, one of the Batch I Type 22 AS frigates. (*Mike Lennon*)

Ship	Date*	Est Cost	Corrected cost**
Whitby	1956	3.1	20.1
Torquay	1956	2.8	18.2
Scarborough	1957	2.75	17.3
Eastbourne	1957	2.8	17.6
Blackpool	1958	3.3	20.1
Yarmouth	1959	3.5	20.7
Rothesay	1959	3.5	20.7
Londonderry	1960	3.6	21.6
Rhyl	1960	3.6	21.6
Type 12s	1961	3.5	20.3
Leander	1962	4.6	25.7
3 *Leander*s	1963	4.6	25.3
4 *Leander*s	1964	4.4	23.8
Arethusa	1965	4.9	25.0
Cleopatra	1965	5.3	27.0
3 *Leander*s	1966	4.7	23.5
3 *Leander*s	1967	5.5	25.4
Andromeda	1968	6.7	27.6
5 *Leander*s	1969	6.1	26.8
Achilles	1970	6.3	26.5
Diomede	1971	6.0	23.4
Apollo	1972	6.6	23.8
Ariadne	1972	6.6	23.8

* Completion date.

** Corrected to 1984 value of the £ (see Appendix 1).

The cost of *Leander* herself probably includes some 'First of Class Costs'.

There was a slow cost reduction in later *Leander*s, probably due to the 'Learning Curve' (see Chapter 10) which may be identified in those ships built at a single shipyard. Yarrows was the only yard which built in sufficient numbers for the learning effect to be recognised, and its effect was reduced because ships were ordered in ones and twos rather than in bulk. The full benefit of the 'Learning Curve' is seen in the Vosper-built 'Hunts' (Chapter 10) where the man-hours required for the last ship were half that of the first.

Pugh has suggested that the real cost of military artefacts rises at about 7 per cent per annum above inflation.[6] This effect is not obvious in the table above but then the technology changed little over the years concerned – confirming the view that the Type 12s were built over far too long a period. They needed large crews and their equipment was ageing, while the naval staff failed to recognise that a true successor would be bigger and more expensive. There was a marked reduction in the cost of the Type 23 frigates (or at least a reduction in the expected increase) which coincided with a much more aggressive approach to competition. Whilst competition played a part, it is probable that the introduction of building very large modules, outfitted under cover, was what made low tenders possible.

Weapon-Platform Ratio

The Nott Defence Review made great play with the so-called 'Weapon-Platform Ratio'. In its crude form, as used by Nott, the cost of weapons was taken as bills paid by DG Weapons (Ensleigh) whilst that of the platform was the amount paid by DG Ships (Foxhill). The diagram, prepared by Peter Chamberlain, then head of forward design, shows the fallacy of this approach. The top bar shows the Nott breakdown (with items not included in either heading).

However, weapon and sensor crews are part of the weapon system and their accommodation, stores, etc are part of the weapon capability. The second bar shows this breakdown, painting a very different picture of a frigate's capability. The third bar goes further and gives a truly functional breakdown of cost, showing that a frigate is a truly cost-effective mobile fighting machine.

The make-up of cost can be shown in various, equally valid, ways. This diagram shows how the money is spent with about 50 per cent of the production cost going to the shipbuilder for labour, materials, overheads and profit.

Navy Estimates

Again due to the changing value of the pound, Defence Estimates and warship building in particular showed massive numerical increases. The reality is that when formed NATO was promised 70 frigates and today the figure is 'about 30'. True, today's ships are far more capable, but numbers do matter. However, the number in active serv-

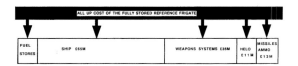

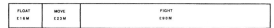

Left: The so-called Weapon/Platform Ratio and functional breakdown of warship costs.

MAKE-UP OF COST

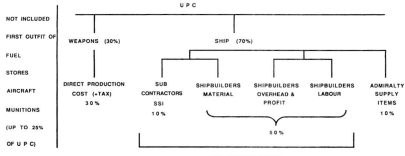

The make-up of cost showing that only about 50 per cent of total cost is attributed to the shipbuilder.

ice has declined to a much smaller extent. This is only partly due to the abolition of the large reserve fleet; improved corrosion protection (see Chapter 13) has meant a great reduction in time spent replacing rusted plates, so a much smaller part of a ship's life is spent in dockyard hands. The introduction of gas turbines, with 'Repair by Replacement', further reduced the time in refit. Personnel numbers shrank from 144,000 in 1949 to 70,000 in 1985, only partly reflecting the much smaller crews needed in automated ships with gas turbine propulsion. It is hard enough to recruit even to this lower level.

The conflict of quality versus quantity is an eternal one, but it has intensified in the years since the Second World War. No longer can designers seek the best, or even justify extra cost on the basis of greatly increased capability, but there is a fixed price and the problem is to get the best within that limit – all you want for £100 million!

Design Approvals Procedure

Warships are the most expensive single artefacts in the Defence Budget and it is essential that the Navy gets a capable ship at a price which the country – the taxpayer – can afford. Unlike almost all other defence equipment there is usually no prototype – 01 has to be operational after trials. Over the period covered in this book, approval procedures became steadily more elaborate, depending more on formal submissions and less on the subjective judgements of a few individuals, however well informed.

[6] P Pugh, *Cost of Seapower* (London 1986).

A traditional representation of the reality of the design process.
(*Redrawn by John Roberts*)

ORDER 24 FIRST OF CLASS REAL PROBLEMS COMMENCE	COSTS 23 ESCALATE OR PROGRAMME SLIPAGE BACK TO 17	FULL 22 DEVELOPMENT (CONTRACT DEFINITION)	MINISTERS 21 APPROVE IF NOT APPROVE RESIGN
PROJECT 17 DEFINITION (SHIP DESIGN)	BOARD 18 APPROVE FINAL DESIGN	ORC 19 AND DEPC APPROVE	CHIEFS 20 OF STAFF APPROVE
DEPC 16 APPROVE NST	ORC 15 APPROVE NSR	NPC 14 OR BOARD NOT SATISFIED	NPC 13 OR BOARD APPROVE GO STRAIGHT TO 15
ORC 9 APPROVE NST	FEASIBILITY 10 STUDY	STUDY 11 DELAYED BY COST DIFFICULTIES OR COLLABORATION	NSR 12 PREPARED
ORC 8 APPROVE NST	NAVAL 7 PROJECT COMMITTEE OR ADMIRALTY BOARD APPROVE	NST 6 PREPARED	DISCUSSIONS 5
IDEA 1 OR NEED	CONCEPT 2 AND OPERATIONAL STUDIES IF NOT REQUIRED GO TO 6	RESEARCH 3 WORK REQUIRED MISS A TURN	DRAFT 4 STAFF TARGET

[7] No longer true.

[8] There was a less formal review when the design study agreed for development was selected. I think this involved Controller and ACNS.

[9] Admiral Sir Lindsay Bryson, 'The Procurement of a Warship', *Trans RINA* (1985), p21. This was a very brave paper, read at the height of the 'Short Fat Frigate' controversy.

[10] Note that UK terminology is used here. In the USA the meanings of Concept and Feasibility are reversed.

These procedures changed frequently, perhaps too frequently, during the period and the titles of the committees involved changed even more frequently. However, the basic problems have not changed very much. The designer's view is well represented by the game of Snakes and Ladders above.

Against a background of the Navy's perceived role and an awareness of the likely extent of funding, ideas will be floated for new ships within the Staff. There will often be an input from technical departments on the introduction

Design Programme. This chart from the mid-1970s outlines the tasks in each phase and who does them.

DESIGN PROGRAMME

Years	Approval	Ship	Weapon	Staff	Other
?		Research General Studies (eg Min manning) Ship Studies Standards	Research Development Bread Board	NRO Policy Sub concept	Private R & D Government Budget Replacement
5	EPC	CONCEPT STUDIES Option, ANV Big/small Role definition Identification Technical definition	PROTOTYPE Test	Outline Requirements Role	
4.5	ORC MPC	CONCEPT DESIGN Style Collaboration Batch II Convert Base line variants Cost/ capability		ST (Sea)	Shipbuilder Input Producibility Sales
3.5	ORD MPC	FEASIBILITY		SR (Sea)	
2.5	Admiralty Board	DESIGN CONTRACT DESIGN Order long lead	PRODUCTION		
0.5	Ministry	Approval to go to tender			
0	Treasury	Approval to order ORDER			

of new technology. Freelance designs were welcome;[7] though rarely adopted *in toto*, they quite frequently provoked a new line of thought – 'Requirements pull, technology pushes' – whilst the obsolescence of the existing fleet will be borne in mind. Politicians will wish to help industry and to provide employment.

Taking the 'Tribal' class frigates as an example of 1950s practice, formal design reviews were infrequent, and even those there were little more than rubber-stamp decisions already made informally. There were two formal reviews:[8] the first at Sketch Design when the ship was basically defined, and the second when the design was ready to go out to tender. For both, the drawings and a statement of particulars would be laid out and approval would be given by the Board of Admiralty in a short minute. Since the Board included ministers, senior administrators (responsible to the Treasury for financial probity) as well as admirals, it was a more representative body than modern readers may imagine, although there were no engineers or scientists.

The informal contacts were frequent and invaluable. The most important was with the Staff (DTSD) – the 'Tribals' had a great advantage in being designed in Whitehall. Staff officers and constructors in Whitehall had offices very close together, and even quite substantial changes could be agreed in a few minutes of friendly conversation. Contact with the main design organisation in Bath was more formal and prone to misunderstanding.

A very detailed review of design procedures was given by Admiral Sir Lindsay Bryson, then Controller, in 1985, taking the Type 23 frigate as an example, and this will be taken as the end-point of this review, though they have changed again since.[9] The requirement for a new design could arise from one or more of the following: a change in concept of operations, a need to replace old ships, a new threat, or the introduction of new technology, together with a window of opportunity for funding! Major weapon systems, and other systems such as communications that could be deployed in more than one class of ship, had a similar but not identical approval system. Note that the weapon system usually had several years' lead over the ship programme.

The staff's ideas resulting from these topics would be melded with the views of technical departments, leading to a series of design studies which might take from two weeks to a year, and might include unconventional craft such as hovercraft, SWATH, etc. These were considered by the Fleet Requirements Committee (FRC), who would decide which, if any, fitted best into the future role of the Navy and the resources available. This guidance permitted the Staff to start work on a formal Staff Target and Ship Department to develop their studies into a Concept Design.[10] Note that weapons had a similar but separate approval system corresponding to the separation of Ship and Weapon Department on opposite sides of Bath.

There was an inherent problem in that the timescale for the development of a new weapon was very different from that of the ship that was to carry it. The diagram (left) shows that ship concept should start when the weapon is still in development, perhaps with a prototype on trial. It is useless to start the ship design earlier, as the weapon is sure to change, whilst if the ship design is left until later, it will go to sea with obsolescent weapons. This problem is exacerbated in collaborative projects and was a major factor in the demise of the NATO frigate programme.

Industry would be consulted at this stage on cost and export prospects, and a few study contracts might be placed on specific systems. The Staff Target and the Concept Design are as the chicken to the egg, and interact to a very considerable extent. During concept design risks and problem areas should be identified but not necessarily solved. Some quite major decisions are taken early, which may pre-empt other aspects. For example, it was decided at an early stage that the proposed Type 43 destroyer should have four SM-1A engines, which made a proposed increase in speed impossible.

The Concept Design and Staff Target then go together through a two-stage approval process. The Naval Projects Committee is a naval committee chaired by the Controller, and they will ensure the Navy is getting what it wants within the constraints of money, manpower, etc. When endorsed, the papers go to the Operational Requirements Committee, a tri-service organisation who will look at the proposals in terms of the national defence policy and resources.[11] At this stage very little effort or cost has been incurred.[12] Hence it is proper to consider some quite unlikely options, as it will be almost impossible to insert a new approach at a later stage. Many studies will be rejected at this point.[13]

The next design stage is Feasibility and this is concurrent with the development of the Staff Requirement. Feasibility takes the approved Concept Design and re-works it in greater detail; for example, weights and the positions of the centres of gravity are calculated in detail rather than scaled from previous designs, permitting a more accurate estimate of stability.[14] Some structural design work may take place and layout will be developed. Overall, the object is reduction of risk; there should be no remaining technical problems and cost estimates should be accurate. Approval of the Staff Requirement and Feasibility design go through the NPC and ORC as before but, as the following design stages involve considerable spending and committal of in house resources, the Defence Equipment

[11] Attempts would be made to schedule major programmes for each service so that peak spending did not occur at the same time. 'Slippage' made this difficult.

[12] At this stage there will only be a single option, perhaps with a few minor points left open. Unusually, the OPV had two options, which led to the 'Castle' class and to the hydrofoil *Speedy*.

[13] Many good engineers hate to see their work discarded whilst others enjoy the exploration of novel schemes.

[14] The author has doubts, see 'Design Methods' below.

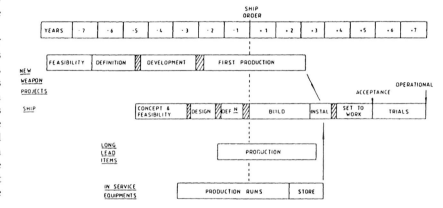

Above: The phasing of design: weapons and ship. The weapons programme must usually start some years ahead of the ship programme.

Left: The procurement cycle around the middle of the 1970s, with approval stages.

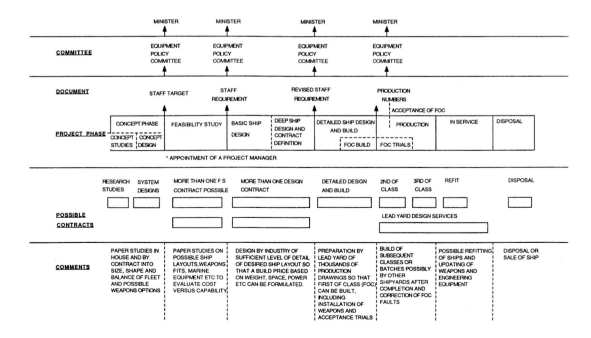

15 The Common Hull Frigate, designed for mass production in wartime, was cancelled very shortly after the explosion of the first hydrogen bomb – a correct decsion, since the bomb rendered a long conventional war highly unlikely.

16 The Treasury tends to have the brightest administrators and submissions need to be written with great care.

17 I am sure this could be overcome but, so far, it has not been.

Policy Committee (DEPC) must also agree. The DEPC is concerned with the overall Defence Budget, its impact on national industry, collaboration and sales prospects. For simple ships, a contract may be placed at this stage. Feasibility design involves a considerable use of design effort and cancellation should be very rare at this stage.[15] Approval to go ahead with the procurement of long-lead items may be given at this point.

Ship design proper can now begin. This may be divided into two phases, with Admiralty approval at the end of the first. When the design is complete, approval of the Minister and then of the Treasury is required before negotiations on a building contract can begin. The Treasury can take an active role supporting or opposing a particular proposal.[16] The lead shipbuilder would probably be selected and they would participate fully in the later stages of design.

The approval procedures are long and complicated, but it is not easy to see how such important decisions that impact so much on the future Navy and on the national budget can be much simplified, particularly with some twenty staff and technical organisations involved. The time taken can be reduced by frequent contact at working level to ensure that the facts are clearly understood. Problems have arisen when junior staff have not ensured that their seniors know what they have agreed to. If the design is being carried out within the ministry – 'in-house' – work can continue during the approval process at each phase. Design by contract will usually come to a halt for many months while collaborative projects are delayed even more.[17]

The Procurement Cycle diagram on the previous page

attempts to show how the technical task interacts with the staff, shipbuilder and minister, whilst the smaller diagram attempts to put a timescale on the process and re-emphasise the interaction with weapon programmes. Though the committee names (and initials) differ, the principles did not change greatly over most of this era – and ship projects were generally close to programme and budget.

Ship and Weapon Design Co-ordination Group

Ship and weapon design approvals took similar but separate routes. The Ship and Weapon Design Co-Ordination Group (SWDCG – pronounced 'Shwepcog'), was a semi-formal grouping, usually chaired by the Director of Warship Design, to ensure that the programmes were consistent in both objective and in timetable. The Group operated through working parties, one for each ship project, usually chaired by the head of preliminary design (Chief Constructor). The preliminary design section was allowed to freelance for a short time, but if they wanted to develop any study, approval of the SWDCG was needed at the next meeting. Concept designs were approved by the SWDCG before being sent to central committees.

The main problem was that one man could represent the 'ship (including machinery and electrics)' but weapon work was so specialised that numerous representatives were needed from both AUWE and ASWE. Though the working parties did not work by voting, it was usual to add one or two extra men from Ship Department to avoid a single representative being overwhelmed by weight of numbers. A design working party is essential to bring

Northumberland, one of the numerous 'Duke' class Type 23 frigates. (*MoD*)

together all departments involved. It needs a strong leader and a clear objective if it is not to break down into factionalism, as enshrined in the engineer's adage:

> *The Irregular Verb 'To Design'*
> I create
> You interfere
> He gets in the way
> We co-operate
> You obstruct
> They conspire

Design Methods

The problem is eternal but the methods used to reach a solution have changed dramatically in the last half-century.[18] The problem is to design a ship capable of fulfilling operational requirements – interpreted as a specified weapon fit and performance – with economy and safety. The translation of an operational requirement into a technical specification is sometimes referred to as the 'Interpretation' phase, and it is essential to get it right.

The first stage, concept studies, involves a series of trade-offs between cost and capability. It is a time for lateral thinking: novel solutions can only be introduced at this stage. Later stages are convergent, eliminating the less attractive options. It will take some 10 years to get the first ship into service so that, with a 20-year life, the designer will have to look ahead at least 30 years – more if the class is built over several years.[19]

The benchmark will almost always be a conventional, propeller-driven displacement ship, but it will sometimes be necessary to consider alternative vehicles such as hovercraft. Such comparisons are difficult: the 'Advanced Naval Vehicle' (ANV) will usually have exceptional performance in one role whilst being inferior in other aspects.[20] Cost, too, is difficult, as the pattern of spending may be very different – the hovercraft MCMV would have been much cheaper to buy than a 'Hunt', but much more expensive to run, and would have required new training facilities.

Comparison of different conventional vessels is straightforward. One foot on the beam hardly affects the cost, so stability need hardly be thought about in most cases, whilst a weight of structure scaled from an existing ship should be sufficient to satisfy strength criteria.[21] Mutually consistent values for Weight, Space and Layout must be found, leading to cost estimates of the right order overall but accurately reflecting the differences between variants. Weight of the hull and its equipment can usually be scaled quite accurately from previous ships. However, a new ship will usually have novel weapons and sensors that may not even exist and are unlikely to be beyond the prototype stage. An intelligent guess is needed for their weight.[22]

'Space' is more difficult as it may refer to volume as in tanks, to area as in mess decks, or length for the upper deck. Upper deck length impinges directly on layout governed

The designer's desk: a mock-up created for the RCNC Centenary exhibition at Greenwich. At bottom left is an integraph (see text) with a pile of foolscap workbooks beside. Further back is a set of ship curves for drawing and a drum slide rule (Fullers) with a scale 84ft long. Centre is an integrator (a baby one – most were more than twice this size). Near the designer's arm is a lead weight used to hold a batten to form a curve; it was said that if you needed more than six weights, the curve had no place in a ship. Behind, a photo shows students at work on the 8ft drawing benches typical of a real design office.
(*D K Brown collection*)

by physical and electronic clearances needed. The superstructure and mast arrangement of the 'Tribals' was constrained by the trajectory of the AS mortar projectile. Upper deck length governed most post-war designs. Most design sections had equations (today they would be called 'mathematical models') based on experience with their class of ship. For frigates there was a complicated formula involving armament weight, crew number, speed, endurance, etc, all leading up to a figure for deep displacement.[23] Speed and power could be reconciled by intuition backed by R E Froude's magical Iso-K books, which codified the hydrodynamic results of 80 years of model testing.[24]

All this was done by hand using only a slide rule and a hand-cranked calculating machine and if the study was of a conventional type, two assistant constructors could produce a reasonable answer in half a day. All calculations had to be recorded in a foolscap workbook, dated and indexed.[25] Figures could not be altered but, if necessary, the old figure could be crossed out and replaced with a new one in red ink. The next stage, originally 'Sketch Design' later 'Feasibility', went over the same ground but in more detail using direct calculation rather

[18] For a more detailed history of older design methods see D K Brown, 'British Warship Design Methods 1860-1905', *Warship International* 1/1995. Methods changed little between 1905 and the computer age.

[19] It was always said that the principal design tool was the Admiralty Pattern Crystal Ball, Mk I, with lucky pin attachment.

[20] The OPV was remarkable in that several very different displacement ships were considered, together with hydrofoils (three types), hovercraft and airships.

[21] Hull weight varies as LxBxD for most ships – $L^{1.3}xBxD$ is slightly more accurate. L^4B/D is often quoted but this applies only to <u>fully stressed</u>, longitudinal material, less than 25 per cent of the total.

[22] My 'guesstimate' for the Type 965 radar aerial on the 'Tribal' was 2½ times the quoted weight, which proved right. Since it was at the top of a tall mast, this was very important.

[23] It was about 50 tons out in 2250 tons for the early studies of the 'Tribals'.

[24] D K Brown, *Warrior to Dreadnought* (London 1997).

[25] Many have been preserved in the National Maritime Museum. They make it clear that obedience to the rules on index, date, corrections etc, were rarely observed.

26 I was never very happy with this approach and believe scaling was actually more accurate than an approximate calculation, which, all too often, omitted something.

27 All drawing work was supposed to be carried out by draughtsmen and they strongly resented graduates (assistant constructors) doing such work. On the other hand, the graduates had the hydrodynamic background needed to shape the form. There was usually a compromise in which the graduates drew for about one day producing a 'guidance sketch' after which draughtsmen did the fairing. The converse came when I was head of preliminary design and passed out a note giving the form parameters I wanted for the 'Castle' class. A few minutes later, the Senior Draughtsman came to see me – none of the draughtsmen had worked on a Sheer Draught since apprenticeship and would I tell them how to start.

28 The work was eased (slightly) by using a special body plan with sections at a special, non-uniform spacing – Tchebycheff spacing – which eliminated one stage of arithmetic.

29 John Roberts, *British Warships of the Second World War* (London 2000), includes reproductions of many such drawings.

than scaling where possible. A general arrangement drawing would be produced based on the form of a selected type ship that might be quite different in size and style. The form of the 'Tribals' was based on heavy cruiser 'Y' of 1944, itself derived from the *Glorious* of the First World War. This general arrangement formed the basis for many weight calculations. A small panel of deck structure would be designed, using the best method available at the time, and the weight per square foot calculated. Measuring the number of square feet on the drawing produced the answer.[26]

The 'elements of form' which make up part of the Iso-K books include the midship section, load waterline and the curve of areas of the type ship in non-dimensional form. The curve of areas shows the area up to the waterline of transverse sections along the length. This still leaves the designer of the new ship plenty of scope to make changes to the form. In particular, the shape of bow sections to improve seakeeping was (and is) a matter of debate. There were real difficulties as the requirement for section shape below the waterplane would often conflict with that for the shape above water. Then began the 'fairing' process in which transverse and horizontal sections (waterplanes) had to be adjusted to obtain a consistent shape. (One or two diagonal sections would often assist this process.) It would take a draughtsman about a working week to get what was wanted.[27] Model testing would usually improve a form derived in this way, reducing power requirements by some 3-5 per cent.

Hydrostatic curves showing to a scale of draught the displacement, height of the centre of buoyancy, height of the metacentre, etc were calculated using lengthy arithmetic methods, converting breadth at each point to area and then to volume. It was usually more simple to measure half breadths from the centreline to one side and multiply the result by two. Forgetting to multiply was a common error and at least one design office had 'x 2' painted in large letters on the end wall. Curves of stability at large angles of heel (righting levers – GZ) were produced using a mechanical integrator, a large triangular device made of brass, running on a rail. It would take about 20 minutes to trace the pointer round each section in turn up to the heeled waterline for each point and some 20-25 points were needed.[28]

Next came the strength calculation, in which the ship was assumed to be floating head on to waves of length, crest to crest, equal to the ship and with a height of $\frac{1}{20}$ length; firstly with wave crests at bow and stern (Sagging) and then with the crest amidships (Hogging). Getting the draughts right in these conditions involved more lengthy and repetitive arithmetic. The distribution of weight along the length was estimated, the ship being divided into some twenty sections for the purpose. A curve of load (Weight minus Buoyancy) would be drawn and then another ingenious machine, the integraph, would be used to calculate shearing force and bending moment. The integraph

was a beautiful device – poetry in motion – with chromium-plated levers moving fast in all directions and pens drawing graphs in coloured ink.

A later structural design approach involved calculating the probability of occurrence of different loads in random seas over the life of the ship. This was hard to apply and undervalued the effect of the largest seas, which imposed the greatest loads. In turn, this was replaced by a return to standard waves of length equal to the length of the ship, but the height used for all classes was 8m. The figure of 8m was justified from many years of wave height recordings, world-wide.

The bending moment, together with a decision on acceptable stresses, enabled structural design to begin. The midship section came first (the only section for sketch design) and usually two more would be drawn and calculated in detail, changing scantlings until stresses and buckling strength were acceptable. These sections enabled a more accurate estimate to be made of the weight of structure and the position of its centre of gravity, both height and longitudinally.

The sketch design (Feasibility) accurately expressed the design intention but the level of detail was insufficient to seek tenders for building. The whole process would begin again. There would be a much more detailed general arrangement with most individual spaces laid out. More accurate weight estimates of machinery and weapon systems should be available, while weighed weights from ships of earlier design but still under construction would be used to improve the estimates of weight for the so-called 'judgement items' such as electric cables and piping systems, which were always difficult. There would be a number of detailed calculations, including propeller design, shaft bracket strength, rudder and pintle strength, masts, etc.

The detailed design stage would end with the production of the building drawings, specification and book of calculations. The building drawings, 6-8ft long, comprised the sheer draught, inboard profile, plans of each deck, a 'sketch of rig' (outline profile showing masts, yards and aerials), and structural sections.[29] The specification was a thick book laying down the size of each item of structure, where it was to go and how it was to be painted. The equipment to go in each compartment was listed and so on. By about 1960 this had been replaced by the 'General Hull Specification' which, with a few exceptions, would apply to all classes. The book of calculations would summarise calculations of weights, stability, strength, etc made by two calculators working independently and checked and signed by the constructor and chief constructor.

All these drawings and documents would then be laid out for formal approval by other departments. They had to sign a special book that they agreed (subject to very minor changes at most). Finally the day came for the Director of Naval Construction to sign the drawings. This was a near-religious rite and was taken very seriously. At this point the Director accepted personal responsibility for the design.

Early Computers

Early computers were hard to program and the programs were difficult to use. In consequence, only very lengthy calculations, used often, went on the machine (work marked as lengthy arithmetic in earlier passages). The input of data was often difficult and as each program was 'stand alone', data input had to be repeated. These problems were exacerbated by staff moves, generally every three years.[30] It was not only 'reactionaries' who wondered over the value of computers at first.

There were exceptions: for the first time it was possible to study complicated flooding incidents causing both heel and trim.[31] The so-called 'finite element analysis' was developed in other areas of work and applied to ship structures. The whole ship would be broken down into a mesh of tiny elements and the reactions one on the other studied. This technique was particularly valuable in identifying and correcting stress concentrations. The preparation and input of data was very lengthy.[32] More recently, the use of finite element analysis has been extended to the flow round the hull.[33]

Computer Aided Ship Design

About 1965, Ian Yuille, a naval architect working in a Science grade post, proposed an integrated suite of design programs – Computer Aided Ship Design (CASD). There was considerable opposition to this proposal, mostly on the basis that it was merely a device to interpolate between existing designs and would discourage innovation. There is some truth in this argument, but it was all too common in the past to stick firmly to old approaches while if one wished to innovate, the CASD system was an invaluable helpmate.

The author and his chief strongly supported the approach but thought that it was wrong to separate the development from Ship Department. The key to the system was that the hull form should be developed within the computer and then its definition could be used by any other sub-routine such as stability. This proved a very difficult problem and the first solution was still very difficult to use. A later method mimicked the action of the draughtsman (B-spline) and was fairly simple to use. It was 1988 before the system called 'Goddess' was ready to go but it worked from the start.[34] It has been updated and remains a world leader, proven by the number of requests to explain its workings at computer meetings. It was a little cumbersome to use in concept studies and a very simple system, CONDES, was devised to run on a desktop machine in some eight weeks' intensive work led by Dennis Pattison and Simon Rusling.[35]

Goddess was not just a quicker way of carrying out the design calculations. It enabled a large number of calculations to be performed that had previously been the subject of informed judgement, like flooding of large extent, buckling of large areas of stiffened plating, and many others. It could also produce detailed drawings, fully lettered.[36]

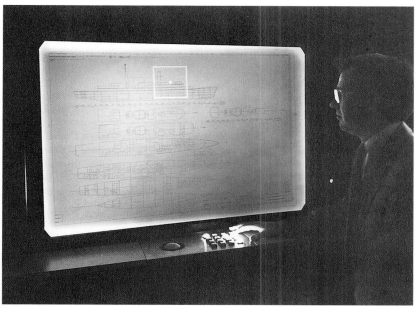

Above: A frigate on the computer screen of GODDESS, the modern design office. The operator is Doug Pattison, now Director of Naval Architecture. (*D K Brown collection*)

Forms to suit. There is no one hull form appropriate to all ships. Each of these is 'right', reading clockwise from right, for minesweeper, frigate, destroyer, fast patrol boat, and landing craft. Note that they are not all to the same scale. (*D K Brown collection*)

Conclusions

A major warship is the most complex manmade artefact and the most expensive item in the Defence Estimates, supported on a turbulent sea rather than on solid foundations. There is normally no prototype – 01 has to operate at the conclusion of trials – and the life from concept may approach 50 years. No wonder that great care is needed to get both the requirement and the design right.

[30] At least three times I completed a course on a particular machine only to be moved before I could apply my skill. Radiation-shielding calculations for nuclear submarines were the first use of computers in ship design (see Chapter 9).

[31] I did such calculations for the 'Tribal' class, but that was a very simple case – even so, it took about three months – and time was available because of delays in the machinery programme.

[32] I still feel that this technique is used too often in simple cases which can be solved by judgement – or even worse, used in place of judgement.

[33] Sometimes referred to as CFD – Computational Fluid Dynamics

[34] Government Defence Design System for Ships. The logo is the head of the Goddess of Wisdom, Minerva.

[35] This system illustrated the problem associated with the meaning of 'Space', which it read as Volume. In consequence, if there was a lack of space, it would increase depth to get more volume when it was deck length or area which was needed.

[36] One young man having shown that a set of deck plans and profile for a frigate could be produced in 20 minutes said: 'And what's the use? Whitehall will still take 20 years to make up its mind.'

1 The Wartime Legacy

[1] ADM 167/121: 1944 Admiralty Board Minutes and Memoranda (PRO).

Bow view of *Eagle* at speed on 2 May 1954. Note axial deck and eight Westland Whirlwind helicopters. (*D K Brown collection*)

THE END OF THE Second World War saw the Royal Navy at the zenith of its strength in material terms. The only superior power was the United States of America, which was now the undisputed leading military and economic power in the world. The fleets of the Axis Powers and those of France and the USSR were devastated, so there was now no major foe which the Royal Navy would have to counter.

The end of the war in the summer of 1945 came rather more rapidly than expected, but the first steps towards planning for peace began in the summer of 1944, following the invasion of France, when it was anticipated that the Japanese war would be won by the end of December 1946. The object was to move the shipyards back to a normal peacetime footing and to this end it was decided that only warships which could be completed by the end of 1946 should proceed, with the exception of some vessels where construction would continue in order to clear the slipways.[1]

The warship building programme was in a somewhat chaotic state when the war ended. Plans had been badly dislocated by the needs of the invasion fleet and the tank landing ship programme began for the Pacific campaign. Repairs to both warships and merchant ships, as well as delays in the delivery of equipment, were also constraints on efficient warship production. As a result the construction of the fleet carriers ordered under the 1940 (*Ark Royal*), 1942 (*Eagle* and *Audacious*) and 1943 Programmes

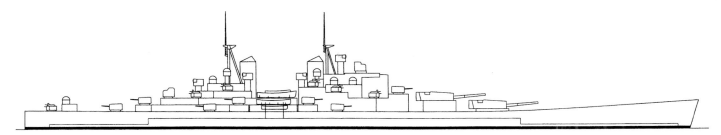

(*Gibraltar, Malta, New Zealand* and *Africa*) had either not started or was severely delayed by shortages of labour and steel. The situation was compounded by late design changes in the 1943 ships. The eight light fleet carriers of the *Hermes* class also suffered and, through the intervention of the First Lord of the Admiralty, A V Alexander, only four were allowed to proceed, although all of them had been formally sanctioned by the War Cabinet.

The cruiser situation, where the programme had been curtailed in 1942 by the orders for sixteen light fleet carriers of the *Colossus* class which lead to the immediate cancellation of four cruisers and work slowing on a further four, was no better. Other priorities, such as the construction of the battleship *Vanguard*, also took their toll. The result was that *Blake* (1942), *Defence* (1941 Supplementary) *Tiger* ex-*Bellerophon* (1941 Supplementary) and *Hawke* (1942) were well behind schedule and far from completion when the war ended. The 1944 Programme included five ships of the *Neptune* class which were also the subject of considerable design and policy changes. From being small cruisers (Design N2) of some 8650 tons mounting eight 5.25in guns of a new design they gravitated to expensive vessels (Design Y) of 15,560 tons mounting twelve 6in guns in triple turrets, again of a new design. The smaller cruiser design was thrown out in January 1944 at the instigation of the new First Sea Lord, Admiral of the Fleet Sir Andrew Cunningham. A sixth ship was added to the programme when it was decided that the original *Tiger* should be built to the new design. No work had been done or material ordered for these ships when the war ended, although the original *Tiger* (now renamed *Bellerophon*), remained formally on order from Vickers Armstrong's Tyne yard. Destroyer construction was also in some disarray with 'C' (1942), 'Battle' (1942 and 1943) and 'Weapon' (1943) class destroyers all well behind schedule. One cause was delays in the delivery of 'K' director towers for the 'Ca' class destroyers and Mark VI directors for the later 'C' and 1942 'Battle' class destroyers. In addition, the 1944 Programme authorised the construction of twenty-two *Daring* class and eight *Gallant* class destroyers. Submarine construction had shifted from the production of the pre-war designed 'S', 'T' and 'U' classes to the new 'A' class design in 1943, which required less man hours to build than the earlier designs. The end of the war saw the conclusion of the earlier programmes with the completion of the last stragglers of the 'S' and 'T' classes.[2]

The 1945 Programme approved by the Board of Admiralty included the reinstated battleships *Lion* and *Temeraire*, where new designs were being considered, as well as four escort vessels of a new design and one experimental submarine. The war was to end before these aims were formally placed before the Cabinet.[3] The cessation of hostilities inevitably resulted in an substantial curtailment of the planned new construction programme. Some deletions had, however, occurred in 1944, when three 'Weapon' class destroyers were cancelled. Twenty 'A' class submarines ordered under the 1943 Programme and a further twenty members of the class planned under the 1944 Programme but not yet ordered were also abandoned. Three of the latter group were reinstated for a few months under plans to build them as units of an improved 'A' class. The autumn of 1945 saw the cancellation of the fleet aircraft carriers *Gibraltar* and *Africa* and four of the 1943 light fleet carriers. However, no work had been done on any of these ships and, although construction was approved by the Cabinet, their existence as firm projects was purely notional. The cruiser *Hawke* also went, perhaps surprisingly, for although she was still on the slip in Portsmouth Dockyard, her boilers and machinery were complete whilst her 6in gun armament was nearly so. The destroyer programme saw the demise of sixteen 'Battle' class destroyers, eight of which had been launched. Eight 'Weapon' class destroyers also went, together with twelve more submarines of the 'A' class. The planned battleships *Lion* and *Temeraire* also died at this point although, incredibly, development of the 16in Mark IV gun intended for the ships continued – albeit slowly – until 1948.

The final tranche of cancellations in December 1945 cut into the planned post-war new construction programme. The aircraft carriers *Malta* and *New Zealand* were abandoned; here preparatory work, largely paid for by the Admiralty, had been completed at John Brown so that work on *Malta* could get underway. The aircraft carrier *Eagle*, which was said to be 26 per cent complete at Vickers Armstrong's Tyne yard, also had to go: another cancellation where work had been done and material manufactured. Some 3000 tons of armour plate intended for the ship cluttered up the yard for a while after her demise. Eight *Daring* class and the eight *Gallant* class destroyers were also cancelled with some work being underway on both. Four 'Weapon' class destroyers, close to being launched, were also abandoned. The 1945 New Construction Programme was reduced further with two escort

Lion and *Temeraire* (1945 Design). Conjectural drawing of 1945 Battleship design which was included in the original 1945 Programme. Although the names are the same there was little relationship with the *Lion* class of 1938. (*Drawing by John Roberts*)

[2] G L Moore, *Building for Victory: The Warship Programmes of the Royal Navy 1939 – 1945* (World Ship Society 2003). Although construction of *Hawke* at Portsmouth Dockyard had been severely delayed, work continued on other equipment. Her boilers and machinery were complete and the nine 6in Mark XXIV mountings were nearly ready. The earlier 'Z' class were also fitted with 'K' director towers.

[3] CAB 66/67: New Construction Programme 1945 dated 29 June 1945 (CP (45) 54). Although this paper was prepared for presentation to the Cabinet it was never formally considered (PRO).

[4] ADM 1/19096: 1945 Trial Programme Cancellations (PRO). Sections of *Malta* were completed and used for underwater explosive trials (see Ian Johnston, *Ships for a Nation – John Brown and Company, Clydebank* (Dumbarton 2000).

[5] CAB 129/4: New Construction (Revised) Programme dated 22 November 1945 (CP(45)291) and CAB 128/ 2: Cabinet Minutes dated 27 November 1945 (PRO). An admirable source outlining British naval policy since the Second World War is Eric Grove, *Vanguard to Trident* (London 1987)

vessels deleted, the remaining major ships being only two escort vessels and one experimental submarine.[4]

The six cruisers of the *Neptune* class remained in the long-term programme at this point and indeed the First Lord of the Admiralty, A V Alexander, had hoped to make a start on two of them immediately when the 1945 Programme was finally presented to the Cabinet. However, the Cabinet effectively deferred the matter and then the design was changed yet again early in 1946 when the *Minotaur* class with ten 6in guns in twin mountings was substituted. By 1947 the economic situation was so bleak that these ships died, although their armament was to live on. Destined to be completed for the post-war fleet of the 1950s, 1960s and 1970s were the two fleet aircraft carriers *Eagle* (ex-*Audacious*) and *Ark Royal*, the light fleet carriers *Centaur*, *Albion*, *Bulwark* and *Hermes*, the cruisers *Blake*, *Defence* and *Tiger* and the eight *Daring* class destroyers. The two escort vessels surviving from the 1945 Programme ultimately appeared as the aircraft direction frigate *Salisbury* and the anti-aircraft frigate *Leopard*, whilst the submarine evolved into *Explorer*. Also launched but incomplete at the close of 1945 were the last six units of the *Colossus* class, which at this stage had been modified to incorporate new messing arrangements and were now known as the *Majestic* class. Their future was uncertain and four of the class came very close to being abandoned in the 1945 economies. The contracts for three of them, *Hercules*, *Leviathan* and *Powerful*, were ultimately cancelled in the spring of 1946. The ships were not scrapped but laid up effectively in the care of the Reserve Fleet organisation or the shipbuilder. None was to see service in the Royal Navy.[5]

Gallant. The clear relationship with the 'Weapon' class can be seen. The class was cancelled at the end of the war but the design formed the basis of the austere design 'A1' which was considered in the early post-war years.
(Drawing by Len Crockford from an original in NMM ADM 138/711)

Fleet Aircraft Carriers *Ark Royal* and *Eagle*

The origins of these ships go back to 1940 when *Irresistible* was authorised as a unit of the *Implacable* class. Nothing was done about building her, initially due to the war situation. The 1942 Programme provided for a new aircraft carrier design and after the loss of the *Ark Royal* it was decided that *Irresistible* (by then renamed *Ark Royal*) should be built as a unit of the new class. Principal changes from

Right: Ark Royal, an overhead view on 26 August 1955. Note interim angled deck, which has caused little impact on the structure of the ship.
(D K Brown collection)

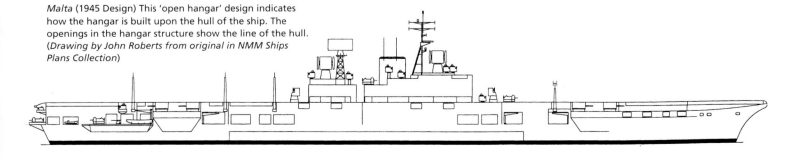

Malta (1945 Design) This 'open hangar' design indicates how the hangar is built upon the hull of the ship. The openings in the hangar structure show the line of the hull.
(Drawing by John Roberts from original in NMM Ships Plans Collection)

Eagle, an overhead view early in her career, illustrating the formidable anti-aircraft armament. (*D K Brown collection*)

the *Implacable* design were improved underwater protection, the disposition of machinery spaces so that total loss of motive power by enemy action was unlikely, more electric generating machinery, thicker flight deck armour and larger lifts. The height of each hangar was 14ft 6in. Displacement, when the design was originally approved by the Board of Admiralty in July 1942, was 31,600 tons (standard). By November 1942 it was clear that the new carriers would have to operate American aircraft, which meant increasing the hangar height to 17ft 6in. With deck armour being kept at 4in thickness it meant that the beam of the vessel had to be increased by 4ft in order to retain stability. The standard displacement now grew to 32,600 tons. The next major change was to enhance lifts, arrester gear and catapults so that aircraft weighing 30,000lbs could be operated. Many other piecemeal changes were made as war experience was incorporated in the ships, with the result that by 1946 the standard displacement had increased to 36,800 tons. This was a substantial development from the 1942 project but inevitably a better result would have been achieved had it been feasible to incorporate all the new requirements in a revised design. One example of a short-

Below: Ark Royal on 3 January 1957. Aircraft visible are Sea Hawks and Sea Venoms. (*D K Brown collection*)

[6] D K Brown, *The Design and Construction of British Warships 1939 – 1945. Volume One – Major Surface Warships* (London 1995), contains the design history of the class up to the point when *Eagle* was completed in March 1952. See also D K Brown, *Nelson to Vanguard* (London 2000). The adoption of jet propulsion later resulted in more fuel being carried in the same space; lower levels of fire precaution being needed.

[7] ADM 1/28639: 1963 Aircraft Carrier Programme: Date of placing order for replacement of HMS *Ark Royal* (PRO).

[8] ADM 229/29: Department of the Director of Naval Construction (Unregistered Papers March to May 1943); also ADM 205/32: First Sea Lords Records (PRO).

coming was that far less aviation fuel could be carried than was now needed to operate the new aircraft designs coming forward effectively and in sufficient numbers. However, with work underway in the shipyards and most of the design work completed, it was just not practical to scrap all that had been achieved: the in-service date of the ships would have slipped dramatically. The *Eagle* (ex-*Audacious*) was built to the revised design and was finally completed in 1952. Her sister-ship *Ark Royal* lingered in the shipyard until 1955. Her design embodied four further major changes: a deck-edge lift, steam catapults, a repositioned forward lift and an angled flight deck. The result of these additions and other improvements was that displacement increased to 43,060 tons (standard), a far cry from the 31,600 tons anticipated in 1942. The two ships were now the main elements of the aircraft carrier fleet, but the speed of technological change was such that even better ships were wanted in order to retain effectiveness, which meant that modernisation had to be contemplated.[6]

The weakness of *Ark Royal* in particular was highlighted in 1963 when the ship had only been in service for some eight years. She had been laid down in 1942 and much of her equipment dated back to this era. The result was inevitable deterioration due to age as well as usage, which affected reliability. Furthermore, the old DC electrical system in the ship produced inadequate power to meet the demands of new and more capable equipment. Habitability was also regarded as poor whilst the design of the flight deck restricted operations. The ship was then not expected to remain in the fleet beyond 1972 unless very heavy expenditure was incurred, an option which was not felt to be desirable by the Director of Naval Construction.[7]

Centaur, Albion and Bulwark

These ships, *Hermes* class light fleet carriers, were originally part of a group of eight ships to be built under the 1943 New Construction Programme. Initially the ships were expected to be members of the *Colossus* class but the design was modified following a report produced at the end of December 1942 by the Joint Technical Committee on Aviation. Significant new requirements were for the maximum allowable weight for carrier-borne aircraft to be increased from 20,000lbs to 30,000lbs and for the hangar height to be increased to 17ft 6in. The design also called for an increase in maximum speed from 25kts to 30kts. The penalties for this enhancement in the new light fleet carrier specification were that the standard displacement increased from some 14,000 tons to 18,300 tons, with the building time increasing from a scheduled 1¾ years in the case of the *Colossus* class to 2½ years for the new class. Four of the class, although not formally cancelled at the end of the war, were effectively abandoned in June 1943 and it was not until early 1944 that approval was given for the first four ships to proceed. They were laid down during the year but with priorities assigned elsewhere progress was inevitably slow.[8]

Above: Albion as a commando carrier exercising with RFA *Tidereach* in September 1962. (*D K Brown collection*)

Right: Bulwark as a commando carrier with Wessex and Sea King helicopters in April 1979. (*D K Brown collection*)

Construction of all four ships continued slowly after the war, basically to clear the slips, for after the first three members of the class were launched in 1947 and 1948 they were laid up with little or no work being done. The fourth ship, *Hermes*, languished on her slip until 1953 when she was eventually launched. The design, although modified at the end of the war when it was decided not to carry four 4.5in twin mountings, was clearly dated by the end of the decade. The speed and size of newly planned jet aircraft was far in excess of expectations when the class was conceived. *Centaur*, the first to complete in 1953, benefited from an interim angled flight deck, which did not involve any structural modifications. *Albion* soon followed, with *Bulwark* completing in 1954. The design was now obsolete, so it was decided to complete the *Hermes* to what was effectively a new design, which involved reconstructing the ship. Her evolution will be covered in Chapter 3. *Centaur* served with the fleet with few modifications until 1966 after which she remained in reserve until scrapped in 1971. Her short operational life reflected her obsolescence. *Albion* and *Bulwark* were both altered to enable them to operate as commando carriers between 1959 and 1961, which resulted in the loss of their ability to operate fixed-wing aircraft. Alterations were, however, far from elaborate and their appearance was little changed from their days as light fleet carriers. Their manpower demands must have made them quite expensive to operate. *Albion* only survived until 1972 when she was discarded as an economy measure, but *Bulwark* was in commission in 1980 and she was finally scrapped in 1984 after a life of 30 years.[9]

Majestic class light fleet carriers

This class consisted of the last six ships of the *Colossus* class. Initially the only difference between the two classes was the incorporation of central messing arrangements. Work on *Hercules, Leviathan* and *Powerful* was stopped on 10 April 1946 with contracts cancelled, but this did not mean that plans for the modernisation of the class ceased, for work was still continuing on *Magnificent, Majestic* and *Terrible*. The major items involved were a stiffening of the flight deck so that aircraft on landing could weigh 20,000lbs compared with 15,500lbs specified for the *Colossus* class; the accelerator was also to be improved and more up-to-date radars and armament fitted, whilst 180 kW generators were to be replaced with 400 kW ones. The island spaces were also to be rearranged. *Magnificent*, lent to Canada, and *Terrible* which had been renamed *Sydney* on transfer to Australia, were both completed to the new specification in 1948.[10]

A more comprehensive plan to modernise the class was approved by the Board of Admiralty in October 1949. The aircraft lifts were improved so aircraft weighing 24,000lbs at take-off could be operated. Dimensions of the aircraft lifts were also increased from 45ft x 34ft as fitted in *Colossus* and *Sydney* to 54ft x 34ft. The arrester gear was

strengthened so that it could accept a 20,000lb aircraft landing at 87kts. The *Colossus* and *Sydney* both carried 80,000 gallons of aviation fuel, increased to 130,000 gallons in *Majestic*. By 1951 the ships' aviation fuel storage had been further expanded to 146,000 gallons, almost double that in the wartime design. Generating capacity showed a steady increase, being 1580 kW in *Colossus*, 1800 kW in *Sydney* and 2200 kW in *Majestic*. There were also improvements to the armament and radar and many other modifications of a more modest nature. Initially the only ship proceeding with the revised design was *Majestic*, which by now was scheduled for transfer to Australia. Before completion in 1955, *Majestic*, which was renamed *Melbourne*, incorporated further improvements, being fitted with a steam catapult and an angled flight deck.[11]

The three laid-up ships were not wanted by the Royal Navy unless an emergency arose, in which case they could be considered for completion as escort carriers. *Powerful* and *Hercules* were ultimately sold to Canada and India, both being completed essentially to the *Majestic* design but with the Canadian ship (now renamed *Bonaventure*) able to accept aircraft with a landing weight of 23,000lbs. The Indian ship, which was renamed *Vikrant*, was virtually indistinguishable from *Majestic*. The only member of the class not to see service was *Leviathan*, which was laid up at Portsmouth Dockyard for some 20 years. Her boilers and turbines were ultimately used in the Dutch *Colossus* class carrier *Karel Doorman*.

The modernisation of the *Colossus* class was also considered, and in 1951 Draft Staff Requirements were produced which sought improvements generally on the lines of *Majestic*. The only ship to be improved was *Warrior* where a limited modernisation was completed.[12]

Melbourne in 1959 flying off Gannet ASW aircraft. She is accompanied by the Australian-built *Daring* class destroyers *Voyager* (to starboard) and *Vendetta*. (RAN, by courtesy of Ross Gillett)

[9] *Conway's All the Worlds Fighting Ships 1947-1995* (London 1995), p496.

[10] ADM 138/744: *Majestic* class (NMM).

[11] ADM 167/133: 1949 Admiralty Board Memoranda (PRO); and ADM 138/772: *Majestic* class (NMM).

[12] ADM 138/811: *Colossus* Modernisation (NMM).

The 'Weapon' class destroyer *Scorpion* refuelling from the carrier *Eagle* during a NATO exercise in September 1953. (*D K Brown collection*)

'Weapon' class destroyers

This class was designed in late 1942/early 1943 as a successor to the 'Q' – 'Z' and 'C' group of intermediate destroyers. New features were three twin 4in Mark XIX mountings in place of four single 4.5in ('Z' and 'C' flotillas) or four 4.7in ('Q' – 'W' flotillas) and a staggered machinery layout with boiler pressure and temperature raised to 400lbs/750° against 300lbs/650° in the earlier classes.

In March 1946 the design of the four survivors was modified. One 4in mounting was given up and replaced with a double Squid anti-submarine mortar (20 salvoes). The class, now described as anti-submarine escort vessels, were completed in 1947-8. They gave valuable experience which assisted in the design of the limited and full destroyer conversions to anti-submarine frigates.[13]

Daring class destroyers

These were the last major warship design to be approved by the Board of Admiralty during the Second World War to enter service. They proved to be a bridge between the war-built destroyers and the first post-war frigates, which were similar in size. In order to save weight and increase strength, construction was all welded and substantial sections were prefabricated in the shipyards before being assembled on the slipways. Aluminium alloys were used in parts of the structure, an option not available during the war because of the scarcity of the metal resulting from the demands of the aircraft industry. Braided cables were used instead of lead-based cable, whilst in four ships an AC electrical system was installed which was to become standard practice in later years. The machinery was designed to operate at a higher pressure, 600psi compared with 400psi in the 'Battle' class destroyers, which brought practice nearer to the standards accepted in the United States Navy a decade earlier. All these developments were to lead to savings in weight and improvements in the performance of the ships. The class was also the first to mount the twin 4.5in Mark VI gun in operational service. This gun was specified for the Type 12 series of frigates where construction continued until the early 1970s for the Royal Navy and it had an operational life of some 40 years.[14] The *Daring* class, the last true destroyers, were considered successful but no significant modernisation was undertaken largely due to budget constraints.

[13] G L Moore, 'The *Weapon* and *Gallant* class Destroyers', *Warship 2000 – 2001*.

[14] ADM 167/24: 1945 Admiralty Board Minutes and Memoranda (PRO); machinery particulars are recorded in NCD 31 (NMM).

2 The Demise of the Cruiser

[1] The legend of the 1944 5.25in cruiser is in ADM 167/118: 1943 Board Admiralty Board Minutes and Memoranda (PRO). See also G L Moore, 'The Royal Navy's 1944 Cruiser', *Warship 1996*.

[2] The minutes of the Sea Lords meeting on 2 February 1944 which instigated the new 6in cruiser design and details of Design 'Y' are held in ADM 205/40: First Sea Lord's Papers (PRO). The cancellation of the *Neptune* design is recorded in ADM 205/64: First Sea Lord's Papers (PRO). Details of the revised *Neptune* design are recorded in a memorandum by the Director of Naval Construction, C S Lillicrap, dated 11 April 1946 held in ADM 167/127: 1946 Admiralty Board Minutes and Memoranda (PRO).

AT THE END OF THE WAR, four *Tiger* class cruisers remained under construction. One, the *Hawke*, was cancelled whilst the remaining three were in the end reconstructed and completed to a new design which will be discussed later. The 1944 New Construction Programme authorised the building of five cruisers of a new design, increasing to six when it was decided that one ship already ordered from Vickers Armstrong's Tyne yard should also be built to the new design rather than proceed as a unit of the now outdated *Tiger* class.

The 1944 cruiser had a long history and initially in the summer of 1943 the Board of Admiralty approved a design (N2) displacing 8650 tons standard with a main armament of four twin 5.25in mountings of a new design then in the very early stages of development. One significant feature was the acceptance of a speed of 28kts in deep condition, which meant less space was required for boilers and machinery, which in turn reduced vulnerability. Considerable debate over many months had resulted in this compromise, which produced an affordable and potentially effective cruiser.[1] The 5.25in design remained in the proposed 1944 Programme until early February 1944 when the new First Sea Lord, Admiral of the Fleet Sir Andrew Cunningham, expressed his opposition to the construction of these new cruisers, wanting nothing less than a 6in design. Unfortunately no modern 6in mounting existed and it was estimated that it would take 4 years to produce one. There was clearly considerable resistance to the new proposals. However, he got his way and it was decided that a new cruiser would be developed with low-angle 6in guns and an adequate number of 4.5in HA/LA guns. By November 1944 the new cruiser design (Y) had evolved into a very large ship mounting twelve 6in guns in triple turrets with 80° elevation and not the low-angle mountings as originally suggested. Twelve 4.5in in twin mountings were also carried. Speed in deep condition was 32kts. This dramatically enhanced ship now displaced

15,560 tons and clearly the design was a very expensive alternative to the original 5.25in cruiser. Nevertheless the proposal was pressed forward and what was now a long-term project survived the initial post-war cancellations. By June 1946 improvements were being considered to provide increased amenities. A flush deck was incorporated, which would have taken the standard displacement to 16,410 tons. The Board of Admiralty, however, decided that the design – now known as the *Neptune* class – was out of date and larger than needed, the result being the cancellation of the project but not the cruiser requirement.[2] Names approved by the King were *Neptune*, *Bellerophon*, *Centurion*, *Edgar*, *Mars* and *Minotaur*.

The *Minotaur* Class

The escalation in the size of *Neptune* and the resultant cancellation lead to a new design being developed. The inspiration was the US cruiser *Worcester* (CL-144) which towards the end of the Second World War was seen as an attractive proposition by many RN officers. She mounted twelve 6in HA/LA capable of rapid fire (10 rounds a minute of heavy 130lb shell from each gun) in six turrets and a secondary armament of twenty-four 3in/50 cal on a standard displacement of 15,210 tons. With engines developing 132,000shp at 10 per cent overload a speed of 32.5kts could be achieved.

Four new Sketch Designs (A – D) were produced. In Sketch 'A' the main armament comprised ten 6in in twin HA/LA turrets, the secondary armament being sixteen 3in/70 cal in twin mountings. Both the 6in and 3in mountings were new designs where development was at an early stage. One significant change was the elimination of any close-range armament, the new twin 3in covering both the medium and close-range requirements for anti-aircraft fire. Compared with *Neptune* the length had been reduced by 10ft and the beam by 1ft. The new design had

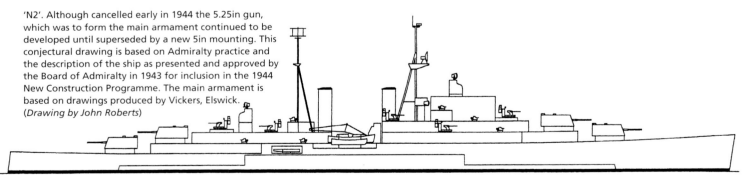

'N2'. Although cancelled early in 1944 the 5.25in gun, which was to form the main armament continued to be developed until superseded by a new 5in mounting. This conjectural drawing is based on Admiralty practice and the description of the ship as presented and approved by the Board of Admiralty in 1943 for inclusion in the 1944 New Construction Programme. The main armament is based on drawings produced by Vickers, Elswick. (*Drawing by John Roberts*)

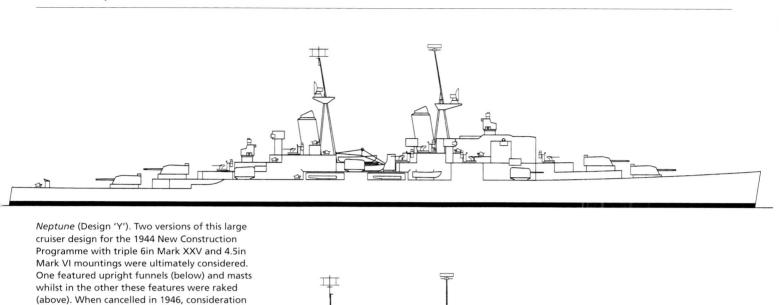

Neptune (Design 'Y'). Two versions of this large cruiser design for the 1944 New Construction Programme with triple 6in Mark XXV and 4.5in Mark VI mountings were ultimately considered. One featured upright funnels (below) and masts whilst in the other these features were raked (above). When cancelled in 1946, consideration was being given to extending the forecastle to the stern as seen in the *Minotaur* design. (*Drawing by John Roberts from original in PRO ADM 1/17285 and NMM ADM 138/729*)

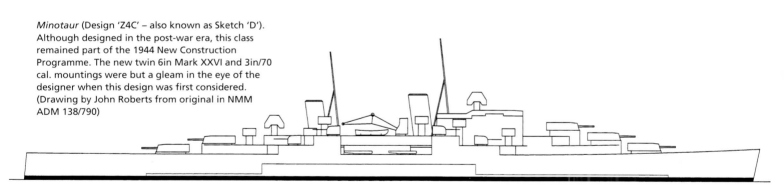

Minotaur (Design 'Z4C' – also known as Sketch 'D'). Although designed in the post-war era, this class remained part of the 1944 New Construction Programme. The new twin 6in Mark XXVI and 3in/70 cal. mountings were but a gleam in the eye of the designer when this design was first considered. (*Drawing by John Roberts from original in NMM ADM 138/790*)

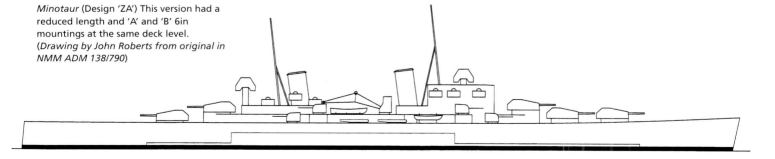

Minotaur (Design 'ZA') This version had a reduced length and 'A' and 'B' 6in mountings at the same deck level. (*Drawing by John Roberts from original in NMM ADM 138/790*)

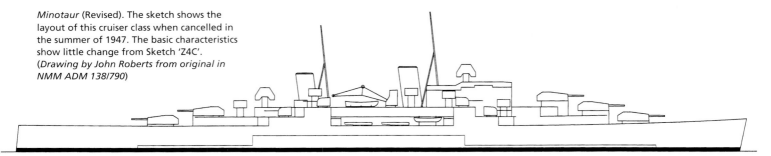

Minotaur (Revised). The sketch shows the layout of this cruiser class when cancelled in the summer of 1947. The basic characteristics show little change from Sketch 'Z4C'. (*Drawing by John Roberts from original in NMM ADM 138/790*)

a flush deck, which resulted in a saving of only 40 tons over Design 'Y' but nearly 585 tons against the ultimate flush-forecastle *Neptune* design. Only 30 tons was expected to be saved in the armament weight but 300 tons was gained in the weight of the machinery, which produced 100,000shp to achieve 31.5kts, when compared with the ultimate *Neptune* design. Displacement was 15,070 tons, a saving of only 490 tons over design 'Y'.

Sketch 'B' was a four-turret design which displaced 14,088 tons (standard), 25ft shorter than the *Neptune* design. Other arrangements, including machinery, speed and secondary armament, were the same as those in Sketch 'A'. Sketch 'C' was a revised version of Sketch 'A' with a new engine-room layout consisting of four combined boiler-rooms and engine-rooms. Sketch 'A' had a boiler-room/engine-room/boiler-room/engine-room layout which followed the *Neptune* design. One effect was to shorten the length of Sketch 'C'. Sketch 'D' had the same armament and engine-room layout as Sketch 'C' but length was restored to that in Sketch 'A'. The Sea Lords decided that Sketch 'D' should be developed.[3]

There must have been some doubts about the size of the new *Minotaur* design, which at 15,280 tons standard offered only a small saving in displacement and no doubt also in cost over the *Neptune* design. Early in 1947 two revised designs, 'ZA' (13,870 tons standard, 16,760 tons deep) and 'ZB' (14,300 tons standard) were considered which although carrying the same armament were 616ft long at the waterline as against 645ft length in design 'D' (Z4C). The main saving was 770 tons in the weight of the hull in 'ZA'. Design 'ZB' had a beam of 74ft as against 73ft in Design 'ZA'. The machinery arrangements were as specified for Sketch 'D'. In March 1947 a range of options P / P1 – S / S1 with various armaments were produced by the Director of Naval Construction, Sir Charles Lillicrap. At the extremes were Design 'Q1' (six 6in, sixteen 3in in twin mountings, no torpedoes, length 600ft, deep displacement 17,500 tons) and Design 'R' (ten 6in, thirty-two 3in in quadruple mountings, torpedoes, length 710ft, deep displacement 21,000 tons). Displacement was escalating as the design process went on, the main reason being that it was now found necessary to place the 3in magazines close to the mountings to achieve the desired rate of fire, which resulted in a need to lengthen the ship. Lillicrap pointed out that the designs had been considered off and on for a

very long time and that they seemed no nearer finality than they were at the beginning. He had been involved when the process started with the 5.25in Design in 1943-4. He suggested that Design 'P' without torpedoes was now the most attractive option. This ship displaced 18,500 tons with eight 6in in twin mountings and twenty-four 3in in quadruple mountings, the length being 635ft. The complement was approximately 1030 officers and men.

The Sea Lords discussed cruiser design on 11 April 1947. The First Sea Lord initially drew attention to the financial stringency faced by the United Kingdom, which meant that it was most unlikely that cruisers could be laid down for some years. The function of cruisers was then debated and it was agreed that the two main tasks were (a) the provision of anti-aircraft defence for herself and aircraft carriers, and (b) the attack and defence of trade in which the cruiser and the carrier were complementary. No agreement was reached on which of the functions should take precedence or to the extent in which carriers would replace cruisers as escorts for convoys. It was decided to take no further action on cruiser design until the latest American views were known, for there were now even doubts about the 'ideal' calibre of gun for the long-range AA armament.[4]

There were still six ships planned which, in spite of the change in design remained part of the 1944 New Construction programme. Names were the same as those allocated to the *Neptune* class. In March 1947 when the year's New Construction Programme was being considered it was clear that building could not proceed in the immediate future and to tidy up the financial considerations it was decided to regard the class as cancelled. The contract for *Bellerophon*, which still remained in place, was finally cancelled on 28 February 1947. However, this did not mean that the quest for the ships was abandoned, for in a ten-year expenditure forecast prepared in July 1947 it was indicated that two ships could be laid down in 1951, 1952 and 1953. By August 1947, however, the Board of Admiralty decided that there would be no new construction larger than frigates during the next five years and for all practical purposes this point can be regarded as the end of the *Minotaur* class cruisers. But this was not quite the end of the story for in March 1948 there was still talk of six ships being built, with construction starting in 1954. Design work was suspended but a space analysis of existing cruisers was being undertaken which

[3] ADM 167/127:1946 Admiralty Board Minutes and Memoranda; and ADM 205/64: First Sea Lord's Papers contain details of Sketch 'A' to Sketch 'D'. Designs may well have been known earlier as Z1 – Z4; Sketch 'D' is known to have been designated Z4C.

[4] Details of Designs ZA and ZB are included in a paper titled 'USS *Worcester* – Comparison with *Minotaur* Design' held in the DNC's papers at the NMM. The proposed 6in Cruiser Designs of 1947 and the record of discussions are held in The First Sea Lord's Papers ADM 205/67 (PRO). The order in which the minutes of the Sea Lords' meeting sets out the function of a cruiser is indicative of the uncertainty prevailing. Anti-aircraft defence of the cruiser herself is surely not the primary task.

was expected to assist in the preparation of the design.

The influence of United States design practice was strong in the *Minotaur* class. Superficially, when comparisons are made with the *Worcester,* they favour the US ship. In particular *Minotaur* only carried ten 6in guns in five twin turrets. The British gun, however, could fire 20 rounds a minute, although it proved not to be very reliable when it came into service in the *Tiger* class. The US gun at best could only manage 10 rounds a minute with two of the turrets having very restricted arcs of fire. The British secondary armament of sixteen 3in/70 cal. was, however, greatly superior to the US twenty-four 3in/50 cal.

Comparison of weights is difficult as US and British definitions differed considerably. One comparison showed hull savings in the British ship over the American cruiser as 205 tons in structure caused by the effect of welding and use of aluminium. A further 285 tons was saved in fittings, mainly electrical items such as cables. Machinery installed in the *Worcester* developed 120,000shp compared with 100,000shp in *Minotaur*, the former using considerably less space with the more powerful US machinery being about the same weight as the British. The space per man differed only slightly but was used very differently, British office space being much greater.[5]

1948 Future Cruisers

Although there were no immediate prospects of building new cruisers, it was nevertheless a fact of life that the existing ships were ageing and, in spite of some modernisation, suffering from creeping obsolescence. In late 1948 the Ship Design Policy Committee considered the problem and opened up a debate on the function of the cruiser and the shape of the cruiser of the future.

The response of the Director of Naval Construction was firstly to consider the projected equipment, which was likely to be available for ship fitting in the next ten years. This analysis indicated that the anticipated dates were:

6in Mark XXVI	1953 (end)
New 5in/70 cal.	1957
3in/70 cal.	1957
New close-range DA Weapon	1957
LRS1 Director and MRS3 Director	1953
MRS IV Director	1957
TIU Mark III	1954
Type 992 radar	1954
Sea Slug Guided Missile	1958

For propulsion there was no practical alternative to the steam turbine in the relatively near future and it was expected that the type of machinery used would be of an improved *Daring* type as envisaged for the *Minotaur* class cruiser design.

In order to focus ideas four preliminary design studies, known as the 1960s Cruisers, were then prepared with none of the ships including all features in the design, as

this would have resulted in a cruiser which was too large to be produced in any numbers. Particulars are given on the following page.

The Ship Design Policy Committee expressed the hope in January 1949 that two cruisers could be laid down within the next eight years. The outcome was a proposal that the Director of Naval Construction should prepare a sketch of a cruiser with six 6in (3 twin), eight 3in/70 cal. (4 twin), four fixed torpedo tubes on each side, DA or close-range Bofors mountings and Type 984 radar. By March 1949 a new 5in cruiser design was in the subject of preliminary discussions. The result of this new line of thought was that this series of sketches and the preliminary ideas for a new ship were destined to be a cul-de-sac in the development of the cruiser.[6]

The Cruiser/Destroyer

With there being no prospect of building any cruisers in the immediate future a fresh look was taken in the spring of 1949 with thinking encompassed in a paper entitled 'Ships of the Future Navy'. There were three controversial conclusions:

- The replacement of the conventional cruiser and destroyer by an all-purpose light cruiser.

- It was argued that in wartime some sort of quickly-produced escort carrier and the aircraft to fly from it would be needed.

- The value of a completely specialised second-rate anti-submarine frigate should be investigated.

The result was the development of the Cruiser/Destroyer design and the construction of the second-rate *Blackwood* class Type 14 frigates. The escort carrier option never evolved. [7]

At the end of the War when, as we have seen, the size of cruiser designs was escalating, there was perversely a reaction to the ever-increasing size of destroyer designs. The result was the production of a small destroyer design in June 1946 known as 'A1'. The vessel carried the same main armament and utilised the same machinery as the cancelled *Gallant* class but many other features were stripped back with the result that some 30ft in length and 500 tons in deep displacement were saved. The ship could be described as austere with far more use of a depot ship for support being required. The design was still alive in June 1948 when DNC made comparisons with the new Swedish *Oland* design. By August 1948 ideas were changing for two new options were the subject of rough estimates by DNC. The first was an all-purpose fleet destroyer with a main armament of eight 4.5in in twin turrets, close-range AA, two torpedo tubes and a single Limbo anti-submarine mortar in a ship which would have had a standard displacement of 3500-4000 tons. The second ship mounted what were described as 'future weapons'. The main armament was two 5in dual-purpose single mount-

5 'The Royal Navy's 1944 Cruiser' and DNC's papers held at the NMM. The comparison between *Worcester* and *Minotaur* was produced by D K Brown.

6 ADM 116/5632: 1948-1952 Ship Design Policy Committee – meetings and recommendations (PRO); and DNC Papers (NMM); ADM 138/790: Cruisers – general 1948-1958 (NMM). The DA weapon was probably the six-barrelled 40mm Bofors. See also Anthony Preston, 'The RN's 1960 Cruiser Designs', *Warship* 23 and clarification by Professor Michael Vlahos ('As & As') in *Warship* 26. The *Daring* class funnel was designed to counter the effect of a nuclear blast.

7 DNC's papers (NMM). The Short Seamew was developed as a utility anti-submarine aircraft to operate from small aircraft carriers.

The 1960 Cruisers. This series of studies were essentially design exercises although there was a short-lived proposal in January 1949 to develop a new design using Sketches IV and V as a basis. Note the two Type 984 radar sets. It is doubtful if this feature would have proved practical due to mutual interference. (*Drawing by John Roberts from original in NMM DNC Records and PRO ADM 116/5632*)

Sketch I (Large Cruiser) – about 14,500 tons (standard), 17,500 tons deep. Eight 5in in twin mountings, twelve 3in in twin mountings, two DA close-range weapons, four 21in QR torpedo tube mountings. Protection – 3¼in side belt plus box protection to machinery spaces etc. shp 95,000 = 30kts at

deep displacement. Endurance 7500 miles at 20kts. Important features were all-round training for the guns, four self-contained combined boiler/engine-rooms, a single funnel in order to permit all-round training and a closed bridge.

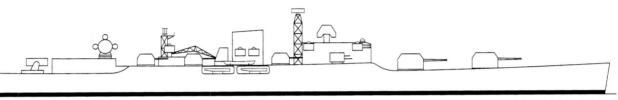

Sketch II (Large Cruiser) – about 14,000 tons (standard). Based on Sketch I, this sketch showed how a guided missile launcher might be fitted aft in place of two 5in mountings. Weight and space requirements relating to the

Sea Slug missile were still very tentative but it was anticipated that the ship would have an outfit of 48 missiles.

Sketch III (Small Cruiser) – about 10,500 tons (standard), 13,000 tons (deep). Four 5in in twin mountings, six 3in in twin mountings, four DA close-range weapons, four QR torpedo tube mountings. This cruiser was described as in effect a modernised *Tiger* and it was thought possible that the *Fiji* engine-

room arrangements might have to be adopted except that forward and after machinery units would be separated. The anticipated speed was 31kts. The funnel arrangements followed those of the *Daring* class.

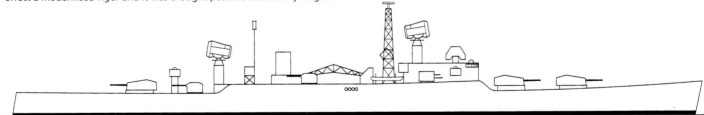

Sketch IV – Deep displacement just under 15,000 tons. Six 6in in twin mountings, six 3in in twin mountings, two DA close-range weapons, four fixed torpedo tubes each side, Type 984 radar. Machinery based on *Daring* class – 4 x 30,000 = 120,000shp (4 shafts). This sketch was produced early in 1949 incorporating features proposed by the Director of Plans. Sketch V

was also produced (below), the difference being machinery – 3 x 30,000shp (3 shafts). Also considered was an arrangement of two 30,000shp sets (*Daring* type) driving the outer shafts and two 15,000shp sets (Y100 type) driving the inner shafts. Funnel arrangements again followed those in the *Daring* class.

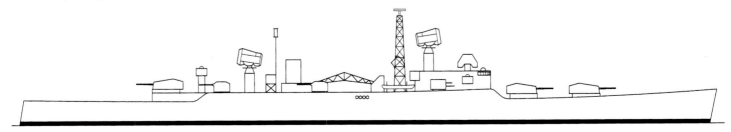

ings. There was to be short-range AA, up to eight torpedoes and a single Limbo. Standard displacement was in the range of 2700-2900 tons. It was concluded that the 5in design should be developed, but with the advent of the new all-purpose light cruiser the design died.

The new proposals in 'Ships of the Future Navy' produced in the Spring of 1949 were revolutionary, for on a long-term basis they envisaged replacing up to fifteen cruisers with 6in guns, eight cruisers with 5.25in armament and fifty-eight fleet destroyers with fifty 5in gun light cruisers. Initial thoughts were that the ships should mount four 5in dual-purpose weapons with four singles being preferred to two twin mountings. The ships were to have close-range AA, eight torpedoes (possibly singles), a single Limbo and good radar. Standard displacement was 4000 to 5000 tons. The 5in gun and mounting at this stage were possibly a development of the 5.25in originally specified for the 1944 Cruiser. The project was very much alive in the summer of 1948 when it was described as the basis of a dual-purpose gun and mounting required as main armament for cruisers and destroyers.[8]

The first attempt at what was now known as the Cruiser/Destroyer design was produced in July 1949. The word 'Destroyer' was included in the title to facilitate preparation of the design to destroyer standards. If purely described as a cruiser it was felt that demands for such items as damage control, stores, protection, sick bay etc, to a cruiser standard would prove difficult to resist! The main armament was three 5in single dual-purpose mountings controlled by one LRS1 and two MRS3. Also wanted were two close-range weapons (STAAG or equivalent), one Limbo and eight fixed torpedo tubes. The main radars were to be Air Warning Type 960, Target Indication Type 992 and Warning Combined and Heightfinding Type 277Q. Deep displacement was 4600 tons, length 465ft and beam 48ft. Endurance required was 4500 miles at 20kts with speed 30.5kts (deep and dirty). Two sets of YE47A machinery produced 60,000shp. There was to be accommodation for a crew of 500.

The length of the ship was governed by the main armament, with mountings located forward, amidships and aft. The amidships gun arrangement resulted in a good separation of the two propulsion units, which reduced the risk of both being put out of action by damage. The forecastle was continuous, eliminating the need for large deckhouses, which would have interfered with the gun arrangement. An inner bottom was provided to improve protection and stiffen the lower part of the hull as well as providing valuable space for oil storage. It was aimed to fit the smallest possible bridge consistent with meeting the needs for an operations room. Two masts and two funnels would be needed in a confined area. The problem was overcome by incorporating the funnels in plated masts.

By March 1950 sketch staff requirements were prepared but it was quickly realised that if they were met in full then a ship considerably larger than 4600 tons would be the result. Essential requirements were three 5in, one Limbo

and latest asdics (sonars), two fixed anti-submarine torpedoes with reloads, one Ruler (an anti-torpedo weapon), one or two close-range weapons and radars Type 960, 277Q and HDWS (High Definition Warning Surface Search Radar). At least four surface torpedoes, three close-range weapons and the new Type 984 radar were regarded as desirable. The principle problem, however, was the endurance requirement, which the Director of Naval Construction considered completely unbalanced the design. It was decided to seek a reduction to 3000 miles at 22.5kts, which DNC expected to achieve. Other issues considered were the armament where a reduction to two 5in was suggested but ruled out on the grounds that mechanical failure could mean a reduction in the armament available. Items such as centreline torpedo tubes, Limbo and the big Type 984 radar were also questioned. It was agreed that one 5in mounting could remain sited amidships and that stores for 45 days should be carried, which was in line with destroyer standards. At this stage just one ship was in the proposed 1953-4 Building Programme.

In February 1951 three design studies were under consideration, the arrangement of the main armament being largely determined by alternative schemes for radar. Design I had one 5in mounting forward, one amidships and one aft with the minimum radar requirements, which were now Types 960, 277Q and HDWS. The estimated deep displacement was 4710 tons. Design II had two mountings forward and one aft, which enabled two Type 984 sets to be carried. Limbo was mounted amidships and the displacement increased slightly to 4770 tons. Design III had all three mountings forward which allowed an intermediate radar scheme to be fitted, two Type 982 (one in lieu of Type 984). Deep displacement remained 4770 tons. All the studies were to have two 30,000shp units of YEAD 1 (Yarrow/English Electric Advanced Development) machinery which were to installed 50ft apart. This design which operated with a boiler pressure of 700psi at a temperature of 950° F, was developed for installation in major warships. Although it never went to sea, it had a major influence on steam plant design. It was an English Electric/Admiralty project which was built and tested at Pametrada. Design Study II appears to have been the scheme adopted.

In February 1951 plans were being drawn up for an emergency construction programme to cover the period 1 April 1952 to 1 April 1953. Four new cruisers would have been in the programme and as the new 5in cruiser/destroyer design was not ready, resort would have had to be made to the *Dido* class but armed with eight 4.5in (4 twins) instead of 5.25in mountings. This contingency plan was never implemented.[9]

Progress with the cruiser/destroyer was slow and by January 1952 a higher endurance was wanted. There was still a hankering for the original requirement of 4500 miles but initially the best prospect was expected to be 3250 miles on a deep displacement of 4770 tons. The controlling constraint was an imposed deep displacement ceiling of 5000 tons. By February 1952 the Director of Naval

[8] ADM 138/830: Destroyers and Frigates General Cover (NMM). The comparison between 'A1' and *Oland* is in the DNC's papers (NMM). Brief details of the destroyer designs produced in August 1948 are recorded in the paper 'Ships of the Future Navy' held in ADM 205/83: First Sea Lord's Records (PRO). Limbo was the project name given to a prototype anti-submarine mortar which when produced was known as the Mark X.

[9] Details of the Light Cruiser design are dated 13 April 1949. See 'Ships of the Future Navy', ADM 205/83 (PRO). The financial record for the 5.25in gun is recorded in ADM 1/25240: 1944-1953 5in Medium Calibre Dual Purpose (MCDP) single weapon: design, development and manufacture of prototype; estimate of financial liability (PRO). A later 5in mounting is believed to have been a development of an anti-aircraft gun designed for the Army. The Emergency Cruiser Programme is recorded in ADM 1/22760: 1951 Emergency Cruiser Programme – Gun Armament (PRO).

[10] ADM 138/830: Destroyers and Frigates General Cover (NMM). See also ADM 116/5632: Ship Design Policy Committee meetings and recommendations 1948-1952 (PRO). There would have been two problems to overcome if the Type 984 radar had been installed. Firstly there were doubts if two could operate in a fleet let alone in one ship and secondly there were production constraints. The planned production rate in 1953 indicated that one set a year would be produced in 1955-7 with two sets a year thereafter. ADM 167/143: 1953 Board Minutes and Memoranda 1953 (PRO).

[11] ADM 1/23473: 1952 5in DP Gun in conjunction with the concept of the Cruiser/Destroyer (PRO).

[12] ADM 167/143: 1953 Admiralty Board Memoranda (PRO); and ADM 1/24610: Consideration and Armament of New Destroyer Design (PRO). Brief details of the 5in destroyer design presented to the Sea Lords' meeting on 30 November 1954 are held in ADM 138/789: Guided Weapon Ships 1 (NMM). There is a good account of the development of the Cruiser/Destroyer in Norman Friedman, *The Postwar Naval Revolution* (London & Annapolis 1986).

Construction was asked to produce a further design study. The minimum equipment requirement now included three 5in single with three Type 903 radar, two Bofors Mark XII with two further Type 903 radar, six fixed torpedo tubes on each beam or eight tubes sited aft (no reloads), Limbo and a Type 984 radar. By April 1952 a detailed examination of the requirements indicated a substantial increase in displacement. As a result the Bofors and associated radars went, which saved about 200 tons. The torpedoes were also deleted as was the Type 984 radar set. The latter was replaced by Type 960, Type 982 and Type 983 sets.[10]

By July 1952 further difficulties appeared when it was found that the required 5in gun performance of 60 rounds per minute per gun could not be achieved within the weight specified. If the weight was unaltered then it was expected that 35 rounds could be fired against a surface target with perhaps up to 40 rounds per minute in the anti-aircraft role. It was decided that planning would proceed on the basis that a simplified gun was produced which met the reduced expectations.[11] By this stage the Radical Review was underway and the Cruiser/Destroyer came under scrutiny. It had been evolving for four years and there were now forward plans for four ships. They were deleted from the programme in October 1953 and replaced initially by one Guided Weapons Ship. The concept did not totally die away for a version with two twin 5in mountings was being evolved in 1954 as part of a wide range of studies including fleet carriers and cruisers for presentation to the Sea Lords in November 1954. The 4750-ton (deep) design was, however, not recommended by the Director of Naval Construction.[12]

The Guided-Missile Cruiser

Although construction of the traditional cruiser seemed to have ended when the decision was made to develop the cruiser/destroyer in 1949, it was not long before new cruiser-style designs began to emerge. What had changed was the realisation that an anti-aircraft guided missile would be available as a valuable addition to the armament. Studies into guided missile development for naval use had started in October 1945 and by 1948 the Sea Slug missile

had become recognisable. Between 1949 and 1951 most of the studies initiated involved converting existing ships, such as the aircraft carrier *Formidable*, the battleship *Vanguard*, a *Majestic* class light fleet carrier and various merchant ships. In December 1951 the Board of Admiralty decided that three types of guided-missile ship were required. In order of priority they were the 12kt coastal convoy escort (Type C) armed with one triple launcher, a 30kt task force guided-missile ship (Type A) with two triple launchers, which seems to have equated with a cruiser. Lastly there was to be a 17kt ocean convoy escort (Type B) with one triple launcher. None of the conversions proved worthwhile other than *Girdle Ness*, which was originally earmarked as the prototype for the coastal convoy escort, a role she was destined not to perform. However, she was used as a trials ship for the Sea Slug system.

It was to be September 1954 before the first guided-missile cruiser sketch designated GW25 was produced. An amended version GW25C was presented to the Sea Lords in November 1954. This cruiser was a large ship displacing 18,300 tons full load. Length was 645ft and beam 79ft. She carried one twin Sea Slug launcher with 48 missiles. Two Type 901/2 directors were fitted. The main gun armament was two 6in twin mountings, which were the same as those specified for the *Minotaur* and *Tiger* classes. Also carried were four 40mm twin Bofors mountings. Machinery was four sets of YEAD 1 which generated 120,000shp and gave the ship a speed of 32.5kts when deep and clean. Endurance was 4500 miles at 20kts. There were some 1300 officers and men to be accommodated. There were four studies in this initial series, GW25 and GW25A – GW25C. All had the same hull and machinery but it was in the suggested armament where the debate was clearly not settled. GW25 carried two twin missile launchers (84 missiles per ship) and also two twin 6in mountings. Both GW25A and GW25B carried the same missile armament but had gun armaments of one twin 6in mounting and two twin 3in mountings respectively. Also considered was an all-gun large cruiser with two twin 6in turrets forward and one aft which was effectively an insurance policy for implementation if the guided-missile armament failed to materialise. The Director of Gunnery Division, however, took the view that there was no reason why the new guided-

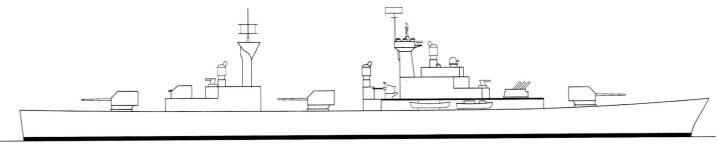

The Cruiser/Destroyer. This is Design Study I produced in February 1951. Two other studies were included in this series. Design Study II was arranged with two single mountings forward and one aft. Two Type 984 radar sets were included with Limbo moved amidships. In Design Study III all gun mountings were placed forward. Radar was to be Types 982 and 983 in lieu of Type 984. (*Drawing by John Roberts from original in PRO ADM 116/5632*)

missile armament could not be trusted, with the result that the all-gun cruiser design never proceeded.

Also presented at the Sea Lords' meeting was an all-gun light cruiser mounting six 5in guns in twin mountings, two forward and one aft. The secondary armament consisted of a six-barrel 40mm mounting interposed between 'B' 5in mounting and the bridge with two twin Bofors 40mm sided aft. Four sets of triple torpedo tubes were wanted for both anti-ship and anti-submarine purposes. The design embodied Y102 COSAG machinery developing 60,000shp, a type later fitted in the 'County' class destroyers. A speed of 29.5kts (deep and dirty) was anticipated. The deep displacement was 8000 tons. However, this cruiser, which was not dissimilar in concept to the 1944 5.25in design, was not pursued any further. Also considered by the Sea Lords was fitting a Sea Slug installation in a *Fiji* class cruiser retaining only 'A' 6in mounting. But the age of the ships, the latest of which would have been twenty years old by the time it went to sea with guided missiles incorporated, quickly lead to this idea being dismissed.

The concept of the guided-missile cruiser was initially given the highest priority by the Sea Lords and over the next 8 months a plethora of studies was produced. Preparatory work on the large cruiser GW25C, however, ceased in January 1955, with efforts now concentrated on a variety of smaller ships. The first, GW35, had been considered by the Sea Lords in mid December. This study instigated by the Director of Naval Ordnance displaced 8000 tons full load, carried two twin 5in mountings of a new design forward and a Sea Slug aft with 20 missiles. The study was sent back by the Sea Lords for further consideration. Other options also evolved: GW38, for example, carried a twin Sea Slug launcher and two twin 6in mountings on a deep displacement of 12,200 tons. The penalty was that only 24 missiles could be carried. Another study, GW42, had one launcher and 48 missiles, four 5in in twin mountings with

a displacement of 12,560 tons. GW45 carried the same missile armament but two 6in single mountings were specified on a displacement of 14,340 tons. The design with twin 5in mountings, although desirable, ultimately had to be ruled out because it would take at least 8 years to bring forward the gun mountings, even though it was a simpler concept than the 5in single developed for the cancelled cruiser/destroyer. Resources just did not exist to develop both the Sea Slug missile and a new gun. By May 1955 it was clear that a main armament of two twin 6in with a secondary armament of twin 3in mountings would be the way ahead. A new study, GW52A, had a deep displacement of 15,100 tons.[13]

The culmination of all this effort was the production of Design Study GW58, which was presented to the Board of Admiralty in July 1955. The ship carried one twin Sea Slug launcher and 48 missiles (radar one Type 901/2), two twin 6in Mark XXVI mountings, two twin 3in Mark VI and two twin Bofors Mark XI mountings. Each gun mounting was controlled by a Type 903 (MRS3) radar. Other radar carried included Types 974 (navigation set), 984 (comprehensive display system) and 992 (surface and low-level air search). The cruiser had a deep displacement of 15,400 tons, length on the waterline was 625ft with beam being 78ft; machinery generated 105,000shp on four shafts. There were separate boiler, engine and gearing rooms, the two locations being isolated from each other by the 3in magazine. Speed when deep and clean was 32kts whilst endurance in operational condition was 4500 miles at 20kts. A crew of 1050 officers and ratings was envisaged. Protection was provided by 1½in protective plating at the sides and decks over the main machinery spaces, missile stowage, magazines and steering gear compartment, although the thickness was reduced to 1in over the machinery spaces. This was lighter than usually seen in the conventional cruiser. The Board of Admiralty

[13] ADM 138/789: Guided Weapon Ships 1 (NMM). This cover has particulars of a wide range of guided-missile ship designs. Whether cruiser, destroyer or convoy escort they all follow in the sequence. GW1, for example, is an ocean escort. The debate over a new all-gun cruiser design is recorded in ADM 205/102: First Sea Lord's Records (PRO). Study GW25 was produced as a result of the deliberations of the Admiralty Air Defence Working Party. Up to this point the first guided-missile ship known as *Blue 01* was planned as an escort. Supply difficulties meant that only one Sea Slug system could be operational by 1960-1, another two years being needed before additional systems were produced. The evolution of this policy is recorded in ADM 1/25609: Introduction of Ship borne Guided Weapons (PRO).

Cruiser/Destroyer. This is Design Study II of the February 1951 series. Note the two big Type 984 radar sets and the *Sverdlov* class cruiser in the background. The ship was expected to be able to counter Soviet cruisers by the weight of firepower from the new 5in mountings. A rate of 60 rounds per minute per gun was specified at this time. (*D K Brown collection*)

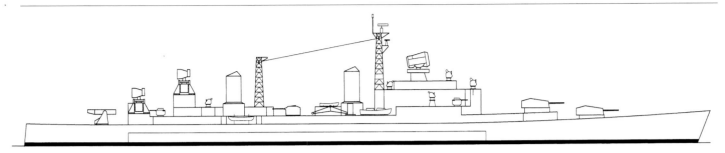

Guided Weapon Cruiser 'GW25C'. The first Guided Weapon Cruiser Designs were the four sketches in the 'GW25' series produced in September and October 1954. The uncertainties can be seen in the options, which were a feature of these sketches. 'GW25' had two twin 6in mountings and two launchers with 84 missiles; 'GW25A' one twin 6in and two launchers with 84 missiles; 'GW25B' two twin 3in and two launchers with 84 missiles. The preferred 'GW25C' had 48 missiles. Note: The number of missiles carried is missiles per ship.
(*Drawing by John Roberts from original in NMM ADM 138/789*)

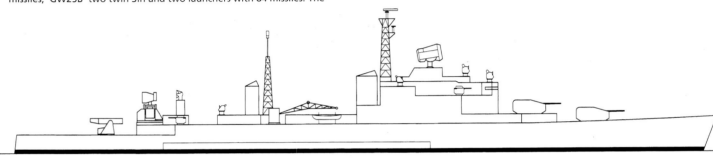

Guided Weapon Cruiser 'GW50A'. This study produced in April 1955 included a proposed twin 5in mounting. The idea proved fleeting for it was found that eight years were needed to develop the new mounting.
(*Drawing by John Roberts from original in NMM ADM 138/789*)

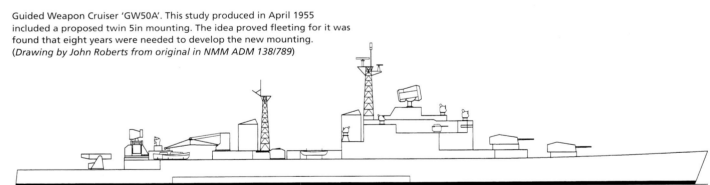

Guided Weapon Cruiser 'GW58A'. This design, produced in June 1955, was selected for development by the Board of Admiralty. Capability and cost were reduced with one Type 901 tracker wanted rather than two in 'GW25C'.
(*Drawing by John Roberts from original in NMM ADM 167/139*)

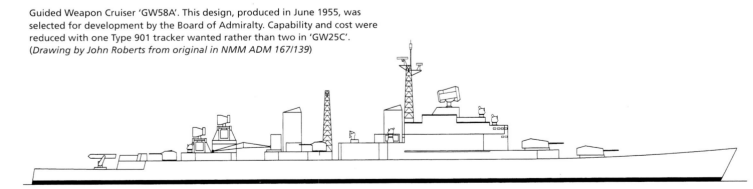

Guided Missile Cruiser 'GW96A', the last design. Two Type 901 trackers are again a feature and there are now four twin 3in/70 cal. mountings.
(*Drawing by John Roberts from original in NMM ADM 138/789*)

approved the development of Design Study GW58, the aim being to order two guided-missile cruisers in the New Construction Programme for 1955-6. Also included in that year's programme at this stage were two fast escorts and the Board were asked to approve the design study for these new ships on the same occasion. They were the ancestors of the 'County' class guided-missile destroyers.[14]

The new cruiser design was now the subject of intensive development but it was not long before warnings about the cost of the project began to emerge. In February 1956 A J Sims, later Sir Alfred Sims, DG Ships, had grave doubts about the design and he felt that there would be considerable opposition to their construction. Nevertheless, planning continued and by July 1956 the Programme consisted of three ships to be ordered in June 1957, June 1958 and June 1960 with completion scheduled for October 1962, March 1964 and October 1965. At the end of August, however, the programme was put back by a year; in October further doubts were expressed by Sims and in November he was joined by other voices within the Admiralty. The Suez crisis was now upon the nation with its necessary strictures, which resulted in the project being wound up in January 1957. The *coup de grace* was given by the First Sea Lord, Admiral of the Fleet the Earl Mountbatten of Burma. In a memorandum to the Deputy Chief of the Naval Staff he intimated that he was originally opposed to the cruiser which he thought far too big for Sea Slug and that he had in fact succeeded in getting the destroyer design (fast escort) increased by some 900 tons in order to take the missile. At that time he had been told that the cruiser was needed to carry the Type 984 radar and that the 6in guns were wanted for shore bombardment. He countered by saying that surely the 4.5in guns of a destroyer were adequate for shore bombardment and could not one destroyer in every squadron of four carry the Type 984 radar instead of a gun armament. This latter idea was later investigated but not pursued. There were also thoughts that the guided-weapon cruiser could be used as some sort of depot ship for a squadron of guided-weapon destroyers. Mountbatten considered that a guided-weapon carrier could perform this function, an idea again investigated but not pursued.

At cancellation the cruiser had grown into a very large and expensive vessel. The final design (GW96A) displaced 18,450 tons (deep), with length on the waterline being some 675ft and a beam of 80ft, increases of 50ft and 2ft respectively over GW58. The principal causes of this escalation in size were an increase in missile capacity from 48 (GW58) to 64 (GW96A) and a doubling of the 3in armament from two to four twin mountings. Another two Type 903 radars (MRS3 mod 1) were required to control the additional gun mountings. The crew increased by 65 to 1115 officers and men whilst to maintain the required speed the Y200 machinery now specified had to develop another 5000shp. Although never formally approved by the Board of Admiralty, a considerable amount of effort was put into its design. Possible names were also consid-

ered by the Ships' Names Committee for the first ship, the choice being *Duke of Edinburgh*. However, it is unlikely that the formalities reached the stage where the Queen gave her approval.[15]

On 11 April 1957 the Board of Admiralty confirmed that the cruisers had been abandoned 'in spite of high expectations that had been aroused concerning these ships'. To the public it was justified 'that in building guided-missile destroyers instead of guided-missile cruisers, the Admiralty would be making the best use of limited resources now available.' The change in strategy, however, was more fundamental, for the staff of the Cruiser Section responsible for designing the ship were moved to become the nuclear submarine design team.[16]

The 'County' Class Guided-Missile Destroyers

With the cancellation of the cruiser/destroyer there was now a requirement for a new destroyer. Initial ideas produced a development of the *Daring* class mounting a 5in gun developed from the Army's weapon known as 'Rate-fixer'. A major revolution was the decision to install gas turbines in addition to the conventional steam plant (an arrangement later known as COSAG), the aim being to give a boost for top speed. Escort destroyer designs were also under consideration. In June 1953 there were two separate designs with different hulls: an anti-submarine ship and an anti-aircraft/aircraft direction vessel. By October 1953 the displacement of the AA/AD version was 3600 tons and the main armament would have been the tried and tested 4.5in Mark VI mounting; but there was a debate over whether it should carry two or three mountings. The machinery would again have been a COSAG installation. The escort destroyers were superseded at the concept design stage by a fast escort displacing 4800 tons with an all-gun armament of six 4.5in in three twin mountings, two forward and one aft. Other versions mounted two 4.5in twin mountings forward with a a twin 3in/70 cal. mount aft, again displacing 4800 tons. The last version of some twenty studies produced displaced 4500 tons, the gun armament comprising one twin 4.5in and one twin 3in/70 cal. The ship was 425ft long with a beam at the waterline of 47ft 6in. Additional armament comprised six fixed torpedo tubes with six anti-submarine torpedoes and a Mark X anti-submarine mortar. This study was produced following a request of the Sea Lords made on 28 January 1955. The Controller considered the design to be unbalanced and under-armed and in May 1955 recommended acceptance of the fast escort design incorporating a twin guided-missile launcher.[17]

A study for what was called a Destroyer GW Ship was produced for the Sea Lords' meeting in November 1954. Displacing 3550 tons deep, the ship carried one twin Sea Slug launcher with 12 missiles and three L70 Bofors mountings. The machinery was the Y102 COSAG installation as specified for the 5in cruiser study presented to

[14] ADM 167/139: 1955 Admiralty Board Memoranda (PRO). The memorandum makes the point that as originally conceived the guided missile cruiser was intended to displace 11,000 tons. Design study GW49, which was one of five produced in April 1955 displaced 11,100 tons deep. Main armament was one Sea Slug launcher with two 5in twin mountings. The first Guided-Missile Destroyer studies emerged in May 1955, the first one meeting the displacement guideline. The 5in cruiser studies were not developed. ADM 205/789: Guided Weapon Ships 1 (NMM).

[15] ADM 138/789: Guided Weapon Ships 1 (NMM). ADM 205/170: First Sea Lord's Records contains memorandum dated 4 January 1957 by First Sea Lord (PRO). Minutes of the Ships' Names Committee (Naval Historical Branch, Whitehall).

[16] ADM 167/149: 1957 Admiralty Board Minutes (PRO); and D K Brown, *A Century of Naval Construction* (London 1983). See also Chapter 9.

[17] D K Brown, *A Century of Naval Construction*. Displacement of fleet escort and suggested armament are recorded in ADM 1/24610: Consideration of Armament of new Destroyer Design (PRO). See also paper presented in 1974 to the Royal Institution of Naval Architects, 'Post War RN Frigate and Guided Missile Destroyer Design 1944-1969', by M K Purvis RCNC. First mention of fast escort (escort destroyer) is in ADM 138/818: Fleet Aircraft Carrier. New Design 1952 (NMM). The memorandum by the Controller which signalled the abandonment of the all-gun armed Fast Escort is held in ADM 205/104: First Sea Lord's Records (PRO).

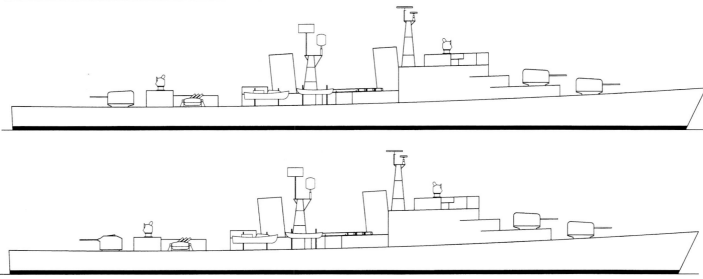

Fast Escort. These two conjectural drawings illustrate how it is believed this design appeared. The first study shows the ship with a main armament of three twin 4.5in Mark VI mountings, which was the main armament originally specified. The second drawing shows the aft twin mounting replaced with a twin 3in/70 cal. This was then in turn superseded by a Sea Slug guided missile launcher in the first studies, which were to lead to the 'County' class guided missile destroyer.
(*Drawings by John Roberts*)

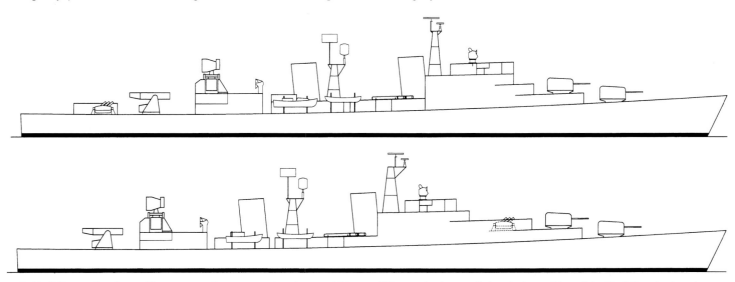

Guided Weapon Fast Escort. These two studies were produced very quickly in May 1955. They were based on two existing fast escort designs with the guided missile installation replacing a twin 3in/70 cal. mounting. The difference in the two designs is the position of the Mark X anti-submarine mortar.
(*Drawings by John Roberts from original in PRO ADM 167/139*)

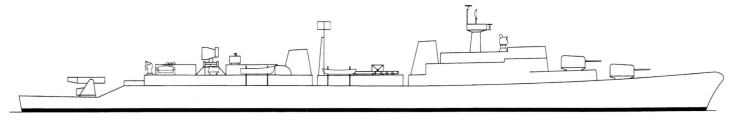

Guided Weapon Destroyer. This drawing was produced in May 1956. The ship now incorporates features of the final 'County' class design. The Mark X anti-submarine mortar is still included and there is no provision for helicopter operation.
(*Drawing by John Roberts from original in PRO ADM 205/109*)

the Sea Lords. Speed achieved was only 0.5kt more than the cruiser, which was more than double the destroyer's displacement. The cause was the differing lengths of the two designs. This concept with surface armament reminiscent of the Type 14 *Blackwood* class then under construction was not pursued.

Development of the escort destroyer design proceeded and two ships were included in the 1955-6 New Construction Programme. However, as we have seen, there were concerns about the viability of the large guided-missile cruiser design and in May 1955 the first studies for a guided-missile destroyer were produced, which would seem to have evolved from the escort destroyer design. What probably happened was that the aft 3in/70 cal. mounting and magazine of a study mounting two twin 4.5in mountings forward and one 3in/70 cal. mounting aft was replaced by a Sea Slug installation. There are indications that the studies were prepared in a hurry, the instigator being Admiral Mountbatten. Four options were produced by the Director of Naval Construction (Studies GW54-57). Displacement ranged from 4550 tons to 5400 tons. The gun armament was either one or two twin 4.5in, two carried six anti-submarine torpedoes whilst the number of MRS3 carried ranged from one to four. All carried a twin Sea Slug launcher with 12 missiles and had COSAG machinery.[18]

Two versions based on GW57, which was now known as the GW Fast Escort, were presented to the Board of Admiralty on 14 July 1955, just two months after the first studies were prepared. This was the largest and most capable of the studies produced in May 1955. Also before the Board was the Guided-missile Cruiser (GW58). Length on the waterline was 470ft with beam 50ft 6in; displacement was 5400 tons deep and the gun armament, consisting of two 4.5in twin mountings, was sited forward of the bridge. The machinery produced 60,000shp to give 31kts deep and clean. Endurance was 3500 miles at 20kts. The difference in the two studies was the location of the anti-submarine mortar. In Study 1001 the weapon was located at the stern aft of the missile launcher whilst in Study 1002 the location had moved to a position before the bridge and aft of the two twin 4.5in mountings. The great advance was that it was now hoped to carry about 20 missiles which were located in a hanger forward of the missile launcher with storage space extending for two decks below this structure. The Board approved the design as a basis for further elaboration. Doubts were expressed about the location of the missile launcher, which it was felt might be subject to vibration at the after end of the ship, affecting the launch of a missile. The Naval Staff were also asked to consider the inclusion of Bofors guns. The Controller indicated that if the missile armament was not available then the ship would be completed with the 3in/70 cal. as a temporary expedient.[19]

Cancellation of the big guided-missile cruiser gave the project increased impetus and by March 1957 the design had evolved sufficiently for presentation to the Board of

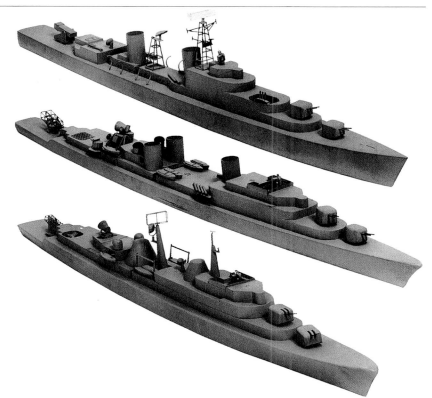

Admiralty. The ship now displaced 6000 tons deep and had a waterline length of 505ft. The machinery (Y102A) comprised two 15,000shp steam turbines with four 7500shp gas turbines to boost power. The ship was designed to achieve 30.5kts deep and dirty in temperate waters. A speed of 26kts in this state could be achieved using steam power alone. Two large propellers were fitted with the aim of both reducing noise and vibration. The hull was to be built of a special notch-tough medium tensile steel whilst the superstructures were of aluminium suitably reinforced with steel frameworks. Lessons learned during the post-war Ship Target Trials by the Naval Construction Research Establishment, Rosyth (NCRE) were incorporated.

The main gun armament remained two twin 4.5in mountings forward whilst two twin 40mm Mark V Mod 2 were also to be fitted. There were also to be eight anti-submarine torpedoes and a Mark X anti-submarine mortar located on the deckhouse forward of the missile launcher. The Sea Slug outfit was now to be 14 missiles with conventional warheads and four with special (nuclear) warheads (see below). The midships deckhouse (abaft the funnels) was made one deck higher to provide additional space for the special weapons. The main change in appearance was the provision of a split after funnel arrangement, the aim being to simplify the gas turbine uptake arrangements.

At this stage it was realised that changes were going to have to be made. The provision of four nuclear Sea Slug missiles exerted a penalty, which meant that the anti-submarine torpedoes would have to be surrendered as com-

Three models of studies which were to lead to the 'County' class guided missile destroyers.
Top: Study 1002. One of the first studies with Mark X anti-submarine mortar mounted forward.
Centre: A later study with the split after funnel.
Bottom: Study with hull raised by one deck over most of the length of the ship. Mark X anti-submarine mortar still carried aft and no provision for helicopter operation. (*D K Brown collection*)

18 ADM 138/789: Guided Weapon Ships 1 (NMM).

19 ADM 167/139: 1955 Admiralty Board Memoranda (PRO); and ADM 167/142: 1955 Admiralty Board Minutes (PRO). A third design was also submitted to the Board meeting, the 'Tribal' class general purpose frigate, which at this stage had a main armament of two twin 4in Mark XVIII. The operation of a Fairy Ultra Light helicopter was considered in December 1956. It was decided to retain the Limbo anti-submarine mortar but the question remained open pending further assessment of the capabilities of the helicopter. ADM 205/112: First Sea Lord's Records (PRO).

[20] ADM 167/150: 1957 Admiralty Board Memoranda (PRO). The first post-war warships built which incorporated the lessons of the NCRE trials were the Type 41 and Type 61 frigates. Chapter 5 covers this topic. A series of articles by D K Brown on the post-war trials was published in *Warship* 41-44 inclusive.

[21] ADM 167/149: 1957 Admiralty Board Minutes (PRO). In the discussion there was talk of the Sea Slug Mark II showing promise of doing all that was required whilst the Green Flax missile was not proven.

[22] D K Brown, *A Century of Naval Construction*. ADM 167/149: 1957 Admiralty Board Minutes (PRO); and ADM 167/151: 1958 Admiralty Board Minutes (PRO). According to a draft Board Minute dated 5 June 1958 held in ADM 205/176: First Sea Lord's Records (PRO). The hangar for the helicopter was initially described as a movable cover of telescopic design which could be pulled out over the helicopter on the flight platform. The change from a three-funnel to a two-funnel layout was initiated after the retirement of Sir Victor Shepheard.

[23] Dr John Coates confided his experiences on the shakedown cruise in a conversation with D K Brown in March 2002. He gained his doctorate for work on the Greek Trireme project after his career with the RCNC.

[24] ADM 167/162: 1963 Admiralty Board Minutes (PRO).

[25] T 225/1539: 1946-1959 Admiralty R & D of Guided Missiles for use afloat (PRO); and DEFE 30/2: Defence Board – The Naval Programme 29 November 1960 (PRO). There are references to Blue Slug missile in ADM 138/888: SCC Project 35 (Aircraft Carrier CVA-01) (NMM).

[26] *Conway's All the World's Fighting Ships 1947-1995* (London 1995), p508.

pensation. This loss resulted in consideration being given to the provision of facilities to enable a Fairy Ultra Light helicopter to be operated, including a hanger, which in turn meant sacrificing the anti-submarine mortar. The helicopter had, however, not been evaluated and it was suggested that its provision be reviewed in twelve months time. What could be quickly achieved was a landing space for an S.55 helicopter without a hanger, maintenance or fuelling facilities. The prototype was expected to cost £9 million with subsequent ships costing £8 million, including the cost of the guns.[20]

The Board of Admiralty approved the sketch design and legend of particulars and confirmed that work on the detailed design could proceed as proposed. They also congratulated the Director of Naval Construction, Sir Victor Shepherd, and all those concerned, on the originality and ingenuity, which had been displayed in the design. Two ideas came out of the meeting. One was a suggestion by the Parliamentary Secretary that the Army's new guided-missile 'Green Flax' could take the place of Sea Slug. The other by the Director of Naval Construction was that it might be possible to install a Type 984 radar with reduced circuits in place of the main gun armament. It was thought possible that one in four vessels of the class would carry this radar, reflecting Mountbatten's thoughts. Both ideas were studied but duly died away.[21]

The first change to appear as the detailed design work proceeded was the replacement of the three-funnel arrangement by two funnels which were not dissimilar to those ultimately fitted. The next alteration, which had evolved by November 1957, was more fundamental. Up to now the sketch designs had all had a conventional superstructure but it was now decided to raise the main hull by one deck over most of the length of the ship. The effect

was a major increase in internal space, a better structure, better survivability and improved protection from nuclear attack. It was now possible to stow 24 missiles, a major gain. They were now stored in a long hanger which extended over the machinery spaces through the middle of the ship high in the hull. This was a radical departure from conventional practice and as a safeguard a constantly pressurised automatic fire-fighting system was installed. There was no armour, for the ship was built to destroyer standards. By June 1958 it had been decided that the ship should operate a Wessex helicopter with hanger and support provided. The cost of the first ship had, however, now risen to £10.5 million.[22]

The first pair, *Devonshire* and *Hampshire*, were laid down in March 1959 by, respectively, Cammell Laird and John Brown, who were responsible for the detailed design. *Devonshire* was completed in November 1962, exactly 7½ years after the first studies were instigated, a fine achievement. The Constructor who as Head of Section in charge of designing the 'County' class for six years was John Coates RCNC. He was present on an extended shake down cruise to the United States and Caribbean, one of the purposes of which was to test the air-conditioning system in tropical conditions, the class having been the first to be designed from scratch with this feature. *En route* the ship visited Philadelphia where people from the Bureau of Ships expressed astonishment at the lavish standard of furnishing in *Devonshire*. They were also surprised at the absence of pillars in machinery spaces. Coates told them that, being responsible for the design as a whole, he had decided that the structural arrangements in the class made them unnecessary. In the Bureau of Ships decisions were more departmentalised and codified.[23]

The original plan was to build ten ships but by 1963 the

The 'County' class destroyer
Devonshire firing a Sea Slug missile.
(*MoD*)

escort cruiser and the Type 82 frigate, both of which were to be armed with the new CF299 (Sea Dart) missile, were under development. The last four 'Countys' had consequently been deferred. However, by the end of the year it was apparent that there would be delays in the escort cruiser programme and there were uncertainties surrounding the Type 82 programme. In view of these reservations it was decided to proceed with two of the deferred ships, assurances having been given that the missile armament would be effective into the 1980s.[24]

The Sea Slug missile had rather a chequered career. Development clearly proved difficult and in 1957, long before it entered service, the missile was described as 'not as good as it might have been'. A major weakness was that it was a beam-riding missile with no homing device which would attract it to its target, accuracy diminishing with distance. There were also doubts about the ability of the missile to cope with low-level targets. The requirement for an nuclear warhead (special weapons) existed to extend the range at which the missile could operate, less accuracy being needed, and also to give it surface-to-surface capability, enabling the ships to deal with Russian cruisers and land targets. The Mark I missile did not carry a nuclear warhead, the Admiralty having rejected that proposed as too hazardous for stowage and operation on board ship. However, by 1960 a Mark II version was being developed to overcome the weakness in the Mark I. Improvements enabled it to engage supersonic targets and a Russian Komet-type missile, capabilities which the initial version did not possess. The Komet, NATO code name 'Kennel' was an air-launched beam-riding missile based on the MiG 15 fighter. The Mark II Sea Slug could also be fitted with a nuclear warhead, improved manufacturing techniques enabling a smaller and safer warhead to be made. Initially it was planned to install the Mark II system in the second group and then retrofit it in the first group; but only the second group received the new system. A related project was Blue Slug, a surface-to-surface guided weapon which flew at about 50ft and was altimeter controlled. It outranged the 6in guns in a *Sverdlov* class cruiser. Development of the Sea Slug Mark II probably caused its abandonment.[25]

The first four members of the class, *Devonshire*, *Hamp-*shire, *Kent* and *London*, were completed to the original design. The second group, *Fife*, *Glamorgan*, *Antrim* and *Norfolk*, were armed with Sea Slug Mark II and they also had an improved version of the Type 965 long range radar. Service life was relatively short, with *Kent* the last member of the first group becoming a harbour training ship by 1980. All the second batch were sold to Chile, the last to go being *Fife* which was transferred in 1987.[26]

Top: *Antrim* as originally completed with two twin 4.5in mountings and double Type 965 radar. (*D K Brown collection*)

Above: *Norfolk* on 26 January 1976. Note Exocet surface-to-surface missile fitted instead of twin 4.5in mounting in 'B' position. (*Mike Lennon*)

3 The Reconstructions

THE RECONSTRUCTION OF WARSHIPS to counter both age and obsolescence developed between the wars as an expedient to ensure that both numbers and quality were to some extent maintained in the face of both budgetary constraints and treaty restrictions. Major warships reconstructed before the outbreak of the Second World War included the battleships *Warspite*, *Queen Elizabeth* and *Valiant*, the battlecruiser *Renown* and the cruiser *London*. There is a fine line between reconstruction and modernisation, and in this account the main criteria used to distinguish between the two will be the submission of a project for approval by the Board of Admiralty.

Victorious

At the end of the war the Royal Navy possessed six fleet carriers all of which unfortunately lacked hangars with sufficient height to accommodate modern aircraft, a disadvantage of the armoured hangar design. A limitation on the weight of the aircraft carried was another constraint. Hangar heights and aircraft weights were: *Illustrious* 16ft and 20,000lbs; *Formidable* and *Victorious* 16ft and 14,000lbs; *Indomitable* 14ft upper hangar, 16ft lower hangar and 14,000lbs; *Implacable* and *Indefatigable* 14ft both upper and lower hangars and 20,000lbs. A hangar

height of 17ft 6in and the ability to handle aircraft with a weight of 30,000lbs was needed, features which were incorporated in the design of the new *Ark Royal* and *Hermes* classes. The deficiencies were a major constraint on the effectiveness of the existing carriers and tentative steps towards the necessary modernisation were being considered as early as September 1945.

In November 1945 the Deputy Controller indicated that nine fleet aircraft carriers would be needed in 1950, of which three would be the *Ark Royal* class (the contract for the original *Eagle* had not then been cancelled), the other six being the *Illustrious* and her five contemporaries. Anything less than a full reconstruction was not recommended. The cost of reconstruction was said to be £2.5 million compared with £7 million for a new aircraft carrier. Nevertheless, the Fifth Sea Lord, who was responsible for aircraft in the fleet, considered it was not worth while modernising *Illustrious*, the money saved being better put towards the cost of a new ship. In any case there was now no money for the project so the subject was deferred for 6 months.[1]

The subject came up for discussion again in the summer of 1946. Part of the debate centred around the question of closed or open hangars, a controversy which had plagued the design of the cancelled *Gibraltar/Malta* class carriers. The Director of Naval Construction, Sir Charles Lillicrap, was far from convinced that an open hangar was the way ahead and he was anxious to avoid any vacillation. The arguments were finely balanced, with the Americans initially in favour of an open hangar, a position changed after wartime experiences in the Pacific. The penalty of the closed armoured hangar was a constraint on aircraft operations, but the advantage was that it was not so easy to put the ship out of action. Lillicrap was particularly anxious to avoid the *Gibraltar* state of affairs where firstly a closed hangar design was approved, then an open hangar was wanted and later it was decided that the redesigned ship was 50ft too long, only for the project to be finally cancelled, with a considerable waste of design effort. He also indicated that 9 to 12 months notice would be needed before the ships could be taken in hand. The outcome of these deliberations was the setting-up of a small committee under the Assistant Chief of Naval Staff (Air) which was to decide the future of each carrier on its merits. No decision on what was described as the 'vexed question' of open versus closed hangars was to be taken until the results of the Bikini Atoll atomic experiments had been examined.[2]

In January 1947 the committee held its first meeting. The Director of Naval Construction indicated that the carriers should have a life of a further 20 years, which would take them up to 1967. It was decided that the order in which modernisation should be undertaken was *Formidable*, *Victorious*, *Indomitable*, *Illustrious*, *Implacable* and lastly *Indefatigable*. The easiest projects were *Formidable* and *Victorious* with the *Implacable* and *Indefatigable* being the most difficult. The committee held a second meeting later

in the month when broad decisions were taken. An intermediate modernisation was felt not to be worthwhile, but owing to financial constraints a full modernisation was not possible at that time. All six carriers were said to have long defects lists and, prior to placing in reserve, repairs were to be confined to remedying critical defects only. It was also concluded that the Bikini tests did not affect the plan, which indicates that it was decided to retain closed hangars. The final report of the committee was submitted in April 1947. Full modernisation of *Formidable* and *Victorious* was approved to what was described as an 'improved *Hermes*' standard. The ships, which were described as a 'Fast Armoured *Hermes*', would carry 48 aircraft. By comparison the *Hermes* carried 45 whilst *Ark Royal* carried 84. It was to be January 1948 before the Board of Admiralty approved this project in principle.[3]

Preparation of the design commenced in February 1948, the aim still being for *Formidable* to be the first ship. Progress was slow, however, and it was to be June 1950 before a Legend was prepared. The ship now had a deep displacement of 33,000 tons (27,180 tons standard). The eight 4.5in twin mountings were to be replaced by six twin 3in/70 cal. The 3in flight deck armour was retained but the ship was to be rebuilt from the hangar deck upwards. The beam was increased, which in turn meant moving the side armour and generally rearranging all compartments outside the machinery spaces. All cables and wiring was to be renewed with generating capacity doubled and new auxiliary machinery installed. The island was also reconstructed. The cost of the project was unclear, however, as the Director of Dockyards did not have sufficient information to formulate an estimate, an ominous portent. By now it had been decided that *Victorious* would be the first ship as she was in a better state than *Formidable* which had a distorted flight deck, propeller shaft defects and other outstanding problems which would need a lengthy refit to correct.

Work on the reconstruction started at Portsmouth Dockyard in October 1950, the intention being to complete the work by April 1954; but the project was to be dogged with alterations, the first of which was a decision to install the US 3in/50 cal. which was taken in February 1951 owing to delays in the development of the British 3in/70 cal. By June 1952 the provision of an angled deck was being considered following successful trials in the light fleet carrier *Triumph* in February 1952. By May 1953 it was decided that an 8½° angled deck should be fitted. In July 1953 it was decided to fit a Type 984 radar, a not inconsiderable undertaking. It was also now realised that the boilers would only run until 1964 without a further extensive refit, so it was decided to re-boiler the ship. This turned out to be a somewhat contorted and expensive exercise. The first difficulty was removing the old boilers, reconstruction having already reached the point where the armoured deck had been refitted, resulting in a considerable amount of completed work being dismantled. The original idea had been to produce boilers of similar design

[1] ADM 138/767: Existing Fleet Carriers Modernisation 1945-1949 (NMM).

[2] ADM 1/19161: 1945 Modernisation of Fleet Carriers; ADM 1/19977: 1946-47 Modernisation of existing Fleet Carriers (PRO) and ADM 138/767: Existing Fleet Carriers Modernisation 1945-1949 (NMM). The nature of the argument over closed versus open hangars changed with the advent of nuclear weapons and jet aircraft. See Chapter 4.

[3] ADM 138/767: Existing Fleet Carriers Modernisation 1945-1949 (PRO).

4 ADM 138/ 770: *Victorious*
(NMM), and D K Brown, *A
Century of Naval Construction.*
'The Developments in Reboilering'
are recorded in ADM 167/143:
1953 Admiralty Board Minutes
and Memoranda (PRO). The cost
estimates are recorded in ADM
167/144: 1954 Admiralty Board
Minutes and Memoranda (PRO).
The insidious effects of inflation
were a factor in the escalating costs
but by no means the dominant
influence.

5 ADM 138/806: *Implacable*
Modernisation, and ADM
138/818: Fleet Aircraft Carrier
New Design 1952 (NMM).

to those originally fitted with existing auxiliary machinery and systems being retained, at an estimated cost of £250,000. The old boilers were removed and duly destroyed, but it was then found that modern boilers would be needed to meet the large intermittent steam requirements of the steam catapult. Provision of these new boilers plus some new auxiliary machinery resulted in the additional costs rising to £607,000. The Board of Admiralty approved the scheme in December 1953, the figure quoted being £650,000 to provide a small margin.

A new Legend produced in July 1955 quoted a deep displacement of 35,500 tons (30,532 tons standard). Completion was now due in June 1957. The complexity of the task proved to be much greater than any earlier project and it was clear that there was a need for improved production control systems and procedures. It was to be 1958 before the work was completed. The cost of the conversion escalated throughout the life of the project. In December 1947 it was anticipated that £5 million (excluding the cost of the guns) would be spent on each ship. By August 1950, when the *Victorious* was in dockyard hands, the total cost was £5.4 million. By October 1950, with more reliable data available on dockyard costs, the figure had escalated to £7.7 million. By March 1952 an up-to-date estimate came out at £11 million, which itself increased to an estimated £14.16 million by December 1953, taking into account re-boilering, the angled flight deck and the Type 984 radar. The final figure, £30 million, was far more expensive than ever envisaged; nevertheless the reconstruction was a success for a very useful modern carrier equipped for handling, operating, controlling and detecting modern jet aircraft was the result.[4]

The next ship in line was now *Implacable*, which it was planned to take in hand at Devonport in April 1953 and modernise her on the lines of *Victorious*. She would have

been followed by *Indefatigable*. Deep displacement would have been 36,000 tons. But by October 1951 the project had been postponed for 2 years and the delays to *Victorious* were becoming a cause for concern. By June 1952 the Admiralty decided that it was the wrong policy to spend large sums of money on the modernisation of old carriers and that *Victorious* would be the only major conversion.[5]

Hermes

This light fleet aircraft carrier, originally named *Elephant*, was ordered from Vickers Armstrong, Barrow under the 1943 New Construction Programme. She was one of eight ships of the *Hermes* class, four being cancelled at the end of the Second World War, including the 'original' *Hermes*. Progress on all the class was slow, with three of the ships being completed in 1953-4. In the case of *Hermes* the Admiralty indicated to the shipyard in December 1948 that the ship was to be completed by the end of 1952. However, priority was given to the completion of the aircraft carrier *Melbourne* for the Royal Australian Navy with the result that delays became severe and there were periods when construction stopped altogether. However, advantage was taken of the delays to substantially modify the design.

The first batch of major changes was made in 1951 when it was decided to fit two steam catapults, incorporate a side lift and provide improved arresting gear. The installation of a side lift in an aircraft carrier with a closed hangar is far more difficult than it may appear at first sight. The structure of the ship acts as a box girder with the flight deck and the bottom taking most of the bending stresses whilst the sides of both the ship and the hangar resist the shear forces and prevent the whole structure from buckling. Cutting a large hole in the hangar and ship's side

Hermes in 1966, with a pair of Scimitars on deck. Originally a sister of *Centaur*, as completed this ship revealed little beyond the general appearance of the hull to signify their relationship. (*Royal Naval Museum*)

weakens this structure considerably. A workable solution was produced by NCRE (see photograph of the structure in Chapter 12). They used what was then the fairly new method of photo-elasticity in which a large model of the structure was made in Perspex. This was illuminated with polarised light and put under load. Bands of light and dark showed the stress pattern and the number of fringes would give an indication of the magnitude of the stress. The model was fairly easy to alter so amendments could be made until the best answer was obtained. Sliding doors were then fitted in the ship to keep the hangar 'closed' as a fire precaution. The side lifts installed in *Hermes* and *Ark Royal* worked, but they were heavy and there was a limitation on the size of aircraft carried.

The structure needed to support a steam catapult also proved difficult to design, one major problem being the severe impact at the fore end where the heavy shuttle had to be brought to a stop in a few feet. A replica of the catapult structure was built and tried in a large test frame measuring 69ft x 33ft x 39ft where loads of up to 2000 tons could be applied. The structure of the catapult for *Ark Royal* was tested there in 1953 and the lessons learned incorporated in the design used in *Hermes*.

In 1953 further major works were authorised, including the fitting of a fully-angled deck and a Type 984 radar system. The result of all the additions incorporated was that the standard displacement rose from 18,410 tons (23,800 tons deep) in 1944 to 23,460 tons (27,800 tons deep) in 1954. The deep displacement was at the acceptable limit and was a cause for concern as the design of some of the radar and gunnery equipment had not been fully developed. If further additional equipment weight had to be accepted then the weight of other features in the design would have to have been reduced as compensation. Measures to save weight were fairly extreme, ranging from 50 tons being saved by using plastic-covered cable wherever possible instead of lead covering, to 5 tons saved by using light alloy in the bridge structure. Careful attention to detail saved about 120 tons over seventeen items. The speed of the ship was inevitably affected but it was still expected that 25kts could be achieved when the ship had been out of dock in tropical waters for six months. However, when the steam catapult was operating under the most severe requirements then a further reduction of in full speed of 1.5kts was expected. Endurance was also reduced. The original requirement was 6000 miles at 20kts in the tropics when the ship had been out of dock for six months. This figure now reduced to 4800 miles, a small part of the reason being that a change in the calculation rules meant that the original figure would have been 5 per cent lower.

The aircraft complement in 1954 was expected to be eight Scimitars and eight Sea Vixen fighters, eight Gannets, four Skyraiders (presumably for ASW and AEW respectively), and two helicopters. Larger aircraft could not be accommodated as their weight would place them beyond the capacity of the catapults.[6]

Hermes displays her revised layout as a commando carrier while replenishing at sea from USS *Neosho* in June 1974. To starboard of the oiler is USS *Vreeland*, a *Knox* class destroyer escort. *(Royal Navy)*

Hermes operated as a front-line aircraft carrier from completion in 1959 until 1971 when she was converted into a commando carrier operating Wessex helicopters, losing catapults, arrester wires and her Type 984 radar, which was replaced by a Type 965; but the basic structure of the ship was largely unaltered. In 1977 she became an ASW carrier with a complement of Sea King helicopters, which were quickly supplemented with a squadron of Sea Harriers for air defence, a 7° ski jump ramp being installed to improve the performance of the aircraft. The ship filled a gap pending the arrival of the three *Invincible* class, which at that time were described as through-deck cruisers, and as such she played a key role in the Falklands War of 1982. She was finally paid off in 1984 and sold to India who have renamed her *Viraat*.[7] Although too small to be an effective fleet carrier in her later years, *Hermes* proved to be a remarkably flexible ship which served the Royal Navy well. She can be regarded as highly successful.

[6] Vickers Archives (Cambridge University Library) and ADM 167/144: 1954 Admiralty Board Minutes and Memoranda (PRO). Weight saving measures are recorded in ADM 167/143: 1953 Admiralty Board Memoranda (PRO). The photo-elasticity technique was introduced to NCRE by J A H Paffett and applied to the side lift structure by K J Rawson. Side lifts proved not to be really compatible with closed hangers and the installation was removed from *Ark Royal* when the ship was fitted with an angled deck. The *Ark Royal* side lift served only the upper deck.

[7] *Conway's All the World's Fighting Ships 1947-1995*, p499. The Constructor Commander who served in the *Hermes* in the Falklands War described her as 'A bloody great steel fort'.

Hermes comes home from the Falklands battles on 10 February 1983. Note the streaks of rust on the sides of the ship. All other members of the task force returned with their paintwork in virtually pristine condition. Work on *Hermes* started in 1944 when techniques for preserving steel were not so advanced. D K Brown worked on her as an apprentice in 1947/48. (*Royal Navy*)

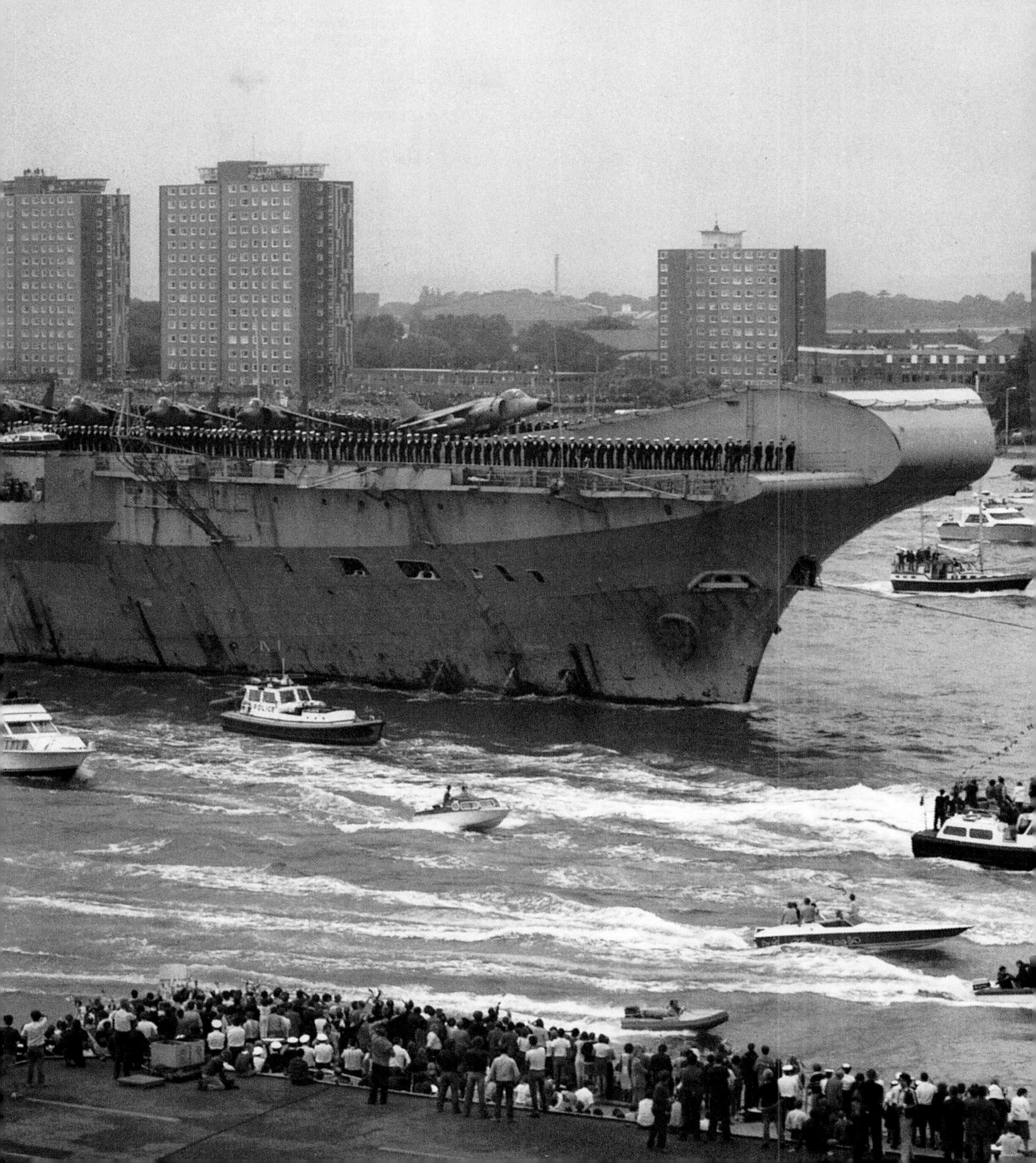
POLICE

8 The stabilisation trials were recorded in J Bell, 'Stabilisation Controls and Computation', *Transactions of the Institute of Naval Architects* (1957) . The author points out that 'stabiliser' is a misnomer: they are rolling damping devices. The full power trial with the three-bladed noise reduced propellers was dubious given the state of the ship's boilers. From memory D K Brown believes that she reached c25kts safely.

Cumberland being given a thorough dousing in 'pre-wetting' trials to test ability to disperse contamination. (*Crown Copyright*)

The Trials Cruiser *Cumberland*

In 1951 the old 'County' class cruiser *Cumberland* completed a refit as a trials cruiser. The obvious trials were of new gunnery systems but there were also other important tests. At first she mounted a single 4.5in and a 40mm STAAG with a 'Battle' class director, all situated on the starboard side abreast the funnels. Another 4.5in mounting was later fitted on the port side. By 1953 the ship had a twin 3in/70 cal. in 'Y' position followed by a twin 6in Mark XXVI in 'B' position. Both mountings, which were fitted in the *Tiger* class, were controlled by an MRS3 located on the bridge. Other trials included pre-wetting to reduce the effect of nuclear fallout. She was also fitted with four pairs of small non-retractable stabiliser fins. These were less effective than a single pair of high aspect ratio retractable fins but were much easier to install. Most

of the work was devoted to improving the control system. The ship was also fitted with three-bladed noise-reduced propellers based on those successfully tried in the wartime destroyer *Savage*, but for some reason they did not work so well in *Cumberland*. The old cruiser paid off at the end of 1958.[8]

The 'Ca' Class Destroyers

The eight destroyers of this group were all completed in the last months of the Second World War. By 1951 they were obsolete and required modernisation to make them effective units of the fleet. The main function of the ships as modernised would be to screen heavy forces against attack by submarines, aircraft and light forces and to attack enemy light forces and trade. Secondary functions were to supplement cruisers for independent operations, sup-

port combined operations and attack heavy ships with torpedoes. The work was extensive and the most comprehensive given to any of the wartime destroyers which were not converted to frigates. The result was a class of ships with improved anti-submarine and anti-aircraft capabilities.

The bridge structures were all rebuilt, incorporating an enlarged operations room, four of the class acquiring a frigate-type bridge. The No. 3 4.5in mounting was removed to enable a double Squid anti-submarine mortar to be fitted. Also removed was the after set of torpedo tubes, which enabled the after deckhouse to be extended forward. The three remaining 4.5in guns were controlled by a Mark 6M director fitted with FPS 5 (Fly Plane System). A Type 275 radar was also provided for this purpose. The close-range armament consisted of a twin 40mm Bofors Mark V with STD (Simple Tachymetric Director) on the aft superstructure and two single 40mm Bofors Mark VII abreast the bridge. Provision was made for Type 147F, 162 and 166 sonars and an enlarged sonar instrument room. The depth charge store was converted to a Squid magazine, which could stow 60 projectiles (10 salvoes). Radar carried included Type 293Q, a surface and low-angle air search target indicator set, and Type 974, a Decca navigation set. The generating capacity was increased with a 150 kW machine replacing a 50 kW set in No. 1 boiler room; a 150 kW set was installed in No. 2 boiler room with a 50 kW set in the gearing room being retained. All the additions exacted a price. Deep displacement was now 2675 tons against the original designed displacement of 2485 tons. The maximum speed was now 30kts with the ship clean in temperate waters. Some 50 tons of permanent ballast was needed to maintain stability. The ship had also reached the point where no further weight additions were possible, any increase in the stresses imposed on the ship's structure being unacceptable. The class proved useful units of the fleet, the first of the class not being broken up until 1967. One ship, *Cavalier*, has been preserved and is now at Chatham Historic Dockyard.[9]

The *Tiger* Class

The three surviving cruisers of the *Tiger* class were a prewar design with some war experience incorporated in improvements. The main development had been the substitution of the triple 6in mounting Mark XXIV for the Mark XXIII, the gain being an increase in elevation from 45° to 60°. Manufacture of this armament was nearing completion when construction of the three ships was suspended in the summer of 1946.[10]

In November 1947 a full investigation was made into fitting the new twin 6in Mark XXVI mounting in the class, this armament having been specified for the cancelled *Minotaur* class cruisers. Two mountings could be carried, one forward and one aft. In addition three of the new twin 3in/70 cal. could be mounted. Another scheme considered at this time was the elimination of the 6in armament and the fitting of six twin 3in/70 cal. in substitution. By March 1948 it was decided that the 6in scheme should proceed, the all-3in armament not being worthwhile because it would leave the ship vulnerable if it ever had to encounter an armed merchant cruiser. The ships, however, remained suspended, with *Blake* and *Tiger* being the responsibility of the shipyards whilst *Defence* was part of the Reserve Fleet Organisation. When the Korean War broke out there were thoughts of completing the ships with two 6in Mark XXIV mountings. These guns would have been mounted forward in 'A' and 'B' positions. Two twin 4.5in Mark VI were to be mounted aft in 'X' and 'Y' positions, with either a further pair of sided twin 4.5in Mark VI or two single 4.5in Mark V sided in 'P1' and 'S1'

Royalist in July 1956 after a major refit. She was the only *Dido* or Modified *Dido* class cruiser to be given extensive modernisation which included a new bridge structure, lattice masts, new sensors and Bofors 40mm close-range anti-aircraft armament. The result was a particularly handsome ship, but like many warships of her era she suffered badly from hull corrosion in later life. (*MoD*)

[9] ADM 167/140: 1951 Admiralty Board Minutes and Memoranda (PRO).

[10] Vickers Archives (Cambridge University Library).

Tiger class with all 3in/70 cal. armament. This option with six twin 3in/70 cal. mountings was considered in November 1947 with the adopted twin 6in Mark XXVI and three twin 3in/70 cal. design. Note the size of the 3in/70 cal. mountings, which do not look out of place on a hull designed in 1936/37 to carry four triple 6in Mark XXIII mountings. (*Drawing by John Roberts from original in NMM ADM 138/777*)

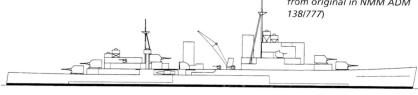

Tiger in 1959. She is a new ship, but her replacement in the fleet, the 'County' class guided-missile destroyer, is only a few years from completion. (*Royal Naval Museum*)

[11] ADM 138/ 777: *Tiger* Class Cruisers (NMM). It was hoped that a *Tiger* class cruiser could defeat a Soviet *Sverdlov* class cruiser. The *Tiger* had the advantage of a faster rate of fire with heavier shells and better cross-level correction (D K Brown).

[12] ADM 167/144: 1954 Admiralty Board Minutes and Memoranda (PRO); and ADM 138/777: *Tiger* Class Cruisers (NMM).

[13] *Conway's All the Worlds Fighting Ships 1947-1995*, p504. The cost of the cruisers is quoted in *Jane's Fighting Ships 1970-71*. There were two designs of Mark XXVI mounting. Of the six in service three had hydraulic drive and three had electric drive. *Lion* had one of each.

positions. The 6in mountings were in store at Rosyth Dockyard, some incomplete. This option was quickly abandoned when it was found that the ships would not be ready before the end of 1953, unfinished work on the gun mountings being a major part of the task.[11]

Design work moved forward slowly and as late as 1954 there were considerable doubts within the Admiralty as to whether it was worthwhile completing the three ships, the Radical Review being underway. They had now been laid up for 8 years. *Blake* and *Tiger* were said to be 'in first class condition' although *Defence*, which languished on moorings, was said to be 'not so good'. In July 1954 the Board of Admiralty at long last approved the legend and sketch design of the redesigned ships. The class was now seen as providing escort and anti-aircraft support to convoys and carrier task groups. There were clearly severe limitations for by the time the ships were complete they would have been in the water for at least 12 years, whilst the hulls and machinery were of pre-war design and layout in all major respects. There was also going to be considerable congestion within the hull structure with accommodation standards being low due to the incorporation of equipment not specified in the original design.

The reconstruction was extensive. All the superstructure, gun supports, minor bulkheads and most of the services were stripped out. In addition all auxiliary machinery and equipment had to be modified or replaced so that it could operate on an entirely AC electrical system. Reboilering was considered but was ruled out by the Board of Admiralty, as the advantages would not compensate for the delay and expense incurred. The displacement in deep condition was now 11,900 tons, the result of this increase

and other improvements such as air conditioning being a reduction in speed to 29.25kts when the ship operated in the tropics and had been out of dock for 6 months. Endurance was reduced by 440 miles to 4190 miles when the ship had a clean bottom. The revised main and secondary armaments were as first envisaged in 1947. The cost was put at £6 million each with 3 years being taken to complete each ship. A new cruiser of comparable size and armament was said to cost about £12 million and would require 5 years to complete. When it was decided to complete the ships it was appreciated that vessels mounting guided missiles would be their ultimate successors, but it was expected that they were at least 10 years away. The *Tiger* class at this stage in their careers can be considered as very much a stop-gap.[12] The work took rather longer to complete than was anticipated, with *Tiger* completing in March 1959, *Lion* (ex-*Defence*) in July 1960, and *Blake* in March 1961, the latter ship only 20 months before the first of the new 'County' class guided-missile destroyers was commissioned. It also proved more expensive than projected with *Tiger* costing £13,113,000, *Lion* £14,375,000 and *Blake* £14,940,000. The effects of inflation made themselves felt but were again not the only factor in the escalating figures.[13]

The entry into service of the guided-missile destroyers and a need to modify long-term new construction plans due to the advent of the Polaris submarines caused the postponement of an escort cruiser programme. The result was a new role being found for the *Tiger* class. The escort cruisers would have provided an anti-submarine helicopter force for the fleet, a requirement which continued. It was concluded in the autumn of 1963 that the conversion of the *Tiger* class provided the quickest and most practical means of meeting the need for anti-submarine helicopters in the fleet. The War Office, however, were concerned at the reduction in bombardment support for the Army but after consideration this was accepted.

Three schemes were considered:

• Scheme 'X' provided deck space for one Wessex helicopter with rotors spread and hangar stowage for three. There would have been no maintenance facilities and the after 6in mounting would have been removed.

• Scheme 'Y' provided deck space for two Wessex helicopters with rotors spread but there was only enough space to land one at a time. There would have been hangar space for four helicopters and maintenance facilities would have been at the level provided in the new guided-missile destroyers. The after 6in and both after 3in mounts would have been removed.

• Scheme 'Z' provided deck space for two Wessex helicopters with rotors spread and two could take off and land at the same time. There was hangar space for four and the same level of maintenance could be achieved as specified in Scheme 'Y'. The after 6in and both the after 3in were again removed.

Initially it was expected that the work could be completed quickly in conjunction with long refits which were now unavoidable because of the long delay imposed on the escort cruiser programme. The time needed to do the work was 9 months ('X'), 12 months ('Y') and 15 months ('Z'), with costs put at £1.25 million, £1.5 million and £2 million per ship respectively.

Scheme 'Z' was regarded as the best option and although the most expensive was the one chosen. The total cost of the programme was soon found to be somewhat larger being put at £12 million in total for all three ships for Dockyard work which included the refits, plus an additional £10.5 million for Wessex 3 helicopters spread over 1964-8. The programme was considered worthwhile even though the converted ships were initially expected to have a life of only 6 years, soon prolonged to 10 years. One gain achieved by the scheme was in the political sphere, for criticism of the *Tiger* class in their role as conventional cruisers was still being felt. One problem anticipated was the provision of trained aircrew. There was already a deficit of 37 helicopter pilots in the Fleet Air Arm and now it would be necessary to train 75 pilots in 1964. It was thought possible that the entry would fall short and that provision of the pilots would take a year longer than the work on the ships. However, work on the reconstructions

Blake on 6 May 1969 reconstructed as a helicopter cruiser. (*Crown Copyright*)

14 ADM 1/28609: 1963 Fleet
Requirements Committee:
proceedings 1963; and *Conway's
All the Worlds Fighting Ships 1947-
1995*, p504. The concerns of the
War Office at the loss of shore
bombardment capability were
expressed at a meeting of the
Operational Requirements
Committee (ORC) held on 16
February 1964. See DEFE 10/457
1963-1964: Minutes of Meetings of
ORC (PRO). The Board of
Admiralty discussions in October
1963 and January 1964 are
recorded in ADM 167/162: 1963
Admiralty Board Minutes, and
ADM 167/163: 1964 Admiralty
Board Minutes (PRO). The cost of
conversion to carry helicopters is
quoted in *Jane's Fighting Ships
1974-75*. These costs look suspect
as quoted, the disparity being so
great. The figures for *Tiger* may
include additional overheads.

took longer than anticipated, with *Blake* in the hands of Portsmouth Dockyard between 1965 and 1969 whilst *Tiger* was modified by Devonport Dockyard between 1968 and 1972. Delays and an increased workload in the Dockyards resulted in the reconstruction of *Lion* being abandoned and she was placed on the disposal list in 1975. The cost of the conversions proved to be far higher than the original estimates: *Blake* cost £5.5 million whilst *Tiger* cost £13.25 million. *Blake* was sold in 1982 having been laid up in 1980 whilst *Tiger* survived until 1986.[14] Always regarded as a stop-gap in both their roles, these ships were open to criticism on grounds of both cost and manpower. New ships would have been a better answer but a financial constraints meant that second-best had to be accepted.

Eagle

The first scheme to modernise *Eagle* was considered in 1955 when the ship had been in service for barely four years. It was extensive, expecting to cost £16.5 million and take 6 years to complete, so it was considered unaccept-

Eagle in 1964, the second fleet carrier to be reconstructed. The Types 984 and 965 radar, modified superstructure, and fully angled deck are notable differences from the ship's appearance in 1951 when first completed (see Chapter 1). (*Royal Naval Museum*)

able. A more austere scheme was worked out which was expected to cost £11 million and take 4 years. The aircraft complement was initially to be 12 NA.39 (Buccaneer), 10 N.139 (Sea Vixen), 12 P.177 (a combined jet/rocket fighter cancelled in 1957, a concept flight-tested in the SR.53), 14 Gannet ASW aircraft and 2 rescue helicopters. In operational service the aircraft carried included Buccaneer strike aircraft, Scimitar and Sea Vixen fighters, and Gannets. This modernisation was approved by the Board of Admiralty in July 1958.

The reconstruction was still extensive. A completely new island was fitted and a fully-angled flight deck (8½°) installed. The 4in armoured deck was removed and replaced with 1½in NC armour, producing a weight saving of 1294 tons whilst changes in the armament saved a further 442 tons. Strengthening the structure cost 605 tons whilst an extra 183 tons of aviation fuel could be carried. The major gain was 892 tons growth allowance to cope with the inevitable alterations and additions to come. The deck was strengthened to enable it to bear a static load of 45,000lbs and for a total landing reaction of 150,000lbs. Two steam catapults were fitted, one initially to be placed on the starboard side having a stroke of 151ft. This was later situated on the port side forward. The second catapult was located on the angled deck and had a stroke of 199ft. Deck blast deflectors and cooling panels were fitted. To handle the increasing weight of aircraft a new crane was provided which had a working load of 35,000lbs with overload of 45,000lbs. Both lifts were upgraded with capacity to accept a working load of 40,000lbs. The arrester gear was also upgraded.

The four forward twin 4.5in mountings were to be replaced, initially by two 6-barrelled Bofors and two twin L70 Bofors; the Bofors L70 were, however, replaced in the specification by Sea Cat close-range anti-aircraft missiles. Other modifications to the close-range anti-aircraft armament included new MRS8 directors to control the 6-barrel Bofors. The radar installations were also substantially upgraded with a Type 984 long-range air warning radar being the principal feature. The communications systems were completely updated and generating capacity was increased by 3000 kW to 8250 kW. Accommodation and air-conditioning were also improved. Originally stowage was to be provided for 283 tons of High Test Peroxide (HTP) in four pure aluminium tanks fitted in the spaces where the forward 4.5in magazines had been located. With the cancellation of the P.177 aircraft this requirement was deleted.

Although the modernisation was expected to provide the best of the fleet carriers when the work was completed, she was not up to the standards that could have been achieved in a new ship. Steam conditions and quantities were lower than needed and the electrical system now being a complicated DC/AC arrangement was barely adequate to satisfy the new demands. Improvements in habitability were limited and increases in wiring and pipework resulted in lower headroom. It was also calculated that had the ship been damaged by conventional weapons then the heel of the ship would have been greater than that expected in a ship of modern design. Nevertheless, it was initially believed that the cost of a new ship would have been two or three times greater than the £11-14 million it was expected to cost reconstructing *Eagle* over a period of 3½ years, the time being reduced from the earlier 4-year estimate.[15]

By October 1959 the modernisation was expected to cost £23.5 million and to take 4½ years to complete. Members of the Board of Admiralty expressed grave disquiet that such a large adjustment in the estimate should be found necessary in such a short space of time. The Board considered if there was any acceptable means of reducing the cost but the conclusion reached was that any loss of capability would not be acceptable. However, the sanction of the Treasury and Ministry of Defence were needed and in the meantime the Board directed that there should be no extensive stripping of the armoured deck. This support was forthcoming and the work proceeded, the ship being in the hands of Devonport Dockyard from mid-1959 to May 1964, the cost ultimately reaching £31 million.[16]

Eagle returned to service for less than 8 years before being paid off in January 1972. As part of a refit in the late 1960s the ship was due to have been modified to enable her to operate Phantoms, but in February 1968 it was decided this would not take place.[17] She was retained while her erstwhile sister *Ark Royal* remained in commission, before being finally towed away to the shipbreakers in 1978.

Girdle Ness

The development of the Sea Slug guided missile required the use of a ship for sea trials. Initial studies from 1948 to 1950 called for the conversion of an LST 3 to fulfil the role, with the proposal being considered in some detail. It was however decided that the poor sea-keeping qualities and the short rolling period of the LST meant that it was not the ideal vehicle for the trials. *Girdle Ness*, a Canadian-built landing craft maintenance ship completed in September 1945, was chosen in December 1950 as both the trial ship and the prototype 'Type C' missile ship. As the project progressed it was found that after the ship had performed her role as a trials ship there would be difficulty in accommodating the full war complement. It was therefore decided that she would not become a 'Type C' operational warship, with the result that the completed conversion did not incorporate guns, armour protection and other operational features. In March 1951 there were thoughts that the ship could also carry out trials of another new missile codenamed 'Mopsy', which was designed to replace the 3in/70 cal. gun, which had yet to go to sea on trials aboard *Cumberland*. In the event this suggestion soon died.

The Board of Admiralty approved the sketch design in

Girdle Ness in September 1956. Note the triple Sea Slug launcher, which was not ultimately adopted in the 'County' class. (*MoD*)

July 1953, the ship being taken in hand at Devonport Dockyard. The superstructure was stripped away and replaced by new upperworks with the guided missile launcher placed forward of the bridge. All the necessary radars, displays and communications equipment were installed and the ship was duly commissioned in July 1956. At this stage some missile handling, testing and control items were not ready, but the ship was capable of firing missiles unguided. *Girdle Ness* was commissioned for a further series of trials in April 1959 when presumably all the missile systems were operational. A triple launcher was installed for the tests but the production system installed in the 'County' class was a twin launcher. She was fitted with a Type 901 radar for missile control and a Type 293 for target-finding. A Type 960 long-range air warning set and Type 982/983 intercept and height-finding radars were also carried. *Girdle Ness* successfully completed her role and paid off as a guided-missile trials ship in December 1961 after which she served as an accommodation ship for many years.[18]

The Radar Picket Destroyers

The need for radar picket destroyers was initially met by converting the four ships of the 'Weapon' class. The radar picket was a requirement indicated by war experience which was to be met by the 1947 Fleet Aircraft Direction Escort (FADE) project, which considered a lengthened *Daring* class destroyer and the conversion of either the cruiser *Scylla* of the *Dido* class or the fast minelayer *Ariadne*. These ideas were followed by the Type 62 frigate project. All were destined to fail. It was to be 1958 before a start was made in converting the 'Weapon' class to fulfil the new role. The conversion was not radical and very much an interim measure. The torpedo armament was removed, the space being utilised to install the Type 965 (AKE 1) early warning radar and deckhouses. The main twin 4in armament and anti-submarine mortars were retained, thus keeping an anti-submarine capability.

15 ADM 167/152: 1958 Admiralty Board Memoranda, and ADM 167/153: 1959 Admiralty Board Memoranda (PRO). In the Ship's Cover ADM 138/866: Aircraft Carrier *Eagle*, three schemes are recorded in November 1955. Scheme I – all Staff Requirements met; cost £7m over 4 years. Scheme II – as I but interim deck retained; cost £6.5m over 4 years. Scheme III – interim angled deck and existing radar retained; cost £5.75m over 3¼ – 3½ years. Scheme I seems to have been the one adopted but the costings are very different. A double headed Type 984 radar was considered. The weight adjustments are taken from the Legend in the Ship's Cover. The deletion of the need to provide stowage for HTP was a gain, for this fuel is difficult to maintain, a pollution-free environment being needed. The explosion of a torpedo on the submarine *Sidon* in 1959 brought home the risk of handling HTP.

16 ADM 167/155:1959 Admiralty Board Memoranda. The final cost of the modernisation is quoted in *Jane's Fighting Ships 1966-67*.

17 DEFE 13/952: *Ark Royal* (PRO). About this time D K Brown was asked why she was not originally designed to operate bigger aircraft. His reply was, 'You were flying Swordfish when she was designed.'

18 ADM 138/737: *Girdle Ness*, and ADM 138/789 Guided Weapon Ships 1 (NMM). *Jane's Fighting Ships 1959-60* and *1962-63* describe the ship.

Scorpion in 1961 as a radar picket, with a Type 965 array and obsolete torpedo armament removed. As reconstructed this 'Weapon' class ship carried a Mark X mortar and remained a useful anti-submarine vessel. (*World Ship Society*)

Aisne in 1966, a 'Battle' class radar picket conversion with Type 965 double aerial. (*Royal Naval Museum*)

Well before the conversion of the 'Weapon' class destroyers had commenced, work had started in 1954 to design a fleet picket based on reconstructed 1943 'Battle' class destroyers. Initial ideas were to substitute the single 4.5in Mark V gun mounted immediately aft of the funnel and a set of torpedo tubes with the new radar installation. As an alternative a full modernisation and conversion was to be considered with an extended forecastle as seen in the Type 15 frigates. By March 1955 three schemes were being investigated: Scheme 'A' involved a full conversion, re-boilering, a new AC electrical system and generators, a revised close-range and anti-submarine armament and an improvement in habitability achieved by the extension

of the forecastle. Scheme 'B' was less ambitious, with boiler and electrical systems only modified and the forecastle deck extended. Scheme 'C' incorporated modifications to the boilers and electrical systems.

By May 1955 it was decided that Scheme 'A' would proceed. But in January 1957 when general arrangement drawings had been completed which incorporated the ship being bulged in order to meet stability, strength and buoyancy considerations, Scheme 'A' was abandoned and an 'austerity' conversion took its place. By July 1958 this scheme was ready to proceed and general arrangement drawings were sent to the Dockyards in February 1959. Four ships were converted: *Aisne* at Chatham, *Agincourt* at Portsmouth, *Barossa* at Devonport and *Corunna* at Rosyth. The work was scheduled to take between 24 and 28 months, a schedule, which largely seems to have been met.[19]

The main changes seen were the replacement of the mast by a substantial installation which carried a Type 965 (AKE 2) early warning radar and the Type 277Q height finding radar. The short-range 40mm Bofors and torpedo tubes were removed and replaced by a Sea Cat missile system and two single 20mm guns. The electrical requirements of the new radar and Sea Cat meant that the electrical system had to upgraded with an AC system being installed. The two twin 4.5in mountings with the American Mark 37 director were retained. The class were in service with the fleet for about 8 years, being disposed of between 1970 and 1978.[20]

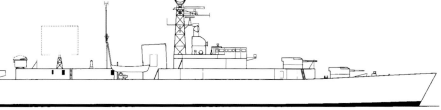

'Battle' class radar picket. The original proposal to convert all eight of the 1943 class produced a very handsome ship, which was unfortunately abandoned on grounds of cost. Note the extended forecastle. (*Drawing by John Roberts from original in NMM ADM 138/860*)

Ark Royal

Originally a sister-ship of *Eagle,* the *Ark Royal* was laid down in 1942 and finally completed in 1955. There were thoughts about giving her an extensive reconstruction on the lines seen in *Eagle* but this plan was abandoned. By 1963 the decision had been made to replace the ship with a new aircraft carrier even though she was only 8 years old. The problem was that much of her equipment and structure dated back to the war years and had deteriorated due to age and heavy usage during her operational life. In 1963 there was already a tendency for her equipment to break down and it was concluded that the planned refit over 2 years, which would commence in 1966, would only extend the life of the ship until 1972. If the ship were to run on for a further 2 years until 1974, the 1966 refit would take 3 years against the 2 years planned, additional work being inevitable. The result would be that one extra year of refit would only achieve 2 extra years' service, a net gain of only a year. One particular problem area was the electrical system. *Ark Royal* was a DC ship and power was already inadequate for her equipment and duties. The distribution system was described as overloaded and even dangerous. Additional AC generators would have to be fitted, communications needed to be bought up to date, and it was necessary to extend the air conditioning. Habitability would remain poor. The cost at this stage was said to be of the order of £9 million.[21]

The scope of the refit changed with the cancellation of the new aircraft carrier CVA-01 and aircraft projects such as the P.1154. The ship now benefited from what was described as a 'special refit and modernisation' between March 1967 and February 1970 at a cost of £32.5 million. The result was that *Ark Royal* could now operate the Phantom and Buccaneer Mark II. The catapults and landing gear were improved and an extension added to the island. Two Type 965 search radar systems were carried with a Type 982 for aircraft direction and Type 983 for heightfinding.[22]

There had been doubts about completing the special refit in the months after the demise of the new aircraft carrier early in 1966 and in March 1969 it seemed that her operational life would be short as the ship was due to de-equip in mid-1972. The refit did not always go smoothly, because a shortage of coppersmiths resulted in the pipework running behind schedule. The medical authorities advised that asbestos lagging was dangerous and then the substitute material proved even more toxic in the short term. A substitute for the substitute had to be found! There were then problems with gas turbine-driven generators which meant that electrical output might have to be downgraded. Nevertheless, the preliminary sea trials in December 1969 went well, but by January 1970 vast numbers of defects and deficiencies were said to be showing up, thus vindicating the warnings given 7 years earlier. In the end the ship ran on until December 1978, well beyond her allotted lifespan, being nominally replaced by the newly-built *Invincible.*[23]

The retention of *Ark Royal* was important, for it gave the fleet air cover while she was the sole operational fleet carrier during a period of financial stringency when inflation was rampant, devaluation of the currency a fact of life, and the economy in a severe recession. For all her faults she was a valuable ship.

[19] ADM 138/860: Destroyers 'Battle' Class – Conversion to Fleet Pickets (NMM).

[20] *Conway's All the Worlds Fighting Ships 1947-1995,* p506, and Norman Friedman, *The Post War Naval Revolution.* The AKE 2 was double the size of the AKE 1. For implications see problems with weight in 'Tribal' class frigates.

[21] ADM 1/28639: Aircraft Carrier Programme – date for placing order for replacement of HMS *Ark Royal.*

[22] *Conway's All the Worlds Fighting Ships 1947-1995,* p498.

[23] DEFE 13/952: *Ark Royal* gives background on the special refit. The health concerns raised by the medical profession have proved to be well-founded for asbestosis is fatal.

Ark Royal towards the end of her long service career, with Phantom and Buccaneer aircraft on deck. (*Royal Naval Museum*)

4 Aircraft Carriers

I**N MID-1945** four of the new light fleet carriers of the *Hermes* class had been laid down with a further quartet nominally in the new construction programme. The latest fleet aircraft carrier design was the *Malta* class where there were plans to start building two ships, with a further pair again nominally part of the long-term programme. But only a matter of weeks after the end of the War two fleet carriers and four light fleet carriers were cancelled. By December the financial situation had deteriorated to such an extent that the final two ships of the *Malta* class, as well as the original *Eagle* of the earlier *Ark Royal* class, had to be abandoned. The *Malta* class were large ships, displacing some 46,000 tons. The original 1943 design had 'closed' hangars but by 1944 an assessment of American practice was to lead to an 'open' hangar being specified in spite of objections expressed by the Director of Naval Construction.

Considerable work had gone into the closed-hangar design. The first open-hangar design was 900ft long and again not a little effort went into developing this design but misgivings about the length of the ship resulted in the Board of Admiralty cutting back the length by some 50ft. Yet more design effort was wasted. The advantage of the open-hangar design was the ability to get aircraft warmed up on the hangar deck and thus launch them more quickly, which was felt to be crucial by the airmen. The advent of the atomic bomb placed a new complexion on the subject and the *Malta* class was destined to be a dead end in design terms. The ability to close down the ship and wash off exposed surfaces to protect against radioactive fallout became vital and counteracted any advantages of an 'open' hangar. Furthermore, the introduction of jet aircraft, which needed less time to warm up than piston-engined ones, made an open hangar less necessary.

The 1952 Fleet Aircraft Carrier

The aircraft carrier fleet of the 1950s and early 1960s was initially to be provided by *Eagle* and *Ark Royal*, the four ships of the *Hermes* class then under construction, and the reconstruction of the six wartime fleet aircraft carriers. However, by June 1952 it was clear that the reconstruction of the *Victorious* was proving difficult and the Board of Admiralty came to the conclusion that it was the wrong policy to spend money on modernising the old carriers. Instead a new design was to be developed with a view to completing the ship in 1958. Steel for the new ships, then in short supply, was to be found by scrapping *Formidable* and the early 'Hunt' class escort destroyers.[1]

The Ship Design Policy Committee first considered the development of a new aircraft carrier design in April 1952. It was suggested that the ship should displace 55,000 tons, have a flight deck 1000ft long, be capable of 30kts 'deep and dirty', and have an economical cruising speed of 20 to 25kts. The endurance wanted was 6000 miles at 22kts whilst the carrier was to handle 80-90 aircraft with a weight of 60,000lbs. There was talk of a 'skew' landing deck. It was suggested that the ship be laid down in 1956.[2]

In July 1952, with the Board of Admiralty clearly supporting development of the new carrier, the requirements were further debated. The ship now had to be capable of carrying an aircraft the size of a Canberra bomber weighing 70,000lbs, with a length of 65ft and a 70ft wingspan. A single hangar with a height of 22ft was required, a considerable advance on the 17ft 6in built in to the *Ark Royal* design. It was to have an area of 50,000-55,000ft[2]. Three catapults were specified and ideally four were wanted. The flight deck was still to be 1000ft long so that the Canberra, Scimitar and successors could be operated.

This ambitious specification meant that docking was going to be a major problem. No. 10 Dock at Devonport was the only Admiralty-controlled dock capable of reliably taking the *Eagle* and *Ark Royal* and it was said that had the aircraft carrier *Malta* been built then a new dock would have been needed to accommodate her. The draught of the new vessel had to be limited to 33ft on the insistence of the Director of Naval Construction. The speed of the ship was now to be 32kts clean in temperate waters. Endurance and economical cruising ranges showed no change from the original specifications. There was to be a capacity of 750,000 gallons of aviation fuel including 250,000 gallons of AVGAS. The advent of jet aircraft operating provided one potential advantage, for jet fuel was less flammable, which meant that stowage arrangements were easier to design as safety precautions took up less space. Protection was 2in plate to the waterline but the full specification was to be worked out at a later date. The main anti-aircraft armament was to be the new 3in/70 cal. twin mounting, whilst the main radar array was a pair of Type 984, then under development.[3]

By September 1952 the parameters of the ship were: length 815ft, hull beam 115ft, a figure which the angled flight deck, by now a firm feature, extended to 160ft. The ship displaced some 52,000 tons; four sets of machinery were to produce 200,000shp to give a speed of 30kts with the ship 'deep and dirty' in the tropics. The flight deck was to have 2in NC protection with the structure of the ship being largely welded. The size of the design, although now less than in the first designs, meant that the only dry docks capable of accommodating the class were No. 10 Dock at

[1] ADM 138/818: 1952 Fleet Carrier – New Design (NMM). The merits of the options considered in the *Malta* design are outlined in D K Brown, *Nelson* to *Vanguard*, pp53-6.

[2] ADM 1/24145: 1952 New Design Aircraft Carrier (PRO). The 'Skew' landing deck was soon being described as an 'Angled' deck.

[3] ADM 1/24508: 1952 New Design Fleet Aircraft Carrier. When the *Malta* design was approved by the Board of Admiralty in August 1945 the only Admiralty-controlled dock in the British Isles capable of handling the ship – and then only with difficulty – was *AFD 11* then located at Portsmouth Dockyard (ADM 167/124, PRO). The building slip at Devonport was extended to 1000ft with the aim of constructing large carriers. Land was also purchased which would have enabled the slip to be extended to 1500ft (information from D K Brown).

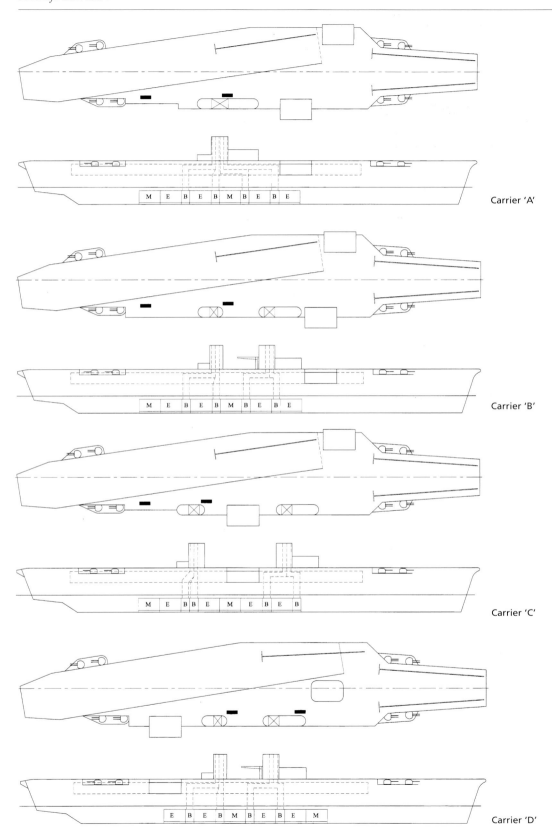

Carrier 'A'

Carrier 'B'

Carrier 'C'

Carrier 'D'

1952 Fleet Aircraft Carrier. Four versions are illustrated. The engine / boiler / magazine layout as illustrated in Sketches 'B' and 'D' was preferred. Note the angled deck, a feature tested in the light fleet carrier *Triumph* in February 1952.
(*Drawing by John Roberts from original in NMM ADM 138/818*)

Devonport, the Gladstone Dock at Liverpool and No.1 Dock at Gibraltar. The tentative programme at this time was:

1 September 1952 – Preliminary Studies complete.

1 December 1952 – Sketch Design to Board and commence Building Drawings and Specifications.

1 December 1953 – Building Drawings to the Board.

1 January 1954 – Order Ship.

1 May 1954 – Lay Down Ship.

1 July 1955 – Steel Deliveries complete.

Mid 1956 – Launch ex-Machinery or mid 1957 launch with Machinery.

31 December 1958 – Complete Ship.

This programme quickly saw slippage, with the preliminary deadlines not being met. Early developments in the life of the ship showed interesting innovations, with two funnels being preferred, and hinged funnels also being considered. An angled deck on the starboard side was also investigated but abandoned in favour of the original port-angled configuration. By June 1953 the design staff were clearly under pressure, indicating potential problems in evolving the design of such a complex warship. Other new projects also underway or planned included a new cruiser, two designs of fast escort each with different hulls, the Type 42 coastal escort, the stage two aircraft-direction frigate, a medium fast patrol boat and a new midget submarine. There were also industrial considerations. The only three shipyards capable of building the new aircraft carrier were John Brown, where No. 4 slip was available in January 1955, Cammell Laird's No. 4/5 slip, available in June 1955, and Harland and Wolff's No. 14 slip, available in June 1953 but earmarked for a liner. Important criteria in the choice of contractor would have been the availability of electricians and the attitude to welding in the yard. There would also have been problems in manufacturing the machinery, for had the ship been built with the aim of completing her in 1958, it would have had to have been ordered in October 1952, which was clearly impossible.

By April 1953 doubts were being expressed about whether building the large fleet carrier, two of which were included in the long-term programme, could be justified, and it was agreed to aim for smaller carriers. The cost of each ship was said to be £26 million. The end finally came in July 1953 when the ship was cancelled as part of an evolving Radical Review. However, development of the machinery – by now designated Y300 with each unit now expected to produce 45,000shp – continued at the request of the Engineer-in-Chief, who clearly had future projects in mind. The design had reached the Sketch Staff Requirement stage when it was abandoned. The dimensions were unchanged apart from the beam where the width on the waterline had been increased to 116ft. The deep draught was 33ft 6in with the deep displacement now 53,150 tons. There were

two catapults, one with a 200ft stroke, the second with a 150ft stroke. The maximum aircraft take off weight was to be 60,000lbs with a maximum landing weight of 45,000lbs. The aircraft complement was undecided but calculations were based on a complement of 12 strike aircraft x 33,000lbs, 33 fighters x 22,000lbs and 8 anti-submarine aircraft x 16,500lbs. The hangar height was the standard 17ft 6in, and the main anti-aircraft armament was six 3in/70 cal. twin mountings. Protection of both the hangar deck and sides was 2in NC with 3½in NC armour for the magazines and steering compartment. Group weights were:

	Tons
Hull structure	18,460
Hull fittings etc	9855
Armour and protection	4665
Equipment	2479
Aircraft equipment, weapons and fuel	5725
Armament	987
Machinery	4125
Reserve feed water	280
FFO and DIESO	6400
Margin	174
Deep Displacement	53,150 tons.[4]

The 1954 Medium Fleet Aircraft Carrier

The demise of the large fleet carrier did not mean that interest waned in the provision of new ships. As early as May 1953 the possibility of constructing cheaper carriers was raised, with thoughts that a ship of some 20,000 tons could be produced. By February 1954 it was found to be difficult to accommodate the necessary requirements within a 24,000-ton hull. The Director of Naval Construction commented that a larger carrier would give a steadier flight deck, a more flexible layout of aircraft equipment, better aircraft control arrangements and greater scope in making allowances for future aircraft development. Nevertheless, in November 1954 a 28,000-ton design was included in the book of studies produced for the Sea Lords. The design had a similar capability to *Hermes* and was able to operate 38 aircraft which could include 12 Scimitars (N.113), 12 Sea Vixens (DH.110), 5 Gannets, 4 airborne early-warning aircraft and 2 search-and-rescue helicopters. The deck was fully angled. The defensive armament had to be twin Bofors with MRS3 directors as it was impossible to accommodate the 3in/70 cal. mounting. Machinery consisted of a two-shaft arrangement with 50,000shp per shaft, which gave a speed of 28.4kts 'deep and dirty'. Endurance was 5500 miles at 20kts under operational conditions. However, the Director of Naval Construction did not consider the design to be a balanced one, particularly as regards the defensive armament. On 22 December 1954 the Sea Lords concluded that the ship

[4] ADM 13/818: 1952 Fleet Carrier – New Design (NMM). The machinery order requirement is recorded in ADM 1/24508 (PRO). A meeting of the Sea Lords in April 1953 which discussed the 'Shape and Size of the Fleet after 1960' and concluded that the new Fleet Carrier was too large is recorded in the First Sea Lord's Records held in ADM 205/102 (PRO). See also ADM 205/163: 1947 – 1960 Size and Shape of the Navy (PRO). The final set of particulars are recorded in a note produced by G Bryant on 15 January 1960, which is held in Ship's Cover ADM 138/888: CVA-01. There is an excellent discussion of the 1952 Fleet Aircraft Carrier in Norman Friedman, *British Carrier Aviation*.

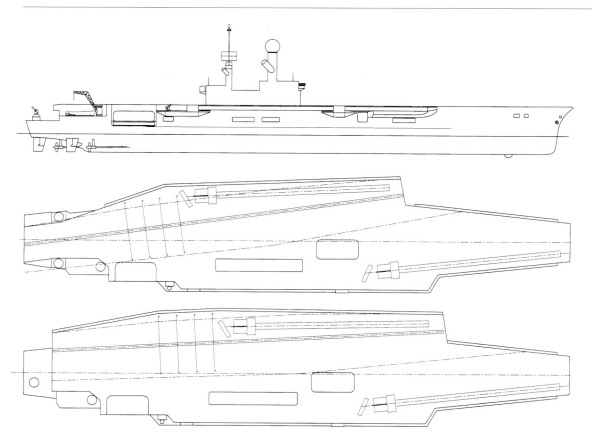

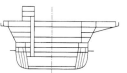

CVA-01, also known as Project 35. The drawing illustrates the design in March 1963. There were many modifications made but the basic layout does not seem to have changed. The deck plans show the angled and parallel deck layouts as at December 1962. The parallel layout was adopted. (*Drawing by John Roberts from original in NMM ADM 138/888*)

[5] ADM 1/25149:1953-54 Design of cheapest possible Aircraft Carriers to operate modern fighters: proposals (PRO). Details of the 28,000-ton Aircraft Carrier were recorded in a book of studies presented to the Sea Lords on 30 November 1954. The description but not the drawing is held in ADM 138/789: Guided Weapon Ships 1 (NMM). The minutes of the meeting which rejected the 28,000-ton design are held in the First Sea Lord's Records in ADM 205/106 (PRO).

[6] ADM 205/97 contains the Amended £1610 Million Plan – New Construction Programme dated May 1954 (PRO). The cost of Medium Carriers is recorded in a memorandum by the Director of Plans dated 15 September 1954 held in ADM 205/102 (PRO). A description of the design is held in ADM 138/789: Guided Weapon Ships 1 (NMM). No drawings of the design have been found and the dimensions are not known. ADM 205/170 includes an extract from a Sea Lords' meeting dated 8 October 1957. The First Sea Lord's first visit to Bath is said to be in 1955, but it was actually in 1954. In addition to wanting aircraft carriers designed to accommodate VSTOL aircraft, he also wanted them to have a guided-missile armament. This idea was, it seems, adopted and guided missiles were also incorporated at Mountbatten's suggestion in the new escort destroyer design which evolved into the 'County' class.

[7] ADM 138/888: SCC Project 35 (CVA-01) (NMM). The three planned 45,000-ton ships are recorded in DEFE 13/186: 1957-1960 New Construction Programme (PRO). A note on the table indicates that they were previously described as ' Guided Weapon Carriers'. Note how the displacement has escalated.

seemed too small for a big carrier and too big for a small carrier. The project then died.[5]

Contemporaneously with the smaller carrier studies, consideration was being given to the design and construction of a larger 35,000-ton ship. By May 1954 one ship was included in the ongoing amended £1610 Million Plan – a figure first settled upon in the 1953-4 Estimates – with the aim of producing Staff Requirements in the autumn of 1954, laying the ship down in August 1957 with completion in May 1962. A second ship was also envisaged. The cost of each new carrier was very approximately placed at £18 million. One interesting aim was embodying suitable characteristics to enable the ships to be adapted for the operation of vertical take-off aircraft – a far-sighted ambition included as a result of his first visit to Bath by Lord Louis Mountbatten, the new First Sea Lord. The design was duly included in the Book of Studies prepared for the Sea Lords, the ship being considered the smallest carrier that would operate modern aircraft in reasonable numbers, being regarded as 'in effect a general purpose carrier which while not being so large as to be wasted in the trade protection role, could carry a considerable strike force as an alternative when required'.

She could operate 47 aircraft, a typical mixture of types including 12 Scimitars, 12 Sea Vixens, 8 Gannets, 9 Buccaneers, 4 airborne early-warning aircraft and 2 search-and-rescue helicopters. The defensive armament consisted of four twin 3in/70 cal. with MRS3 directors and a secondary Bofors armament provided below the flight deck on the transom. Some 2700 tons of protection was worked into the design, the hangar being protected at the top by 1¾in plate, the sides being 1¼in. There was 3in side armour by way of a citadel, whilst the top of the citadel and vital compartments in the island benefited from 1½in protection. The ship had an angled deck and two catapults. The machinery was to be a three-shaft arrangement with 45,000shp on each shaft which produced a speed of 29.9kts 'deep and dirty'. Endurance was 5000 miles under operational conditions. The design was still evolving at this stage, with the armament and the machinery subject to discussion. In the latter case a twin-shaft arrangement was being considered, each unit having greater power. It was expected that weight would be saved. The ship would have accommodated a crew of 300 officers and 2100 ratings.[6]

Development of the design continued throughout 1955 with Staff Requirements being discussed and as late as 1956 outline drawings of a fleet carrier were shown at a meeting in Bath. How the project evolved thereafter is not known but three 45,000-ton aircraft carriers were included in the 1959-60 Long Term Costing. They were to complete in the 1970-1, 1971-2 and 1972-3 financial years. This project was, however, succeeded by CVA-01.[7]

8 ADM 138/888 (NMM); and
ADM 167/159: 1961 Admiralty
Board Memoranda (PRO). Six
studies were presented: 'Study 27'
(42,000 tons), 'Study 23D' and
'23E' (48,000 tons), 'Study 29'
(50,000 tons), 'Study 24' (55,000
tons) and 'Study 30' (68,000 tons).
All would have carried the
American Tartar missile with the
exception of 'Study 27', which
carried Sea Cat. The main radar
outfits in all options were Type
985, a 3D radar which was later
abandoned, and Type 978. Sonar
types fitted were 182 and 184. The
project was designated SCC 35 by
the Ship Characteristics
Committee. A full list of projects
as at September 1962 is held in
DEFE 24/90 (PRO).

Artist's impressions of CVA-
01 as the design appeared
in the summer of 1965. Note
the slight angle (3½°) of the
flight deck, Type 988 Anglo-
Dutch radar, deck-edge lift,
opening to hangar aft, and
Sea Dart launcher on the
quarterdeck. The aircraft
are Phantoms and
Buccaneers, with a Sea King
helicopter parked aft.
(*Author's collection*)

The Fleet Carrier – CVA-01

In November 1958 the Director of Naval Construction
drew attention to the age of the aircraft carrier force. At
that time they were expected to end their lives in: 1972
(*Victorious*), 1973 (*Eagle* and *Centaur*), 1974 (*Albion*),
1975 (*Ark Royal*) and 1980 (*Hermes*). Little seems to have
been done immediately but by January 1960 the Fleet
Requirements Committee was giving consideration to the
size of the ship. A displacement in the range 45,000-50,000
tons was envisaged. The issue was also discussed on 19
January by the Board of Admiralty, where the First Sea
Lord expressed the view that the Government of the day
would feel able to afford no more than four new carriers.
By June 1960 the Ship Characteristics Committee had
drawn up a timetable of the approach required; an abbreviated version is set out below:

Staff Requirement approval needed – end of 1961.

Approval of the Sketch Design – end 1962.

Provisional order including main machinery – early
1963.

Approve building drawings and complete
specification – early 1965.

Confirm order – 1965.

Lay down ship – mid-1965.

Launch ship – mid-1967.

Ship in service – mid-1970.

Operational – mid-1971.

By November 1960 the Fleet Requirements Committee
were considering a range of six studies with deep displacements between 42,000 tons and 68,000 tons. A fleet
of four 42,000-ton ships was estimated to cost £180 million, whilst four 55,000-ton carriers were estimated at £240
million, but these figures were regarded as very tentative.
There were key advantages in size, for the 55,000-ton ship
had an aircraft capacity which was 80 per cent greater than
the smaller vessel, and was expected to be suffer less interference to flying operations due to weather and have a
lower aircraft accident rate. Doubts were expressed about
the value of the smaller carrier which could accommodate 27 Buccaneer or Sea Vixen aircraft as opposed to 38
in the 48,000-ton ship or 49 in the 55,000-ton carrier. The
Board of Admiralty concluded in January 1961 that a ship
of at least 48,000 tons would be needed. The aircraft complement indicated two main roles for the ship: firstly to
act as a strike carrier, a function which included attacking enemy airfields; and secondly to provide air defence
for the fleet. Other functions included supporting radar
early-warning aircraft and, a later addition, the embarka-
tion of anti-submarine helicopters.[8]

Discussions between the Naval Staff Divisions duly proceeded on the basis that the ship would displace about
50,000 tons. Some forty design studies were made, whilst
the *Forrestal* of the United States Navy and the *Foch* of the
French Navy were also considered. The former had to be
ruled out as too expensive, whilst the latter was thought
to be unstable and too small to carry enough aircraft to
make the ship worthwhile. A design study known as
'A1/1D' emerged early in 1962. Length overall was 890ft,

beam at the waterline 118ft, the maximum width of the flight deck being 177ft with displacement 50,000 tons deep. On 2 April 1962 the Board of Admiralty considered the merits of the design in some detail. They decided that a quick study be made of a carrier of up to 60,000 tons capable of embarking more aircraft (including the possibility of carrying more aircraft on deck), the types of aircraft which the carrier could carry, and a comparison between the new ship and the modernised *Eagle*. The implication of using commercial docks in the early life of the ship was also considered.

By May 1962 another series of five design studies emerged in response to the Board Minute, with deep displacements ranging from 50,000 tons to 58,000 tons. The studies were presented to the Board of Admiralty, who after deliberation decided that 'Design 53' should be developed as the replacement for *Victorious* as the best compromise available in the circumstances. The cost of the ship was constrained to £55-60 million at current prices, with the added proviso that no additional equipment could be added which increased this cost. There was, however, one dissenting voice, namely the Civil Lord of the Admiralty, Lord Carrington. He suggested that the Board give serious consideration to a design of about 40,000 tons carrying 24 aircraft costing around £43 million, an ominous portent for the future. The new design displaced 53,000 tons and carried 35 aircraft and 5 anti-submarine helicopters. Length overall was 920ft, beam at the waterline 120/122ft, the maximum width of the flight deck being 180ft.[9]

Development of the design now proceeded, but complications due to a stretched budget soon emerged. By May 1963 there were still four ships in the Long Term Pro-gramme, but CVA-01 had been put back 10 months with her planned sister-ships all delayed by 6 months. The main cause was the addition to the building programme of four Polaris ballistic missile submarines ordered in April 1963. Expenditure of £1.6 million had been agreed to fund development of the design, but from October 1962 difficulty was experienced in getting the Treasury to approve individual projects within this ceiling, creating problems in maintaining the design effort as a result of this parsimony. By July 1963 the Sketch Design had been developed sufficiently for it to be placed before the Board of Admiralty. The length of the ship had increased from 870ft to 890ft at the waterline, the overall width of the flight deck rising from 180ft to 189ft. The ship had three shafts with the machinery developing 135,000shp, which gave a speed of 28kts and an endurance of 6000 miles at 20kts 'deep and dirty'.

The aircraft complement was 30 strike and fighter aircraft, which initially would be the Buccaneer and Sea Vixen with the planned variable-geometry ('swing-wing') aircraft being designed to meet Operational Requirement 346 being embarked later. Four early warning aircraft, 2 search and rescue helicopters and 5 anti-submarine helicopters were also to be part of the complement. Aircraft weighing up to 70,000lbs could be operated, with two 250ft catapults and two lifts (70ft x 32ft) installed. The angled deck in 'Study 53' was originally 7°, while the sketch design had a parallel deck with an angle of 4°. The 3D surveillance radar, originally to be two systems, was reduced to one because of space and interference problems. Electrical power output was increased from a planned 18,000 kW to 20,200 kW. Both designs had a defensive armament of one Ikara anti-submarine system and one CF299 Sea

[9] ADM 167/160: 1962 Admiralty Board Minutes, and ADM 167/154: 1962 Admiralty Board Memorandum (PRO). According to a Treasury minute the displacement of the design studies ranged between 25,000 tons and 68,000 tons. T225/2788: MOD Navy Department – Replacement and Modernisation of the present generation of Aircraft Carriers (PRO). The five studies presented to the Board were 'Study 50' (50,000 tons), 'Study 52' (52,000 tons), 'Study 53' (53,000 tons), 'Study 55' (55,000 tons) and 'Study 58' (58,000 tons).

[10] ADM 167/161: 1963 Admiralty Board Memoranda (PRO); and ADM 138/ 888 (NMM). Many of the early studies did not carry anti-submarine helicopters as this task was to be performed by the new escort cruisers developed from c1959. The extent of the conflict between the Royal Navy and the Royal Air Force over the aircraft carrier project is illustrated by a forthright memorandum dated 16 January 1963 sent by the First Sea Lord, Admiral of the Fleet Sir Casper John to the Chief of the Defence Staff which is held in ADM 205/197 (PRO). Other ideas for coping without large fleet carriers were guided-missile cruisers with long range surface-to-air guided weapons, more escort cruisers and 15,000-ton aircraft carriers. All were quickly dismissed. See ADM 205/201: 1963 The Navy without Carriers (PRO).

[11] ADM 138/888 (NMM). The cost of the dock in October 1964 was said to be £5 million. T225/2788: 1964-65 Replacement and Modernisation of the present generation of Aircraft Carriers (PRO).

[12] ADM 138/888 (NMM). Had two aircraft carriers been ordered simultaneously it was estimated that £2 million would have been 'saved' (ADM 167/164: 1964 Admiralty Board Minutes, PRO).

Dart anti-aircraft missile launcher. With an eye to the future there were four take-off positions for VSTOL aircraft. On 17 July 1963 the Board of Admiralty approved the Sketch Design and Staff requirements and decided that a price of £58 million should be shown in the long-term costings. On 30 July the Cabinet agreed that the aircraft carrier fleet be maintained at three vessels in the 1970s, a reduction of one ship from the earlier planned levels and that the new aircraft carrier should be built to replace the *Ark Royal*.

Pressure on the project was intense throughout the early months of 1963, with the Chief of the Defence Staff, Admiral of the Fleet The Earl Mountbatten of Burma, attempting to resolve the now bitter dispute between the Admiralty and Air Ministry over the planned new aircraft carriers. The project survived but various ideas were explored which investigated how the Royal Navy would operate without aircraft carriers. One option, a 20,000-ton off-shore support ship, was considered to the extent that Draft Staff Requirements were drawn up, but the idea was not considered practical.[10]

Building a new aircraft carrier of this size and complexity was not going to be a straightforward operation. There was, firstly, the physical problem at the shipyards, where there were no berths which could meet requirements without expenditure on widening and/or dredging fitting-out berths. There was also a perceived technical problem to resolve, for one-third of the structure was to be built with QT35 steel which required specially-trained welders. This steel was used in nuclear submarines and here work was said to have been placed with subcontractors because the shipbuilders could not find welders of the right quality. In practice, it was found that a 2-week training course was all that was needed to develop the necessary skills. Subcontractors could well have been used to make up a numerical shortage of welders. It was also believed that all work with QT35 had to be done under cover. In fact early nuclear submarines with this steel were built in the open.

Another problem was that none of the shipyards possessed sufficient drawing office capacity and even combining the staffs of two shipyards such as John Brown and Fairfield meant that virtually all the draughtsmen employed in the hull and engineering sections would be needed, and there was still a shortfall in electrical draughtsmen. When it came to construction there were again going to be difficulties. The worst area was the provision of electrical fitters, where the requirement was estimated to be 800 men whereas in late 1964 the largest number employed in any one yard was 338 at Harland & Wolff. There were also worries about the quality of the management at the shipyards where better planning, inspection and quality control was deemed necessary. Another requirement was a new dry dock to take the ship at Portsmouth where planning was progressing but there was no approval to take it forward beyond this stage.[11]

The project progressed and in April 1964 there were even thoughts that the Royal Australian Navy would buy one of the class. Had this occurred the draft programme would have been to order CVA-01 and the Australian ship in the last quarter of 1966, with the completions seen in the third and fourth quarters of 1973, CVA-02 being ordered in late 1969. Changes to the design inevitably occurred. The Ikara system was deleted in February 1965 when a role as a commando ship was also considered. At that time there were long-term plans to build three commando ships to replace and enhance the capacity currently provided by the converted aircraft carriers *Albion* and *Bulwark*.[12]

The design of CVA-01 incorporated many novel features. She has been described as a 'furniture van' with a novel light structure and until very late in the day had no armour, not even over the magazines, but she did possess new, effective torpedo protection based on work at the Naval Construction Research Establishment. The power needed to achieve 27-28kts was thought to be too much for a two-shaft layout in Bath (but not by the propeller designers at Haslar), so three shafts were chosen in spite of worries about vibration. This arrangement enabled one unit to be shut down for maintenance while maintaining a fairly high speed on the other two engines. The steam plant was novel, operating at 1000psi at 1000°F. The electrical distribution system was at 3.3 kV with step-down transformers, also new to the Royal Navy. The steam catapults were longer than in existing carriers and required as much steam as the propulsion plant. Bigger boilers were therefore needed. New hydraulic arrester gear and a scissors lift were incorporated. The flight deck layout was another new feature, the small angle finally being 3½°. Outboard of the island on the starboard side was a wide passage for moving aircraft aft. There were also doors at the after end of the hangar opening on to a quarterdeck to enable aircraft engines to be run in the hangar. The size of the island proved a difficult problem to solve, for early studies incorporated two surveillance radars. The matter was resolved when one Anglo-Dutch 'Broomstick' Type 988 radar was specified.

Another problem was the lack of staff in Ship Department: the number required was 30 rising up to 80, but the maximum number employed was 45, with inevitable penalties. Very late in the day it was decided to incorporate better protection. This ranged in thickness from 2½in at the magazine sides, 2in at the Sea Dart magazine sides and ends, to 1½in at the ship's sides, with 1in protection being given to the hangar. The result was an increase in displacement from the constrained 53,000 tons to 54,500 tons. The ship was, however, still said to displace 53,000 tons in 'average action condition'. The Project Managers were J C Lawrence (1958-62) and L J Rydill (1962-7), and the latter was particularly concerned about the extent of the new features and equipment incorporated in the design. Not only new features and equipment were specified but also weapons such as the untried and developing Sea Dart missile and aircraft such as the new variable-geometry project. A particular problem was the association of displacement with cost, which was proving a fallacy as complex (and expensive) solutions were accepted to save weight to keep the ship within the agreed displacement of 53,000 tons.[13]

The first ship was to be named *Queen Elizabeth*, with *Duke of Edinburgh* being reserved for the second member of the class. The Board of Admiralty approved the final design of CVA-01 on 27 January 1966, at the same time warmly congratulating the DG Ships and his staff who were responsible for the design. A Legend had been drawn up in December 1965. There were no changes to the length of the hull but the length overall including the bridle arrester boom was 963ft 3in. The extreme breadth of the ship was 231ft 4in. The weight of the hull and the protection were quoted as one item at 33,900 tons. The aircraft complement was now 36 Buccaneers or Phantoms, 4 early warning aircraft, 5 anti-submarine helicopters and 2 search-and-rescue helicopters. Orders for long-lead items costing £3.5 million had been placed in spite of Treasury procrastination, of which £1.5 million would be nugatory expenditure if the project did not go ahead. Less than a month later, with detailed plans ready for dispatch to the shipbuilders, the aircraft carrier was cancelled. The event was traumatic, and the whole structure of the Royal Navy came under review with the formation of the Future Fleet Working Party. Although desirable, this class of aircraft carriers was more than the nation could afford, since building the ships was but 20 per cent of the through-life cost of operating the vessels.[14]

The Escort Cruiser

The first studies for a new helicopter ship to carry 22 helicopters were probably completed in 1959-60. The result was a series of designs, the largest being a vessel displacing 19,000 tons. Clearly it was going to be impossible to build such a ship within existing budgets, so the requirement was scaled back to a ship capable of operating 6 (later 8) helicopters. Studies in 1960 now concentrated on ships with speeds of 26kts 'deep and dirty' and armed variously with a twin 3in/70 cal., US Tartar or British Sea Slug missiles. Three series were produced.

In Series 6 'Study 6C' displaced 5400 tons deep with a waterline length of 430ft, carrying 8 Wessex helicopters and armed with a twin 3in/70 cal. mounting. 'Study 6D' substituted a Tartar missile system for the gun mounting.

[13] D K Brown, *A Century of Naval Construction*. The last Legend was drawn up in December 1965 and is held in the Ship's Cover. It does not indicate a tonnage figure for protection. D K Brown worked on problems associated with the propeller arrangements at Haslar. There were worries about the uneven flow into the central propeller, which could cause longitudinal vibration in the shaft. This could wreck the thrust block, which occurred in *Illustrious* in 1945, and also lead to an early onset of cavitation noise.

[14] ADM 1/29044: Proposed Name for CVA-01 (PRO). The name of CVA-01 was approved by the Queen in May 1964. The design approval and subsequent cancellation are recorded in the 1966 Minutes of the Board of Admiralty held in ADM 167/166 (PRO). The Legend of CVA-01 (SCC Project 35) is held in the Ship's Cover ADM 138/888 (NMM).

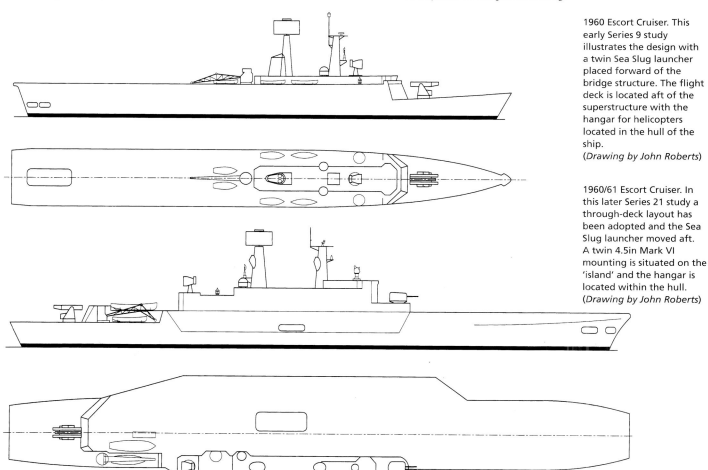

1960 Escort Cruiser. This early Series 9 study illustrates the design with a twin Sea Slug launcher placed forward of the bridge structure. The flight deck is located aft of the superstructure with the hangar for helicopters located in the hull of the ship.
(*Drawing by John Roberts*)

1960/61 Escort Cruiser. In this later Series 21 study a through-deck layout has been adopted and the Sea Slug launcher moved aft. A twin 4.5in Mark VI mounting is situated on the 'island' and the hangar is located within the hull.
(*Drawing by John Roberts*)

15 ADM 1/27685: 1960-61 Case for the Helicopter Carrier/Escort Cruiser (PRO). This series of studies illustrates the impact of requirements such as increased speed and increased complement.

16 ADM 205/193: 1961-1963 Naval Staff Presentations and Studies on Carriers, Escort Cruisers and Nuclear Submarines (PRO). The initial logic behind developing the escort cruisers was to enable the aircraft carriers to concentrate on the operation of fixed wing aircraft, adding to efficiency. In July 1962 Escort Cruiser EC 01 was to replace *Tiger*, EC 02 was to replace *Blake. Lion* was to remain in commission after a long refit in 1967-8. The redesign with the CF299 missile (later Sea Dart) caused delay. EC 01 was now due to complete in 1969, EC 02 in 1970 with EC 03 and EC 04 completing in 1971. A fifth ship was also wanted. The CF299 version was designated SCC 36A by the Ship Characteristics Committee. The earlier studies were presumably designated SCC 36.

17 ADM 167/162: 1963 Admiralty Board Minutes, and ADM 167/163: 1964 Admiralty Board Minutes (PRO). There had been no intention to convert the *Tiger* class cruisers until the escort cruisers had to be postponed.

Opposite: Illustrious on 23 February 1983, with the full normal complement of Harrier aircraft and Sea King helicopters on deck. The Sea Dart installation, with its blast deflector, is prominent forward, with the Vulcan Phalanx CIWS to starboard.

(D K Brown collection)

The complement of both ships was 50 officers and 400 men. 'Study 6E' was equipped as '6C' and '6F' as '6D' but the ships were fitted as guided-missile destroyer style flagships. The crew increased to 61 officers and 534 men, with the result that the length of both studies increased to 460ft and displacement to 5900 tons.

The Series 9 studies were larger ships armed with 28 Sea Slug missiles, 12 ready for use and 16 stowed broken-down. 'Study 9C' was 485ft long with a displacement of 6400 tons. The twin-shaft turbine machinery produced 36,000shp. The hangar height was 16ft 6in with the decks capable of handling an all-up weight of 12,600lbs. In 'Study 9D' the hangar height was increased to 18ft 6in with the strength of the deck increased to take a 22,000lb helicopter. In 'Study 9E' the superstructure was placed to starboard as an island, with the flight deck extended to port by means of a sponson. Displacement increased to 6730 tons. Four helicopters could be operated simultaneously. Series 6 and 9 were designed to destroyer standards for maintenance, complements and endurance.

Flagship cruiser variants were produced in Series 21. 'Study 21D' had an armament as in Series 9 but was fitted with some splinter protection. Length was 535ft, the machinery produced 40,000shp and displacement was 8350 tons. 'Study 21H2' had an island structure, a twin 4.5in Mark VI sited above the flight deck facing aft, and an increase in freeboard forward to ensure maximum dryness for the Sea Slug launcher. The missile stowage was increased to 12 ready-use and 32 broken-down missiles. Displacement was 9500 tons. 'Study 21J2' had two twin 4.5in mountings facing aft, displacement rising to 9700 tons. In 'Study 21K' the guns were mounted forward and the Sea Slug launcher aft. Length increased to 560ft and deep displacement to 9860 tons. Missile stowage, however, dropped to 28 rounds and the arrangements were regarded as awkward. The final variant, 'Study 21L2', was the same as 'Study 21J2' with an island superstructure but with machinery power increased to 60,000shp to give 28.5kts 'deep and dirty'. Displacement rose to 10,250 tons, with the waterline length being 550ft. All the cruiser studies had an endurance of 4500 miles at 20kts.[15]

The largest cruiser study was developed, for by December 1961 the First Sea Lord was presenting details of the latest design to the Chiefs of Staff Committee. The ship now displaced 13,250 tons, with length at the waterline was 610ft and beam 73ft. Machinery producing 60,000shp gave the ship a speed of 28kts whilst endurance was 5000 miles at 12kts. The main armament remained Sea Slug with an outfit of 28 missiles. There were also two Sea Cat short-range missile launchers and a twin 4.5in Mark VI. Nine helicopters were operated. The complement was 106 officers and 970 ratings. Cost was in the order of £19.25 million, with the first ship to be ordered early in 1964 and completed by mid-1967. The ships were required for the effective deployment of anti-submarine helicopters and guided-missile air defence. They also had the ability to operate as fleet units or independently for long periods.

Four ships were placed in the long-term programme, part of the cost being found by deleting the last two units of the 'County' class (DLG 09 and 10). Two of the *Tiger* class cruisers were also to be replaced.

By July 1962 the ships had been redesigned. The alterations were substantial, for 4 Chinook-type helicopters were to be carried. The weapons were also modified, with two launchers for the new Sea Dart (CF299) guided missile and the Ikara anti-submarine weapon system installed. There was also to be accommodation to enable 700 troops to be embarked in an emergency. The displacement was reduced to 10,000 tons and the cost to £16.5 million.[16] The decision to purchase the four Polaris submarines, however, resulted in the deferment of the escort cruisers but not their deletion from the long-term plans. The cause was not only financial but also inevitable design delays due to resources being concentrated on the new carrier and the Polaris SSBNs. The plan was now to bring them into service 10 years after conversion of the *Tiger* class, which was authorised when the escort cruiser programme was delayed.[17]

This new class was destined not to be built, for in February 1966 the new aircraft carrier CVA-01 was cancelled and it was decided to review the whole structure of the fleet. Nevertheless, they did have an influence on the studies undertaken by the Future Fleet Working Party. One lesson learned from this affair is that constraints on size do not necessarily lead to a reduction in cost. The new aircraft carriers being designed in the first decade of the twenty-first century are being made bigger to help 'reduce' the price of the ships.

The *Invincible* Class

The cancellation of CVA-01 and ultimately the decision to abandon conventional fixed-wing aircraft flying from carriers in the Royal Navy was to lead to a major reappraisal of the make-up of the fleet. Early in 1966 the Future Fleet Working Party was formed to consider the problem and provide the Board of Admiralty and the Government with recommendations.

The studies included a commando cruiser, initially described as an escort cruiser/commando ship. The design probably owed some of its characteristics to the earlier escort cruiser designs, which had remained in the long-term construction programme up to the time of the review. The primary tasks of the new design were ASW helicopter operation, the transport and loading of an embarked force, the provision of a self-contained air strike/reconnaissance capability, some fighter defence and, lastly, command and control of a naval task force or an amphibious operation. In June 1966 there was talk of producing six ships, the first vessel being accepted in June 1975. Studies were produced with the superstructure forward, the superstructure aft and a conventional aircraft carrier arrangement. It was concluded that the traditional arrangement was clearly superior to the alternatives. The

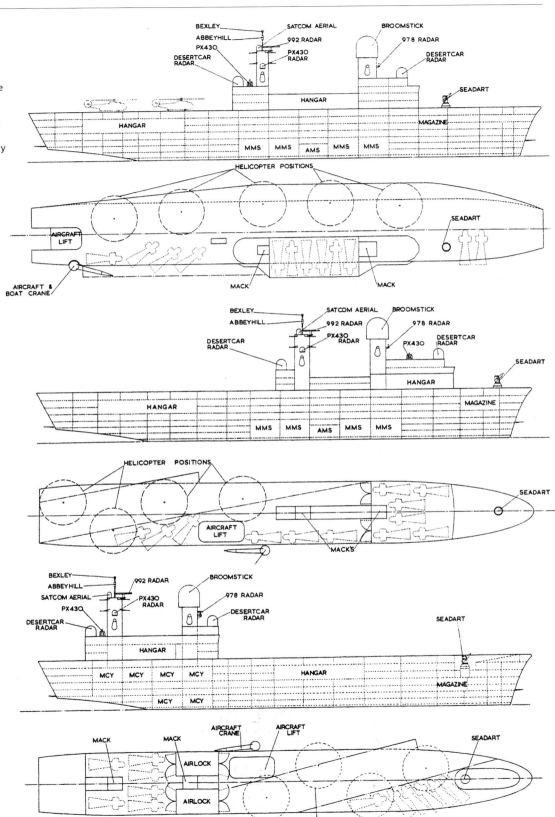

Future Fleet Working Party 1966 – Large Ship Studies.
Eight studies were produced of cruiser carriers, cruisers and a commando ship. Features will have appeared earlier in the escort cruisers, which were still in the forward programme in 1966. They were also an influence on the *Invincible* design but only indirectly as the design of this ship started afresh. (*PRO DEFE 24/238*)

Cruiser Carrier – Study No 1.
Design capable of operating helicopters and V/STOL aircraft with full command and control facilities. The ship had a commando capability.

Cruiser Carrier – Study No 2.
Design has limitations effecting the operation of both helicopters and V/STOL aircraft. Ship has full command and control facilities and a commando capability but there is less accommodation.

Cruiser Carrier – Study No 3.
General capabilities as Studies Nos 1 and 2 but poor layout for operating helicopters and V/STOL aircraft. Hangar arrangement was bad because doors would have needed an air lock. Machinery arrangement was not satisfactory because machinery and gearing could not have been placed in line.

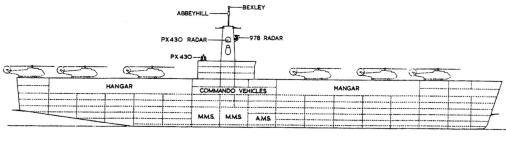

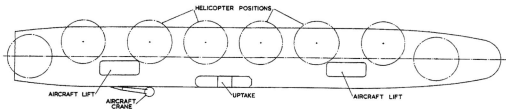

Commando Ship – Study No 4. A 'cheap' ship constructed to merchant standards. Internal volume comparable with USS *Iwo Jima*.

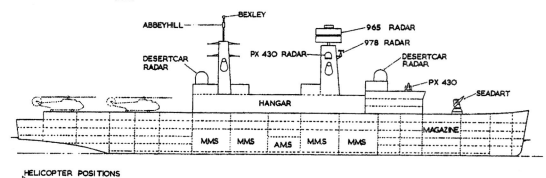

Cruiser – Study No 5. A ship intended to operate 6 SH3D (Sea King) helicopters with full command and control facilities.

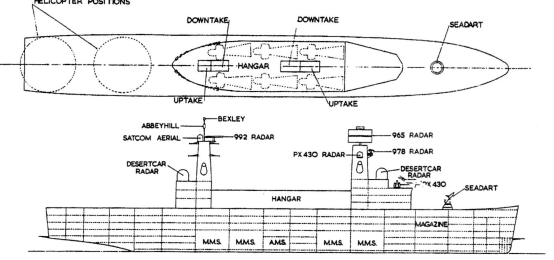

Cruiser – Study No 6. A ship intended to operate 9 V/STOL aircraft with full command and control facilities.

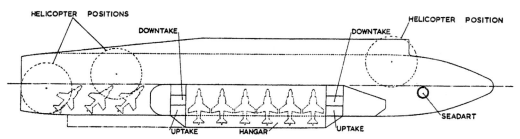

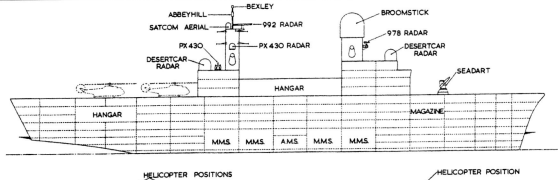

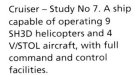

Cruiser – Study No 7. A ship capable of operating 9 SH3D helicopters and 4 V/STOL aircraft, with full command and control facilities.

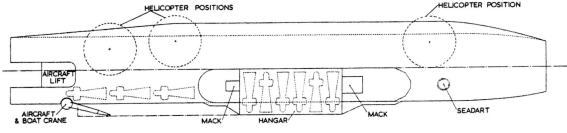

Cruiser Carrier – Study No 8. As study No 1 but with commando capability removed.

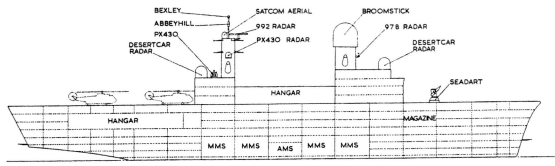

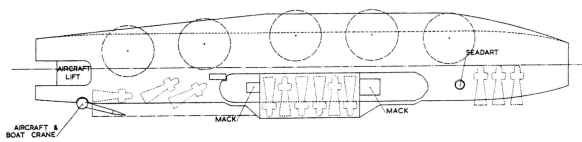

[18] DEFE 24/234: 1966 Future Fleet Working Party – Papers (PRO). Forward-facing hangar doors were ruled out; when open there was too much wind inside the structure.

[19] DEFE 24/238: 1966 Future Fleet Working Party – Report (PRO). Note that the Commando Cruiser was now styled as a Cruiser Carrier.

helicopters carried would have been the Sea King for both the ASW and commando roles, whilst the fighter requirement was to be met by the VSTOL Kestrel, the immediate ancestor of the Harrier and Sea Harrier. It was envisaged that gas turbine propulsion would be provided. The main weapons were the Sea Dart and PX430 (later named Sea Wolf) anti-aircraft missiles. The big Anglo-Dutch 'Broomstick' Type 988 radar was to be installed. By August 1966 an increased complement was being called for in the 16,000-ton design, the numbers being increased from 1390 to 1712 officers and men. The effect of this demand was that length increased by 30ft, the beam by 1ft, draught by 6in, displacement by 1500 tons and cost by £1.5 million to £31.5 million.[18]

The results of these deliberations were produced in a report for the Board of Admiralty entitled 'Ship Design Recommendations and Studies' which duly appeared in August 1966. Included were four cruiser carrier studies, three cruiser studies and a commando ship. Other details and drawings appear in Chapter 6.[19]

The Board of Admiralty discussed the Future Fleet Working Party report in October and November 1966. The idea of a combined cruiser and commando ship was rejected, the intention now being that the cruiser should be kept to the smallest size consistent with its primary function of command and control. It was estimated that the displacement of the ship would be about 10,000 tons. There was also opposition to the inclusion of Kestrel VSTOL capa-

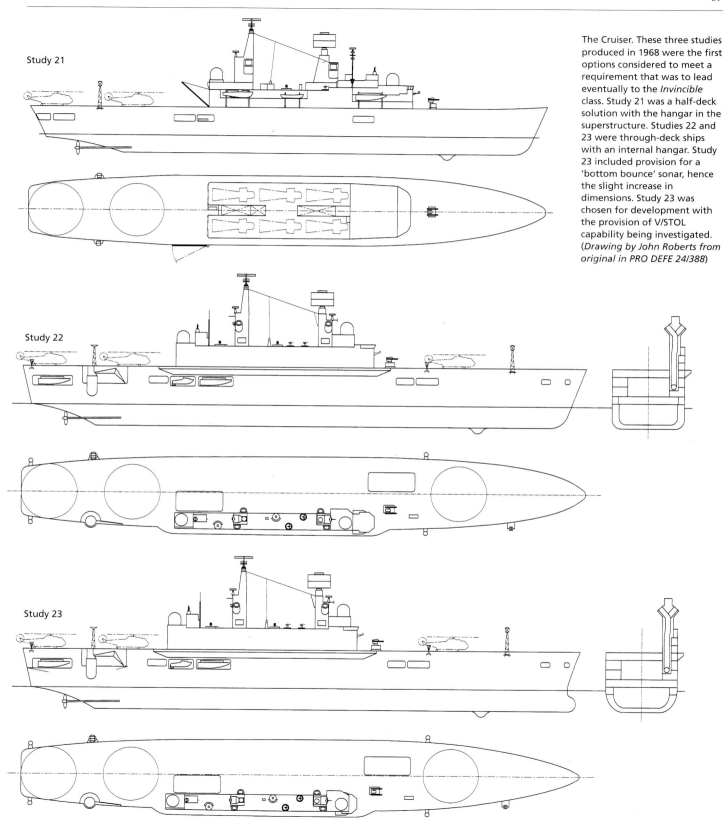

Study 21

Study 22

Study 23

The Cruiser. These three studies produced in 1968 were the first options considered to meet a requirement that was to lead eventually to the *Invincible* class. Study 21 was a half-deck solution with the hangar in the superstructure. Studies 22 and 23 were through-deck ships with an internal hangar. Study 23 included provision for a 'bottom bounce' sonar, hence the slight increase in dimensions. Study 23 was chosen for development with the provision of V/STOL capability being investigated. (*Drawing by John Roberts from original in PRO DEFE 24/388*)

20 ADM 167/166: 1966 Admiralty Board Minutes (PRO).

21 T 225/2963: 1966-68 Future Shape of the Fleet following the Report of the Future Fleet Working Party 1966. A Treasury official, J A Patterson, considered it highly unlikely that all six ships would be built.

22 DEFE 24/385-388: The Command Cruiser. By July 1969 there were three ships in the programme. The target timetable was for the Admiralty Board to approve the Sketch Design in October 1970 with the lead ship ordered in February 1972, the ship being accepted in November 1976 and then operational in May 1978. The second and third ships were to follow at about yearly intervals. According to a Treasury memorandum dated 21 October 1969 it was concluded that the original concept of a £30 million cruiser providing for six Sea King helicopters did not provide a big enough capability to be worth the money. (T225/3200: 1967-1969 Design and Construction of a new Command Cruiser for the Royal Navy, PRO).

bility with the majority of the Board regarding this option as not cost effective. The Deputy Chief of the Naval Staff, however, had reservations on this point. In his view the cruiser required a better offensive capability against surface ships and an increase to 13,000 tons would not only keep the option open but would also provide a better potential to exploit any future VSTOL developments. Final decisions were not taken, with Dennis Healey, the Minister of Defence, who was present at the meeting indicating that further consultations were necessary.[20]

The attitude of the Treasury at this time was far more supportive of the plans then envisaged than compared to the attitude shown to the big aircraft carrier. The deliberations of the Future Fleet Working Party were regarded as sensible at this juncture and there were still six cruisers envisaged in the long-term costings. These were now being seen as a development of the Type 82 destroyer, with command facilities and helicopters but no Ikara ASW system, displacing around 10,000 tons and costing £30 million. The first ship was expected to enter service at the end of 1975.[21]

By July 1967 Ministers had approved that planning of the fleet of the 1970s and beyond should be based on three new classes of warship: a frigate to succeed the *Leander* class, a destroyer to carry Sea Dart, and a cruiser to succeed the converted *Tiger*s. Capabilities of the cruiser were to be force command, control of shore-based aircraft, and contributions to area ASW defence and to area air defence. Based on these requirements, the Staff Target was produced and endorsed by the Operational Requirements Committee in December 1967 (NST 7097). The Director of Naval Construction duly produced a series of three studies in January 1968:

	Study 21	Study 22	Study 23
Approximate Deep Displacement	12,750 tons	17,500 tons	18,700 tons.
Helicopters	6 Sea Kings	9 Sea Kings	9 Sea Kings
Hanger	External	Internal	Internal
Flight Deck	Aft	Through	Through
Main armament	Sea Dart	Sea Dart	Sea Dart
Machinery	Gas Turbine	Steam Turbine	Steam Turbine
Maximum Speed	28kts	26.5kts	25kts
Approximate Dimensions	550ft x 72ft	595ft x 78ft	595ft x 82ft
Radar	965R / 992Q	965R / 992Q	965R / 992Q
Sonar	184M	184M	184M
	New Duct Sonar FBNW		
			HG Sonar FBNW
Complement	959	1068	1067
Order of Cost	Within £30 million	Within £35 million	Within £36 million

It was decided that the Naval Staff requirement should be based on 'Study 23'. Also decided was that a VSTOL capability should be investigated within a total mix of 12 aircraft and that the cost bracket of the studies should be within the range of £32 million to £38 million. The design

was still very much in its early stages and there were many problems to solve. Propulsion options were either four Olympus gas turbines on two shafts, two Olympus and two Ruston diesels, four boilers and two sets of steam turbines, or four Ruston diesels with two on each shaft. The number of Sea Dart missiles to be carried was debated and here it was concluded that 22 would be an acceptable minimum. Other issues to be resolved included helicopter numbers, the provision for future aircraft, the avionic and weapon fit, speed and endurance. Performance in the ranges 24-28kts, 5000-7500 miles at 18-20kts was debated. Further matters to resolve were hull configuration, provision of a high grade hull-mounted sonar, degree of self-support including storing intervals, plus the possible provision of an admiral's bridge.[22]

The Sketch Design was completed by the end of 1970 and then refined over 18 months, after which an invitation to tender was placed with industry. The design team was lead by A A Austin and some 5 million man-hours were spent on design work alone. The final result – now described as a command cruiser (CCH) – was no longer based on any earlier design of completed warships, having departed from the aircraft carrier *Centaur* and the command cruiser *Tiger* which were both an influence on the early studies. Comparisons with *Centaur* show just how the relationship between volume and displacement had changed. Internal volume of *Centaur* was 92,000ft² with a full load displacement of 28,500 tons. By comparison the new CCH had a volume of 90,000ft² and a full load displacement of 19,500 tons. The complement was halved, from 2000 in *Centaur* to 1000 in the CCH. Displacement was now a poor guide to size, a process which began with the post-war frigate designs. The reasons were the replacement of guns by guided missiles, sophisticated sensors making demands on space, the demand for improvements in accommodation, the replacement of heavy steam boilers and machinery with lighter gas turbines, upkeep by exchange and structural design refinement which enabled some lighter steelwork to be used. The deployment of helicopters plus the necessary maintenance and stores backup also lead to a demand for space.

All these factors produced a voluminous ship with a small draught (6.4m against *Centaur*'s 8.5m) and a high beam-to-draught ratio to maintain stability. The large exhausts from the gas turbines meant extensive trunking and this plus a substantial communications and radar suite resulted in a long island structure. The trunking also impacted on the hangar deck with the result of some loss of space. The provision of gas turbines for propulsion (Olympus TM3B) reduced the engineering complement by half compared with *Centaur*. However, more senior and skilled grades were required. Provision was also made to enable a gas turbine to be removed from the ship via the trunking, a massive advantage over steam practices. The ship's high freeboard and the provision of two pairs of non-retractable stabilisers resulted in a very seaworthy design with little water being shipped over the bow.

Illustrious arriving at Portsmouth on 27 January 1983. Note the Vulcan Phalanx CIWS right aft on the starboard side, an emergency fit for the Falklands deployment, since replaced by the Goalkeeper system in the CVLs.
(*D K Brown collection*)

Construction was not always straightforward, for there was some buckling problems during building which were overcome by the use of horizontal stiffeners. Damage control requirements meant that the communal deck below the hangar deck included the main passageway in the ship, no through passages being permitted below this level. There were no longitudinal bulkheads within the hull. Fresh air filters also had to be worked into the design for use if there was a nuclear, biological or chemical attack. The flight deck was angled slightly to port to clear the Sea Dart launcher. Six helicopter spots and four run-up points for Sea Harriers were incorporated. A further innovation was the aircraft lift. In previous designs this structure involved the use of heavy chains and balance weights, but in this case a new system involving hydraulic rams, probably

evolved from that specified for CVA-01, was produced by MacTaggart Scott, achieving a considerable weight-saving. Another innovation was the 'Ski Jump' ramp designed by D R Taylor in the early 1970s which result in the disposable load on an aircraft being increased by 30 per cent and the deck run reduced, leaving more space for Sea King operations, a massive increase in effectiveness.[23]

The first ship, *Invincible*, was ordered from the lead yard Vickers, Barrow in 1972 and completed in 1980, being followed by *Illustrious* and *Ark Royal*, which were both built by Swan Hunter and delivered in 1982 and 1985. They were described as a 'new beginning' when first delivered and ultimately came to be known as aircraft carriers, an immensely politically sensitive term following the cancellation of CVA-01 in 1966. *Invincible* cost £184.5 million at 1980 prices, the original estimate in the early 1970s being £60 million. They have proved of immense value to the Royal Navy, having operated as commando ships on occasion and, now that they can also operate RAF Harriers, have become effective small attack carriers, a tribute to their flexibility.[24]

[23] A F Honnor RCNC and D J Andrews RCNC, 'HMS *Invincible*: The First of a New Genus of Aircraft Carrying Ships', *The Naval Architect* (January 1982). It seems likely that a group of four Exocet SSM launchers was originally specified, space being provided forward in the vicinity of the Sea Dart launcher. The design of the ship always made provision for operation of the Sea Harrier, but it was to be May 1975 before the politicians formally approved incorporation and an order for the aircraft. D R Taylor is reported to have claimed that Ship Department was opposed to the Ski Jump. This was not so. The problem was that the Treasury had forbidden Ship Department from altering the contract as this had proved a loophole for cost escalation in the past. As a consequence it was necessary for Ship Department to 'play hard to get' until a separate contract was negotiated.

[24] *Ark Royal* was originally to be named *Indomitable*. The cost of *Invincible* is quoted in *Jane's Fighting Ships 1986-87*.

Invincible on 31 October 1980 undertaking first launching of a Sea Harrier using 6½° ski jump. (*D K Brown collection*)

5 The Frigate Programme

THE END OF THE Second World War found the Royal Navy in possession of a massive fleet of escorts, ranging from the early-war 'Flower' class corvettes and 'River' class frigates, to the later and more capable vessels of the 'Castle', 'Loch' and 'Bay' classes. Also in limited production throughout hostilities were the *Black Swan* class sloops, which were constructed to full naval standards. All the classes were limited in effectiveness by their speed, which was no more than 20kts. This was adequate when faced with opponents whose submarines could barely exceed 7kts or 8kts submerged and the 'Loch' class in particular were very efficient submarine hunters. The enemy, however, was changing, for in 1944 production was underway in Germany of the Type XXI ocean-going U-boat and the Type XXIII coastal boat which were capable of 17kts and 12.5kts submerged respectively. Also planned by Germany were the 'Walter' Type XXVI boats which were designed to achieve 24kts underwater using a newly-developed HTP turbine. These developments made the entire vast escort fleet potentially obsolete.[1]

Even before the new German threat was known, in the summer of 1943 the Allies were working on a standard class of escort vessel which could be produced in both Great Britain and the United States. The aim was to give the best surface and anti-aircraft protection possible to convoys without prejudicing the endurance and anti-submarine requirements. The main improvement over existing designs was an increase in speed to 24kts through the use of more powerful geared-turbine machinery. It was anticipated that displacement in trial condition would have been about 1700 tons. The gun armament was to be two twin 4in mountings forward with two twin 40mm 'Buster' and either six or eight 20mm Oerlikons. The anti-submarine armament was to be an as then unspecified ahead-throwing weapon. By August 1943, with the U-boat threat under control, the project died as there were other more urgent production requirements. This project, although not pursued, does give us a small window on the way that anti-submarine frigates were going to develop.[2]

By December 1944 a need for new sloops was becoming apparent. It was clear that a new design was needed and the first attempt was essentially a *Black Swan* class sloop redesigned to be capable of 25kts. Displacement went up to some 1660 tons full load from the 1429 tons of the 1944 version of the class, and the shaft horsepower rose from 4300shp to 15,000shp. In January 1945 it was realised that anti-submarine and anti-aircraft versions were going to be needed for convoy protection and the frigate and sloop types then began to converge. The main armament considered for the anti-aircraft version was either two twin 4.5in or three twin 4in mountings. The anti-submarine version was to carry a gun armament of either one twin 4.5in or two twin 4in mountings. The 4.5in option, however, was preferred, as this gun was destined to become the standard high angle/low angle gun in the future; it also had the advantage of an enclosed turret whilst the open-backed twin 4in Mark XIX was then considered to have reached the limit of its useful development. By the end of the month Staff Requirements were being considered, one of which was to limit displacement to 1400 tons. The Director of Naval Construction did not consider this constraint feasible. It was also indicated that the ships should be capable of mass production and that the hulls should be interchangeable and possible to complete as either anti-submarine or anti-aircraft vessels.

By the end of February it was accepted that the anti-submarine version would displace some 1560 tons whilst the anti-aircraft escort would displace 1650 tons. At this time the incorporation of aircraft direction facilities in the anti-aircraft version was considered but ruled out in view of the loss of armament. By the end of April 1945 it was confirmed that the versions considered in February should proceed. It was also now concluded that an aircraft-direction version was indeed needed and that a further version, 'A Headquarters Ship for the Senior Officer of a Convoy Escort', was also a requirement. The increase in size and complexity of the new escorts meant, however, that it would not be possible to produce the new ships in sufficient numbers. This was to lead to thinking that corvettes would still be required and it was decided that a separate design for this type of ship should be begun. This will be considered later.[3]

The end of the war resulted in a reappraisal of the planned 1945 New Construction Programme. The Programme, which originally incorporated plans to build four of the new escorts, was scaled down to just two ships for financial reasons, one to be an anti-aircraft version, the other an anti-submarine ship. The Cabinet approved construction of the new frigates in November 1945. There was soon a further debate amongst the Naval Staff as to which type of frigate should be built. The conclusion was that one anti-submarine and one aircraft-direction frigate should be constructed, the aim being to lay the ships down in 1946. The designs of the frigates were far from settled at this point in time and by January 1946 the displacements were increasing, that of the anti-aircraft frigate rising to 1750 tons mainly due to an increase of 50 tons in the weight of the machinery. This development gave rise to the possibility that two designs would give better-balanced ships with the anti-aircraft and aircraft-direc-

[1] The design history of the German U-boats is admirably told in Eberhard Rossler, *The U-Boat* (London 1981). A prototype 'Walter' U-boat (Type XVIIB), *U1407*, was commissioned for trials by the Royal Navy and named *Meteorite*.

[2] ADM 1/13479: Standardisation of Escort Vessels (PRO).

[3] ADM 138/830: Destroyers and Frigates General Cover (NMM). The Draft 1945 New Construction Programme included four vessels. By the end of June the Programme had been printed for presentation to the War Cabinet. Approval was sought to proceed with the design of four escort vessels of a new type, each of about 1400 tons with a speed of about 25kts. They were described as largely for experimental purposes, with two to be finished as AA ships and two as AS vessels. (CAB 66/67, PRO).

tion versions being capable of 20kts whilst the anti-submarine and Senior Officer Convoy variants retained the 25kt speed requirement. At this time the suggestion was not implemented as there was still a desire to retain the standard hulls with their consequent production flexibility. The theory was that an anti-submarine, anti-aircraft or aircraft-direction version could be produced at a late stage in construction to meet the most pressing need. In practice the designs, although theoretically capable of mass production, were becoming very complex, with the result that any change would not be easy to achieve unless demanded at an early stage in construction.[4]

In March 1947 the need for standardised hulls for all versions was again being questioned. It was decided that the anti-aircraft and aircraft-direction versions should use diesel machinery in order to achieve the Staff Requirement for an endurance of 4500 miles at 15kts, which current designs of steam machinery could only achieve if the weight of machinery and fuel were increased by 800 tons. A subsidiary reason was the limited capacity available to

produce steam turbine sets within the United Kingdom should quantity production be wanted. By April a revised hull design for the two diesel-powered frigates was underway. These became the *Leopard* and *Salisbury* classes.[5]

The number of frigate designs under development or evolving was ultimately to lead to the Admiralty instituting a system of Type Numbers, which came into practice in July 1950. It was clearly becoming difficult to differentiate between the various designs, some of which had rather clumsy titles. What became the Type 18, for example, had been simultaneously referred to as 'The improved limited conversion' and 'The fused conversion'. Clearly something had to be done to rationalise the titles. All ocean convoy escorts, including converted destroyers, were to be known as Frigates, which in turn were divided into anti-submarine (Type 11 and following), anti-aircraft (Type 41 and following), and aircraft-direction (Type 61 and following). An Admiralty Fleet Order defined multi-role ships as destroyers if they could attain fleet speed, or sloops if they were slower.[6]

[4] ADM 138/830 (NMM). Details of the 1945 Programme are set out in CAB 129/4 (PRO). The two escorts sanctioned ultimately appeared as the AA frigate *Leopard* and the AD frigate *Salisbury*.

[5] ADM 138/830 (NMM); and Director of Naval Construction Correspondence Files – memo by Engineer-in-Chief, 21 July 1949 (NMM).

[6] ADM 167/135: 1950 Admiralty Board Minutes and Memoranda (PRO).

Salisbury, first of the Type 61 aircraft-direction frigates, in November 1956. Note how radar and sensors dominate the upper deck layout. The low air-warning radar Type 960 is located aft of the second combined mast and funnel.
(*D K Brown collection*)

12 ADM 138/795: 1945 Frigates AA
and AD Types (NMM). The
Legends are recorded in Naval
Construction Department Records
(NCD 24, NMM). Machinery for
one AA and one AD frigate was
ordered from Vickers Armstrongs
(Barrow). One set was
subcontracted to Peter
Brotherhood, Peterborough.
(ADM 138/795, NMM).

8 ADM 167/131: 1948 Admiralty
Board Memoranda (PRO). A
memorandum concerning
prefabrication of frigates and the
elaborate electrical equipment was
written by a Deputy Director of
Naval Construction in 1951.
Arthur Honnor RCNC commented
on the difficulties experienced by
the shipbuilders in a note to this
author. He also commented on the
relative unreliability of the diesel
installations in service, perhaps
countered by the gain in
endurance, which gave a
considerable advantage over steam
turbine machinery. The ASR 1
teething troubles were overcome
and the type proved very valuable
until later commercial diesels
became available. They are now
well liked by the Bangladesh Navy.
The early history of the 'Muscovin'
V16 is recorded in ADM 265/1:
Engineer in Chief – Miscellaneous
correspondence 1938-1940 (PRO),
and J K .H Freeman, *To Invent or
Assess* (1982), a history of A E L.
The profile with maximum
freeboard carried aft was thought
to keep the ship dry. Opinions still
differ on effectiveness, but D K
Brown used the approach on the
Type 23, although mainly for
aesthetic reasons.

Lynx, Type 41 anti-aircraft
frigate, in May 1957. The
ship is dominated by the
two twin 4.5in Mark VI
mountings.
(*D K Brown collection*)

The Anti-Aircraft and Aircraft-Direction Frigates (Types 41 and 61)

These two classes were the first post-war frigates to be designed in detail and their development was to run in tandem. Legends were prepared in December 1947. The anti-aircraft version displaced 1770 tons, whilst the aircraft direction version displaced 1665 tons. The armament was as anticipated – the anti-aircraft version mounted two twin 4.5in Mark VI, the aircraft-direction type having one such mounting and a much more comprehensive air-warning radar system in place of the second. The 4.5in gun was, however, regarded as an interim fitting for it was anticipated that in due course the new twin 3in/70 cal. mounting then under development would be carried in all the planned new frigates when the Stage II equipment option was implemented. It was to be January 1955 before this plan was finally abandoned.[7] The anti-submarine weapon was a single Squid with 10 salvoes carried.

It was initially considered that these frigates would be produced in large numbers in wartime but the nature of the hull construction and the elaborate electrical equipment meant that this aim would just not be met. The hull was constructed using a large number of longitudinals in the hull structure, a technique introduced after explosive tests against the hull of the *Nonsuch* (the ex-German destroyer *Z38*). The structure was designed by E W Gardiner, who had carried out these trials. Although effective, the technique gave the shipbuilders considerable difficulty in constructing the vessels. A high degree of standardisation was achieved in the two classes, with the engine installation and the hulls being identical. However, the engine installation was complex, involving the fitting of eight ASR 1 diesels driving two shafts. A three engine-room arrangement was adopted, with the first and third engine-rooms each containing two more ASR 1 diesels driving generators. The main engine exhausts were originally to lead through the ship's side at the waterline but technical considerations meant that this idea was dropped in 1951. The ASR 1 design evolved from a high-speed V16 diesel for

submarines, the prototype of which was under construction at Chatham in 1939. It was further developed in 1941 and it was initially intended to install the design in the new 'A' class submarine. The idea did not progress and the plan lapsed, but the design was not abandoned and shortly after the war it was converted to direct injection and supercharged, becoming the ASR 1 prototype.

The new diesel installation was 100 tons heavier than the steam plant which was first considered, but the major gain achieved by the diesel engine over the steam turbine was in endurance, where the anti-aircraft version could achieve 4500 miles at 15kts whilst the aircraft-direction frigate achieved 5000 miles at the same speed, the difference being due to the ability of the latter type to carry more fuel because less space was taken up by armament and ammunition. The ship was also slightly lighter in displacement. One weakness was the lack of speed, performance being below that needed for both classes to operate as effective units of the fleet, but then they had been conceived as convoy escorts. The distinctive forecastle was an aid to improved sea-keeping in a design where there was a need to keep the heavy forward 4.5in mounting low in the ship. A small 60kW generator was also fitted in the eyes of the ship, as far as possible from potential harm. Both designs carried a comprehensive radar fit, each having the Type 275 anti-aircraft fire control and Type 960 air-warning radar. The Type 41 frigate also carried the Type 262 close range anti-aircraft control system and the Type 992Q surface/low level search system, reflecting its anti-aircraft role, while the Type 61 frigate was fitted with Type 277 height-finding, Type 960 air-warning and Type 982 low air-warning radar for its specialised task. Each class was fitted with Types 162, 170 and 174 sonar. In June 1950 Legends of both types were again prepared, the Type 41 being 1835 tons standard, the Type 61 displacing 1738 tons standard. Growth from the displacement calculated some 2½ years earlier was relatively modest as the detailed design evolved.[8]

The prototypes were ordered from Portsmouth (*Leopard*) and Devonport (*Salisbury*) Dockyards, a deci-

sion made as early as January 1948. Arrangements were also then being made to order the engines, a task which the Engineer-in-Chief found difficult. The numbers of each class planned varied from year to year, the requirement being eleven Type 41 and ten of the Type 61 in early 1953. Ultimately only four vessels of each class were built for the Royal Navy, with a further three Type 41 frigates being purchased by India, one of which was originally intended for the Royal Navy.[9] The time taken to build the ships was prolonged, ranging between 3½ years and 6 years, reflecting deliberate delays to constrain costs in given financial years, and design complexity. The ships were also competing for resources with the merchant ship owners and other major industries in an era of full employment. Both classes proved to be dead ends in design evolution, for no further frigates using diesels solely for propulsion were produced for the Royal Navy with the exception of *Mermaid*, a design based on the Type 41 but with a far weaker armament, the main offensive weapon being a twin 4in Mark XVI. This vessel was ordered by Ghana as a presidential yacht and laid down in 1965 but the contract was cancelled following a change in government. The ship served in the Royal Navy for only some 4 years before being sold to Malaysia.[10]

The Anti-Submarine Frigate (Type 15)

The first thoughts on converting 'Emergency' wartime destroyers into anti-submarine escorts emerged in March 1947, but it was quickly decided to wait until experience had been gained with the new 'Weapon' class anti-submarine destroyers before deciding how best to evolve the design. By November 1948 design work was given high priority on both this and also a simplified version which was being developed in parallel. Ten ships of both types were initially envisaged. The destroyers *Rocket* and *Relentless* were selected to be Type 15 prototypes, the functions of the type being to protect convoys of all types against submarines and to hunt and destroy submarines in co-operation with aircraft.[11]

By 1949 the international political situation was deteriorating and it was clear there would be a severe shortage of anti-submarine frigates capable of dealing with fast submarines such as the Russian 'Whiskey' class, and that it would not be possible to remedy this shortage by building new frigates. There were, however, considerable numbers of the wartime 'Emergency' class destroyers whose armament was outdated but with sound hulls and machinery. The programme now expanded to make use of these assets. The proposed armament was to be double Squid ASW mortars sited on the after deckhouse. In the event the prototype Limbo was installed in *Rocket* and *Relentless*, with Squid carried later on an interim basis in sistership until Limbo, as the Mark X was in production. Eight (the original Staff Requirement asked for twelve) anti-submarine torpedoes, the 'Bidder' (Mark XX), were carried and it was proposed that four tubes be fitted for launching them. The original proposal was for reloads to be held in a centreline deckhouse, but this lead to reloading problems. There was also concern over the drop from the forecastle deck level to the sea, but this was overcome. Eventually, eight single tubes were fitted (no reloads) but few ships carried the system and eventually the 'Bidder' was dropped. The supporting sonar sets were Type 170 and 174. The main gun armament, the twin 4in Mark XIX controlled by a CRBF director, was sited aft instead of on the forecastle where it would have obstructed the view from the new low bridge structure and would also been very exposed when the ship was driven into head seas. Also carried was a twin 40mm Bofors Mark V controlled by a ST director. This armament seemed light but it weighed considerably more than the original destroyer fit (179 tons compared to 150 tons). Space was also needed and weight-saving, particularly high up, was clearly important. Some thought was also given to fitting 'Fancy', an anti-surface ship HTP torpedo, but this idea died as did the weapon itself.

Assistant Director N G Holt was instrumental in the design, incorporating an aluminium forecastle extended well aft, a very brave decision as it involved manufactur-

[9] The difficulty surrounding the supply of engines is recorded in DNC Correspondence Volume 74 (NMM). The best source for the history of the warship building programmes in the post-war era is Eric Grove *Vanguard to Trident* (London 1987). Type 41 class AA frigates built for the Royal Navy were *Leopard*, *Lynx*, *Jaguar* and *Puma*. Type 61 class AD frigates were *Salisbury*, *Chichester*, *Lincoln* and *Llandaff*. The Type 41 frigate *Panther* was sold to India before completion. Two further vessels of this class were built for India. Further names suggested by The Ships' Names Committee were *Cougar* and *Cheetah*. Three Type 61 class frigates planned were named *Coventry*, *Exeter* and *Gloucester*. Other names suggested by the Ships' Names Committee were *Truro*, *Winchester*, *Durham*, *Ely*, *Lichfield*, *Armagh* and *Canterbury* (Minutes are held in the Naval Library, Whitehall).

[10] *Conway's All the Worlds Fighting Ships 1947-1995*, pp516-17.

[11] DNC Correspondence Volume 72 and Volume 76 (1) (NMM); and ADM 167/133: 1949 Board of Admiralty Memoranda (PRO).

Rocket, the prototype Type 15 full conversion, in July 1951. Trials with the ex-German destroyer *Nonsuch* (*Z38*) suggested that the spray deflector on the side near the bow helped to keep the forecastle dry. A similar deflector was fitted to *Rocket*, as shown here, but no benefit was found and no other ships were fitted.
(*World Ship Society, Abrahams Collection*)

[12] ADM 167/133: 1949 Admiralty Board Minutes and Memoranda (PRO). The design of the structure was by Norman E Gundry, then Assistant Constructor, whose assistance in the preparation of this section is gratefully acknowledged.

[13] ADM 138/798: Aircraft Direction Frigate Conversions (NMM).

ing what was probably the largest aluminium structure afloat. The design of the structure was comparatively straightforward but, because of the low modulus (load/extension) of aluminium, the design was governed by deflection rather than stress. The connection of aluminium to the existing steel structure was a potential problem due to the danger of electrolytic corrosion. The scheme adopted was to weld a steel bar flat to the deck and then bolt or rivet the aluminium to it using insulating material between the two metals. There seem to have been no problems in service.

A big operations room stood on 1 deck; there was no bridge in the conventional sense as the captain was expected to handle his ship from the operations room – he was given a periscope with which to see out – but the last three ships had a small bridge over the operations room. At the fore end of the superstructure on 1 deck there was a steering position with big windows. Unfortunately, no model tests were carried out to assess the viability of this feature in all weathers, and they turned out to be obscured in any sea. The big openings in the keel for sonar domes were a problem, as structural theory of the day could not cope, but 'engineering judgement' produced an effective solution. Fore and aft access under cover proved a major advance in comfort, and hence efficiency, for the crew, who no longer had to cross an open deck in heavy seas and risk a soaking.

Altogether twenty-three Royal Navy destroyers were converted, twelve in Dockyards, the rest in commercial yards. Four Australian and two Canadian destroyers were also converted on similar lines. A conversion took about 2 years and although the initial cost estimate at £600,000 seemed excessive at the time, they were amongst the best anti-submarine ships in the world and most had service lives of 15 to 20 years after conversion.[12]

The Aircraft-Direction Frigate (Type 62)

This proposal first emerged in August 1948, the basis being the conversion of an 'R' class destroyer. The radar installation initially planned was Type 293Q, two Type 277Q, Type 960 and two Type 262. Armament comprised a twin 4in mounting, a twin 40mm Bofors, and a single Squid. By September 1949 the programme was to start with the conversion of the five surviving 'M' class destroyers at a cost of some £386,000 each. The class title at this time was 'Aircraft Direction Frigate Limited Conversion Fleet'. The allocation of a Type number was a very necessary simplification.

By December 1951 the radar outfit had been modified. It now consisted of Types 293Q, 960, 974, 982 and 983. The prototypes were to be *Marne* ('M' class) and *Myngs* ('Z' class), which were to be followed by the four remaining 'M' class and the intermediate destroyers *Kempenfelt*, *Troubridge*, *Wager*, *Whelp*, *Savage* and *Ursa* (substituted for *Grenville*). The intermediate destroyers, however, could not mount the Types 982 and 983 radar wanted in the revised design so they were eliminated from the Type 62 Programme. The 1954 Radical Review resulted in the deletion of four of the 'M' class conversions, leaving just *Musketeer* in place as a potential prototype. However, *Salisbury* (Type 61) was expected to be ready by September 1955 so, with no need for *Musketeer* as a trials ship, it was decided that it was not economic to proceed with her conversion.[13]

The Anti-Submarine Frigate (Type 16)

This class was a simplified conversion of wartime destroyers to anti-submarine convoy escorts. Development evolved in parallel with the Type 15 and initially ten vessels were to receive the limited conversion, the aim being that they should follow the first ten destroyers receiving the full conversion. At one stage eighteen conversions were said to be planned. The Staff Requirement was exactly the same as that expected of the full conversion but inevitably the capability was to be less. The basic destroyer hull outline was retained but there were modifications made to the bridge structure so that AIO compartments, radar offices and a closed navigation bridge could be provided. The fore end of the hull was fitted with additional stiffening so that the ship could be driven into head seas. A twin 4in Mark XIX was originally to be mounted in 'A' gun position, but this position was later altered to 'B' position, which reduced exposure in heavy seas. A twin 40mm Mark V mounting was also to be carried, but this was replaced by five single 40mm Bofors Mark IX mountings in the final design; on completion most carried one twin Mark V and three single Mark IX 40mm Bofors. The Type 293 target indication radar was installed. The anti-submarine armament consisted of a double Squid capable of firing 20 salvoes, 120 projectiles being carried. It was also planned to mount four anti-submarine torpedo tubes

Teazer, a Type 16 limited conversion, in May 1955. The ship retains one set of torpedo tubes which were pertinent to the ship's previous role as a destroyer. Note the Squid anti-submarine mortars sited on the deckhouse aft of the torpedo tubes.
(*D K Brown collection*)

without reloads but these were not installed and four of the 21in torpedo tubes, which the class carried as a destroyer, were retained. A Type 170 attack sonar and a Type 174P medium-range search sonar were fitted.

The prototype conversion was *Tenacious* and ultimately six further units of the 'T' class emergency destroyers received the limited conversion. Also converted were one 'O' class and two 'P' class destroyers, which made up the full complement of ten conversions originally planned. The 'O' and 'P' classes had less endurance than their near sisters: 1700 miles as against 3000 miles at 20kts. The cost of a 'limited' conversion at £260,000 was considerably less than the £600,000 price of the full conversion. The other advantage was that theoretically a destroyer could be modified in 10 months as against the 18 months budgeted for a full conversion, an important consideration in the early years of the programme. The weak link was a relatively poor anti-submarine armament and once production of the full conversions was coming forward there was no need to convert any further limited versions beyond those planned, for which equipment had been procured.[14]

The Anti-Submarine Frigate (Type 12)

Up until the end of 1947 the anti-submarine frigate was still expected to achieve a speed of 25kts with 20,000shp, with endurance of 3000 miles at 15kts. But by early 1948 the Naval Staff Target had changed, with a speed of 27kts and endurance of 4500 miles at 15kts now wanted. The threats to be coped with were now threefold. First, the typical Second World War submarine with an underwater speed of 7kts, the answer to which was the 'Loch' class.

Second, an enemy equivalent of the Intermediate 'B' Type Submarine (*Porpoise* class) capable of 17-18kts, requiring a 27kt frigate to counter it. Third, there was also the HTP submarine able to achieve 25kts underwater: two boats of this type, *Explorer* and *Excalibur*, were being designed for the Royal Navy and the Russians also had access to German HTP technology. A 35kt ship was needed against such submarines. It was to take more than 10 years to overcome a threat with this speed, shipborne helicopters providing the answer. By the end of the year the Board of Admiralty had sanctioned development of the upgraded design to cope with the Intermediate 'B' Type threat.[15]

Initially work on the design was slowed by a lack of staff, priority being given to designing the conversion of destroyers into anti-submarine frigates. Indeed, at one time there were thoughts of postponing the first-rate design for 5 years in favour of a less-capable version, but this idea was ruled out. By February 1950 the Sketch Design was ready for approval by the Board of Admiralty. The standard displacement had risen to 1840 tons whilst the engines now produced 30,000shp using the new Y100 steam turbines. A compromise had to be made with the endurance. Instead of achieving 4500 miles at 15kts, this could only be achieved at 12kts. Initially the main anti-submarine weapon was to be a double Squid but by the time the design was placed before the Board of Admiralty the double Limbo had been substituted. There were also to be anti-submarine torpedoes, but these had not yet been developed and ultimately they proved a failure. The gun was the twin 4.5in Mark VI as long planned, but provision was made for fitting the new 3in/70 cal. mounting. The initial radar fit was to be Type 277Q for height find-

[14] ADM 167/133 and /135: 1949 and 1951 Admiralty Board Minutes and Memoranda (PRO).

[15] ADM 116/5632: Ship Design Policy Committee (PRO). Asdics at the end of the Second World War were inefficient above 18kts.

Torquay (Type 12 first-rate anti-submarine frigate) in August 1956. Note the small cylindrical funnel which was designed to resist a nuclear blast; this was later replaced with a larger, domed design. (*D K Brown collection*)

ing and Type 293Q for target indication. Also fitted in service were Type 262 for close-range anti-aircraft fire control and Type 275 for long-range anti-aircraft fire control. The sonar sets mounted were Types 162, 170 and 174, the latter set being later replaced by Type 177.

The funnel was originally designed to resist a nuclear blast but it was later considered ugly and replaced. Accord-

The refitted Type 12 *Rothesay*, seen here modernised to *Leander* standards. The helicopter deck to operate a Wasp helicopter (which displaced one anti-submarine mortar), a hanger for the helicopter and a Sea Cat short-range missile system in the place of a 40mm Bofors are clearly visible.

(*D K Brown collection*)

Below: *Rothesay* in 1960 as originally completed, first of the second group of Type 12 frigates. The main visible difference from the *Whitby* class was the larger funnel. They were fitted for the Sea Cat short-range missile system, but carried a 40mm Bofors mount in lieu until refitted later in their careers. (*World Ship Society*)

Right: An overhead view of *Torquay* (Type 12 first-rate anti-submarine frigate) in August 1956. Note the fine bow lines. There are chocks amidships for the single AS torpedo tubes that were only fitted in a few of the class. (*D K Brown collection*)

16 ADM 167/135: 1950 Board of Admiralty Memoranda, ADM 281/149: 1950 Director of Naval Construction – Progress Report (PRO); and *A Century of Naval Construction* by D K Brown. The 'Tribal' class had to have the bridge placed further forward, which resulted in these ships giving a rough ride. The first production propeller designed by Honnor was known as C256, Brown was the trials officer. Quiet propellers were previously effective at 6 to 8kts.

17 D K Brown, 'The 1945 Sloops – Designer's View', *Warship World* Vol 3, No. 3.

ing to Arthur Honnor RCNC, the hull design was simplified in that the number of longitudinals was reduced when compared with the earlier anti-aircraft and aircraft-direction designs. The hull form developed by N G Holt and R W L Gawn incorporated a high freeboard carried aft, a deep draught and fine lines forward which gave a centre of buoyancy well aft (see photographs of *Leander* and her model in Chapter 12). To maintain stability as fuel was consumed, water ballast tanks were fitted under the fuel tanks, water being admitted via an elaborate system of pumps as fuel was used up. The utilisation of these features was based on practical experience at sea and an extensive series of tests by Gawn at the Admiralty Experiment Works, Haslar.

A conspicuous feature of the Type 12 frigate, and to some extent of the Types 41 and 61, was the raised fore end. The fine lines forward in the Type 12 hull form could only accommodate the large-diameter gun bay of the twin 4.5in Mark VI gun bay if this installation was placed well aft. This in turn forced the bridge further aft than was usual. The Mark VI turret was both high and heavy and to enable watchkeepers to see over it the mounting was placed as low as possible in the ship, which assisted stability. With the bridge forced into the low-motion zone amidships, watchkeepers were given an easy ride, accounting for some of the reputation of the class as good seaboats. The Type 41 and 61 classes had fuller lines, but it was still desirable to keep the Mark VI turret low and they were given a similar profile. It was widely believed that this peculiar profile accounted for their good seakeeping qualities and in particular keeping the deck dry. The ideas were translated to the Type 23 frigate in a modified form by D K Brown at the concept design stage, the aim being to maintain the maximum freeboard a little aft of the stem as there is evidence that waves come over the deck in that position. In the Type 12s the raised fore end was a convenient place for the diesel generators, as far as possible from the turbo generators, good practice for damage limitation. Unfortunately, because the diesel exhaust made the paint dirty; they were moved in the *Leander*s so that they could exhaust up the mast, which Brown considered a retrograde step.

The Type 12s and later twin-screw frigates had twin rudders in the propeller slipstream for improved performance, giving a turning circle of about 3½ times the ship's length. Also incorporated were slow-running 12ft

propellers, which revolved at 220rpm instead of conventional destroyer propellers of 10ft 6in diameter. This feature was eventually to contribute to the quiet speed being virtually doubled.[16]

Soon after the Board of Admiralty approved the Sketch Design the class was described as the 'Type 12 Anti-Submarine Frigate First Rate'. Six frigates were produced to the original design, the *Whitby* class, and nine slightly modified versions, the *Rothesay* class, for the Royal Navy. In addition, two were built for India, which were originally intended for the Royal Navy, three for South Africa and a further four were constructed in Australia. The external differences between the two groups were small, the main gain in the *Rothesay* class being the ability to fit Sea Cat. The cruising turbines were also eliminated, which reflected the increased use of the ships with the fleet rather than as convoy escorts as originally planned. The *Rothesay* class were all later rebuilt to *Leander* standards, but the original six *Whitby* class were little changed throughout their lives apart from much of the thin hull plating having to be replaced due to corrosion.

The Anti-Submarine Frigate (Second-Rate) (Type 14)

The role of the second-rate frigate during the war years was performed by the 'Flower' and 'Castle' class corvettes. With new threats appearing it was concluded that a new corvette design was needed. A study made in June 1945 resulted in a vessel displacing about 1000 tons armed with a single 4in gun, one twin 40mm Bofors and four twin 20mm Oerlikons. A twin Squid with 20 salvoes was provided, together with 15 depth charges. Speed was 20kts with the endurance sought being 4000-5000 miles at 15kts. No development seems to have taken place beyond the production of this brief outline and with the cessation of hostilities the idea was dropped.[17]

A new intermediate anti-submarine frigate was considered in March 1947 when there seemed to be possibilities that the first-rate vessels would be delayed. There was a resemblance to the vessels built later in that they were steam-driven with a strong anti-submarine armament and light surface weaponry. However, this was an idea which again quickly died. In October 1948 there were ideas that that an anti-submarine frigate could be produced with 'Hunt' type machinery, but studies soon showed that this

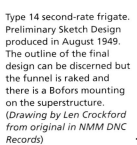

Type 14 second-rate frigate. Preliminary Sketch Design produced in August 1949. The outline of the final design can be discerned but the funnel is raked and there is a Bofors mounting on the superstructure. (*Drawing by Len Crockford from original in NMM DNC Records*)

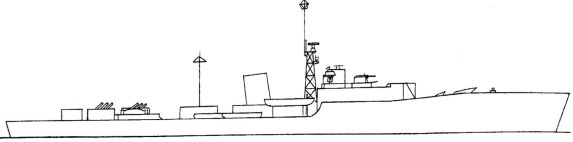

proposition was ineffective and again the idea was dropped.[18] The summer of 1949 saw a need for a second-rate frigate again emerging, this time the aim being to increase numbers without increasing costs. Initial thoughts veered towards a diesel version, but this was ruled out because of cost, with the result that half the installed power of a first-rate frigate became the only option at this time. The ships again concentrated on the anti-submarine role through the double Limbo and anti-submarine torpedoes supported by the best asdic (sonar) sets available at the time. The sonar outfit was the equal of that mounted in the Type 12 class. The anti-aircraft armament was originally to be one twin 40mm Bofors mounting located on the bridge structure, and one single. Tests at the Admiralty Experiment Works, Haslar, however, indicated that such an arrangement was not satisfactory and ultimately three single 40mm Bofors with a simple form of direction were fitted.[19]

Building times were meant to be a mere 3 months longer than seen in the Second World War when the 'Flower' class were in production. The new design was, however, far more complex than the wartime vessels and most of the twelve vessels (the *Blackwood* class) built for the Royal Navy took over 3 years to complete. Structurally the class proved rather frail and they needed considerable strengthening, particularly after fishery protection duties in Icelandic waters. They also had problems at the break of forecastle where there was a two-deck step which caused a major stress concentration. They were also prone to slamming under the flat stern in following seas. The Type

14 had a big single rudder behind its single propeller. The rudder could not be removed on normal dock blocks so the lower part was separate and could be removed before docking. The problem with this attachable piece was that it often fell off at sea and it is believed that it was often not replaced. The 'Tribal' class tried to overcome this problem by fitting two large rudders close to each other. It was also hoped that this pair of rudders would channel the propeller slipstream and aid turning at rest. Experiments were run with rudders turning through 45° and with flapped rudders in which the after portion moved through double the angle of the forward section.

The accommodation was also rather sparse and 50 per cent hard-lying money was paid to crews when they were on fishery protection duty. The Ships' Names Committee originally considered names such as *Cromarty Firth* and *Dornoch Firth* for the class following the Second World War tradition, but the idea was quashed within the Admiralty.[20] The ships were then named after famous naval officers. The *Blackwood* class proved to be very competent anti-submarine vessels, a reflection of their focused role.

The Type 11 Frigate

The nature of this design is one of those rather tantalising mysteries which gives rise to speculation. Logically it should have been the first of a line of anti-submarine frigates. Amongst ideas forthcoming, the most quoted version is that it was an anti-submarine version of the Types 41 and 61 with the same engines. However, such a ship

The Type 14 second-rate anti-submarine frigate *Keppel* in June 1956. The AS Mark X mortars aft dominate the armament, and despite their reputation for being 'under-armed' in terms of weight the weaponry (including the sensors) was heavy for a ship of this size. (*D K Brown collection*)

[18] ADM 138/830: Destroyers and Frigates General Cover (NMM); G L Moore, 'The *Blackwood* class Type 14', *Warship 2001 –2002*

[19] ADM 167/135: 1950 Board of Admiralty Memoranda (PRO).

[20] Ships' Names Committee Minutes (Naval Library, Whitehall). Other names suggested were *Beauly Firth, Moray Firth, Pentland Firth, Solway Firth,* and *Westray Firth.*

would have been too slow for the task, less effective than the new second-rate design then being developed and as costly to produce as the first-rate frigate. It seems unlikely therefore that this arrangement was ever suggested.

Another possibility is that a frigate with 'Deltic' diesel engines could have been considered. A memorandum was presented to the Board of Admiralty in October 1950, close to the date when the Type numbers were instigated, which indicated that a 'compounded' version of the engine was to be developed. The note made the point that 'this should give us 6000shp on an engine about the bulk of the First Lord's desk'. Someone might have thought of using this engine in a frigate which with eight engines would have possessed sufficient power to counter any HTP submarines that the Soviets might possess. The speed of 35kts wanted for this task could have been achieved. However, the engine was destined for motor torpedo boats, and in a de-rated form, in the interest of a longer life, for coastal minesweepers. The new version was probably years away from production.

One final thought is that the first version of the Type 14 *Blackwood* class, which had some fundamental differences from the production version, may have been given the Type 11 designation. It was after all the submission of this design to the Board of Admiralty which caused the institution of the 'Type' numbering scheme which has survived for well over 50 years. No record has, however, been found.

It may well be that a Civil Service 'quirk' is the cause of no Type 11 appearing and that for some unexplained reason the number was not used. No evidence has been discovered to substantiate any facts which have appeared in print and no one alive who was close to the design process at the time has any knowledge which could lead to the mystery being solved.

The Third-Rate Frigates (Types 17 and 42)

In June 1950 with the international situation deteriorating it was decided that a truly austere vessel was needed which could be mass-produced. The first- and second-rate frigates, although initially planned for mass production, clearly could not be quickly produced even in wartime. Initial studies produced two diesel-powered options of 950 and 800 tons respectively. The larger ship carried a Limbo anti-submarine mortar and four fixed torpedo tubes. Four ASR 1 diesels gave a speed of 22kts. The second ship was even more austere, with an armament of one Squid and two anti-submarine torpedoes, whilst two ASR 1 diesels gave a top speed of only 19kts. Both carried a twin and single 40mm Bofors mounting.

Within 5 months there were calls for a gun-armed coastal frigate able to operate on the East Coast of the United Kingdom against both aircraft and fast attack craft, the requirement harking back to the days before the war when the 'Hunt' class were designed. Both designs were now developed in parallel, but progress was slow and it proved difficult to reconcile the two differing requirements. By late 1951 the machinery to be installed in the anti-submarine version, now designated the Type 17, evolved to a utility steam turbine installation with one shaft and one boiler, with displacement approaching that of the Type 14 frigate. The anti-aircraft version, now designated Type 42, had two shafts and two boilers. The main armament of the Type 42 was initially three 3in/50 cal. supplied by the United States. By January 1952 there were doubts about supplies coming from this source so it was decided to mount three single 4in Mark XXV. This gun was being developed by Vickers as a utility mounting which could be produced by engineering firms with no previous armaments experience.

Type 17 third-rate anti-submarine frigates. These two austere designs were produced in June 1950. They were effectively diesel powered and simplified versions of the Type 14, but with their slow designed speeds their effectiveness would have been questionable.
(*Drawings by John Roberts from originals in PRO ADM 1/22001*)

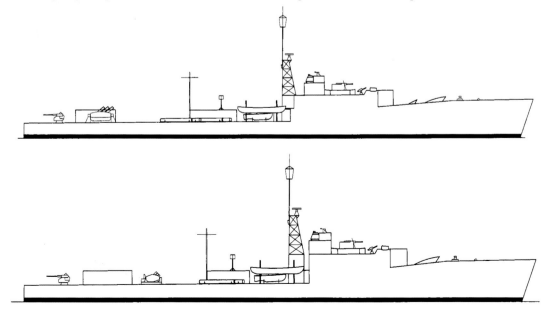

There were serious thoughts about building a prototype of each type under the 1954-5 Estimates but by late 1953 it was clear that there was no possibility of ordering the ships before December 1954. The designs were far from being ready, with Staff Requirements being revised yet again in the summer of that year. For example, various options for the Type 42 hull design were still being considered. The Ships' Names Committee suggested new names in June 1953. For the Type 17 the 'Firth' names were revived, whilst it was suggested that the Type 42 be given names of precious stones, *Agate, Amber, Jade* and *Topaz* being four of twelve suggested. The Type 17 design reached the stage where it went to the Board of Admiralty but was stopped at that point before formal presentation. By the end of the year the decision had been made to abandon both types and also not to order any more of the second-rate Type 14, which was in production. It was, however, decided to develop new, less-constrained designs which emerged as the Common Hull Frigates (see below).[21]

The Anti-Submarine Frigate (Type 18)

This conversion was originally conceived in the summer of 1950 as a replacement for the Type 16 limited conversion, the origin of the project being the not-infrequently expressed dissatisfaction of the Naval Staff with the Type 16's anticipated operational performance. The DNC was also not impressed with the limited conversions; he considered it wrong to waste valuable destroyer hulls and machinery on equipment which was inadequate to cope with modern submarines. By early 1951 it was suggested that this new class should replace both the limited and the full Type 15 conversions. The key improvement over the Type 16 was the mounting of the double Limbo anti-submarine mortar supported by a Type 170 sonar. The improved Type 177 sonar was to be fitted at a later date. The ship would also have a better anti-aircraft performance with the 4in twin mounting being controlled by the Close Range Blind Fire (CRBFD) system instead of the Simple Tachymetric Director (STD). This armament achieved virtually the same effectiveness as the full conversion, the only loss being the Type 277Q height finding radar and four anti-submarine torpedoes. The cost of the conversion was reduced from £600,000 to £400,000; in addition there was a saving of 3 months in conversion time – all useful gains.

In April 1951 the destroyer *Noble* was initially planned for the prototype conversion and it was expected that the remaining four 'N' class destroyers would follow. By July 1953 the programme had expanded, with *Troubridge* and *Savage* and four 'Z' class destroyers earmarked for conversion, with the remaining four 'Z' class also to be considered. None of these plans were to progress, for concern was expressed about the multiplicity of frigate types being built and converted and the Radical Review seems to have finally brought about this project's demise.[22]

The Common Hull Frigate

Following the demise of the Type 17 and the Type 42 frigates, the search for a cheap frigate to be built in numbers continued with a larger ship which could be completed with either anti-submarine or anti-aircraft armament, as with the wartime 'Loch' and 'Bay' classes. It was again intended to build a prototype of each variant, sort out any problems and prepare drawings for mass production should it be needed. The anti-aircraft version carried two twin 4in Mark XIX mountings, one twin 40mm Bofors and one Squid. The anti-submarine version had one Limbo and two twin 40mm.

The design, which was worked out in some detail, was loosely based on the *Black Swan* and looked attractive. However, it was becoming increasingly clear that the weapons and sensors were nearly obsolete and capability against both aircraft and submarines was limited. The final blow came with the explosion of the first hydrogen bomb, making mass production in war unlikely. The cancellation was followed by an interesting period looking for frigate designs which could be built in numbers and yet have a worthwhile capability.[23]

The 'Tribal' Class Frigate (Type 81)

With the demise of the Common Hull Frigate the next idea to emerge was a ship with the capability of a second-rate frigate in all three main aspects – anti-aircraft, anti-submarine and aircraft-direction tasks. They were also expected to be valuable for Cold War 'police' duties. Since a frigate was defined as a single-role ship, this multi-role design was referred to as a sloop.[24] Initial studies carried two twin 4in Mark XIX mountings, one twin 40mm, a

[21] This account is based on G L Moore, 'The 1950s Coastal Frigate Designs for the Royal Navy', *Warship 1995*. Other names suggested were *Cairngorm, Coral, Cornelian, Crystal, Jacynth, Opal, Sardonyx* and *Turquoise*.

[22] ADM 167/137: 1951 Board of Admiralty Memoranda (PRO); and ADM 138/810: Type 18 Frigate (NMM).

[23] This account has been provided by D K Brown, who worked on the project.

Type 81 Sloop. This study from mid-1955 shows the ship as then perceived. She mounts two twin 4in Mark XIX, a Mark X anti-submarine weapon and there is no provision for a helicopter. Note the austere funnel design, as wanted by the DNC, Sir Victor Shepheard. The design changed soon after he retired.
(*Drawing by John Roberts from original in PRO ADM 167/139*)

[24] Someone discovered that the Royal Navy had committed 70 frigates to NATO and to reach that number, the 'Tribals' had to be classified as 'General Purpose Frigates, Type 81', a contradiction in terms.

[25] There were a number of possible profiles pinned up in the design room and visitors were asked to vote on them. The Director of Naval Construction, Sir Victor Shepheard, reminded us that the team was not a democracy and duly told us his choice (D K Brown).

[26] This method was proposed by Ken Rawson, just back from an appointment with NCRE and writing a new structures course for the RN College. He used Schade's graphs to re-examine the structure of wartime destroyers and showed the new method predicted problem areas better than the traditional approach (D K Brown).

[27] Examination of one ship towards the end of its life, after an exceptional wave impact, showed he got this right (D K Brown).

[28] It took D K Brown 3 months of difficult and tedious calculation and re-calculating existing masts to prove the method.

[29] ADM 167/146: 1956 Board of Admiralty Memoranda (PRO).

Limbo and anti-submarine torpedo tubes. For aircraft direction a US-supplied SPS 6C radar was to be fitted. The main gun armament was, however, wanted mainly for shore bombardment so the twin 4in were replaced by two single 4.5in Mark V. The radar was replaced by a British Type 965. Tartar anti-aircraft missiles and twin 3in/70 cal. were also considered.

Despite its old-fashioned appearance, the 'Tribal' class frigate had many technical innovations.[25] Foremost in these was the machinery fit – single-shaft steam turbine with gas turbine boost. The size of the steam plant was set by the requirement for astern power, which gave a rather bigger forward power than was needed. With surplus power the required top speed was easily achieved and it was decided to optimise the hull form for high-speed cruising at about 18kts. The maximum speed was 24kts when the ship was in deep condition and out of dock for 6 months. The form was a 'low prismatic' with buoyancy concentrated amidships and very fine ends, then believed (mistakenly) to improve seakeeping. The form selected was the cruiser *Neptune*, Design 'Y' (1945), itself based on the First World War light battlecruiser *Glorious*.

The hull structure used a novel approach by the American, Schade, in which for the first time the buckling strength of complete stiffened panels of plating could be considered.[26] The design philosophy was that it was inevitable cracks would start in a complex structure built under shipyard conditions but that careful design would ensure such cracks did not spread.[27] The original design had an aluminium superstructure. One study had all aluminium above 2 deck, which was finally dropped following gun-blast problems on the Type 15s.

To avoid vibration problems the mast had to have a natural vibration frequency clear of propeller blade rate and this posed a difficult problem in those pre-computer days.[28] This led to a very wide base to the mast – with one leg passing through the wardroom table in the initial designs. Because of the asymmetric machinery the layout was heavily constrained and it took a redesign of the whole forward half to separate mast and table. The upper deck was dominated by the firing trajectory of the anti-submarine mortar which stood on 2 deck in a well and this pushed the bridge forward. Although the overall motions of the 'Tribal' class were not different from those of the *Leander*, the forward position of the bridge gave much greater motions at the compass platform.

The 'Tribals' were the first class designed for bunk sleeping and to be fully air-conditioned. The cost was much greater than that of the successor design, the *Leander* class, even though they were quite simple ships. Only seven were built, a number dictated by the production of machinery where intricate licensing (and by implication contract) arrangements were involved. With considerable design effort having been put into the class the Controller also considered it uneconomic to stop at just four ships.[29] They were, however, a valuable addition to the fleet, since they provided experience in the operation of gas turbines in warships before the 'County' class destroyers and their successors came into service. They were regarded as successful and most had service lives of 20 years in the Royal Navy.

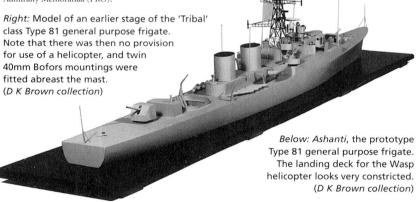

Right: Model of an earlier stage of the 'Tribal' class Type 81 general purpose frigate. Note that there was then no provision for use of a helicopter, and twin 40mm Bofors mountings were fitted abreast the mast. (*D K Brown collection*)

Below: Ashanti, the prototype Type 81 general purpose frigate. The landing deck for the Wasp helicopter looks very constricted. (*D K Brown collection*)

The *Leander* Class Frigate (Improved Type 12)

This design was initiated in 1959 and was a development of the successful Type 12, which had then been in service for 3 years. The armament changes involved two Sea Cat launchers instead of the Bofors anti-aircraft armament, anti-submarine torpedoes reduced from the twelve sanctioned in 1950 to just four (which never seem to have been fitted), and one Limbo anti-submarine mortar instead of two. The most effective gain was the ability to operate a P.531 Wasp helicopter which could carry Mark 43 or 44 anti-submarine torpedoes. A Cast 1 variable depth sonar was specified (Type 199) and the newly available Type 965 air-warning radar, as fitted in the new 'County' class destroyers, was carried. The machinery arrangements were based on the installation fitted in the Type 12 but the cruising turbines were dispensed with, as seen in the *Rothesay* class. The ships were now regarded as fleet escorts rather than convoy escorts, the higher cruising speed required being beyond the range of the cruising turbines. The ships were now used as the outer screen of a fleet which had the aircraft carrier at its core and an inner screen of guided missile destroyers. The endurance was 4500 miles at 12kts in deep condition 6 months out of dock in temperate waters. Fuel stowage was increased to 450 tons, achieved by abolishing separate ballast tanks, the ballast being car-

ried in the fuel tanks. This, however, opened up the possibility of pollution when ballast was ejected from the fuel tanks. Habitability was also improved, with air conditioning installed in the accommodation spaces whilst the bridge and operations room arrangements were improved. Diesel generators were moved from the eyes of the ship to a position where the exhaust was emitted through the foremast, but nevertheless the distinctive raised forecastle was retained. With the advent of this design it was decided not to build any more units of the 'Tribal' class. Another decision taken was to complete three of the Type 12 frigates already on order to the new design. The cost of these ships increased from £4.1 million to £4.2 million, the new ships being expected to cost £4.25 million.[30]

A total of twenty-six *Leander*s entered service with the Royal Navy between 1963 and 1973. They were not built to a uniform design, the first sixteen ships having a 41ft beam, increasing to 43ft in the last ten. There were also differences in the machinery with Y100 being fitted to the first ten units, the next six ships having an improved version designated Y136, and the last ten the Y160 system, which incorporated further benefits gained from operational experience. All had a 440-volt AC electrical supply producing 1900 kW in early ships, which was increased to 2500 kW in later vessels. They were intended to serve three commissions with two short refits and then after 10 years have a major refit.[31]

Euryalus (Type 12 general purpose frigate) in August 1969, showing the appearance of the early *Leander* class ships as completed. Later ships carried a Sea Cat missile launcher instead of the two single Bofors on the hangar roof. Note the well in the stern for the Type 199 Variable Depth Sonar. (*D K Brown collection*)

[30] ADM 167/157: 1960 Board of Admiralty Memoranda (PRO). *Fowey, Hastings* and *Weymouth* originally ordered as *Rothesay* class were built as *Ajax, Dido* and *Leander*.

Above: Leander in 1973. The ship has now been rearmed with the Ikara anti-submarine system, shown being fired from its forward 'zareba'.
(*D K Brown collection*)

Right: Galatea, as an Ikara *Leander*, entering the frigate refit complex at Devonport. These huge covered berths were intended to facilitate the major reconstructions of frigates like those applied to the *Leander* class.
(*D K Brown collection*)

The Ikara Leander (Batch 1)

The Australian designed Ikara anti-submarine missile was originally to be installed in the Type 82 destroyers. The 1966 Defence Review, however, reduced the Type 82 class to just one ship, which meant that another ship had to be found if the capability of this weapon was to be retained. The initial plan was to fit the weapon in an 'Ikara Destroyer' but with priority given to the 'Sea Dart Destroyer' (Type 42) other vessels had to be found in order to expedite matters. Five ships were initially wanted and in 1967 a debate ensued over whether the last five *Leanders* then planned (FSA 41-45) or the first five ships due for a long refit should be so fitted. The cost of fitting the

weapon in new ships was estimated to be £700,000. The additional cost of fitting the system in existing ships was initially estimated to be £1.5 million per ship, a figure reassessed in February 1968 at £1.05 million. It was decided that in spite of the additional cost it was better to install the system in the refitting ships on the grounds that Ikara could be deployed earlier and the number of ships with the system could be varied. There was, however, a price to pay, for the final new construction order for *Leander* class frigates was reduced from three ships to two.[32]

The conversion involved the removal of the twin 4.5in Mark VI mounting and the associated MRS3 director. The Type 965 radar was also landed. In place of the gun a zareba and handling room were built forward of the bridge structure whilst the missiles with torpedoes fitted were stored in the magazine. They had an automated 'Action Information Organisation' (AIO), and new sonar and communications. The gun armament now comprised two single 40mm Bofors, whilst the anti-aircraft missile armament now comprised two quadruple Sea Cat launchers. Also included in the reconstruction were enhanced air conditioning, updated machinery converted to burn dieso in the boiler furnaces, all cables replaced, and accommodation brought up to the latest standards. Electrical power was enhanced with two 300 kW diesel generators replaced by two 500 kW units. A water-displaced fuel system was fitted to improve stability, a necessary feature as the stability of the class was always considered marginal and they never satisfied the new Royal Navy criteria in full. The Wasp helicopter was retained. Eight ships (*Leander, Ajax, Galatea, Naiad, Euryalus, Aurora, Arethusa* and *Dido*), were ultimately converted at Royal Dockyards between 1970 and 1978, the cost ranging between £7.6 million and £23 million, with the average time taken being about 3 years.

The Exocet Leander (Batch 2)

The next group of ships were fitted with the Exocet anti-ship missile instead of Ikara. A new anti-submarine tor-

[31] D F Whittam RCNC and A J Watty RCNC, 'Modernising the *Leander* class Frigates', *Trans RINA* (1979).

[32] DEFE 24/239: Ikara/*Leander* (PRO).

pedo was also fitted, together with a new 'Computer Aided Action Information System' (CAAIS). The anti-submarine mortar was removed, the well being plated over to give a larger flight deck and hangar to accommodate the Lynx anti-submarine helicopter. The Sea Cat armament was enhanced, with two quadruple launchers mounted on the hangar roof, and an additional one fitted forward of the Exocet on the forecastle. The pairs of Exocet launchers were angled outboard to port and starboard to prevent any conflict with this Sea Cat. The modernisation included improvements to air-conditioning, accommodation and the replacement of all cables and was very much in line with the improvements worked into the Ikara *Leander*s. It was originally intended that eight ships would be converted to this standard but the programme was cut back to seven (*Cleopatra*, *Phoebe*, *Sirius*, *Minerva*, *Argonaut*, *Danae* and *Penelope*), with the eighth ship *Juno* being converted to a navigation training ship at Rosyth Dockyard. The seven frigates remaining in the programme were in hand at Devonport Dockyard between 1973 and 1982 the cost ranging from £13.8 million to £47.7 million, the average time taken being 2½ years.

The Sea Wolf Leander (Batch 3)

The last ten ships had a wider beam and thus improved stability which enabled the Sea Wolf point defence anti-aircraft missile and Type 2016 sonar to be installed in addition to Exocet. There were still weight constraints and the funnel caps on this group had to be removed to improve margins. It was also estimated that 45 tons of paint (up to 80 coats) was removed, further increasing the stability margin. All ten of the group were originally to be rebuilt but costs escalated still further, now coming out at between £60 and £79.7 million. The programme started in March 1978 and was finally completed in December 1984, the time spent on each ship varying between 3 and 4 years. The result was that only the first five were converted, the remainder of the programme being cancelled under the terms of the 1981 Defence Review.[33] The five ships converted were *Andromeda*, *Charybdis*, *Jupiter*, *Hermione* and *Scylla*. Their unconverted sister ships *Bacchante*, *Achilles*, *Diomede*, *Apollo* and *Ariadne* were all sold for further service with the navies of Chile, Pakistan and New Zealand between 1982 and 1992.

The class proved to be one of the most successful designs produced for the Royal Navy. The production run was longer than desirable as it proved difficult for the Naval Staff to agree on a successor as the Type 22 fit required a much bigger and costlier ship. Additional ships were built for Australia (2), Chile (2), Holland (6), India (6) and New Zealand (2).

Whether the conversions, where costs escalated far in excess of inflation as the programmes progressed, were worthwhile is open to debate. The major gain was that by using existing ships it was possible to get new weapons to sea far more rapidly than would have been the case had new construction been relied upon, and several played an

important part in the Falklands War. They were undoubtedly expensive, approaching the cost of a new ship with similar capability. The work was also difficult, because the class had been built before modern corrosion protection was developed and a great deal of structural renewal was needed before work could begin. *Cleopatra*, for example, needed 85 per cent of her keel replacing. Painting was also a particular problem: the shallow fuel tanks had to be grit blasted before high-duty epoxy paint was applied. It was a difficult and unpleasant task, as D K Brown discovered by venturing inside one tank while the work was going on. He was, however, pleasantly surprised by the standard of workmanship attained. The paint had to be used within 8 hours of mixing and its fumes were toxic and flammable so that work in adjoining areas had to be interrupted. Renewing the chlorinated rubber paint in the machinery spaces was nearly as difficult. All these complications contributed to the decision to curtail the major conversion and reconstruction programmes.

Minerva, a *Leander* class Type 12 Frigate in April 1979 rearmed with Exocet missiles in place of the twin 4.5in Mark VI mounting. (*Mike Lennon*)

[33] Whittam and Whatty, 'Modernising the *Leander* class Frigates', *Trans RINA* (1979). The cost of the conversions is quoted in Richard Osborne and David Sowden, *Leander Class Frigates* (World Ship Society 1990).

Andromeda in April 1981, rearmed with Sea Wolf and Exocet guided missiles. (*Mike Lennon*)

6 Sea Dart Destroyers

The CF299 (Sea Dart) Frigate[1]

The CF299 missile system, later Sea Dart, was completing development in the early 1960s and following the project study it was thought '...will be much cheaper than Sea Slug 2 and small enough to be fitted in frigates'[2] not much bigger than a *Leander*. Sea Dart was a semi-active homing ramjet with tandem rocket boost. Two Type 909 trackers illuminated the target. Using valve technology, it was not very reliable. Two missiles could be fired every 40 seconds. It was stowed vertically in a rotating drum (height 172in).

There were a number of ship design studies, all with the same armament.

One twin CF299 with two trackers and 38 missiles

One Ikara with 20 missiles

One AS mortar Mk 10 with 60 missiles[3]

One SS 11 or 12 mount with 76 missiles

Anglo-Dutch radar, Asdics

Steam-powered options had either two 15,000shp units giving 27kts or two 20,000shp units for 28kts. Endurance varied between 3000 and 5000 miles at 18kts. There were also gas turbine options but these were uncertain and in 1962 Ship Department clearly preferred to stay with steam. YARD carried out a very detailed study of both first cost and through life cost of various machinery options and came down strongly for all steam at that date.

Though CF299 was smaller than Sea Slug and its vertical stowage made it easier to fit into a ship, a drum stowage for 20 missiles was still large, affecting the hull lines forward.[4] Replenishment at sea (RAS) with missiles was difficult, particularly the movement from the landing position to the launcher and alignment of the missile so that it could be struck down. Later, the figure of 20 minutes per missile for RAS would be quoted. Elaborate safety tests were carried out at Shoeburyness to ensure that the accidental ignition of one rocket motor would not ignite the whole magazine. Air-loaded accumulators were arranged to spray water into the rocket mouths in the event of fire.[5]

It was intended that the Type 909 tracker offices should be pre-outfitted but the requirements for alignment and stiffness of support made this impossible. The estimated cost was £8.4 million (1962) when a *Leander* would have cost £5.25 million. Displacement ranged from 3400 to 4300 tons, but the cost did not change much with size, being governed by armament and machinery. Increasing the complement from 275 to 350 increased displacement by 200 tons.

In January 1963 there was a study of the effect of speed on the size and cost of CF299 frigates.[6]

Power (hp)	Speed (kts)	Displacement (tons)	Cost (£ million)	Layout
90,000	33	5900	12.75	Unitised
60,000	31	4600	11.5	Non unit
60,000	30.5	4800	11.75	Unitised
40,000	28	4100	10.5	Non unit

Tupper tells a sad story of another study. He was asked to look at the cost of doubling the endurance. This meant adding 100 tons of structure and 400 tons of fuel, total 500 tons. Everything was done in a hurry and the cost estimators took their standard rate of £1000 per ton for 500 tons making £0.5 million. This was quite wrong as fuel is not included in the first cost of a ship and structure at that date cost much less than £1000 per ton. To make matters worse, the DG Ships then doubled the estimate to be on the safe side. Incredibly, Controller re-doubled and it was decided that the extra endurance was not worth £2 million!

In April 1963, the Director of Plans suggested that an annual building rate of 2½ CF299 frigates and 2 corvettes could be afforded. About this time a 'Post *Leander*' is mentioned as a cheap frigate. The CF299 studies were important as they were to grow into the Type 82 (*Bristol*) whilst from 1963 a series of corvettes were designed to supplement the frigates, a series which was to grow into the Future Light Frigate (FLF) discussed in the next chapter.

Some CF299 Options

Study	53A	53B	53E
Displacement (tons)	4100	3600	4200
L (ft)	400	375	400
B (ft)	45	45.7	45
T (ft)	14.6	13.2	14.8
Machinery	Steam	Steam	GT
shp	40,000	40,000	40,000
Speed (kts)	28	28.3	28
Range/at kts	5000/18	3000/18	5000/18
Complement	275	275	275
Cost (£ million)	8.5	8.4	?

[1] Though early studies were classed as frigates, the outcome was the Type 82 Destroyer and hence the whole family is dealt with in this chapter under destroyers.

[2] ADM 205/183 (PRO).

[3] To reduce complement Tupper suggested that the long-range Ikara and the relatively short-range mortar should be operated by the same men, since they would not be used at the same time. The naval authorities found this too difficult.

[4] Some studies had up to 38 missiles. The '20' missile fit was often rendered as 22 which probably included two training rounds – see N Friedman, *World Naval Weapon Systems 1991/92* (Annapolis, 1991), p397.

[5] This was developed by Harry Melrose of Hawker Siddeley. When the task was complete he found himself without a job and became a highly respected constructor.

[6] ADM 1/28894 of 31 January 1963 (PRO); signed E C Tupper, who has contributed much to this chapter (private letter of 30 August 2001).

[7] By 1965 the long-term plan envisaged eight Type 82s. DEFE 10/511(PRO).

[8] The 'County' class carried Sea Slug with wrap-around boost, stowed horizontally. The new missile, Sea Dart (ex-CF299) was stowed vertically in a rotating drum holding 38 missiles in *Bristol*.

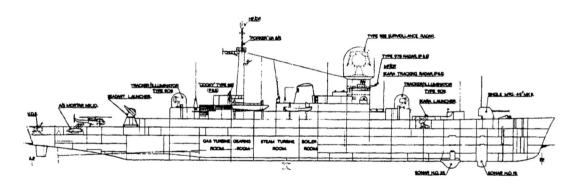

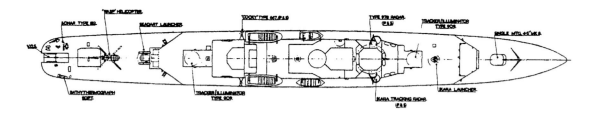

[9] A guided rocket which carried a homing torpedo to the vicinity of a suspected submarine. It had been in development with Australia since 1964.

[10] The name 'Broomstick' was selected by the Dutch, referring to the masthead brush carried by Tromp in the Anglo-Dutch Wars as a boast that he had swept the seas clear of the English fleet – whoever agreed to it in the UK did not know his history.

[11] It was often proposed that a constructor should join the concept group during studies and then take the design with him into detailed design. *Bristol* was one of the few cases when this happened, with Eric Tupper (who has made a major contribution to this section) and was a success. Even extending this policy to overseeing was considered. He was involved in various novel schemes at this time, including a catamaran frigate and a catamaran to launch space rockets.

[12] In fact, the Netherlands cancelled 'Broomstick' and *Bristol* received Type 965.

[13] A naval staff officer said it reminded him of a guardsman – busby on top, nothing between the ears!

Type 82 – *Bristol*

Four of these ships were planned as escorts for the new carriers (CVA-01).[7] They were intended to provide protection against surface ships, submarines and aircraft. They could operate as pickets or as Local Air Defence Control Ship, while the 4.5in Mark VIII gun gave them a considerable capability for shore bombardment.

The Type 82s were seen as following on from the 'County' class though they were designated in the frigate sequence as Type 82 until 1965, but the different configuration of the missile meant a radically different style of ship.[8] As well as Sea Dart with 38 missiles (in development from 1962), they carried the Ikara anti-submarine weapon,[9] an AS mortar Mark X and a 4.5in Mark VIII (three new weapon systems); as they would be operating with the carrier they did not need to carry a helicopter. Their main radar was to be the Anglo-Dutch Comprehensive Display System, Type 988, 'Broomstick'.[10]

Early studies by YARD suggested a new, all-steam plant, but it was decided to develop the COSAG plant of the 'County' class. However, it was found necessary to design a new, larger steam plant and the gas turbines were to be Olympus, so losing any benefit of standardisation. Tupper wanted to put the Olympus over the transom with electric drive to the shafts to save the space needed for uptakes and downtakes – he even considered the use of air jets; very uneconomical but a great saving in weight and space.[11] In later studies twin funnels were arranged aft to ease replacement of the Olympus through the uptakes.

The ships' main role died with the cancellation of the carrier, but it was decided to build one ship as a trials vessel for Sea Dart, the Type 988 radar, other weapons and the

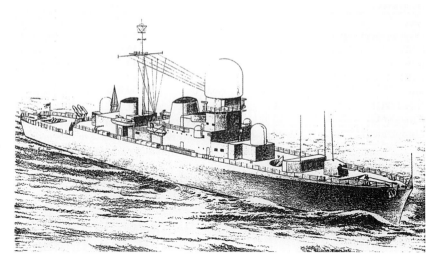

machinery.[12] Type 988 would have had a very large dome and stringent requirements for vibration and environment implied a stiff – hence large – bridge structure. All this obstructed the air flow over the forward (steam) funnel so Tupper devised a scheme with a big air channel under the dome.[13] It was intended to pre-outfit some of the offices. In order to meet requirements for alignment this meant a heavy deck structure. Even so, the normal working of a ship in a seaway and deflection due to solar heating (several inches) meant that such movements had to be measured and corrections fed into the radar system. A particularly valuable system was the Action Data Automation Weapon System (ADAWS-2) which co-ordi-

Type 82 destroyer *Bristol*. Originally intended as an escort for the new carriers, she had no role when CVA-01 was cancelled. This drawing and the sketch show her in original configuration with the Anglo-Dutch Type 988 'Broomstick' radar and an AS mortar Mark X. The second funnel was not divided at this time. (*PRO: drawing DEFE24/38; sketch ADM 205/220*)

14 The desks of the two constructors were alongside each other.

15 T Sarchin and L L Goldberg, 'Stability and Buoyancy Criteria for US Naval Surface Ships', _Trans SNAME_ (1962). Based largely on studies following the loss of three USN destroyers in the Pacific typhoon of 1944.

16 The fire was in the steam turbine room and burnt for several hours. Luckily, she was alongside at Newport and the local fire brigade finally extinguished it with the then novel high-density foam. The author visited the ship a few days after the fire and was told that if she had been at sea, she would have been abandoned.

17 DEFE 16/617 (PRO).

nated input from all sensors and navigation systems and processed it for use in weapon control.

The _Bristol_ was designed in the same room as the 'County' class section to get an immediate feedback from the earlier ships.[14] John Coates, constructor on the 'Counties', had spent 3 months at sea in an early one and written a valuable report on possible improvements. _Bristol_ was the last ship designed 'in-house' and great attention was paid to the passages on 2 deck to get the run of pipes, air conditioning and wiring correct. The environment was tightly specified – temperatures, vibration, shock and noise. The movement of men and stores through the ship was studied and optimised using work study methods. Bathrooms and heads were concentrated in blocks over the sewage treatment plants. There were numerous trials at Shoeburyness on magazine safety, including the novel scheme for injecting water into a burning rocket exhaust mentioned earlier.

In 1965 the estimated cost of the first ship was £16.25 million with follow-on ships £1 million cheaper. This was the same order of cost as the 'Counties' at 1965 money value for a much more capable ship and requiring a smaller crew. The design complement was 380, 70 men less than the 'County', with accommodation for 433 allow-ing for a training margin and additions during the ship's life. The cost of the destroyers could be contained within the planned budget by building a number of 'cheap' Type 19 frigates in parallel (see Chapter 7).

Tupper started to develop a new approach to stability standards but on a visit to the United States discovered that Sarchin & Goldberg were working on similar lines but were well ahead, so their criteria were adopted for _Bristol_ (see Chapter 12).[15] She had no structural problems in service, a rare boast – Tupper thinks this was because there was adequate time in the design stage to get it right. She was laid down at the end of 1967 and completed in March 1973. Used mainly for weapon trials, _Bristol_ received little in the way of updates. She was very badly damaged by a fire in autumn 1973 and for a considerable time ran on gas turbines alone.[16]

In 1967 consideration was given to a stretched Type 82 to replace the _Tiger_ class as helicopter ships.[17]

Destroyer and Frigate Studies 1966

When the carrier CVA-01 was cancelled future plans for escorts envisaged more Type 82s (above, costed at £20.75 million in the report), whilst frigate studies were in hand

Destroyers

Type	82	42 Batch 1 & 2	42 Batch 3	43
Displacement (tons)	7700	4350	5350	c6000
L (ft)	507	410	463	573
B (ft)	55	46	49	59
T (ft)	22-6	19	19	
shp	74,000	50,000	50,000	
Speed (kts)	30	30	31	30
Range/at kts	?	?	?	?
Complement	407	312	312	348

These two views of _Bristol_ show some of the novel equipment which she took to sea – Sea Dart, 4.5in Mark VIII, Olympus gas turbine and the ADAWS-2 data system.
(_Mike Lennon_)

for the Type 19 (Chapter 7). The Future Fleet Working Party (Chapter 4) took the opportunity to review the whole escort programme – destroyers, frigates and even small patrol vessels – in nine studies.[18] Though many of the studies are individually more appropriate to the next chapter it seems best to treat the whole escort scene together. There was the eternal problem of quality versus quantity linked with a desire for a common hull for AA and AS ships. These studies are important as showing what was technically and financially feasible in the mid-1960s and because the studies led directly to the Types 42, 22 and 21. In descending order of size they are reproduced overleaf.

Comparison with the actual Types 42, 22 and 21 suggest that the choice lay near the top of the respective ranges. At the top real savings can be made for a very small loss of capability – was it really necessary to have Match, Ikara and an AS mortar? At the bottom end capability virtually disappears for very little saving in cost.

Type 42

Though the Type 42 is generally – and largely correctly – seen as a 'cut price' Type 82, it also had roots in the Future Fleet Working Party studies outlined in the previous section and in the earlier CF299 studies. The project director for the Type 42 (*Sheffield* class) was M K Purvis who, in 1974, told RINA that the design was constrained by price, initially about £12 million, and displacement limited to 3500 tons, which could only be met by accepting various limitations; in particular, length was to be a minimum in the hope of reducing cost.[19] Design standards were to be similar to those of the later *Leander*s but with gas turbine machinery. There were to be no margins for future updates and there were other economies, such as a single anchor,[20] combined galley for officers and men, and armament was limited to existing equipments.

The Board sub-committee on the report of the Future Fleet Working Party debated margins on cost and possible enhancements.[21] The original DNC estimate was £10.5 million, to which Controller added £0.7 million (10 per cent) to first-of-class costs on the 'ship' side and £0.6M (16 per cent) to that for weapons, making a cost of £12 million for the first ship. There was then lengthy discussion over the possible fitting of a second TIR (Target Indication Radar – later 909). It would add some £0.5-0.75 million but would virtually double the capability in a high threat environment, though in a lesser threat, which was what the Type 42 was primarily designed for, the benefit was less. Various cost saving measures such as deleting either the gun or sonar fit were considered and rejected. DCNS pointed out that over the intended programme of thirteen ships (completing by 1980-1) the total additional cost would be about £10 million, less than the cost of a single ship, and the second TIR was accepted. This is an all too familiar problem: adding weapon capability will always seem cost effective – the phrase 'More bangs per buck' was often used – but with a fixed budget it may mean fewer ships and less rather than more capability in the fleet.

There was also discussion over the fitting of a close-range AS weapon, Terne, a Norwegian rocket-propelled depth charge. Though it was seen as desirable, it was decided not to fit it. The Type 42 had an unusual rounded transom which formed a high stern wave. Some instability in the flow often led to an unsymmetrical stern wave, higher on one side than on the other but there was no adverse effect on performance.

Exmouth

It was clear that Whitehall, politicians and admirals would only agree to an all gas-turbine fleet after a full scale demonstration. Vallis writes, 'Eventually, after much politicking,

[18] Future Fleet Working Party Report Vol 3. DEFE 24/238, 90724 (Originally Secret, now declassified [PRO]).

[19] M K Purvis, 'Post War RN Frigate and Guided Missile Destroyer Design 1944-1969', *Trans RINA* (1974).

[20] There was a second anchor stowed at the bridge front. If the chain broke, the spare anchor could be attached to the remaining chain. Additionally, it was argued that the gas turbines could be started within a few minutes.

[21] DEFE 24/239 (1967) (PRO).

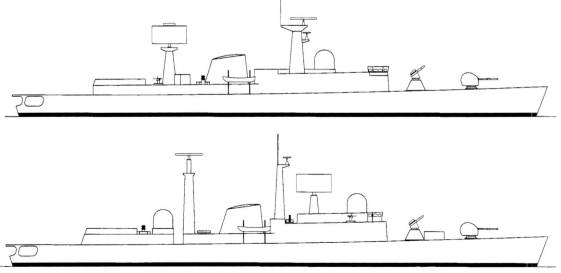

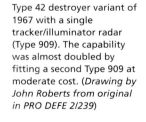

Type 42 destroyer variant of 1967 with a single tracker/illuminator radar (Type 909). The capability was almost doubled by fitting a second Type 909 at moderate cost. (*Drawing by John Roberts from original in PRO DEFE 2/239*)

Type 42 destroyer. This drawing was produced in February 1968 for presentation to the Board of Admiralty. The ship at this stage carried a twin-barrel GWS 30 launcher as developed for the Type 82. (*Drawing by John Roberts from original in PRO ADM 281/291*)

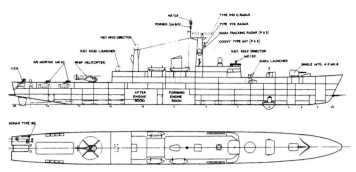

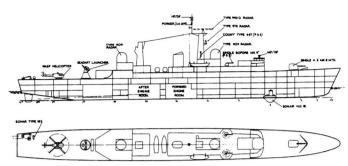

First-Rate AS Frigate (Study 381). This was a diesel-engined ship[22] (four AO16) of 4400 tons deep, also known as the Type 17, dating from 1964. There were two engine-rooms with a slight separation. The armament included Ikara, two AS mortars, Match (Wasp helicopter) and a 4.5in Mark VIII. There was a full sonar fit, including VDS. *(PRO DEFE24/238)*

First-Rate AA Frigate (Study 382). This had the same dimensions and the same machinery fit as the AS ship but the internal arrangements were different. It is probable that a large proportion of the drawings would have been common. It carried Sea Dart with two Type 909 trackers, two 40mm Mark IX and Match.

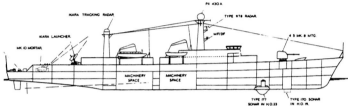

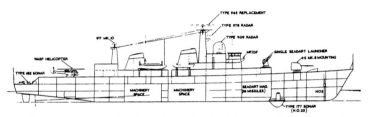

Medium AS Destroyer (Study 392). This design was cost limited to £10.5 million and 3500 tons. It was to carry as many of the following as possible within these limits: Ikara, 4.5in gun, Mortar Mark X, helicopter with hangar and VDS – but only the first three could be accepted within limits. There were two machinery spaces; the engines are not specified but were probably AO16 diesels.

Medium AA Destroyer (Study 391). This ship had the same dimensions and machinery as the Medium AS ship but bulkhead spacing was different. The main weapon system is described as 'Seadaws 100' but the drawing shows a single-arm Sea Dart launcher (26 missiles) with a single tracker. There was also a 4.5in gun and Match. The mortar, VDS and full GWS 30 (Sea Dart) were omitted on cost grounds. Though this may have been the starting point for the Type 42 it differed in almost every aspect.

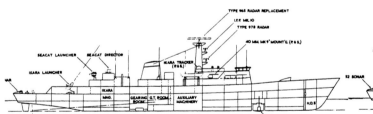

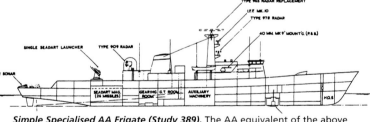

Simple Specialised AS Frigate (Study 390). This was the smallest and cheapest ship which could carry Ikara (vertically-launched, without special weapons). It also had Sea Cat (vertically-launched PX430 [which became Sea Wolf] when available) and two 40mm. The machinery was Olympus/Tyne.

Simple Specialised AA Frigate (Study 389). The AA equivalent of the above with Seadaws 100 (single-armed Sea Dart launcher, 26 missiles with one tracker) and two 40mm. Once again, though the dimensions and machinery were the same, bulkhead arrangement was not. Common-hull AA and AS ships are not an easy undertaking, particularly when designed to a limit. Less obvious, but very important is that the AS ship will almost certainly need more attention to noise reduction.[23]

22 It is noted that the machinery might be altered if the design was developed, probably reflecting development of the Olympus-Tyne fit.

23 These two 'specialised' frigates are described in slightly more detail in DEFE 24/234 (PRO). The aim was to reduce cost and complement by reducing the weapon fit. A 20kt version with a single diesel and shaft would need 10 less men, be 20ft shorter and save about £0.75 million.

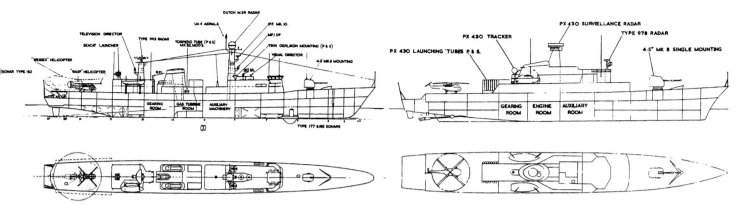

Standard Frigate (Study 387 modified). This was another variant of the Type 19 (*qv*) but with only one Olympus per shaft (30-32kts) and two Venturas per shaft for cruising. Armament was a 4.5in gun, Sea Cat (PX430A – Sea Wolf – in later ships), two twin 20mm Oerlikon, Match with Wasp (ability to land a Wessex in good weather), two torpedo tubes, two Penguin (a Norwegian SSM).

Patrol Vessel (Study 919). The roles were peacekeeping, fishery protection and engaging lightly armed craft. It would work from a base or depot ship – 'accommodation would be cramped'. Armament would be a 4.5in gun and PX430. No sonar and only minimum radar would be carried. (*All* Future Fleet Working Parts drawings PRO DEFE 24/238)

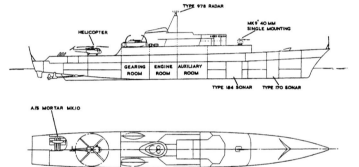

AS Patrol Vessel. (Study 920). Roles as above but also AS escort. Armament: mortar Mark X and one 40mm; Wasp helicopter with limited maintenance. The machinery fit was one Olympus and two Tynes driving two shafts though a single gear box.[24]

The Vosper Mk 5 was also included in the report.

[24] This was proposed for a number of studies and should have worked.

Destroyer and Frigate Studies 1966									
Study	*381*	*382*	*392*	*391*	*390*	*389*	*387m*	*919*	*920*
Displacement (tons)	4400	4500	3500	3500	2500	2500	2600	1200	1200
L (ft)	440	440	390	390	360	360	360	260	270
B (ft)	46	46	45	45	40	40	39	33	33
Depth (ft)	38½	38½	30½	30½	29	29			
Speed (kts)*	28.5	28.5	28	28	28	28	30	28	28
Range (miles @kts)	3500@18	3500@18	4000@20	4000@20			2000@20		
Complement	325	324	210	210	160	160	154	129	129
Cost (£ million)	12	12.25	10.5	10.25	9.75	9.5	6.5	4	3.5

*Speed 6 months out of dock, tropical

The beam looks too small: remember 41ft *Leander*s with heavy steam machinery had to be increased to 43ft.

[25] Rear Admiral R A Vallis CB, 'The Evolution of Warship Machinery 1945-1990', Presidential Address, *Trans I Mar E* (1991).

[26] S J Palmer CB, RCNC, 'The impact of the gas turbine on the design of major surface warships', *Trans RINA* (1974), p1.

[27] A A Lockyer, 'Engineering aspects of the Type 42', *Navy* (Sept 1970).

[28] The consequent diminution of afloat staff and increase ashore led politicians and journalists to complain that the tail was being increased at the expense of the teeth. They could hardly have been more wrong.

[29] The metacentric height in the intact condition could be restored by a small increase in beam but, with extensive flooding, a low centre of gravity is desirable. In most conditions a Type 42 should float with four main compartments flooded – post-sinking studies of *Coventry* with five compartments flooded showed this aim had been achieved.

Exmouth, the first RN all gas turbine frigate. The baffles in the big air intakes fore and aft of the funnel were intended to keep salt water out of the turbines. (*MoD*)

lobbying and persuading … approval was gained to convert *Exmouth* (*Blackwood* class, Type 14) to all gas turbine propulsion.'[25] She was given a single Olympus gas generator exhausting into a special power turbine. There were two Proteus for cruising. Special features were required to keep salt water out of the air supply and the engines had to be screened with blastproof containment. 'Nevertheless, at a stroke fuel consumption was reduced, on-board maintenance was cut, availability was increased and the working conditions in the machinery space were improved beyond imagination.' The gas turbine had arrived.

By this time there was considerable knowledge of the advantages and disadvantages of the gas turbine in warships. The airflow was about three times as much as in a steam plant. Some 75 per cent of the heat of combustion went into the exhaust gas at 500°C and 200ft/sec – in a steam plant 20 per cent went up the funnel and 60 per cent into the sea. The gas turbine air flow had to be unobstructed as 1in water gauge back pressure would reduce the power from an Olympus by 100shp. The ducts also had to be free of obstructions which might excite damaging eddies in the flow. The exhaust ducts for Olympus were about 6m², which meant that they could be used to change engines. The ducts had to be lagged as the inlet could be very cool and the exhaust would certainly be hot. About 40m³ was needed for salt spray eliminators.[26]

The best steam plants needed about the same space and would be 15 per cent heavier. The gas turbine plant would be about 10 per cent more on initial cost but save in life cost. A very important advantage of the gas turbine was that it could start from cold in two minutes.

Olympus/Tyne: Types 42, 21, 22

The Type 42 (*Sheffield*) was to be small, cheap and with a small crew. All gas-turbine propulsion seemed to meet the requirement very well; full power would come from two Olympus, each driving one shaft with a CP propeller. The intended cruising speed was higher than in previous ships and the Tyne fitted the bill. Advice from the principal operator of the Tyne, British European Airways, was that it was the worst engine they had ever used! However, the Navy's luck was in for once, as the effort to remedy these problems in aircraft had succeeded, and the marine Tyne was to prove very reliable. A new free power turbine was needed and many materials had to be changed to suit the marine environment.

The main propulsion system of these classes proved very reliable and led to a revolution in working conditions. The auxiliary machinery posed more problems. The 'Tribals' had Allen 500 KVA gas turbine alternators, which were efficient but complicated. Output fell off quickly due to fouling of the compressors and heat exchangers and cleaning was a lengthy task. The 'County' class had Ruston TA alternators which were simple, rugged and reliable but bulky and inefficient. The machinery was arranged in four spaces – generator, Olympus, Tyne, gearing and generator – used in several other classes.[27]

It was decided to fit diesel generators in the new classes. Experience of diesels in the older frigates had been confined to harbour and emergency use and the change to continuous operation brought many problems. The supply of fresh water was also difficult and in the Types 42 and 21 auxiliary boilers and steam-heated distillers were fitted. This equipment turned out to have a heavy maintenance load.

The biggest changes with the all gas-turbine plant came in the control of the machinery, with much faster response, and in the handling of fuel. Electronic controls, including bridge control, led to a revolution in watchkeeping practice and hence in training. Fuel was stowed in a water-displacement system which meant providing a very elaborate fuel cleaning system and the separation of the least trace of water. Total commitment to 'repair by replacement' was inevitable and demanded a major effort in spares cataloguing and supply.[28] Cruising speed was set by the Tynes, which, at full power, used 0.5 pound per shp hr (1.0 including auxiliaries).

The old, heavy steam machinery made good 'ballast', keeping the ship's centre of gravity low.[29] The downtakes and uptakes for a gas turbine are very large – 6m² for an Olympus – though there was an advantage in that gas turbines could be changed afloat via the air trunks. A hydraulic ring main was fitted, working the capstans, boat davits, winches, RAS mast and storing lift. Since these equipments were not in use simultaneously the power needed for the pump was only 17.5hp.

Controllable-pitch propellers were fitted to give astern power, which led to difficult problems in propeller design, particularly the air supply down the shafts and into the (moveable) blading for the Agouti installation. The big shafts and supporting brackets, together with constraints on blade design, led to an overall loss of 6 per cent in propulsive efficiency. The engine-room staff was about 20

Above: A fine view of *Southampton*, a Batch II Type 42. (*MoD*)

Right: Sheffield with the original funnel intended to reduce infra-red signature from the exhaust plume. Note the absence of an anchor on the port side. (*D K Brown collection*)

Manchester, a lengthened Batch III seen in rough seas off Australia. It is not easy to judge from photographs but it is likely that the weather here is Sea State 5-6, representing 4m significant wave height. (*MoD*)

[30] One of the lessons of the Falklands war was that damage control was easier in a steam ship as they had more technical ratings – you can't win!

[31] Known as the Loxton bend – the Argentine *Hercules* had a similar funnel.

[32] Rather like a paddle wheel with vertical axes; this gear had been developed for CVA-01.

men less than in a steam installation.[30] *Sheffield* completed with a strange funnel intended to reduce infra-red signature.[31] Two pairs of stabiliser fins of the same design as used in the *Leander*s were fitted. A double bottom was incorporated containing fuel tanks, some of which could be water compensated in the light condition. For the first time, rotary vane steering gear was fitted with a considerable saving in space and weight.[32] Twin rudders gave a turning circle whose diameter was 3½-4 times the ship length.

The armament was a twin Sea Dart launcher with two Type 909 directors and 22 missiles.[33] There was a single 4.5in Mark VIII and during and after the Falklands War various close-range guns were fitted, most ending with two Phalanx CIWS. A Lynx ASW helicopter was fitted, with hangar. Accommodation for 300 was generally to the standards of the later *Leander*s. Ship's officers had single cabins with multi-berth cabins for trainees and CPOs. The ships were fully air-conditioned for tropical service.[34]

[33] A single launcher was originally planned.

[34] J C Lawrence, 'The Warship of the "seventies"', *Navy* (Sept 1970).

[35] Perhaps a little overdone, and slightly reduced in later classes with the benefit of experience.

[36] Purvis says that the modification brought them back to his original ideas!

[37] There was a delightful cartoon of a coal-burning Type 42 with 4 tall, thin funnels and a ram bow!

[38] The author took over the concept design in mid-1978.

[39] Typically, a CVS and two AOR.

[40] A new Staff commander altered the target to '36kts desirable' and asked me if it mattered. He was angry at my reply: 'No, you're getting 31.5'. To convince him we did some very quick estimates – four Olympus would give about 34kts at the expense of poor fuel consumption and no more was possible with existing machinery. New machinery, probably steam, would be needed for 36kts.

The class put on weight during building, which might have caused the Argentine *Hercules* failing to reach contract speed. A weight-saving exercise was agreed with Vickers but, unfortunately, too many longitudinals were omitted from 01 deck and the first batch had to be given external stiffening. The second batch were easily corrected in build.

Great attention was paid to corrosion protection, with all 'wet' spaces protected by sprayed metallic zinc, which has paid a considerable dividend in reduced refit work.[35] *Coventry* was the trials ship for improved application of paints. Preparation and painting were done with great care and it was hoped to show that this could be justified by increased corrosion-free life. Alas, the trial was ended by Argentine bombs. *Exeter* had an early application of self-polishing anti-fouling paint – her blue bottom (the only colour then available) caused some amusement but this trial was a great success, leading to considerable fuel saving.

In 1978 it was approved to build the last four ships to a modified design.[36] They were lengthened by 50ft and given 3ft more beam. The extra length was all forward so that machinery and transmission drawings needed little alteration. These much bigger ships were about 1.5kts faster with the same machinery. Their structure was designed using a new, dynamic approach which was very difficult to use and a mistake was made, so that this batch, too, needed stiffening.

Some Comparisons

It was estimated that a steam Type 42 would be 250 tons heavier – 100 tons of machinery, 60 tons more fuel, 50 tons in accommodation and 40 tons of structure. The steam machinery would be 10 per cent cheaper but extra structure and accommodation would take back 7 per cent. However, upkeep of the gas turbine plant would be 5 per cent less through life. Engine-room complement would be reduced in the gas turbine ship by 17 plus 3 support staff leading to a 37 per cent reduction in through-life cost.

A diesel plant would be 250 tons heavier with machinery spaces 20ft longer. In the oil crisis of the early 1970s coal burning was considered, with the conclusion that, overall, the economic solution was to convert coal to oil ashore and continue to burn oil.[37]

The Type 43 and Type 44

The Type 43 was intended to follow on from the Type 42 but armed with the Sea Dart Mark II.[38] The primary role was to protect a task force[39] from air-launched missile attack. This set the requirement for the number of 'channels of fire' – one Type 909 director and a single missile. There were two basic variants. The smaller one resembled a Type 42 with one twin launcher forward and directors fore and aft, while the larger had a twin launcher at each end and four directors. Allowing for refits, the number of big ships needed would have been rather over half the number of small ships.

With launchers at both ends, the helicopter deck had to go amidships in a long gap between the two superstructure blocks. This was not popular with airmen but an acceptable arrangement was found. This forced the engine-rooms (each with two SM1A) apart, with two main compartments between, which was ideal from a vulnerability point of view though some thought the long shaft from the forward space was a hazard. However, intensive study of shaft damage after whipping in the Second World War and in post-war trials showed that the risk of such damage was very slight.

The long gap amidships made the early studies look horrid. Eventually, the pre-war *Southampton* class cruisers provided inspiration and though the Type 43 could not quite match the beauty of their predecessors, they were pretty good – even if I say so myself. The first draft Staff Target was 30kts essential, 34kts desirable and it was soon found that four SM1A would give about 31.5kts in either variant.[40] There were a number of weird variants including one with two Harriers, which served only to confirm that it was grossly uneconomic to carry less than six in one ship (see Chapter 7). There was even a very quick study of a nuclear-propelled ship with two SSN plants.

Increasingly, the bigger ship began to look attractive. The building cost of the whole class was less and, even more important, total crew numbers were less at a time when recruiting was difficult. Control of four 'channels of fire' from one ship was easier than from two. ASWE carried out computer simulations of various forms of mass attack which showed the small ship failing in every

Below: Small Type 43, an updated Type 42 with Sea Dart Mark II. Simulations showed that it had little capability. (*D K Brown collection*)

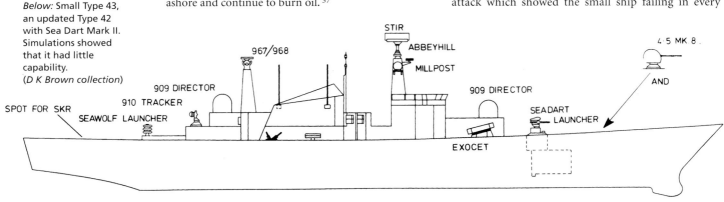

Type 43: artist's impression (left) and profile (below) of the big variant, which seemed much more cost effective than a larger number of smaller ships. The big gap amidships was sufficient to operate a Merlin helicopter, and the aesthetic treatment owed much to pre-war *Southampton* class cruisers. (*MoD*)

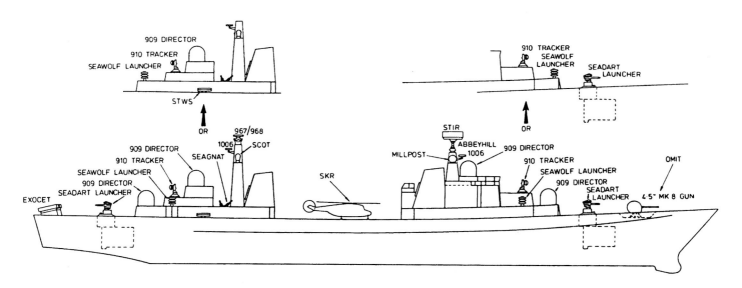

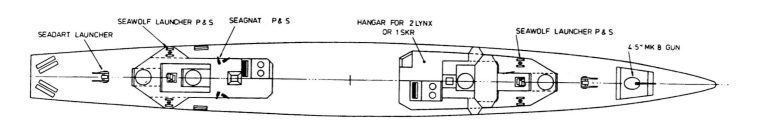

[41] It was later realised that the simulations were flawed as both ships fired several times more missiles than they carried. The true conclusion was that Sea Dart Mark II was inadequate, though the big ship was still better.

[42] In the author's view it would have been cheaper to buy Aegis – even though its unit cost was high – than develop a new system for relatively few ships. The big Type 43 could have been adapted quite easily – we looked.

scenario and the big ship being reasonably acceptable.[41] The big ship was approved by the relevant committees but Whitehall lost its nerve over the high unit cost (about £200 million), and out of committee and without studies the Type 44 was conceived.

This was roughly the small Type 43, already shown to have little capability, with slightly enhanced AS capability. It was put straight into Feasibility design, but before long both it and Sea Dart Mark II were killed by the Nott Defence Review of 1980, one its few correct decision.[42] It was hoped to use the Type 22 hull form though this seems unlikely given the size of the Sea Dart magazine.

The NATO Frigate

The UK joined with USA, France, Italy, Holland, Spain, Canada and Germany to design and build a common frigate. It got off to a bad start as there were considerable differences in national requirements. It was generally agreed that the emphasis was in protecting ships in company from air flight missiles. Existing point defence missile systems were ruled out as they could only cope with missiles aimed directly at them, while the new system had to deal with the much more difficult crossing target. The main threat was seen as coming from missiles launched from submarines at fairly short range, which meant the missile defence system had to have an extremely short response time.

After lengthy negotiations it was agreed to go ahead with a development of the Franco-Italian Aster missile, though it was still uncertain which warning radar would be fitted. Debate on the ship itself centred on USN rules over trunked access to vital compartments, which implied a much larger and costly ship (see Comparisons, Appendix 5). The USN, with RN support, were pressing for the

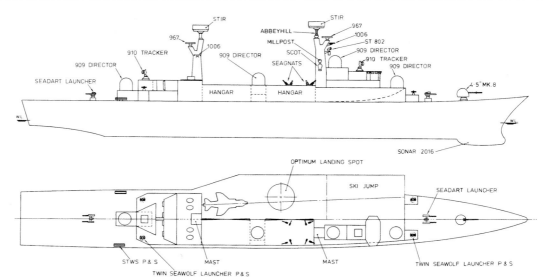

Right: A version of the Type 43 to carry two Harriers. It proved to be not worth the effort. Many studies are carried out to investigate the impact of even unlikely requirements.
(*D K Brown collection*)

Below: An impression of the proposed NATO frigate. (*D K Brown collection*)

compound gas turbine under development in the UK for the USN. The UK was aiming for a cheaper ship than its partners.

NATO collaborative projects are usually approved and funded for one phase at a time, with a contract for that phase only placed with an international consortium. At the end of the phase work stops while all governments have to agree on the chosen option for development in the next phase. There will then be a tender exercise for the next phase so that there is a break of some 18 months between each phase. It is far from certain that the same consortium will win the new contract and, even if they do, only a nucleus staff will have been retained and the next phase will be a new start. The solution seems simple: approve a single consortium for the whole design (subject to satisfactory performance) and fund for each phase plus a continuing team while the earlier stage is being approved.

The NATO frigate as such died at the end of phase two. The head of concept, Peter Chamberlain, then produced his own ideas which was agreed informally by France, UK and Netherlands as the FUN frigate. When Italy showed interest it became the FUNI frigate whilst Greece made it the FUNGI frigate. These informal studies and discussions showed that there was still interest in collaboration.

Project Horizon

Eventually, the UK joined with France and Italy to develop a new ship around the Aster missile, though quite early on the UK decided to fit its own main radar. This design, too, failed. The UK's partners were only proposing to build very few ships and the advantages of collaboration were diminishing. The last straw came over management structure which the UK did not believe was strong enough to control costs. (A note on the succeeding Type 45 is in Chapter 14.)

7 The Later Frigates

[1] The covering paper in DEFE 10/461 refers to actions long forgotten by most people – Palestine patrol, Cyprus, Icelandic 'Cod War', Malaysia, British Guyana, Bahamas, as well as disaster relief and salvage work.

[2] This paragraph is slightly adapted from NSR 7025, originally Secret, now DEFE 10/461 (PRO).

[3] A very good paper on anti-FPB guns was later produced by ASWE during the design of the 'Castle' class. For a quick kill at 6000 yards, by far the best available (and the cheapest at £100,000) was the Centurion tank 105mm (also the basis for CFS 2). Unfortunately, the Staff 'improved' it to a new cost of £6 million, more than the then cost of the ship.

[4] Later ships would have 'Confessor', NST 6522 (this became Sea Wolf).

DURING THE EARLY 1960s the escort programme centred on the Type 82, primarily an AA ship, but with a considerable AS capability. It was a very expensive ship, so escort numbers could only be maintained by building in parallel very cheap frigates, mainly for limited war. It was hoped that the numerous *Leander*s would fulfil the AS role for some years. There were some studies for a bigger AS ship, the Type 17 (see Chapter 6), but these were not developed. The only long-range sonar sets were hull mounted, big, requiring a great deal of power and very expensive (see *Matapan* below). There were numerous attempts at a cheap, capable AS frigate but none was successful until the towed array was developed.

The Type 19 Designs

In the mid-1960s the Admiralty hoped to retain an escort force of some ninety destroyers and frigates, which led to a requirement for four new ships each year, each with a 21-year life. Ideally, all should deploy Sea Dart and Ikara, implying ships similar to the Type 82 (*Bristol*). Forecast budgets of manpower as well as money made such a force impractical and attention turned to a mixed force with a considerable number of cheaper ships requiring small crews. Between 1971 and 1976 it was hoped to complete eight Type 82s and thirteen Type 19s. The balance of

twenty-four ships would include the last two *Leander*s and the first of a Type 82 replacement.

In peacetime the role for the cheap ship, referred to as the Type 19, would include: police, patrol and general peacekeeping duties, including operations against fast small craft engaged in gun-running, smuggling and infiltration, counter-insurgency, fishery protection, disaster relief and showing the flag.[1] In limited and general war it would contribute to the AS escort of a unit in conjunction with more sophisticated vessels. The ship would have an anti-FPB capability for which very high speed was necessary, and also a naval gunfire support capability. She should be capable of a measure of self-defence against air attack.[2] It was hoped to approve the Staff Requirement in mid-1965 and order the first ship at the end of 1967 for completion at the end of 1970. The principal requirements for the peacetime role were seen as a medium-calibre gun,[3] a light helicopter, accommodation for 30 troops, long endurance (5000 miles) at 15kts and very high speed for a short burst (c40kts), sustained top speed 28kts. For war it needed a medium range sonar, torpedoes for the helicopter (Wasp), Sea Cat[4] and limited AIO/EW. In the light of her limited AIO, her weapon systems (Match helicopter) would be directed by a more capable escort.

An early design study showed a 1900-ton ship, 340ft long by 35ft beam. The power available (tropical) would

The 'Battle' class destroyer *Matapan* went into reserve at the end of the war having only completed acceptance trials. In 1971 this 'low mileage' ship was rebuilt as a sonar trials vessel, with an array some 100ft long and a hull packed with the ultimate in valve technology. Though this sonar did not enter service, a great deal was learnt about big hull-mounted sonars. (The USN planned a similar trial in the *Spokane* which was abandoned.) (*Mike Lennon*)

be 64,000shp from two shafts, each having two Olympus gas turbines. There were also two diesels per shaft for cruising.[5] Endurance figures are of interest, particularly in light of future developments, discussed later.

Speed (kts)	Endurance (nm)	Engines in use (per shaft)
39	700	2 Gas turbines
28	1100	1 Gas turbine
20	1700	1 Gas turbine
18.5	4700	2 Diesels (not recommended)
15	7500	1 Diesel

For comparison, *Leander* endurance was quoted as 1200nm @ 28kts, 3530nm @ 18kts.

The gun was specified as a single 4.5in Mark VIII.[6] Complement was 110 (+ 30 troops). This depended on the availability of some automated AIO equipment, then under development. Sonar was Type 177.

The cost was estimated at £5 million and it was emphasised that this was a firm figure, justified as there was hardly any new equipment going into the ship. It was claimed that the cost of a *Leander* built in the same timescale (1970s) would be £9-10 million (as quoted then, but other papers from that date suggest about £6 million for a *Leander*). It is almost unbelievable that this high-performance ship could be built for half the cost of a *Leander*! Problems envisaged in 1965 were the design of a sonar dome that would have to stand up to speeds of 40kts or be able to be retracted. The propeller design was seen as a problem, mainly from the noise at lower speeds (see later), whilst there were unspecified problems expected with the diesels for cruising. None were then thought to be difficult to solve.

About this time A N Harrison (the DNC) compared the Type 19 with earlier ships, showing how the new design was dominated by space.[7] The internal deck area was only 2 per cent (550ft[2]) less than that of the big destroyers of the *Daring* class, while the armament weighed 180 tons compared with 410 tons in the *Daring* yet the space for armament and AIO was virtually the same. The machinery, generators, switchboards and the like weighed 480 tons against 870 tons in the *Daring*, but required 90 per cent of the space. In the Type 19, store rooms were doubled in size, offices and workshops were up by 35 per cent and space per man raised by about 30 per cent.

Within a year the concept had changed radically.[8] In the light of the Indonesian confrontation (1962-6) the requirement was to cruise to Singapore at 40kts, implying a trials speed of 43kts[9] – note the endurance quoted above of 700 miles at 39kts, so needing many refuellings which would much reduce the average speed. Worse was to come. The propeller loading was very similar to a scaled-up 'Dark' class fast patrol boat propeller which, initially, had a life of 20 minutes at 40kts – even the best only

increased this to 20 hours.[10] Therefore, many propeller changes would be needed *en route* to Singapore.[11] The new First Sea Lord thought it was silly to send the world's most expensive propellers into shallow water to chase motor boats – only a Third World navy could afford it!

In the quest for speed the Staff gave some thought to a 50kt hovercraft with frigate capability. They eventually suggested a paper study that would cost £35 million with no guarantee of success. To expose this nonsense the author did a quick study of a 50kt 'conventional' frigate. It had a *Whitby* hull form and four shafts each with two Olympus. The 50kt speed brought the propellers into the super cavitating regime where the design was much easier – they were CP propellers, closely based on those of the 'Brave' class fast attack craft, and should have presented no great problem. All the technology was in existence and the costing section came up with a price tag of £13.5 million. The Staff response was: 'We don't want a 50kt frigate'! However, it did kill the hover frigate.[12]

The original plan for a mix of Type 82s and cheap Type 19s had some merit. This author's views on what is now called the HILO mix are given at some length in another book which suggests that the cheap ship should be first-rate in a limited role, like the Type 14 (*Blackwood*).[13] This is a rather lengthy account of a ship which was not built, but it was important in the search for a cheap frigate and led to the Type 21 and the Future Light Frigate studies, and hence eventually to the Type 23. The Future Fleet Working Party studies, described in the previous chapter, led to the Type 42 for AA work and the Type 22 for ASW.

Type 21, *Amazon* Class[14]

The Future Fleet Working Party, following the cancellation of CVA-01 in 1966 discussed in Chapter 6, saw the need for a cheap frigate to replace the *Leander*s. It was not fully understood in Whitehall that a cheap and effective frigate was not possible with the weapons and sonars of the day – *Broadsword* was the smallest effective ship. It had become obvious, after long argument,[15] that gas turbine propulsion offered large savings in engine-room complement and was necessary above all for this reason. Whitehall – and the Controller, Horace Law, in particular – had been impressed by the performance of the Vosper Thornycroft (VT) Mark 5 frigates for Iran, the first all gas-turbine frigates to be built in the UK. It was believed in Whitehall that a VT frigate for the RN could be built for £3.5 million compared with the current price of £5 million for a *Leander*.[16] (*Amazon* was actually to cost £14.4 million, but much of the increase was due to inflation.)

The new building programme was said to be too great for Ship Department to handle alone, particularly on the electrical side, and it was generally accepted that the cheap frigate could be designed in industry. However, attempts by the Controller to prevent any involvement of Ship Department led to friction and real problems. Many standard design procedures were unwritten, based on common

5 It was recommended that all four diesels should not normally be used together due to the need for maintenance.

6 Later variants had the twin 4.5in Mark VI, presumably due to delays in the Mark VIII. The Mark VI had little anti-FPB capability and the Mark VIII was not brilliant.

7 Quoted in the author's *A Century of Naval Construction*, p230. The original has not been located.

8 The author was running the specialist section covering hydrodynamic aspects and this paragraph is based on his memory.

9 This is a particularly difficult speed band for propellers. Very large cavitation bubbles form at the leading edge and collapse before the trailing edge with impact loading of about 100 tons/in[2]. At higher speeds the bubbles collapse clear of the propeller.

10 The constructor on the propeller section at Haslar was a pessimist and held out for 20 minutes life for the Type 19's propellers. Optimistically, I thought that we could repeat the 20-hour figure.

11 Propeller changes with the ship afloat had been tried with fixed pitch propellers. With difficulty, it should have been possible to change CP propellers afloat.

12 I am a great enthusiast for hovercraft in the right role.

13 D K Brown, *Future British Surface Fleet* (London 1991)

14 This project created much ill-feeling at the time, some of which has endured. The author has tried to be impartial in discussing the problems involved. The draft has been discussed with Peter Usher, who was in charge of the design and later managing director of Vosper Thornycroft, and most of his comments have been incorporated.

15 See Purvis' comments on P J Usher & A L Dovey, 'A Family of Warships', *Trans RINA* (1989).

16 I am assured that Vosper Thornycroft never made such a claim.

Amazon, a Type 21 frigate designed by Vosper Thornycroft. The broad transom gave a good helicopter deck at the expense of increased drag, reduced later when transom flaps were fitted. Four Exocet launchers were later fitted in front of the bridge. (*D K Brown collection*)

[17] The exact mechanism of the improvement is unclear: resistance of the hull is slightly reduced but the major effect is on propeller performance. The author had been involved in the success of a flap on the 'Gay' class fast attack craft (see Chapter 10) and spent about 20 years trying to get a flap on a frigate.

education and training at Greenwich and were hard to codify in the context of a binding contract (see Chapter 12 for stability standards). The Type 82 section were considering the adoption of standards based on those of the USN (Sarchin and Goldberg), and these standards had already been adopted by Vosper Thornycroft for their Mark V frigates. Ship Department remained responsible for stability and strength and asked for major changes to length and beam at the end of the first phase of design so that the new standards could be met in the Average Action condition.

As completed they mounted the new 4.5in Mark VIII gun and carried a small helicopter. After the first two ships, they carried four Exocet MM38 SSMs. They introduced what was to become the standard frigate machinery fit of two Olympus, two Tyne giving a top speed of about 30kts, discussed in the previous chapter. They had a large transom which as they put on weight sank deeper in the water reducing speed. After prolonged argument within Ship Department and Haslar, it was finally agreed to try a flap (elevator) under the transom, which gave a 1.5kt increase in speed when tried in *Avenger*.[17]

Much of the argument over the performance of the class has been concerned with the aluminium superstructure, which was a load-bearing part of the hull girder. An aluminium superstructure is only about half the weight of a steel structure and the lesser topweight permits a reduced beam with further important savings. Attacks on the con-

cept are mostly unsound: aluminium in structural form does not burn, as often claimed, but it does soften at 550° and melt at 650°C. Since a typical oil-fed fire reaches 900°C, it is clear that melting aluminium may add only slightly to what is already major damage. Two Type 21s were lost in the Falklands but in neither case did aluminium contribute to the loss. It is also suggested that the joint between the aluminium and steel structures would lead to corrosion, but this was a well-known problem and the solution adopted by Vosper Thornycroft has given no problems in service.

The one real problem was fatigue cracking in the aluminium, which has a much shorter fatigue life than steel. Cracking in 01 deck began to occur early in service life and got worse. Initially, palliatives were adopted, perhaps the best being patches of carbon-reinforced plastic glued to the aluminium – up to 10ft in length. These cracks were troublesome but not worrying as it was believed that even if the aluminium structure failed completely, the steel alone would cope with almost any loading. Then, in 1981 NCRE discovered, in the course of some basic research, that there was a previously unrecognised failure mode which could lead to the sudden collapse of the steel structure if the aluminium had cracked badly. Whitehall took some convincing, but eventually a study by Lloyd's confirmed NCRE's work. The Falklands conflict broke out before remedial action could be taken and the Type 21s went to war advised to avoid excessive motions. The aluminium structure of *Arrow* was extensively damaged whilst rescuing survivors from *Sheffield* and she was confined to San Carlos Water until a steel reinforcing beam could be fixed in place. After the war, external stiffening was applied at the top of the sheer strake and, 20 years later, the six survivors of the class continue to give good service in Pakistan. Great attention was paid to accommodation, which was unusually spacious, accounting in part for their popularity in the RN.

About 1978 a modernisation scheme was produced which would have given them Sea Wolf and better sonar. Both stability and strength required attention but a solution was found. However, R J ('Jack') Daniel (DGS), who had been involved at the start, recognised that freeboard to 2 deck – the highest watertight deck – was inadequate, and modernisation was abandoned. The Type 21s had a single ventilation system and electric cables under 1 deck passed through openings in the bulkheads which allowed smoke to spread in a fire.

Type 22, *Broadsword* Class

The Type 22 was conceived as an updated *Leander* and there was more similarity than is obvious. In particular, the new ships were to be as good or better sea boats than the *Leander*, so the hull form was very similar to the earlier success. Initial studies were carried out by Jack Daniel, then head of forward design. It was hoped that it would be a collaborative design with the Netherlands but for a variety of reasons this fell through.[18] The length was limited to the then size of the Devonport Frigate Complex.

The Type 22 was proclaimed as the first 'metric' design. However, many equipments were designed in Imperial units and, particularly in the machinery area, it was required to retain standardisation with the Types 42 and 21. The risk of error when working in unfamiliar units is obvious but, perhaps because it was so obvious, no problems were experienced.

It is often asked why two ships so different but of roughly the same size, Types 22 and 42, were designed at the time. (See also Chapter 6 for the Working Party attempts at a common hull, and there were studies for a ship like the Type 42 with Ikara.) The hull form is very different as the big Sea Dart stowage makes the Type 42 very full forward, to the detriment of seakeeping. The Type 22 has more freeboard, a much bigger hangar and flight deck and a very different armament. It would probably have been possible to design a baseline ship which could be completed to either role ('Loch/Bay' style), but such a ship would have been much bigger and the savings, if any, would have been small. Most of the Type 22s were built at Yarrows and the Type 42 elsewhere, further reducing any savings from a common hull. In general, they had the same Olympus/Tyne COGOG plant as the Type 42 and this was an important factor in reducing their complement to 215 (250 with margins).

They had the big hull-mounted Type 2016 sonar which could be used in passive mode but also had an active bottom-bounce capability. This incorporated the lessons from the enormous experimental sonar tried in the trials ship *Matapan*.[19] They mounted four MM38 Exocet and had two GWS25 Sea Wolf for close-range defence, particularly giving very rapid response against submarine launched 'pop-up' missiles, together with a pair of aged 40mm/60 cal. Bofors Mark IX (later replaced by twin 30mm). There were also two triple sets of torpedo tubes for Stingray and two Lynx helicopters (although only one was usually carried). Various funnel designs were tried in an attempt to reduce the infra-red signature.

On joining the fleet they were criticised as too big. They were indeed spacious, in a successful attempt to ease the maintenance task, and it was hoped that there would be a space margin for future equipments. Alas, it was soon found that they were too small to accommodate the Type 2031Z towed array and its associated operations room equipment.[20]

Yarrows were chosen as the lead shipbuilder and the Project Managers, A Bull followed by A J Creighton, set a successful management plan, Creighton being seconded to Yarrows as Technical Director in charge of building the first ships.[21]

Batch II

Even though the four ships of the *Broadsword* group were much bigger than the *Leander*s, they were soon perceived as too small for all the new equipment coming forward. They carried the Type 2031Z towed array sonar which with the CACS-1 control system needed a bigger operations room. It is also said[22] that they carried the US Classic Outboard electronic warfare equipment – SSQ-72 with SLR-16 and SRD-19 – which would have demanded a further large increase in the size of the operations room.

Most of the six Batch II ships had the well tried COGOG Olympus/Tyne plant, but *Brave* was the trials ship for the more economical Spey. Initially the two Olympus were replaced by two SM1A (37,540shp), which reduced her speed by about 1.5kts, but in 1990-9 she received the SM1C

18 See D K Brown, *A Century of Naval Construction*, p258 for a summary of the reasons.

19 H L Lloyd, 'The Type 2016 Fleet Escort Sonar', *Navy International* (August 1979).

20 It is often stated that they were not strong enough to carry the heavy winch. This seems unlikely though the array itself can impose severe loads when towing in a seaway.

21 Some reports say it was intended that up to twenty-six Type 22s would be built. This is a misinterpretation of normal and correct financial planning. It was normal to insert figures into a 10-year spending plan for so many frigates per period, and for financial planning it was assumed that they would be of the latest design.

22 N Friedman, *World Naval Weapon Systems 1991/92* (Annapolis 1991), p531. There is even a photograph showing Outboard antennae on a Type 22.

Broadsword, the first of the Type 22s, in February 1979 with the original (ugly) funnel. (*Mike Lennon*)

(52,300shp), which restored the speed loss.

After the first two ships of the class, the flight deck was enlarged and strengthened to take a Sea King or Merlin helicopter and the hangar altered, though they normally carried a single Lynx. This meant a slightly wider transom. Type 2015 sonar was installed in a bow dome which led to a heavily raked bow carrying an anchor clear of the dome. There are clear advantages in good weather in operating a sonar from a bow dome where it is free from bubbles swept down the stem but in heavy weather the bow dome leads to early slamming. The balance is not an easy one to draw.

Batch III

The government approved the replacement of the four destroyers and frigates lost in the Falklands War with four modified Type 22s, the *Cornwall* class. They had the hull of the Batch II with Olympus/Tyne machinery. They had no specific role and were given an armament of the latest readily available equipments. The need for a gun was seen as a lesson of the war and they had a 4.5in Mark VIII on the forecastle. Eight Harpoon SSM behind the bridge replaced the Exocets, and they had a Goalkeeper CIWS as well as two or four of the new single 30mm. The hangar and flight deck can accept a single Sea King or Merlin.

Cheap Frigates – Types 24 and 25

Around 1970 there were numerous studies for a cheap frigate under the title 'Future Light Frigate' led by Jack Daniel. The records of these designs have not been found but it is clear that none was found attractive since the only long-range sonars were big, hull-mounted sets, expensive in themselves and requiring a big ship.

In 1978 the DG Ships (Daniel) suggested a cheap frigate

Above: Brave, seen here in May 1986, was the trials ship for the Spey SM1B engine, and also had the wider flight deck and hangar for Merlin. The Batch II ships were longer to hold a bigger operations room and towed array. (*Mike Lennon*)

Right: The Batch III Type 22 *Cornwall*, a replacement ship for Falklands War losses. Note the 4.5in Mark VIII forward – the value of such a weapon for shore bombardment was a lesson of the South Atlantic conflict. (*D K Brown collection*)

which would be attractive in the export market and could serve in the RN as a towed-array ship – Type 24.[23] He thought it should look like the 'Castle' class offshore patrol vessel, as customers could be attracted by the armed 'Castle' and then persuaded to move up to a cheap frigate. This made sense, as customer requirements would differ and a very small superstructure as in the 'Castle' made feasible a range of upper-deck armaments. The RN requirement implied sufficient headroom under the quarterdeck for a towed array winch and in the engine-room for noise-insulation mountings. Towed array offered long range detection within the weight and space limits of a cheap frigate.

Daniel rejected the earlier studies and this author took over in mid-1978 with a clean sheet – or perhaps a clean screen, as it was to be the first design to use the new Computer Aided Design System, Goddess. The guiding principle was the old adage 'if in doubt, leave it out', spelt out in a paper jointly written by the author and his deputy, David Andrews.[24] A particular example was the need for a roof aerial and hence a second mast, which increased ship size appreciably, so it was left out.

Though it was a simple design, it had been thought through carefully and we were very pleased with it; we had even taken pains to give it an attractive appearance. The idea was that our outline design should be passed to Yarrows to be developed. They reduced headroom so that it could not take a towed array or engine mountings, so that there was no prospect of it being adopted by the RN (and the second mast came back). Hence there were no sales either.

We toyed with some weird variants. In one a Harrier and ski jump were worked in forward. This was a *reductio ad absurdum* argument to show the fallacy of such ships, then being offered by commercial builders. The maintenance spaces and staff for one Harrier are almost as big as those to maintain six. Another variant had wind propulsion for quietness (Flettner rotors). This was feasible but the auxiliary power needed for the sonar was greater than the power for propulsion, so that wind propulsion did not help much in reducing machinery and propeller noise.

When the Type 24 died we decided to go back to our original study and develop it as virtually the capability of a Type 22 at three-quarters of the cost (one mast!) – Type 25. This began to look very promising; we came up with the idea of diesel-electric cruising engines so that in the ultra-quiet mode a diesel in the superstructure with a long noise path to the sea could be used. At that time Forward Design Group were allowed – even encouraged – to freelance, though we had to seek the agreement of the Ship and Weapon Design Coordination Group at its next quarterly meeting if we wanted to pursue any study.

Just as we were beginning to see the Type 25 as a success, the new government decreed that new frigates should be limited to two-thirds the cost of a Type 22. The idea of a cost limit was novel and proved successful as there was little or no weight growth during the development of the design and there was little ministerial interference with

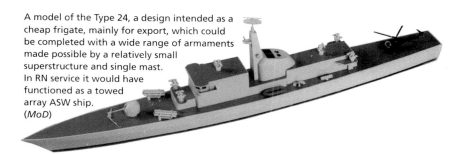

A model of the Type 24, a design intended as a cheap frigate, mainly for export, which could be completed with a wide range of armaments made possible by a relatively small superstructure and single mast. In RN service it would have functioned as a towed array ASW ship. (*MoD*)

the development of the design itself – 'All you want if it does not cost more than £100 million'. Advanced modular construction was introduced in warship yards for the Type 23 and the reduction in building costs enabled capability to be increased within the cash limit. The target set was close enough to our Type 25 for most of that study to be used, including the diesel-electric cruising plant.

Corvettes (*c*1963)

The bottom of the range was Study 352[25] of 1960 tons with twin diesels giving 20,000shp and a speed of 26.5kts.[26] Armament was a single 40mm and twin mortar Mark X, costing £4 million. Its data handling gear could transmit to an Ikara-fitted ship. For £6.5 million (*Leander* £5.25 million) one got a ship of 2700 tons, a 30,000shp steam plant giving 27kts, carrying Ikara (24 missiles and NDB) and a 4.5in gun.

During the development of the 'Castle' class OPV design (see Chapter 10), we had a model made to show at the RN Equipment Exhibition showing possible heavily-armed versions. There were no calculations to support these schemes but they were probably feasible. However, there were no customers and we did not proceed. As Christmas approached, we had a little spare effort and for two weeks the author put the section on to the design of a towed-

Above: Artist's impression of the Type 25. When the Type 24 failed to attract customers the design team developed it into a ship with almost the capability of a Type 22 at three-quarters the cost. It was not adopted, but much of the thinking, including the diesel-electric quiet machinery, went into the Type 23. (*MoD*)

[23] The cachet of RN service was important in export sales.

[24] D K Brown & D J Andrews, 'Cheap warships are not simple', SNAME symposium *Ship Costs and Energy*, New York 1987. We were often asked how big our relative contributions were and gave an agreed answer, 'A quarter each and the rest in discussion between us'.

[25] ADM 1/28609 (FRC/P63.16) (PRO).

[26] It is interesting that Ship Dept gave 20,000 as the maximum power on a single shaft. AEW Haslar, which designed the propellers, would have accepted much higher powers per shaft. Haslar was just beginning to feel confident with advanced propeller design.

array vessel based on the 'Castles'. This was an interesting exercise with some more fundamental implications. The vessel had to be quiet which meant most equipments had to be to warship standards, and electrical power supplies had to be stable in voltage and frequency. All this meant building in a 'warship' yard with high overheads and led to an estimated price of £25 million without armament instead of the £6 million for the OPV. It would have cost about £35 million fully equipped. This is about the most expensive ship that may be seen as 'expendable'. Giving a reasonable self-defence capability would have brought it

close to the Type 23 in cost, well over £100 million. There are 'zones', such as this gap of £35-£110 million in which warships are not viable; there is a similar but bigger gap for cheap aircraft carriers.

The ship was lengthened about 10m to accommodate the towed array abaft the helicopter deck. The deck could accept any RN helicopter and there were refuelling and limited rearming facilities but no hangar or maintenance facilities. After some debate, we added a single 30mm gun 'to prevent hijacking'. We looked at increased speed but the form was unsuitable and a better form would have

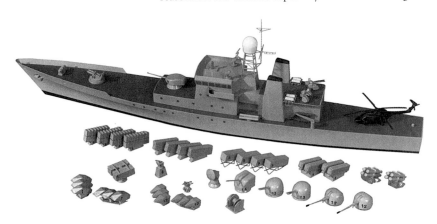

Above: Even some wind-propelled variants were considered. (*MoD*)

Above: A quick study was made of a heavily-armed corvette based on the 'Castle' class OPV. This model demonstrates some of the armament variations possible. (*MoD*)

Right: A more serious study was for an RN towed array ship. It could land and refuel a Merlin helicopter and had a small gun for protection against hijackers. (*MoD*)

1964 Corvette – Design Study 363. This design study dated January 1964 displaced 2075 tons. Dimensions were 320ft x 37ft. Two Ruston V16 diesels driving one shaft produced 20,000shp, which gave a speed of 26kts. The armament consisted of a single Bofors 75mm L/50 and a single Mark X anti-submarine mortar. (*Drawing by John Roberts from original in NMM ADM 1/28609*)

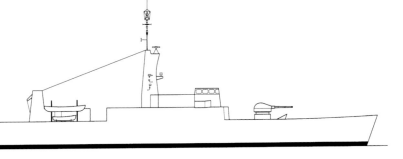

Left: Another study was made of a SWATH (Small Waterplane Area Twin Hull) variant patrol vessel. It could have been much smaller than a conventional craft for the same seakeeping, but there was no effort to develop the idea.
(*MoD*)

Right: A later study of a corvette based on a fast catamaran.
(*MoD*)

An early Type 23 study. Its similarity to the Type 25 is evident. (*MoD*)

Another, cut-price study on the way to the Type 23. (*MoD*)

[27] D K Brown, *Future British Surface Fleet* (London 1991).

[28] The type number 23 had been allocated to a big ASW frigate, which was never started. Hence the out-of-sequence Types 24 and 25.

[29] This should have read EHI 01 (European Helicopter Industries) but a typing error made it EH 101. A second error changed its name from Marlin to Merlin.

[30] Admiral Sir Lindsay Bryson, 'The Procurement of a Warship', *Trans RINA* (1985), p21. The discussion was wide ranging and, at times, acrimonious.

[31] Less than recent COGOG ships but as much as a *Leander*.

[32] I believed that a CP propeller could have been just as quiet at the light loading of the Type 23 propeller.

The Type 23 frigate *Marlborough*. The flat-sided funnel helps to reduce radar signature, as do the sloping sides of the hull and superstructure. *(MoD)*

involved lightweight structure, adding further to the cost. We looked very briefly at a SWATH and also at a very long range version.[27]

It was envisaged that this ship should be additional to the frigate force, adding more sensors. Our proposal was taken very seriously but rejected as it was thought the government would see it as a cheap frigate rather than additional to the force. More recently, the Parliamentary Defence Committee looked at the so-called high-low mix (HILO) with fully-capable frigates backed by cheaper, less capable vessels and these politicians rejected it on the cynical basis that any government would be tempted to build only the cheap ships and 'defer' the more expensive version.

The Type 23, 'Duke' Class

An outline Staff Target was issued in early 1981 for a light ASW frigate, Type 23.[28] This called for a very quiet ship, shaped to minimise Radar Echoing Area (REA), good endurance at moderate speeds, good seakeeping, a flight deck and hangar for the very large EH 101 helicopter[29] and all this for not more than £70 million at 1980 prices.[30] The size of the EH 101 (now Merlin) is often not appreciated; a comparison with a Second World War Swordfish is given in Chapter 11.

The electric cruising propulsion conceived for the Type 25 was adopted and after some thought it was decided that this plant would provide sufficient astern power.[31] Two of the diesel generators stand on 01 deck for noise isolation. The electric motors were connected directly to the shaft, eliminating gearbox noise. This enabled fixed pitch propellers to be chosen, which it was believed would be quieter than a CP propeller.[32] A very low shaft rotation speed was adopted, which made the noise performance at key speeds and frequencies virtually as good as a pump-jet, which would have been much more expensive. The plant (including the large, slow-running propeller) proved very economical, helping endurance, and it has been stated that the class are the world's quietest surface ships. A complete set of the electrical plant, including two diesel generators, was tested on shore.

The main parameters of the form were selected using Goddess programs and confirmed by model tests. The selected form had a low C_P, a high C_M and C_W with deep V sections forward to minimise slamming.[33] The V shape was continued above the waterline to resist pitching and the freeboard was slightly greater than in earlier classes. Very deep, though rather short, bilge keels were fitted, together with fins. Flared hull sides not only helped to reduce radar signature but increased stability if the ship sank deeper in the water due to weight growth or damage. Early reports from sea confirm their seakeeping ability.

The first study was for a 107m ship that exceeded the target price and had serious operational problems. There was no hangar and, unprotected, the helicopter would soon become non-operational; and it had no self-protection system. Desperate measures were taken to reduce cost, including elimination of one main engine![34] Some economy in structural design was also agreed. The design was reconfigured at 115m with a single Sea Wolf system and a basic hangar, though the cost was over £70 million. This was submitted in early 1982 and approved complete with the second engine and a second Sea Wolf tracker. Ability to operate Sea King as well as EH 101 added a further 3m to the length and the extra space reduced congestion in the machinery and accommodation.

The lessons of the Falklands war led to further major changes. A 4.5in gun was added for shore bombardment and vertically-launched Sea Wolf was approved. The number of fire zones was increased from 3 to 5 with no ventilation crossing the boundaries. Cables passed through glands (expensive) rather than openings as in earlier classes. An extensive surveillance system was installed so that damage control would always know the state of ship systems. There was a great reduction in the extent of ship side and deckhead linings[35] as these can obstruct leak-stopping and fire-fighting. Many of these measures had both advantages and disadvantages and there was quite heated debate within the design organisation.

A major feature of the design was a small complement, which meant that many minor items of maintenance had to be done ashore on return rather than at sea. This led to much heart-searching on the reduction in the extent of linings which made it much more difficult to keep the ship clean – how do you balance ease of cleaning against easier damage control? The original complement was 167, increased to 185 when the Falklands additions lengthened the ship to 123m. If the length is determined by weapon and sensor arrangement of the upper deck, then crew are not expensive; conversely, if the ship has to be lengthened to get men in it, becomes very expensive – £80,000 per man. The loss of self-maintenance has caused problems in worldwide deployment, which the class was not designed for. Accommodation has been grouped in three blocks: officers in the superstructure, senior rates forward mostly on 2 deck, and junior rates aft. This grouping reduces the extent of services and aids privacy.

The hull structure is unusual for a warship: deck and bottom are of fairly conventional longitudinal structure but the sides are transversely framed. This has led to an increase of 40 tons in weight but a worthwhile reduction in cost. An incidental advantage is that there are fewer traps where water can lodge causing corrosion. The difficulty foreseen was the connection of the transverse and longitudinal sections. Full-scale sections were tested at NCRE, culminating in a large hull section being subjected to an underwater explosion in the HULVUL trials, where it performed well.

The first ship, *Norfolk*, was built before Yarrow's re-equipment was complete and unit weight was limited to 55 tonnes, with 35 per cent of man-hours achieved before launch, the cost of work alongside after launch being several times the cost of shop work. In later ships the structure was built in 60-tonne blocks that were then assembled into 400-tonne blocks which were largely outfitted in a module hall before being moved to the slip. The 60-tonne units can be rotated, permitting downhand welding and, later, easier installation of electrical cables. As a result, launch displacement has increased by 35 per cent and 80 per cent of man-hours were before launch. *Norfolk* was ordered in October 1984 and delivered in November 1989. Since then eleven have been built by Yarrows and four by Swan Hunter. Building at a second yard meant the transfer of about 12,000 drawings on microfilm.[36]

The 'Short Fat Frigate'

During the early 1980s a number of claims were put forward by Thornycroft, Giles and Associates (TGA) for a frigate with a form derived from their successful motor launches. These claims were supported by an informal committee chaired by Lord Hill-Norton, summarised by them as:

> It is claimed that a radical alternative in the shape of a short/fat form would provide very substantial advantages in building and maintenance costs, in construction time, and in simplicity of layout, with no operational penalties. Indeed it is further claimed that such vessels would be more stable, with better seakeeping and manoeuvring performance, more commodious between deck space and thus better accommodation, and that they would be able to carry a greater weapon outfit.

After a long campaign the government placed a contract for an independent review of frigate design by Lloyd's Register. As part of this review TGA were contracted to design a ship incorporating their views but meeting the Staff Requirements for the Type 23 ('Duke') class (S102). This expensive review vindicated the official view in almost every aspect.[37]

33 See Glossary, roughly, fine ends, full amidships and with a fairly full waterplane.

34 I suspect there was a touch of the *reductio ad absurdum* here.

35 Generally allowed only for hygiene in galley and sick bay.

36 D K Brown, 'The Duke Class Frigates examined', *Warship Technology*, Part I 1989 (3), Part II 1989 (4).

37 *Warship Hull Design Inquiry*, HMSO 1988.

8 Submarines

[1] D K Brown, *Nelson to Vanguard* (London & Annapolis 2000), p117.

[2] The risk of fires was indeed reduced but not abolished: not for nothing were the boats known as *Exploder* and *Exciter*!

EARLY POST-WAR THINKING concentrated on the 'Intermediate B' class with High Test Peroxide (HTP) propulsion derived from the German 'Walter' system. An ex-German Type XVII, *U 1407*, was used for trials as HMS *Meteorite*.[1] An early British study was for a 1700-ton twin screw boat with 6000shp on each shaft giving a top speed, submerged, of about 21kts. It was hoped to lay down the first boat early in 1947 for completion in 1950. By 1948 it was realised that there were too many unknowns to go ahead with operational HTP submarines, and it was decided to build an experimental craft. Later a second boat was added, probably when the need for fast ASW training became apparent.

Explorer, for a short time the fastest submarine in the world at about 27kts. She and her sister were extremely valuable in developing tactics against fast submarines. The machinery was very noisy and they were sometimes referred to as 'sirens under the sea'. (*MoD*)

U1407, an ex-German Type XVIIC submarine, was recommissioned as HMS *Meteorite* during the British development of HTP propulsion. The boat is seen here at Barrow-in-Furness in a dock now converted into an attractive museum. (*W Cloots*)

Construction of these experimental craft was justified on three grounds:

> To prove British HTP machinery.

> To investigate the manoeuvrability and control of very fast submarines.

> To study ASW against fast submarines.

The British experimental boats *Explorer* and *Excalibur* were to complete in 1956 and 1958 and well before this it was clear that their primary role would be ASW training. In order to arrange the HTP stowage and the coolers, a deep section shape was adopted with the outer hull underslung from the pressure hull. The main tank capacity was limited to 9 per cent reserve buoyancy instead of the usual 16 per cent, making them poor sea boats. They had one tank forward, two aft and an amidships tank either side fitted with a Kingston valve. Appendages were done away with as far as possible – there was a single anchor without a capstan. The bridge structure was the minimum for surface navigation – low and hence wet – and accommodated a single periscope, an induction pipe for the diesel, battery vent, indicator buoy and the HTP expansion chambers. There was no Snorkel ('Snort').

For surface propulsion they had a single diesel as used in the 'U' class driving electric motors. The diesel was in the fore ends to obtain longitudinal weight balance, taking the place of the torpedo tubes in these unarmed vessels and, for the same reason, the battery was well forward. All HTP equipment was grouped together at the fore end of the unmanned turbine room, reducing the risk of leaks which could cause fires.[2] Turbine controls were grouped on the fore side of the forward bulkhead of the turbine room, close to the switchboard and control room. The HTP was stowed in PVC bags contained in free flooding tanks outside the pressure hull. Endurance was 3 hours at full speed. Oil fuel was stowed inside the pressure hull, below the control room.

The propellers were large, though not as big as desired for the power, and projected 1ft 5in beyond the maximum beam, protected by guards in the form of stabiliser fins. There were problems in scaling model tests of high-speed submarines to full scale (see *Porpoise* class below) and at the Staff Requirement stage it was said to be sure that they would reach 25kts and that 27kts was probable – and achieved. The power absorbed in the coolers was also uncertain. On *Explorer*'s first trial her escort was a *Blackwood* with a top speed of barely 27kts. However, she had not been warned what to expect and thought she could keep up with any submarine with only one boiler in use!

Trim and compensating tanks followed normal practice but special tanks were provided to compensate buoyancy and trim for usage of HTP. Considerable attention was paid to escape arrangements – this may seem ominous in the light of HTP's characteristics but in reality it was the first outcome of a post-war review of escape equipment. Bulkheads were strong, there was one escape chamber and the conning tower could also be used, whilst the diesel room hatch was fitted for twill trunk escape. She had a very wide, flat keel so that she would remain upright if resting on the bottom.

Despite frightening their crews, the two boats proved invaluable in developing tactics for surface ships dealing with very fast submarines. Both the USN and Soviet navies abandoned their HTP designs, demonstrating the achievement of the UK design teams.[3]

Control

A submarine can only operate in a very shallow band of the sea. Wartime submarines had a safe diving depth only a little greater than their length. *Explorer* is quoted with a diving depth of 500ft, rather over twice her length and thanks mainly to a new steel, UXW (see Chapter 13). Even so, running at 27kts (45ft/sec) it does not take long to reach a dangerous depth.[4] Emergencies include flooding or a jammed hydroplane – a hydraulic failure, running deep at high speed, does not allow long to change to the alternative system. Running fast close to the surface may also be hazardous as the boat may broach in front of a passing ship.

Even without emergencies control and manoeuvrability present many problems and in the early post-war years neither theory nor experimental equipment were fully developed. Very simply, the approach was to measure the forces and moments and how they varied on the hull, appendages and control surfaces of a model submarine both on a straight path and when manoeuvring. In these early years there was no way of controlling a model on a curved path and L J Rydill[5] suggested the results could be obtained by running curved models on a straight path and this approach was used for the *Explorer* design.[6] Later, the manoeuvring tank was built at Haslar, 400ft x 200ft and 18ft deep. It has a rotating arm to which models can be fixed for a curved path of up to 90ft radius some 9ft below the surface. The models may be upright to measure turning forces or on their side to represent diving manoeuvres. Later still, the Planar Motion Mechanism was developed in which a model could be pitched up and down whilst following a straight path. Very large free-running models under magnetic loop control may also be used in control experiments.

The results of these tests, the 'derivatives', were fed into the differential equations describing the path of the submarine. For very many years this work was led by a scientist at AEW, Tom Booth, who received little credit for his work. The obvious feature of control studies is in the positioning of the forward hydroplanes. The RN favoured bow

planes which give better control, particularly at periscope depth. However, bow planes are noisy, degrading passive sonars, and for this reason the USN favoured planes on the sail. The arguments were finely balanced and the author well remembers one Anglo-US meeting at which the American officers argued in favour of bow planes whilst the UK representatives wanted planes on the fin.

Much successful work was also done in developing a re-cycle diesel plant in which the exhaust was replenished with oxygen from HTP and re-used.[7]

Silencing

New and modernised submarines would use acoustic homing torpedoes as their primary weapon, as would enemy submarines. The use of active sonar would be limited since its use would disclose one's own position, and existing asdics (sonar) were not well suited to passive operation.[8] Both of these factors led to a requirement for future submarines to be quiet, to protect them against enemy torpedoes and mines and to provide a silent platform from which the enemy could be heard without being detected by their passive sonar.

Propeller cavitation was a problem at periscope depth but in most cases could be avoided by going deeper where the greater pressure prevented cavitation. However, even at depth the low-frequency pressure pulses from propeller blades passing through a non-uniform inflow were a problem. It is not often realised that streamlining improves the operating conditions of the propeller and makes an important contribution to reducing propeller noise as well as reducing flow noise over the hull. Much had been done during the war to reduce machinery noise by improved design and manufacture and by resilient mounting, but a further major improvement was needed.

A submarine model under the rotating arm at Haslar. The arm had a maximum radius of 90ft and the forces and moments on the model could be measured while turning. For 'rise and dive' manoeuvres the model would be turned on its side. (*MoD*)

[3] One of the leading members of the team, Eleanor MacNair, has helped with this section.

[4] At 30° bow down this would imply a vertical velocity of 22.5ft/sec.

[5] D K Brown, *A Century of Naval Construction*, p315.

[6] A curved model is part of the Science Museum reserve collection at Wroughton.

[7] Eleanor Macnair (personal communication).

[8] In 1951 when this author was serving in *Tabard* the First Lieutenant was devising an elaborate mathematical method of locating an enemy from passive observations.

Scotsman was used for many experiments in streamlining, and also for experimental propellers. (*D K Brown collection*)

[9] Serious consideration was given to a new 'trials' submarine but with the increasing confidence in model tests and computer simulations the cost could not be justified.

[10] *Taciturn* 14ft; *Turpin*, *Thermopylae* and *Totem* 12ft; *Tabard, Tiptoe, Trump* and *Truncheon* 20ft.

[11] 'Fancy' was a slightly modified Mark VIII adapted for HTP. On 16 June 1959 a 'Fancy' torpedo exploded aboard the submarine *Sidon* while she was alongside the depot ship *Maidstone* in Portland Harbour, and sank her.

[12] *Alliance* is preserved in this state on shore at the Submarine Museum, Gosport.

[13] There is a parallel here with *Warrior* (1860) which also used conventional technology in a novel ensemble.

[14] ADM 157/139 (PRO) includes a paper, originally Secret, detailing the way in which performance fell short of the original intention.

[15] They had a very early design of reduced noise propellers; later designs did not lose in efficiency. Some of the problems of scaling from model to ship are explained in Appendix 2 on Reynold's Number.

Modernising the Wartime Submarines

At the end of the war the streamlined *Seraph* had proved valuable as a high-speed target and five more of the 'S' class were similarly converted. *Seraph* was 'padded' so that practice torpedoes could be fired at her. *Scotsman* was given more powerful motors (3600shp) producing a maximum speed of 16.3kts and tried in various configurations, including one in which there was no bridge fin at all. She was a most useful test bed for many ideas and equipments including propellers.[9]

Eight of the wartime 'T' class were modernised between 1951 and 1956. They were lengthened,[10] which provided space for two more electric motors, doubling their power and increasing underwater speed to 15.4kts, and an additional battery section of 6560 amp/hr cells. They were streamlined – gun and external tubes were removed, and a new, tall fin enclosed periscopes, snort, etc. They were armed with Mark 23 (Grog) AS torpedoes and were intended to have 'Fancy', an anti-surface ship weapon using HTP, but after the explosion in *Sidon* in 1959 'Fancy' was withdrawn and they received the venerable Mark VIII torpedo.[11] Sonar fit comprised Types 186, 187 and 197.

Five riveted 'T' class were streamlined but not lengthened, whilst their battery was updated to 6560 amp/hr cells. Their speed was increased by 1.4kts and being fairly quiet, they were used mainly for ASW training. The fourteen surviving 'A' class were given somewhat similar treatment.[12] These updated boats gave valuable service and enabled tactics to be developed both for and against the first generation of fast submarines.

The *Porpoise* Class

By 1948 it was recognised that anti-submarine warfare (ASW) would be the primary role of the Royal Navy's submarine force. Subsidiary to this, it was clear that they would have to spend much operational time providing targets for the training of surface ASW vessels and aircraft and the development of ASW tactics. In addition, it was thought likely that British submarines could operate against Soviet merchant ships supporting their army in the Arctic and possibly the Baltic and Black Sea. The German Type XXI had shown what conventional technology could do when required. The concept was brilliant and original but the individual techniques used for increased diving depth, greater battery capacity, more powerful electric motors and streamlined hull form were all well known.[13] First priority was to use such techniques in modernising existing submarines and then to build a new design diesel-electric boat.

Six *Porpoise* class submarines, designed by R N Newton and E A Brokensha, were ordered in April 1951, and two more in 1954. They were a little bigger and somewhat shorter than the 'T' conversions, but improved design methods and UXW steel together with new structural design methods gave them a considerably increased diving depth. A model of the very long engine-room collapsed during tests at NCRE and a number of extra deep frames were fitted in the final design. They were exceptionally quiet for their day, mostly by careful attention to detail in the design and support of their machinery.

The engines were Admiralty Standard Range I (ASR I) designed at AEL, West Drayton and built first at Chatham Dockyard, an unusual case of 'in-house' machinery development. They were to prove very successful even though some of the design aims proved over-ambitious.[14] Great attention was paid to habitability, including air-conditioning. The six bow tubes had rapid reloading gear so that a second salvo could follow very soon after the first, but this was heavy and not very reliable. Torpedoes could be fired at much greater depth than in previous classes. Submerged endurance was expected to be 55 hours at 4kts, about three times that of any previous RN boat.

The DNC, Sir Victor Shepherd, explained in 1955 that the submerged speed had come down from 17kts to 16kts, which he blamed on the use of reduced-noise propellers of lower propulsive efficiency and on caution in estimating full size performance from model tests.[15] Submerged endurance on batteries had been further reduced following a re-assessment of auxiliary load by the Director of Electrical Engineering. At 4kts the auxiliary load was equal to the power for propulsion. In consequence, the nominal endurance at 4kts was reduced from 55 hours to 40 hours. Problems with the UXW steel, discussed in Chapter 13, led to a reduction in diving depth from 625ft to 500ft. In 1953 the design had been lengthened 4ft to accept an increase in machinery weight. Despite the fact that they fell short of performance targets, they were probably the

	'T' Conversion	'T' Streamlined	*Porpoise*
Submerged Displacement, tons	1734*	1571	2303
Length (oa) (ft)	293	273.5	290.25
Diving Depth (ft)	350	300	500
Diesel power (bhp)	2800	2500	3680
Propulsion motor (shp)	6000	1450	6000
Max sub speed (kts)	15.4	9.5	16
Crew	68	50	71
Torpedo tubes + reloads	6+14	6+5	8+22

* Displacement and length vary slightly

Left: Taciturn, an early 'T' class conversion with enlarged battery and motors; streamlined for higher speed and quietness. (*D K Brown collection*)

Below: Andrew, an 'A' class boat streamlined but not given extra power. (*D K Brown collection*)

best submarines of the day within NATO,[16] and considerably superior to the Soviet 'Whiskey' class. They were deeper diving than either the 'Whiskey' or the German Type XXI (both 400ft), faster than the 'Whiskey' but 1kt slower than the XXI, and far quieter than either.

They had noise-reduced propellers, benefiting from trials on surface ships and on *Scotsman*. Initially, these were very prone to 'sing', in which eddies are shed from the trailing edge, alternately from one side and then the other, exciting a resonant vibration of the blade which, in turn, makes the eddy shedding worse. It is said that *Rorqual* could be heard leaving the Clyde on the west coast of Scotland from a listening station on Long Island.[17] The

USN had similar problems and there was much interesting discussion on both theoretical and empirical solutions either seeking to control the eddy shedding or to prevent vibration by damping. Luckily, the *Porpoise* propellers had been designed before Conolly's work on propeller strength (see Chapter 13) and were stronger than necessary. This made it possible to cut grooves in the blades, which were filled with a damping material which gave a complete cure.[18]

They had a good sonar fit aided by their low noise level and proved successful in a long service life. Top speed was about 16kts submerged and they had an endurance of 9000 miles on the surface.

[16] The USN *Tang*s were designed for 18.3kts submerged but only achieved 16kts. This was part of the evidence leading to a reduction in the design speed of the *Porpoise*. *Tang* could dive to 700ft. Caution is needed in comparing diving depths as it is not certain on what basis these were defined.

[17] With later propellers, she was able to surface off the Statue of Liberty without being detected.

[18] Most other classes were given a V-shaped trailing edge which, with experience, proved successful in controlling the shedding of eddies.

Riveted 'T's were not suitable for the full conversion, but five – like *Tireless* shown here in 1954 – were streamlined, retaining their original machinery. They were quite quiet and useful for ASW training.
(*D K Brown collection*)

[19] British sales successes post-war were the *Whitby-Leander* class frigates and the *Oberon*s, both the best of their category and not cheap. Much the same may be said of the Vosper Mark 10. British Shipbuilders' attempt at selling a cheap frigate may well have been mistaken.

[20] *Onyx* is preserved at Birkenhead, *Ocelot* at Chatham.

Porpoise, the first post-war operational submarine design. For their day, they were exceptionally quiet.
(*D K Brown collection*)

Oberon Class

The thirteen *Oberon*s for the RN were updated *Porpoise*s – one indication of a good design is that it can lead to an even better 'Mark II'. The UXW steel used in *Porpoise* was difficult to fabricate and was replaced by QT28 quality which, together with further refinement to design methods gave a significant increase in diving depth. Special T bar frames were rolled and it was possible to have uniform size, omitting the deep frames which had been so inconvenient in the *Porpoise*s. There were further improvements in silencing. The original sonar fit was the same as *Porpoise* but most were updated in the 1980s. *Otus* carried out trials with the Sub Harpoon SSM in 1989.

In addition to the RN boats there were six Australian, three Canadian, three Brazilian and two Chilean boats.[19] The RN boats had a very long service life, approaching 30 years, but it was claimed that they were still the quietest submarines in the world at the end of their life.[20]

Midget Submarines – *Stickleback*

In the early stages of the Cold War there was a fear that Soviet mini-subs might lay nuclear charges in harbours and estuaries. Four 'X' class midgets were built ostensibly for training in countermeasures, but it has recently been revealed that the RN had plans to return the compliment, laying either Blue Danube (20Kton yield, 10,000lbs weight) or Red Beard (20,000lbs) off Leningrad (now St Petersburg).

Orpheus. Very similar to the *Porpoise* but better steel and improved structural design gave the *Oberon* class a much greater diving depth. They were even quieter than *Porpoise*. (*D K Brown collection*)

One of the four, *Stickleback*, was sold to Sweden in 1958, returning to the UK in 1977 for display in the Imperial War Museum at Duxford. *Sprat* was lent to the USN for ASW training. Commander Richard Compton Hall, who commanded *Minnow*, says that the margin of safety was too small for peacetime operation.

The 1953 Design

By 1952 doubts were being expressed over the cost of the *Porpoise*s and it was suggested by DN Plans that some at least of RN submarines should be of a simpler and less capable design so that more could be built with available funds. For the main ASW role in the Arctic a lower submerged speed would be acceptable (exercises showed speed to be of less importance than previously thought) and a shallower diving depth – 300ft was the maximum for air ejection of torpedoes. Since a single torpedo hit would sink a submarine, there was no need for a large salvo nor for rapid reloading. On the other hand, very elaborate fire-control gear would be needed and hovering gear was fitted.

There would be very little self-maintenance, in order to keep crew numbers down, which meant frequent visits to the depot ship so reducing the stores requirement. Four bow tubes with 10 torpedoes seemed adequate, together with one countermeasures tube (two countermeasures or anti-escort torpedoes). A 4in Mark XXIII gun could be mounted if required but was not carried in the ASW role. It was estimated that this required an extra 2ft on the length of the boat and, in all, some 40 tons on displacement.[21] The smaller submarine resulting would be more suitable than an *Oberon* for Baltic and Black Sea work.

Staff requirements were issued in December 1952 (revised in 1953) and a number of design studies were completed. For the first time there was serious debate over one or two shafts. The single shaft had clear advantages in propulsion (*c*1kt) and would be quieter, but few operators and not many engineers were prepared to risk the lack of redundancy inherent with a single shaft. Stern tubes are virtually impossible with a single shaft. By late 1954 the intention was to build a first batch of six twin-screw boats followed possibly by nine single-screw versions. They were provisionally described as the *Boreas* class.[22] The emphasis was on high silent speed but 10kts submerged was hoped for (8kts snorting) and 11kts on the surface. Endurance on battery was to be 30 hours at 4kts. The result was a submarine of 1100 tons. There was some thought of a later version with re-cycle diesels for use in the patrol area, snorting in transit. Habitability was much improved and cafeteria messing was proposed.

The 1953 design was stopped in 1955. It was argued that its reliance on frequent support from a depot ship was unacceptable in nuclear war. The concept of mass production in wartime was also dead. However, the First Lord, Quentin Hogg, visited Bath personally to apologise for the cancellation and wasted effort, a gesture much appreciated.

[19] British sales successes post-war were the *Whitby-Leander* class frigates and the *Oberon*s, both the best of their category and not cheap. Much the same may be said of the Vosper Mark 10. British Shipbuilders' attempt at selling a cheap frigate may well have been mistaken.

[20] *Onyx* is preserved at Birkenhead, *Ocelot* at Chatham.

[21] For a more detailed discussion of this design see: N Friedman, *The Post War Naval Revolution*, (London & Annapolis 1986).

[22] ADM 205/106 (PRO).

1953 Quiet Submarine Design. This study appears in the files of The Admiralty Experiment Works, Haslar, which carried out experiments in 1955 to investigate the efficiency of single- and twin-screw designs. A single-screw design proved to be more efficient. (*Drawing by John Roberts from original in PRO ADM 226/300*)

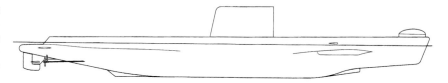

23 P G Wrobel, 'Design of the Type 2400 Patrol Class Submarine', *Trans RINA* (1985). Main source for this section, used with permission of RINA.

24 Torpedo firing gear.

25 A small GRP casing was thought desirable to shroud external fittings such as hatches.

26 H J Tabb RCNC, 'Escape from Submarines, A Short Historical review of Policy and Equipment in the RN', *Trans RINA* (1975), p19.

The Type 2400 Submarine, *Upholder*[23]

During the mid 1970s there was keen debate as to whether the *Oberons* should be replaced by another class of diesel-electric submarine or all the scarce funds be allocated to nuclear boats. SSN were more capable but expensive and the diesel boats might be more suitable in shallow waters and could meet the training role at low cost. As part of the debate five design studies were prepared with sub-merged displacement ranging from 500 to 2500 tons. They were all single-hull boats built of NQ1 steel and had a sub-merged speed of about 20kts.

After lengthy discussion a study of 1850 tons was selected for development under an Outline NST. It used existing weapons and sensors derived from UK, US and German sources. Further investigation caused a growth to 1960 tons. At the final NST stage three options were offered, one being the 1960-ton version. Option 2 was of 2250 tons with a superior weapon fit, including Sub Har-poon, costing 15 per cent more, while the 2650-ton Option 3 cost a further 5 per cent more. Option 2 was selected, with the directive to agree a compromise with Vickers (VSEL), who wanted to attract export orders with a 2500-ton boat having greater endurance and a more flexible weapon fit. Finally a compromise was agreed at 2400 tons. Sensors include a Thompson cylindrical bow array, Micropuffs passive ranging, flank array, sonar intercept with fire control developed from the DCB in the *Trafal-gar* class. Overall, the weapon and sensor fit is more advanced (and more expensive) than a *Trafalgar*. The fea-tures of the new submarine are best shown in compari-son with the highly regarded *Oberon* class of very similar displacement.

	Type 2400	*Oberon*
Submerged Displacement (tonnes)	2400	2450
Length (oa) (m)	70	90
Pressure hull dia. (m)	7.5	5.5
Diving Depth (m)	Over 200	Over 150
Patrol length (days)	49	56
Diesel power (MW)	2 x 1.4*	2 x 1.28
Propulsion motor (MW)	4.0	2 x 2.24
Max sub speed (kts)	20	16
Crew	46	71
Torpedo tubes + reloads	6 + 12	6 + 18

* Supercharged Paxman Ventura.

The pressure hull of NQ1 is very nearly a uniform cylin-der, tapering slightly aft, with internal framing of NQ1 or HY80. The dome bulkhead forward presented a difficult design problem as openings were needed for the six tubes of 0.8m diameter, two for air turbine pumps of 1.0m,[24] and a weapon loading hatch. A Finite Element Analysis supported by large scale model tests confirmed that the design was safe.

The hull form was optimised for submerged perform-ance; it needed about twice the power of the *Oberon* on the surface but slightly over half the power submerged. Numerous model tests and simulations were run at Haslar to ensure good control, in particular the ability to turn at high speed without unwanted depth excursions and to level out after a depth change without overshoot. The hull, fin and casing[25] were shaped to give as uniform flow as possible into the propeller to reduce noise.

All machinery was carefully mounted to reduce noise transmission and to resist the shock of underwater explo-sions. The power-operated weapon storage and loading gear was seen as a particular success. The latest develop-ments in noise reduction coatings were fitted. The fin sup-ports six masts – two periscopes, two snort masts, EW and communications – whilst also containing a five-man diver tower. There are three main compartments with escape equipment in the end spaces and there are two decks for-ward of the machinery. Air purification equipment is of the highest standard. Great attention has been paid to ease of maintenance and upkeep. A reverse osmosis plant is fitted.

Upholder completed in 1990 followed by three more up to 1993 and they proved very successful once problems with their torpedo tubes were overcome. They were put up for sale in 1995 as an economy measure and eventu-ally leased to Canada – who got a splendid bargain, although there have been problems getting them into serv-ice, possibly due to lack of experience with the boats' equipment.

Submarine Escape and Rescue

Up to the end of the war, most submarine accidents hap-pened in shallow water, often due to collision on the surface. A study of ocean depths showed that the con-tinental shelf was rarely over 600ft in depth, shelving rapidly to the deep ocean from which there was little chance of survival. If a submarine is on the bottom and unable to surface it almost certainly implies that one or more compartments is flooded and exposed to sea pres-sure. While it is possible to design bulkheads to with-stand the same overall diving pressure as the pressure hull, such bulkheads would be so heavy as to severely limit the capability of the submarine. In consequence, bulkheads are usually designed to take a much lower pressure and will fail at any greater depth, where there is no chance of survival.

Following the tragic loss of *Thetis* in June 1939, a com-mittee on escape and rescue was set up under Admiral Dunbar Nasmith, but during the war little could be done to change procedures or equipment. In April 1946 a new committee was set up under Rear-Admiral P A Ruck-Keene, who had been a member of the Dunbar Nasmith committee.[26] Their report was most valuable and formed the basis for all post-war work in this area; in particular, it was recognised that the greatest hazard was whilst sur-vivors were still inside the submarine and they should be

The four *Upholder* class were victims of the 'Peace Dividend' and deemed unwanted in the post Cold War era. They were exceptionally quiet and had an unrivalled weapon and sensor fit. They have been leased to Canada. (*Mike Lennon*)

under pressure for the least possible time and that removal of carbon dioxide was more important than supplying oxygen. At that time the normal method of escape involved flooding a whole compartment to equalise the pressure and then, one by one, ducking below a twill trunk to reach the open escape hatch, using the Davis escape apparatus on pure oxygen on the way to the surface. This meant that the survivors would be under pressure for a considerable time, under which conditions oxygen, nitrogen and, particularly, carbon dioxide can be lethal.

A one-man escape tower was developed so that men would be under pressure for the least possible time and it was decided that free ascent should be adopted and taught. Lungs full of air under pressure have more than enough oxygen for the time to reach the surface; indeed the most serious problem was to breathe out fast enough to avoid damage to the lungs. A 100ft tower was built at Fort Blockhouse for training. Further attention was to be paid to air purification, studies of the USN escape chamber were initiated, and location devices, buoys, etc developed

Development of an immersion suit to keep survivors afloat, dry and warm was started but was not in service when *Truculent* was sunk in a collision with a freighter in the Thames Estuary on 12 January 1950. A Standing Committee On Submarine Escape (SCOSE) was set up in October 1951. A simpler One Man Escape Chamber (OMEC) was designed, with the aim that the time under pressure while escaping from 300ft should be less than 3 minutes. A Built In Breathing System (BIBS) provided pure air for those waiting to escape (an oxygen-rich system had been tried).

The USN escape chamber, which could operate to 850ft, was carried in *Kingfisher* (ex-*King Salvor*) from 1954 to 1959. The early *Porpoise* class had a mating ring and escape bulkheads which could resist the water pressure at 800ft. The chamber was abandoned due to the logistics of getting it to the scene in time and difficulty in positioning it

on a sunken submarine.

By the early 1960s it was realised that free ascent was not limited to 150ft. Trained, fit men should be able to escape from 300ft or even 600ft. In May 1963 there was another review under Captain J S Stevens. This aimed at increased depth, escape tower and no twill trunk. Liaison with USN over the use of their rescue submarine (DSRV) led to the decision to abandon the rescue chamber. This review emphasised that submarines are war machines, for which a degree of risk was inevitable. They also considered means of blowing ballast tanks at depth without HP air. This usually involved the use of an explosive, such as cordite, to generate the large quantities of gas at high pressure needed to blow ballast tanks against the pressure in deep water. This high pressure gas had to be vented quickly while surfacing else it might rupture the tanks, sinking the boat again. Large freeing ports were needed. The strength of bulkheads was reviewed as was the performance of pumps. Early location was seen as vital, so indicator buoys were fitted with radio, D/F, smoke candles, and underwater telephone. Three trapped men escaped from *Artemis* the day after her sinking (1 July 1971).

The crews of nuclear submarines with reactor and air purification systems working could survive for a long time.[27] After 1963 thoughts were given to see if pressurisation be quick enough for free ascent from over 300ft. Tests were held at the RN Physiological Laboratory (RNPL) simulating escape from 300-500ft. In the Mediterranean, *Orpheus* in 1965 staged an escape from 480ft (keel 500ft). By mid-1970, instructors from the submarine HQ and training establishment HMS *Dolphin* at Gosport left *Osiris* off Malta at 600ft. Target times were 30 seconds under pressure with the tower flooded before pressurisation. Deeper trials have been carried out with specially-skilled men. The average, fit sailor has a good chance of escaping from 300ft and may even survive 600ft.

27 It is not easy to consider an accident which would keep an SSN on the bottom and leave many survivors. Flooding bow compartment is about all, which is what appears to have happened to the Russian submarine *Kursk* in 2002.

9 Nuclear Submarines

Rowland Baker, later knighted, who led the early nuclear submarine (and Polaris boats) programme, completing them on schedule and within budget. He is seen here as a Constructor Commodore in Canada, where he designed the *St Laurent* class frigates. (*D K Brown collection*)

[1] D K Brown, *A Century of Naval Construction* (London 1983).

[2] R J Daniel, 'The Royal Navy and Nuclear Power', *Trans INA* Vol 90 (1948). Daniel had visited Hiroshima soon after the Japanese surrender and had attended the Bikini trials.

[3] The word 'about' can be inserted in front of all performance figures in this chapter.

[4] I am grateful to Keith Foulger for his contribution to this chapter.

[5] Vice-Admiral Sir Ted Horlick, 'Submarine Propulsion in the Royal Navy', *Trans I Mech E* (1982) (54th Thomas Lowe Gray Lecture).

[6] Reactor functioning but not delivering power.

[7] Assisted by G H Fuller and D Henry.

[8] The US team were suspicious of espionage (see *A Century of Naval Construction*) but this was not so.

THE ADMIRALTY WAS QUICK to appreciate the potential of nuclear propulsion, particularly for submarines.[1] This interest was expressed in Daniel's paper of 1948 to the Institution of Naval Architects which, though dealing mainly with nuclear weapons, also envisaged nuclear propulsion.[2] Early studies by the DNC Submarine Section under Newton and later Starks were based on a gas-cooled reactor somewhat similar to the bulky unit at Calder Hall, Britain's first operational nuclear power station. The submarines were correspondingly large: the first of 1950 was a twin-screw design of about 2500 tons with an underwater speed of 25kts.[3] Within a year, the reactor size had increased and with it that of the submarine. The next study was 3400 tons and speed had fallen to 22kts. A redesign for a manoeuvrable submarine and shock protection brought the displacement up to 4500 tons at 20kts, while the pressure hull diameter had increased from 25ft to 31ft. The obvious conclusion was that a gas-cooled, graphite-moderated reactor was not practical in a submarine.

In the early 1950s submarine studies under Bob Newton were led by Sidney Dale, constructor, with Keith Foulger as his assistant.[4] They were involved in the *Porpoise* class and later HTP designs as well. The team at the Atomic Energy Research Establishment at Harwell were also only part-time on SSN projects. This team included Dr J R Dunworth, later professor of Mechanical Engineering, and a young MEO, Lt Righton. As well as the traditional work on submarine design, the DNC team spent much time in an unsuccessful attempt to mount the complete reactor compartment on springs to protect it from shock. Eventually it was decided that the scheme was impractical and work stopped.

By 1953 further discussions within the naval staff had shown the importance of nuclear submarines, but the Government had decided that scarce resources for research and development in nuclear work should be directed to power stations. Studies at Harwell continued at low priority investigating both water and liquid metal cooling. At the same time the USN prototype water-cooled reactor went critical in 1953 and the submarine *Nautilus* commissioned in September 1954, thanks to the drive of Admiral Rickover.

In 1954 a small naval section was set up at Harwell under Captain (E) S A Harrison-Smith, liasing with the submarine section. This section was considerably enhanced in 1955 when enough uranium (U_{235}) was allocated for R&D to proceed with the aim of getting a submarine plant running on shore by 1961.[5] Attention was concentrated on a pressurised water reactor. A E Reeves was much involved in the design of the shielding, whose weight was an important aspect in the submarine design. This involved the first large-scale use of a computer in ship design. In essence, for each point outside the shielding the radiation dose from every part of the reactor system had to be calculated and added together. This meant a considerable amount of three-dimensional geometry as well as skill in programming the early, clumsy computers. The fact that measurements taken later during the radiation survey were close to the calculated figures reflects great credit on Reeves and the naval section. Newcomers were horrified by the cost of the many tons of lead required to absorb gamma radiation and even more when it was explained that the thick and flawless polythene required to mop up neutrons was much more expensive.

In 1956 Treasury approval was given to build a shore-based prototype at Dounreay, alongside, but not part of, the AEA site. It was hoped that this unit might be running by January 1960 with a submarine by mid-1962. This did not have high priority and progress was slow. The naval section soon concluded that the most suitable plant for a submarine was a pressurised water reactor using enriched uranium. Vickers Armstrong (Engineers) were to be the main contractor with Rolls Royce as the subcontractor responsible for the nuclear reactor. The core design had to be settled by late 1956 in order to have a zero power test[6] by early 1957.

In that year Rickover, on a visit to the UK, invited a British team led by Starks to see something of USN work, which led to some changes in the British plans. Work on the guided-missile cruiser was stopped in 1957 and the design team led by Starks with Daniel as his constructor became the nuclear submarine team. These studies, based on earlier work by Brokensha,[7] led to a nuclear plant very similar in configuration to the US S5W plant.[8] In hull structure the British work was well in advance of the American thanks to the work of Bill Kendrick and others at NCRE (see Chapter 12), while L J Rydill in a paper of 1957 showed the problems of fatigue failure.

By 1957 there were three major projects in hand and all were making progress. The Dounreay prototype had been the lead project and a full-size wooden mock-up of the reactor and machinery spaces was nearing completion at Southampton in the old Supermarine works.[9] The Harwell group had expanded to 160 professional staff and Neptune, a zero-energy reactor designed to provide information for the submarine programme, went critical on 7 November 1957 (it was moved to Derby in 1959). All this work was leading up to the all-British nuclear submarine which became *Valiant*. However, while the US offer to sell a complete nuclear submarine power plant (S5W, as in *Skipjack*) enabled the RN to get a submarine (*Dreadnought*) into service quickly, as discussed in the next section, it delayed the completion of the British work. There were those who were unconvinced that a shore-based prototype was needed now the US plant was available and there was some access to their design philosophy.

The biggest and most controversial decision to be made for the Dounreay plant was in the choice of the type of steel for the reactor pressure vessel and the primary circuit. The advantages and disadvantages of austenitic[10] stainless steel and low alloy steel were argued with some heat, with corrosion of various types and weld reliability at the centre of the debate.[11] Eventually, the low alloy steel was chosen, which did rather better than expected as it formed a corrosion-resistant oxide film that helped to give an active life of over 17 years. Fabrication, however, was not as easy as had been hoped.

The replica submarine hull at Dounreay was built from mild steel which was not strong enough to contain the pressure from a major nuclear accident within the reactor compartment alone. It was planned that the over-pressure should be vented into a void space which had to occur very quickly indeed. This proved much more difficult than it sounds but was solved when toughened glass was suggested. The manufacturers (Pilkington) doubted if their material was consistent enough but some hilarious tests in which a number of panels were broken proved that it was reliable and consistent. The reactor compartment was surrounded by a big water tank which provided shielding and also kept things cool. When the structural work was complete the hull was water tested to 145psi internal pressure and after it was fitted out there was an air pressure test to 126psi. The energy contained in 10,000ft^3 of air at this pressure was equivalent to some 10 tons of TNT, and all sorts of authorities had to be convinced that it was safe (including the author, who was standing on it!). The risk of a catastrophe was quite small but the chance of a valve flying off could not be neglected.

By 1959 most of the research work at Harwell was complete and the naval section was disbanded, with most of the staff moving to the *Dreadnought* project. Professor Edwards moved to the RN College, Greenwich, where he set up the long training courses in nuclear engineering which the submarines would need.[12]

Dounreay (DSMP) commissioned in 1963.[13] There were initial problems with some of the nickel alloy smallbore pipework and this was replaced by chromium-molybdenum low alloy steel in 1964.[14] Since then DSMP has given many years of trouble-free service and has been essential in the development of RN nuclear plants and in training their operators.[15]

Dreadnought

Towards the end of 1956 draft Staff Requirements for a British nuclear submarine (SSN) were agreed, and in February 1957 the Minister of Defence visited the USA when the US offered to release nuclear information. Later that year the uss *Nautilus* visited the UK and the Minister and First Sea Lord were given a demonstration cruise. In January 1958 the President and the Prime Minister signed an agreement for the UK to purchase a complete SSN propulsion plant, later defined as S5W. As part of the deal a small monitoring team from MoD led by Captain 'Shorty' Cotmiston was appointed to Westinghouse, Pittsburg in 1959. Another team with Constructor Commander Keith Foulger and engineer colleagues Roger Berry and Reggie Down worked within the Gorleston shipyard of the Electric Boat Company ensuring that all submarine design information relevant to *Dreadnought* was received in the UK. During this period there were frequent visits by Vickers, Rolls Royce, ship's officers (designate) and by US to Barrow and Derby. Keith Foulger, later Chief Naval Architect, has said that 'seeing the first British nuclear submarine get off the ground' was the most exciting time in his career.

In March 1957 the name *Dreadnought* had been chosen – *Vulcan* was a close second, followed by *Thunder*.[16] In November the *Dreadnought* Project Team (DPT) was set up under Rowland Baker.[17] DPT was responsible for production and programme but the team reported to DG Ships on design aspects.[18] The after end of *Dreadnought* had to be identical to uss *Skipjack*[19] in order to accept the US plant, while the fore end was derived from the earlier British studies and was dominated by the very large conformal array sonar. There was continuing concern that there might be a mismatch or misunderstanding between British and US technology.[20] Rolls Royce set up a new company – Rolls Royce and Associates (RRA)[21]– to deal with Westinghouse and build all British submarine plants.

Dreadnought's diving depth was set by the design of the US machinery systems but was still much greater than British submarines in service. It was realised that the speed, manoeuvrability and strength would lead to frequent dives to maximum depth and hence the fatigue life of the hull was a vital criterion. To ease the problem, the pressure hull ended in torispherical domes and similar measures were taken where the hull diameter was reduced in the machinery rooms. The steel was specially developed – QT35 – and it was decided that a detailed crack-detection survey should be carried out at regular intervals. There were early problems with cracking due to dirt inclusions in the steel but these were overcome with improved welding procedures. *Dreadnought* was decommissioned in 1983, 20 years after she entered service.[22]

The bridge fin was further aft than in the US design, partly to permit an internal layout based on RN practice but also because model tests had shown that roll induced when manoeuvring at speed ('snap roll') would be less. After prolonged debate, it was decided to position the forward hydroplanes near the bow rather than on the fin as was USN practice as this gave better control at low speed, particularly at periscope depth, at the expense of more interference with sonar performance.[23]

[9] The mock-up was started at Dounreay and transferred to Southampton by Vickers.

[10] Austenitic refers to the crystalline structure of the steel. Steel alloys can have several atomic arrangements, with face-centred cubic form in austenitic. When alloyed with about 17 per cent chromium it gives a very corrosion-resistant material.

[11] See Horlick, Note 5 above, for a technical discussion.

[12] Greenwich had a zero-power training reactor, Jason, in the only reactor building designed by Sir Christopher Wren! At that time the local Council proclaimed Greenwich to be a 'nuclear free zone'.

[13] The author carried out the leak test to a much higher standard than *Dreadnought*.

[14] Horlick, Note 5 above.

[15] Horlick refers to some failures in the secondary (conventional steam) machinery.

[16] My memory is that *Upanatom* was a front runner! ADM 1/26779 (PRO) gives this and many others.

[17] See *Warship 1995* for a biography of this remarkable naval constructor.

[18] See *A Century of Naval Construction* for management aspects. Baker introduced many then novel procedures in management.

[19] We did alter the transition pieces where the pressure reduced in diameter as Rydill's work showed a serious risk of fatigue cracking.

[20] There was a sign on the bulkhead between the fore and aft sections which read 'Checkpoint Charlie– You are now entering the American Zone', mimicking a famous landmark of Cold War Berlin. Organisation of spares support from two hemispheres was a nightmare– I chaired the spares committee.

[21] With Vickers Armstrongs and Foster Wheeler.

[22] Rydill got it right on fatigue.

[23] It also permitted a smaller fin– all design is a compromise!

[24] Large diameter, slow-running propellers are not necessarily quiet but are a necessary step to silence.

A considerable number of propeller designs were tested at model scale at Haslar. The interaction between the flow over the hull and into the propeller affected both efficiency and noise. Power is lost due to friction of the water in the flow over the hull and much of this loss can be recovered if the flow is channelled through the propeller. In general the bigger the propeller the more efficient and quieter it would be, but the bigger propellers needed to run at very low rpm– the biggest model propeller had a full-scale diameter well over 30ft and ran at impossibly low speed.[24] To our surprise we were past the optimum and a slightly smaller propeller would have been better.[25] It had long been realised that a single propeller was more efficient than two but the redundancy of two shaft lines was initially preferred by operators in all navies.[26] The success of USS *Albacore* made it clear that the advantages of the single shaft were overwhelming. A small retractable propulsor was fitted.[27]

[25] The author was working on propeller design at Haslar during this investigation. It was said that you became a true propeller designer when you ceased to think of a propeller driving a ship and started to think of the ship as a mere obstruction to the flow into the propeller (this took about 6 months).

[26] There was even a four-shaft study with a propeller in each quadrant!

[27] R P Largess & H S Horwitz, '*Albacore*– The Shape Of The Future', *Warship 1991*.

The launch of the *Dreadnought* at Barrow, Trafalgar Day (21 October) 1960. (*D K Brown collection*)

[28] D K Brown, 'Sir Rowland Baker', *Warship 1995*.

[29] *Dreadnought*'s officers and crew were also outstanding, many of the wardroom making flag rank while several ratings took degrees.

[30] Even so, USS *Nautilus* took 6 months less.

[31] At first I would be on the quayside to meet her after each voyage and sort out the problems. I gave this up when the only complaint was that the wardroom toaster was burning the paint!

[32] Particulars in this chapter are from published sources.

[33] I was actually asked to design a mount for a 4in gun– for shore bombardment!

[34] The original name proposed for this submarine was *Inflexible*, which drew an immediate protest from the E-in-C that a fortune had been spent on <u>flexible</u> mountings and the name was quite unsuitable!

[35] Brokensha was the Principal Ship Overseer at Barrow for both *Dreadnought* and *Valiant*.

Dreadnought, seen on early trials prior to commissioning (note the Red Ensign), still with a pendant number painted up. (*D K Brown collection*)

The fore end had to accommodate the very large sonar and six torpedo tubes using a novel torpedo discharge system which could work at great depths. It was thought that a very smooth surface finish would help to make the submarine quiet as well as increasing speed and *Dreadnought* received a super-fine finish.

By about 1960 there was concern that design changes were delaying the completion date and Baker laid it down that every change would require his personal authorisation. The author had joined DPT in 1961 and initially was responsible for radiation shielding and nuclear safety for all projects (Dounreay and *Valiant* as well); after a year, when the Polaris project started, I found myself with a scratch staff looking after the completion of *Dreadnought*. Getting Baker to sign a change order was a frightening task; one would be sent for a day or so after he had the file and more often than not the file would be thrown at you as you entered. Baker had been brought up on a working Thames barge and had an unusual command of the English language, used to the full when contemplating any change.[28]

Everything possible was tested alongside at Barrow. The designers had promised that if there should be a nuclear accident, the leak rate should not exceed 1 per cent per day. This proved very difficult to achieve and the author spent many weekends at Barrow working on it under the eagle eye of a Health and Safety inspector called Norsworthy, but finally we succeeded. Then came the radiation survey: first a quick sweep when the reactor went critical for the first time to make sure that there was no gross problem; then a wait while the reactor was gradually worked up to full power. After various delays the full-power survey went off without problems. It is maddening to those involved when the media talk of neglect of safety in earlier nuclear plants. Everyone tried hard, supervised

by men like Norsworthy, and got most things right. Speed trials followed off Arran. At that date submerged speed was measured by towing a float whose speed was tracked by a theodolite on shore. The only problem was that the landowner would not permit the use of the site during the rutting season of his deer!

This brief account has only touched on the numerous problems associated with the design and commissioning of a nuclear submarine. For example, it has been said that the air purification gear was a more difficult design problem than the nuclear plant, and, on a personal note, even the instrumentation to check air purity kept the author busy. Oxygen was produced by electrolysis while carbon dioxide was removed by a scrubber – and tobacco smoke by CO and H_2 burner. Rubbish disposal was another long-term problem. Rubbish was bagged and blown out of an ejector like a small torpedo tube. Accommodation standards were vastly superior to those of earlier submarines.

Dreadnought completed in April 1963 on time and on cost, probably the only major defence project of the time to do so, due to Baker's drive and determination and to the enthusiasm he engendered in his staff.[29] She would have completed 6 months earlier had it not been decided to re-braze all the joints in the sea water systems to UK standards[30] (it is believed that USS *Thresher* was lost due to a failure of a brazed joint).

There were a number of teething problems, mainly not very serious. The US-built turbines had to be changed to cure a vibration problem, which caused some difficulty as Rosyth had not begun to train welders to work to Grade A standards on QT35 steel.[31]

Particulars[32]

Dimensions:	265ft 9in x 32ft 3in x 26ft
Displacement:	3500/4000 tons
shp/speed:	15,000/28kts
Complement:	88
Armament:	Six 21in tubes[33]

Valiant

The basic concept was to graft the fore end of *Dreadnought* on to the British machinery under development in the Dounreay Submarine Prototype – Baker's philosophy was to change one of the three main features (fore end, nuclear plant, main machinery) of an SSN in each class. Inevitably, other changes were introduced. The fore planes were moved a little further aft to reduce interference with the sonar; turbulence around the planes accounted for about 10 per cent of the total submerged resistance of *Dreadnought*. The diving depth was slightly increased to the limits of the British machinery, and she was given a retractable propulsor – known as the 'egg-beater' – driven off the battery as a 'get you home' unit in the event of a failure of the main machinery. *Valiant* could also use the main shaft in turbo-electric mode for quiet propulsion

Left: A rare May 1966 photo of *Valiant* with a pendant number, which she carried for a very short time only. (*MoD*)

Below: Churchill, of the later *Valiant* class. (*D K Brown collection*)

Bottom: Conqueror, of the *Valiant* class, built by Cammell Laird. During the Falklands War she sank the *General Belgrano*, ensuring that major Argentine surface warships would remain in port for the rest of the conflict. (*D K Brown collection*)

since the main gearbox was noisy even though both the main engines and gearbox were on a raft resiliently mounted to the hull.[34] Some tanks were resited and to obtain the right longitudinal balance – always a problem in SSN – the forward compartments were lengthened, resulting in a rather larger submarine.

Experience with the American plant in *Dreadnought* led to some changes from the DSMP nuclear plant. In particular, the primary circuit and its components were fabricated from stainless steel, and the reactor pressure vessel was low alloy but with a stainless steel liner deposited by welding. All systems were simplified and the number of valves was reduced.

Valiant was already well advanced when the USS *Thresher* was lost. Two British assistant constructors carried out a computer simulation of the sinking which pointed a finger at the likely cause – failure of a brazed joint in a 5in pipe. Following this loss there were major investigations on both sides of the Atlantic, not only into the loss itself but also into any other potential problems with SSN design or operation. These studies did not show any problems with the *Valiant* design. In the author's opinion, *Valiant* was the finest British post-war design of its day, surface or submarine, and reflects great credit on Brokensha for the initial studies and on the Chief Constructor, Daniel, and his constructor, Foulger, who created the final design and saw it completed.[35] Manoeuvring limitation diagrams were produced for all classes setting out safe limits for speed and plane angle at different depths – *eg* full speed at maximum depth was not 'safe'.

Particulars

Dimensions:	285ft x 33ft 3in x 27ft
Displacement:	4400/4900 tons
shp/speed:	15,000/28kts
Complement:	103
Armament:	Six 21in tubes

[36] For details of the complicated negotiations and organisation see P Nailor, *The Nassau Connection* (London 1988).

[37] Baker asked Flag Officer, Submarines if those involved in DPT could wear the RN Submariners tie. The reply was 'No, you're a lousy lot of b*******s and I've added the bend sinister!' (in British heraldry the bend sinister denotes an illegitimate connection).

[38] The USN class name is *Lafayette* but UK papers always spoke of *George Washington*.

[39] This may not sound much but a nuclear submarine is so tightly packed that a 3in reduction is difficult.

[40] This and much of the section comes from the submission paper for the sketch design now in the PRO as DEFE 24/90.

Resolution, the first Polaris boat, off Portsmouth Dockyard.
(*D K Brown collection*)

Diving depth has been quoted as 300m. Costs for the class varied from £24 million (*Warspite*) to £30 million (*Conqueror*).

Valiant was ordered in August 1960 and completed in July 1966, followed 9 months later by *Warspite*. There was then a gap in SSN orders due to the Polaris programme until *Churchill* (SSN-04) was ordered in October 1965, followed by two more repeat *Valiant*s. (*Conqueror* and *Courageous*). *Valiant* was delayed by the priority given to the Polaris programme and following the problems at Dounreay all nickel alloy pipes and fittings were replaced.

Some cracks had been found in *Dreadnought*'s QT 35 plates and, though these were made good, American HY80 steel was used in some later *Valiant*s until a suitable UK steel could be developed. All five gave good service, *Conqueror* becoming the first SSN to sink an enemy ship – the Argentine cruiser *General Belgrano*. They were paid off in 1990-2 when cracks were found in their primary circuits. Though these were repairable their remaining life under the defence run-down made this uneconomic.

The Polaris Programme

During 1962 the cancellation of the USAF Skybolt missile programme, also intended for the RAF V-bomber force, led to studies of alternative British nuclear deterrents. It was soon realised that the submarine-launched Polaris system was best suited to UK requirements and a technical team led by S J Palmer visited the USA to study the design of USN submarines of the SSBN-627 class. Armed with this information Prime Minister Macmillan and President Kennedy agreed at a meeting in Nassau late in 1962 that the Polaris weapon system and associated technology should be made available to the UK, and the formal agreement was finalised in April 1963.[36] The whole

programme was to be run by Admiral Mackenzie, with Baker responsible for design and building the submarines and installing the weapon system, retaining the familiar initials DPT,[37] this time standing for Director Polaris Technical. At the same time he also retained authority over the SSN Programme.

Various ways of procuring the submarine force were considered, including a total copy of the SSBN-627 design, or the purchase of US-built boats. There was even a suggestion that *Valiant* herself should be cut in half, but this was dropped as likely to cause too much disruption. The eventual design concept was simple in principle: the missile compartments of a USS *George Washington*[38] were to be inserted between the bow and stern of a *Valiant* – but, in real life, nothing is simple. Accommodation was needed for a much larger crew to even higher standards making long patrols more tolerable. About half the increase in length over *Valiant* was due to the missile compartment and the remainder to associated requirements.

Within the missile compartment and weapon spaces the framing, decks, bulkhead, etc had to be identical to the US boats, which meant reducing the pressure hull diameter by 3in compared with 33ft 3in of *Valiant*.[39] External ballast tanks, fore and aft, were fitted as in *Valiant*, giving a surface reserve of buoyancy of 8 per cent. This was thought rather small and internal tanks, designed to take full diving pressure, were fitted to give a total reserve of 12 per cent.

The steam machinery, supplied by the initial reactor core, Type A, would deliver 14,250shp giving 21kts, submerged, clean. The later Type B core gave 19,250shp and 23kts as well as a longer life.[40] Surface speeds were 15.25kts and 16kts respectively. Battery drive would give 4.5kts, whilst a 700hp Ward Leonard turbo-electric mode would give a very quiet 6.75kts as the gearing noise was elimi-

nated. The main machinery was mounted on a raft, as in *Valiant*, with a quiet speed of 15.75kts (6 months out of dock). The electrical load was greater than in *Valiant* and the steam turbo generators were modified to give 2000kW each. There were two diesel generators each giving 290kW on the surface or 230kW snorting. These provided power to start the reactor from cold, for battery charging, to provide DC power and for emergency propulsion. There was a retractable emergency propeller known as the 'egg whisk' which could drive the submarine at 'more than 3kts'. A battery was installed to restart the reactor after a 'scram' (emergency shutdown).

The design diving depth was 750ft and the main bulkheads were designed to take the same pressure. There were two escape towers, one in the fore ends and the other in the motor room. It was noted that the end compartments could not contain the whole crew (with margins) and that the shape was such that the submarine would not necessarily remain upright if resting on the bottom. Any nuclear accident was to be contained within the reactor compartment, which was tested to 240psi, a very severe test.

The submarine had to be kept within a narrow band of depths during missile firing, which required very clever hovering gear. It was decided to develop a British system which worked very well and was thought much superior to the USN system.

Four Polaris boats were ordered in 1963 and completed by 1969.[41] In order not to disrupt the SSN programme entirely, Cammell Lairds was brought in as a second builder, with a constructor lent to the firm as project manager. Baker introduced the PERT management scheme with help from Electric Boat and the co-operation of Vickers, achieving the double of again completing the programme on time and on cost. Baker was awarded the KB on the personal recommendation of Earl Mountbatten (an unusual honour for a civil servant) in the New Year's Honours List of 1968 and retired soon after. Great attention was paid to managing the refits so that the target of keeping two SSBNs on station was maintained throughout the life of the force.[42]

Particulars

Dimensions:	425ft x 33ft x 30ft
Displacement:	7500/8500 tons
shp/speed:	15,000/25kts
Complement:	143
Armament:	16 Polaris A3 (warhead later replaced by the UK-designed 'Chevaline'), six 21in tubes

Swiftsure Class

The design of this class during the mid-1960s provided the first opportunity for an overall review of the features of a nuclear submarine in the light of experience. The principal performance attributes of a submarine are speed,

diving depth and quietness and it was hoped to improve all three in the new class. *Swiftsure* built on the experience with *Valiant* but was in no sense an 'Improved *Valiant*' – it was a totally new design. The design team was led by Norman Hancock,[43] lacking in submarine experience but very experienced in surface ships and supported by a knowledgeable staff. Because of the Polaris programme it was not possible to assemble a full design team until 1964, though studies were in hand a year earlier under Hancock, assisted by W G (Bill) Sanders.[44] Approval was given in 1961 for RRA to develop an improved Core B which would give more power and a longer life.

The pressure hull was made nearly cylindrical throughout its length, eliminating the contractions which reduced fatigue life in earlier boats. This led to a reduction in the capacity of ballast tanks and hence of reserve of buoyancy. A new British steel was introduced which was tougher and cleaner than QT35. Great attention was paid to the safety of systems which might be exposed to full diving pressure, and auxiliary machinery had a fresh water cooling system working at low pressure, itself cooled by the sea in a heat exchanger with very short lengths of piping exposed to full sea water pressure. Many of the components of the sea water systems were large castings of nickel-aluminium-bronze (NAB). It took a great deal of work to develop casting techniques which would guarantee the quality needed to ensure safety.

The external shape of the hull and appendages was improved. There was a very useful report from 1923 by the Royal Aircraft Establishment (RAE) on the shape of airships – also three-dimensional fluid travellers. There was an amusing twist in that two of the best forms tested by RAE had been suggested by AEW Haslar on the basis of the fast 'R' class submarines of the First World War. The aft end was made much more blunt, mainly to provide buoyancy aft but also because there was some small overall benefit in propulsive efficiency due to favourable interaction between propulsor and hull flows. If the ending was too blunt there would be a major loss of efficiency due to separation of turbulent flow. The hydrodynamics of the day was unable to provide a complete answer but it was known that separation would occur more easily on a model than on the full scale. Hence a form was selected which just began to separate on the model confident that there would be no problem on the submarines.

The bridge fin was reduced in size, even though this implied shorter periscopes. The forward hydroplanes were on the axis, just abaft the sonar where they were most effective in slow speed control. They were retractable to reduce noise and drag at medium speed though they were usually extended for safety at the highest speeds.

Some of the class had a pump jet in place of the single propeller.[45] A pump jet is similar to a water turbine consisting of a rotor and a stator, both with a large number of blades, surrounded by a carefully-shaped duct. It enabled the flow to be carefully controlled in velocity and pressure and could be either more efficient or quieter than

41 Five were originally planned but one was cancelled by the new government. This meant that very elaborate maintenance, refit and stores support organisations were needed.

42 D K Brown, *A Century of Naval Construction* (London 1983).

43 An empty space at the aft end of the machinery, needed for buoyancy, was often known as 'Hancock's hole'.

44 A future head of the RCNC.

45 P L Vosper & A J Brown, 'Pumpjet Propulsion– A Splendid British Achievement', lecture to RINA (Western Branch) 1996.

46 Horlick: 'what you don't fit can't give you trouble'.

47 A 'Battle' class destroyer boiler provided steam.

48 Technology advances very quickly and the use of a physical model was soon superseded by computer modelling.

49 Much of this section has been contributed by Brian Wall, Project Director, Trident submarines.

50 British sonar suite 2054.

a propeller or a bit of each. It was the culmination of a lengthy R&D programme at the Admiralty Research Laboratory, Teddington, by Alex Mitchell. Some years later this technology was passed to the USN. During the Cold War it was generally true that Soviet submarines were fast, deep-diving and noisy, while British boats were relatively slow and very quiet, with the USN in between.

Great attention was paid to machinery noise, with even more of the plant on a resiliently-mounted raft. At moderate speeds the cooling water circulated under the ram effect of scoops with the rather noisy circulating pumps switched off. There was a further re-examination of safety and many mostly minor improvements were made. Great efforts were made to simplify the machinery systems.[46] To improve on such a good design as *Valiant* was a real achievement.

The first of class, *Swiftsure*, was ordered in November 1967 and completed in March 1973, while the sixth and last completed in May 1981. Core B was installed at DSMP late in 1967 and went critical in August 1968. Core B was then run at high power for two years to confirm its reliability and check its life.

The Admiralty Development Establishment Barrow (ADEB) had been set up during the development of HTP propulsion and was now refurbished to assemble and test the *Swiftsure* secondary (non-nuclear) machinery.[47] There were a number of problems; the first raft was insufficiently rigid and there were gearbox failures. This meant that the prototype unit had run for a few weeks only, instead of the intended 6 months, when the production unit for *Swiftsure* itself was ready. A risky but successful decision to go ahead was taken and the production unit began trials in April 1970.

Particulars

Dimensions:	272ft x 332ft 4in x 27ft
Displacement:	4400/4900 tons
shp/speed:	15,000/30kts
Complement:	116
Armament:	Five-21in tubes

Pump jet configuration. An accelerating duct will favour efficiency and a decelerating one will be quieter. The choice between pre- and post-swirl will usually be decided by ease of maintenance; the rotor and shaft is more easily withdrawn in a pre-swirl duct. (*RINA*)

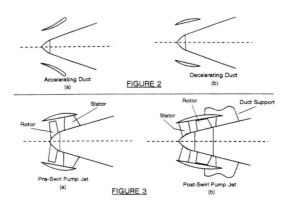

There was rapid inflation while this class were building and hence the quoted cost rose from £37.1 million (*Swiftsure*) to £97 million (*Splendid*). Running costs are £3.8 million per year at 1976 prices.

The main sonar was dropped to the chin position, which necessitated moving the torpedo tubes aft and angling them, leaving room only for five, more than compensated for by very rapid reloading arrangements. Both noise performance and reliability exceeded expectations. Noise performance derived from continuous attention to detail and a vigorous de-bugging campaign of noisy items found during *Swiftsure*'s trials, whilst reliability derived from simplification and further attention to detail.

Trafalgar Class

There were a large number of design studies for the next class known as SSNOX, SSNOY and SSNOZ. These were splendid designs but far too expensive, and it was agreed that the *Trafalgars* should be 'Improved *Swiftsures*'. SSN-13, *Trafalgar*, was launched in July 1981. Work had been started on Core Z in 1968 and completed in 1971. DSMP was due for a major overhaul and Core Z only began tests in 1974. Foulger was project manager from early design until near completion, when Arthur Cook took over.

They had the same machinery as the *Swiftsure* and much the same hull, lengthened slightly to get in extra equipment with a slight speed loss. The *Swiftsure* machinery had proved generally reliable in service and attention was concentrated on noise reduction. Reduction of machinery generated noise had reached a practical limit in most areas, as each further reduction of a decibel was costing more and more to achieve. Attention was therefore focused on attenuation and damping – the *Trafalgars* were the first to be designed for hull damping tiles. The only feature of the *Swiftsures* to give problems in service was the raft and this was redesigned.

ADEB was stretched to the limit and inconveniently situated, far from the building berths, so a new facility was created, the Submarine Machinery Installation Test Establishment (SMITE). It was finished in time for production tests for the last *Swiftsure* (SSN-12) and then used for later boats. Full-scale wooden mock-ups had been built for the machinery of earlier classes. These were time-consuming to build and even more to alter, and very expensive, so for *Trafalgar* it was decided to rely on a one-fifth scale model.[48] This could be scanned using a travelling telescope, passing information direct to the computer. This could then instruct bending machines making pipes and, as a result, *Trafalgar* had some 5000 shop-made pipes as opposed to under 500 for *Swiftsure*. The remainder were made the old fashioned and time consuming way by bending a wire to fit on the ship and taking it back to the shop as a template.

The 'improvements' relate mainly to noise reduction, seen as a continuing process in which quieter items were fitted in successive boats as they became available. They were the first boats to have noise reduction coatings

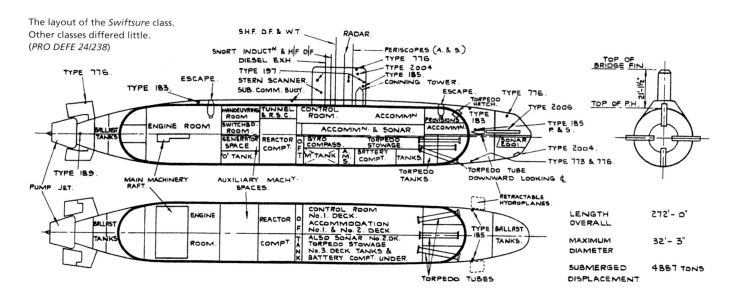

The layout of the *Swiftsure* class. Other classes differed little. (*PRO DEFE 24/238*)

(anechoic tiles) fitted on build, though most earlier boats have since been treated. It has been said that the *Trafalgar*s are even quieter than an *Oberon* on electric drive. They were equipped to fire Sub Harpoon SSM.

No mention has been made of sonar fits, electronic warfare sets or command systems, but it can be understood that all these were greatly improved from class to class.

Vanguard Class SSBN

In 1980 the government announced plans to purchase the US Trident missile system for installation in four new ballistic missile submarines. It was originally intended to buy the C4 missile but this had gone out of production and maintenance could not be guaranteed. In consequence, the D5 missile was purchased with eight independent re-entry vehicles (MIRV) on each missile. The missile compartment is the same diameter as that of the USN *Ohio*, though shorter, since the British boats carry 16 missiles instead of the US 24. The missiles are maintained in the USA at King's Bay, Georgia.

The bow and stern sections were developed from *Trafalgar*, though with many changes. The biggest change was the fitting of an entirely new reactor, PWR2, which had been on trial at Dounreay and represented a significant advance on the *Trafalgar* class.[49] *Vanguard* had an early core which will need one change during the boat's life; later cores will last the whole life of the ship. Forward, a new sonar suite[50] was developed to meet the essentially covert nature of the deterrent role. Advanced noise reduction measures were also embodied to ensure maximum stealth. A great deal of effort was also put in to easing the maintenance task and so maximising the operational availability of the deterrent force.

These are by far the largest submarines to serve in the RN and were built by Vickers at Barrow in an enormous

assembly shop over the old Devonshire Dock, allowing a complete submarine, together with large sections of the follow-on vessels, to be assembled under cover. Conventional launching was replaced by a 'roll-out' procedure in which the complete submarine was transported on a system of synchronised rollers onto a ship lift platform (synchro-lift) which was then lowered into the water. A similar lift is installed at the Faslane base. They were ordered from 1986 to 1992. *Vanguard* completed in 1992 and entered service in 1994 after trials. (A note on the *Astute* class and later can be found in Chapter 14.)

Below: A large replica section of a submarine was used to test the resistance of various equipments to shock from explosions. Those crossing the Forth bridges (in the background) were often surprised by the sight of these blasts. (*D K Brown collection*)

10 Minor War Vessels

[1] D K Brown, *A Century of Naval Construction* (London 1983).

[2] J Maber. 'The "Nearly Non-Magnetic" Ship', *Journal of Naval Engineering* 25/3 (June 1980).

[3] W G S Penman and D K Brown, 'The Chindwin Flotilla', *Warship* 19 (1981).

[4] B Greenhill and A Giffard. *The British Assault on Finland* (London 1988).

[5] D K Brown, 'The Russo-Japanese War. Technical Lessons as Perceived by the Royal Navy', *Warship* 1996.

[6] C A Utz, *Assault from the Sea – the Amphibious Landing at Inchon* (Naval Historical Center, Washington 1994).

[7] Most of the calculations were carried out by a Chief Draughtsman, Steane; my memory is that he filled nine workbooks. Drawing in E Grove, *Vanguard to Trident*. Planned numbers varied. Up to 21 at time of cancellation; replaced by 20 CMS, later also cancelled (ADM 205/97, PRO).

[8] They originally were to have had insect names preceded by a colour adjective – red, blue green, golden – denoting variations in the equipment fitted. Imagine serving in *Green Centipede*! Mountbatten stopped this nonsense in 1952.

Bildeston, a 'Ton' class minesweeper as originally completed with a short funnel.
(P A Vicary)

THE INCREASING TENSIONS of the Cold War and, in particular, the outbreak of fighting in Korea in June 1950 raised the possibility of a Soviet advance into Western Europe with British coastal waters as a battleground. Mines could be laid by aircraft, submarines, fast craft or, clandestinely, before the outbreak of war. Submarines might penetrate estuaries, possibly laying nuclear weapons, while the Soviets were developing a numerous force of fast attack vessels. To counter these threats a large number of minesweepers, seaward defence vessels and fast patrol boats were designed and built. In later years attention was concentrated on the mining threat and a smaller number of very capable vessels were built and some novel ideas were explored.

W J (Bill) Holt

The early programme was directed by W J Holt, who had been in charge of small craft design since the late 1930s.[1] He was a keen sailor and had even served briefly in a windjammer to gain experience with square rig whilst designing the non-magnetic vessel *Research*, which was a brigantine carrying square rig on the foremast.[2] During the war he led the design of the HDML, the 'Fairmile B' and 'D' classes, steam gunboats and the Camper & Nicholson MTBs, as well as MMS, etc; he also improved the structural design of the British Power Boat craft. He also built two small gunboats on the Chindwin River in Burma[3] and devoted a wartime Christmas leave to a voyage in a 'Fairmile B' to Iceland. He was well qualified to lead the design of the next generation. One of his key assistants in postwar boats was J T (Jack) Revans, who has made an important contribution to this section.

Mine Counter Measures Craft (MCM)

The Tsarist navy laid the first free mines in the Baltic in the 1850s during the Crimean War[4] and followed this with further mining success in their war with Japan in 1904-5.[5] Soviet mining in the Second World War does not seem to have been extensive, though they did develop a magnetic mine based on the British 'M sinker' laid in the Dvina River in 1919. After the war there was evidence of massive preparation for mine warfare, partly confirmed during the Korean War.[6]

About 1950 British estimates were that the Soviet Union could lay 4500-6000 mines per month in British waters, and a rule of thumb held that 25-30 mines would have to be laid in order to sink one merchant ship. Losses of 50 merchant ships could be tolerated, which meant keeping the number of effective mines down to 1500-2000. On closer examination, however, the problem got worse: mines might be activated by contact, magnetic, acoustic or pressure signatures and increasingly two or three signatures had to be generated simultaneously and roughly in the right relative position. Ship-based countermeasures meant that each channel had to be swept twelve times for each mine type to ensure it was safe. Clearly a vast number of MCM vessels would be required, and most of them would have to be purpose-built with low signatures. Converted fishing vessels would only have a small part to play in a future war.

A very large number of vessels of different types was planned. The 1951 'War Programme' envisaged 50 improved *Algerines* if the new design was not ready. By May 1954 it was planned to build 5 ocean sweepers, 167 coastal and 167 inshore sweepers, and it was always envisaged that the great majority would be laid up on completion as a war reserve. The ocean minesweeper was a pretty vessel, an updated *Algerine*, and the design was worked up in considerable detail and approved in January 1953.[7] It would have displaced 1522 tons and steamed at 17.5kts free, 11.5kts towing sweeps. However, it was soon realised that a large, steel-hulled vessel had only a small role in modern mine warfare and it was cancelled in January 1955 following the Radical Review.

The Coastal Minesweeper (CMS) 'Ton' class
The coastal sweepers of the 'Ton'[8] class were much smaller, reducing pressure signature, and had non-magnetic hulls with wood planking over aluminium frames. They had a free running speed of 15kts and were intended to tow sweeps with a 9-ton pull at 12kts. At this speed the power required to tow the sweeps and pulse the magnetic sweep

Hickleton, another CMS; this 'Ton' was later sold to Argentina as *Neuquen*. This aerial view shows the bulk and complexity of the gear required to operate wire, acoustic and magnetic sweeps.
(D K Brown collection)

was five times that needed to drive the ship. This required non-magnetic Deltic diesel engines (see later), which were not ready, and early ships completed with the less powerful Mirlees engines, later replaced with Deltics. Another early problem was that the aluminium frames and deck beams formed a conducting loop and when the ship rolled in the earth's magnetic field a current was generated which produced its own magnetic signature. A complete cure was found: a sensor was installed at the top of the mast which measured the current generated and cancelled its effect using a special de-gaussing coil.[9] The design of an all-wood CMS was in hand but dropped when the eddy current problem was solved. A minehunting variant of the CMS (*Thorpe* class) was designed and three were ordered, but they were cancelled before work began.

The 'Ton' class were very successful; 118 were built for the RN, many of which were later transferred to other navies, and still more were built in France, Canada and Holland.[10] In general they lasted well, though there were problems with corrosion of the aluminium frames. Those remaining in service were given a plastic sheath to protect the planking. Eighteen were later converted to mine-hunters, with an 'active' rudder for good manoeuvrability at low speed when using the Type 193 sonar. Some were used for trials – *Highburton* was used for experiments to reduce resistance by the use of long-chain molecules such as polyethylene oxide. It worked, reducing frictional resistance by some 30 per cent, but 'polyox' is expensive and no economic application has been found. She was also used for trials with several experimental propellers, the best of which was fitted in other hunters. *Shoulton* carried the first experimental pump jet units (see SSN, Chapter 9).

One of the main fears was that the fine clearances between rotor and the duct would cause it to jam if debris entered the unit. However, very soon after *Shoulton*'s units went to sea a railway sleeper was seen to enter the pumpjet – it came out as matchsticks without causing damage!

Inshore Minesweepers (IMS)

The 'Ham' class inshore sweepers were even smaller (159 tons deep). The first 37 (numbered 2601-2637) had similar structure to the 'Tons' with aluminium frames. Since they were intended to work in very shallow water, the eddy current problem was more severe and the later 54 craft (2701-2739 and 2777-2793) were of all-wood construction with a slightly greater beam.[11] The 'Hams' were too small to take new equipments and only a few remained in service for any length of time, and these on auxiliary duties only. Mines can easily be altered to play new tricks and

[9] The trials involved forced rolling of a vessel in dock, the roll being induced by men running from side to side; a procedure devised by William Froude in the 1870s.

[10] The author inclined several, see Appendix 4.

[11] The original IMS and the IMS Type 2 came out much overweight and with poor stability, requiring ballast.

Cranham, an all-wood inshore minesweeper. They were good ships but too small to adapt to later sweeping gear.
(D K Brown collection)

Averley, an IMS Type II. Despite the 'minesweeper' designation, they carried no sweeps. They were designed to hunt for mines but the sonar intended for them failed to materialise and they could only use divers to search.
(*D K Brown collection*)

[12] The papers were dug out during debate on the configuration of the *Sandowns*.

[13] I doubt if these made much difference.

[14] The fin drew air down which entered the cooling water inlets, stopping the engines.

[15] ADM 167/135 (PRO).

[16] AEL developed the ASR 1 diesel for bigger ships at much the same time. It is remarkable that for all the problems of commercial diesels, a government laboratory produced two fine engines. The cylinder design but not the Deltic configuration (due to an E-in-C draughtsman, H Penwarden) is said to have derived from the Junkers aircraft diesel. See Le Bailly, *From Fisher to the Falklands* (London 1991), p80.

[17] K Hill, 'The "Deltic Revolution" 40 years on', *Backtrack* (Feb 2001).

hence MCMV must also be adaptable. A similar aluminium-framed hull was used for the twelve 'Ley' class, officially referred to as IMS Type II even though they had no sweeping gear. They were intended as minehunters but there was no suitable gear and they had to deploy divers to search for mines by hand.

All these minesweepers were very seaworthy but, like all small craft, had violent motions in rough seas. Though smaller, many thought the 'Hams' were the better seaboats, probably because the high forecastle of the 'Tons' caught the wind, making them yaw.[12] The 'Ton' class minehunters were given Vosper fin stabilisers.[13] One was used by the National Physical Laboratory for trials with a big fixed foil under the stem to reduce pitching. It did show some benefit but slammed violently if the foil came out of the water.[14]

In the light of the threat as then perceived this programme was necessary and well conducted. Most went straight into reserve as was always envisaged. Fishing craft were of little value against modern mines but their crews, still numerous, could man the 'Tons' and 'Hams'. The designs were sound and many small shipyards were able

to participate. There was still no answer to the pressure mine; much effort went into big plastic bags (later developed as 'Dracones' to carry oil – 'the world's largest condoms' as they were known) or sleeves but no success was claimed, turning minds increasingly to hunting as opposed to sweeping.

The Deltic Engine

In 1943 a committee was set up under Sir Roy Fedden to advise on the development of a high power, lightweight diesel for MTBs.[15] It was decided to develop the Deltic engine invented at the Admiralty Engineering Laboratory (AEL), West Drayton.[16] There were three double-acting cylinders in each bank, arranged in a ∇ (delta) shape. Engines were made with nine or eighteen cylinders.

A contract was first placed with the English Electric Co in August 1946 to develop and produce this remarkable engine. Development cost £1.5 million (estimate £2 million) at Napiers, starting in early 1947 (under Mr Sammons), and took about 3 years. Production engines weighed about one-fifth that of their nearest rival in the same power range. The standard engine was used in fast patrol boats and in de-rated form in the 'Ton' class (also railway locomotives[17]) where its low magnetic signature was useful. An even lower magnetic version was later used in the 'Hunt' class MCMV. A compound Deltic was designed with a gas turbine based on the Nene to be inserted in the centre of the delta using exhaust gases. This would have given about 6000bhp but was stopped when light coastal forces were abandoned.

Seaward Defence Boats, 'Ford' Class

At the time of the Korean war there was a fear that Soviet submarines might penetrate British estuaries and harbours to attack shipping or even to lay nuclear mines. As a counter to this threat a class of 20 seaward defence boats was designed by W J Holt and ordered mostly in 1951 (the

Shalford, the first seaward defence boat to complete. She carried a triple-barrelled Squid AS mortar aft and was very much overweight. (*MoD*)

last two in 1955).[18] The hull form was based on the wartime steam gunboats and, though very seaworthy, they did not have bilge keels and rolled heavily.[19]

They had three shafts with the main Paxman engines on the wings and a small Foden on the centre shaft. They were intended to have a single-barrelled Squid as ASW armament but this did not become available. *Shalford* was given a normal triple-barrelled Squid and the rest had two depth charge throwers and two racks. They also mounted a single 40mm Mark VII. Most remained in service until 1966-7.

Like many of the earlier classes described in the chapter they were a response to the Korean War. DNC department was greatly overloaded and the old rule that key design calculations should be carried out by two Assistant Constructors working independently could not be followed – indeed, neither of the calculators on the 'Ford' class was an Assistant Constructor. Overload was greater still in higher ranks, supervising several designs and there were numerous errors.[20] Even Holt was over stretched. *Shalford* had a design deep displacement of 108 tons and there had been 9 tons of approved additions. When inclined by the author, the displacement was 148 tons![21] On re-checking the original calculations there were a large number of items which had been omitted altogether – funnels, machinery seats etc.[22]

Fast Patrol Boats

At the end of the war there was a perceived role for fast patrol boats, particularly in the North Sea approaches to the Baltic, which the disarmament of Germany left vulnerable to penetration by Soviet forces. Light coastal craft built in the United Kingdom during the war had a number of serious deficiencies and urgent steps were put in hand to overcome them.

The most serious problem was in engines and two approaches were tried – gas turbines and diesels, both of which would ultimately prove successful. The first attempt involved putting a Metropolitan-Vickers Gatric engine in the engine room of the Camper & Nicholson *MGB 2009* driving the centre shaft. This proved the feasibility of gas turbine propulsion but showed two major problems: the need to remove salt water from the incoming air, and the external noise – *2009*'s bridge was between the intakes and the funnel.[23]

The Rolls Royce RM60 was a much more advanced design, using a complicated cycle to obtain good fuel economy at low speeds. Two of these engines were installed in the former steam gunboat *Grey Goose* and ran successfully and reliably. However, the design was too big and heavy for patrol boats and this approach died – probably to return in the Type 45 frigate.[24]

Armament, too, had been a problem for wartime boats. The 4.5in 8cwt went to sea just after the war ended and was to be the main weapon of post-war gunboats.[25] It fired a 15lb shell at about 10 rounds a minute at the low velocity of 1500ft/sec. The first post-war attempt at an effec-

MGB 2009, the first gas turbine test bed. (*D K Brown collection*)

Grey Goose as a test bed with two RM60 gas turbines. The design was ahead of the technology of the day. (*MoD*)

tive patrol boat gun, Coastal Forces System 1 (CFS 1), was abandoned as it grew – and grew.[26] CFS 2 (a 3.3in gun) was developed from the early Centurion tank gun firing a 20lb shell,[27] the mounting being fully stabilised. It went to sea in *Bold Pioneer* in March 1957 and, though on the heavy side,[28] was successful, scoring a high proportion of hits; but the RN had abandoned coastal forces in September 1957 and the project was dropped.[29]

Hull construction was tested in two early prototypes in 1946: *MTB 538*[30] was designed by Vosper using all glued plywood whilst Saunders-Roe (Saunders Engineering and Shipyard Ltd, Beaumaris) designed *MTB 539* in aluminium alloy,[31] both under H R Mason. Both provided useful lessons on what not to do and the majority of later craft had wood planking over aluminium frames.

Two long-hull prototypes (121-122ft) were designed by H R Mason to compare the merits of hard chine and round bilge hull form. Even before they went to sea, the hard chine was seen as the preferred form due to its much greater internal space. As far as is known, they never went to sea together, as the machinery was unreliable. They had two G2 gas turbines, derived from the Gatric, and two Mercedes diesels (from E-boats) – later replaced with Deltics – giving a speed of about 42kts (design speed 48kts). *Bold Pioneer* (hard chine) went to sea in January 1953 and *Bold Pathfinder* in July 1953. E-boats had gained

[18] It would seem that 24 were ordered and 20 completed (see *Conway's All the World's Fighting Ships 1947-1995*, p536). One uncompleted hull was used, upside down, as an office in Chatham Dockyard.

[19] On first going to sea in rough weather the CO of *Shalford* complained that his ship was unsafe. A very experienced assistant was sent who had commanded a Fairmile 'B' in the war. He found that no one in *Shalford* had been to sea in anything smaller than a *Daring* and that *Shalford* was quite normal but needed many more hand holds.

[20] Controller reported the problem with many examples in ADM 167/143 (PRO). Errors were made in relation to the 'Ham' class inshore minesweepers, and all frigates before the Type 81, including a serious error with the *Whitby*, only corrected at the last moment.

[21] Figures from memory – they were seared into my brain and I think they are about right.

[22] For this reason, I tend to prefer scaling from a reliable type ship to direct calculation as there is much less chance of omissions. Certainly I would be worried if the two approaches gave a markedly different answer.

[23] C E Preston, *Power for the Fleet* (Eton 1982), p11: 'a mixture of a scream, a roar and a whine with the scream predominating'.

[24] *Grey Goose* was still afloat in 2001.

[25] *MTBs 528* and *5008* appeared at York in September 1946 with this enormous gun. It was based on an army howitzer, designed by Major Jeffris. Its HE shell was devastating against light structure but with a high trajectory and unstabilised mount hitting was difficult.

[26] It was proposed to fit it in the liner *Queen Mary*.

[27] The complete round weighed 30lbs, the heaviest which could be handled under the high accelerations of an FPB.

[28] The weight included a 5cwt balance weight.

[29] A variant was considered for the 'Castle' class OPV.

[30] Originally the last of the 1944 class but in late 1944 was set aside for experimental work.

[31] Probably an Admiralty hull form.

Right: Bold Pathfinder (seen here in November 1952) and *Bold Pioneer* were built to compare different hull forms. However, the round bilge *Pathfinder* and the hard chine *Pioneer* were never able to run in company, mainly due to unreliability, but the more spacious hull of the hard chine form was preferred. (*MoD*)

Below: Bold Pioneer in 1957 with the prototype CFS2 gun mounting forward. It was very successful on trials but by then the RN no longer required fast gunboats. (*World Ship Society*)

Above right: The 'Dark' class were versatile and could be quickly adapted to various roles: as a gunboat with 4.5in and 40mm guns; as a torpedo boat with one 20mm and four tubes; as a minelayer with one 40mm and six mines; or, as demonstrated here by *Dark Gladiator*, as a raiding craft with a 40mm gun and dinghy.
(*D K Brown collection*)

Right: Gay Centurion. The 'Gay' class fast patrol boats originally ran with severe stern trim, but this was cured by fitting a transom flap, which also increased their speed. The supports for the flap can be seen on the transom in this photo. (*D K Brown collection*)

extra speed by angling their rudders and the 'Bolds' were given the facility to do this, but it was never tried. They were a dead end since the remaining fast patrol boats were differently derived.

Twelve boats of the 'Gay' class were ordered in 1950 following the outbreak of the Korean War, as developments of Vosper's wartime boats, entering service in 1953. As gunboats they carried one 4.5in and a 40mm; as torpedo boats, one 40mm and two 21in tubes. The design was by J T Revans who, on AEW advice, arranged the centre of gravity a little further aft to reduce resistance and increase speed.[32] On first completing they had a top speed of about 40kts, at which they had very marked stern trim. This meant the running waterplane intersecting the bottom in the middle of the longest compartment, leading to structural damage.[33] Jack Revans suggested a flap on the transom to alter running trim, bringing the impact onto a bulkhead. Model resistance tests suggested a loss of speed of about 1.5kts but it was decided to try a flap on one boat.[34] On trial, speed actually increased to 44kts due to much improved propeller efficiency.[35] Turning at full speed, full flap and full rudder was alarming, as the heel would put the deck edge under.

The 'Dark' class were ordered in 1950-3 to a design initiated by Revans.[36] They had the same armament as the 'Gays' in gunboat configuration but as torpedo boats had one 40mm and four tubes. They had two 18-cylinder, opposed piston Deltic diesel engines giving 5000bhp, but which had not run when the 'Darks' were designed. The power available depended very much on rpm (Deltic 960rpm in 'Darks') and on first trials the engines locked up at 22kts and would not go further. Eventually, with a different propeller design, they made 45kts.[37] However, at that speed the life of the propeller was about 20 minutes increased to 20 hours after many designs had been tried. Most 'Darks' were paid off in 1957 when the RN gave up coastal forces.[38]

Studies for the ultimate fast patrol boat began under Revans in early 1954, completing about 1960 after coastal forces had disbanded.[39] The requirement was to 'cruise' to the Dutch coast, fight an action and return, all under cover of darkness. This meant a sustained speed of 50kts and many wild schemes were considered including surface-piercing propellers.[40] A Deltic with a gas turbine using the exhaust arranged in the centre of the delta was under development. However, three Proteus gas turbines proved a relatively conventional solution and was the lightest arrangement for a relatively short range, high speed mission. The two 'Brave' class boats built to this design were to have carried the CFS 2 mount and a single 40mm as gunboats. The armament could be rapidly altered to a number of roles:- torpedo boat, one 40mm and 4 torpedoes in dropping gear; minelayer, raiding craft, etc. Revans paid particular attention to the air intakes which, at full power, had to pass 200 tons of air per hour whilst preventing the ingress of salt particles. Earlier boats tended to come out overweight and for the 'Braves' a

Lindisfarne, an 'Island' class offshore patrol vessel, which gave good service for many years.
(*D K Brown collection*)

scheme was devised in which Vospers carried out the calculations which were then checked in Ship Department and matched to the design calculations. This scheme worked well and the boats completed to the design weight. Weight-saving extended to lightweight cases for standard instruments.

The design was developed by Vosper and made their designed 50kts on first trial. This reflects great credit on the company who had their own hydrodynamics department then under Hermann Rader.[41] Three reduced derivatives of the *Scimitar* class were ordered in January 1969 as fast training boats for surface warships to practise anti-FPB action. They performed well once the right settings for their transom flap had been found.[42] A 144ft Vosper private venture was chartered as *Tenacity* in 1971 and purchased in February 1973 as a fishery protection vessel.

The 'Castle' Class OPV – A Personal Account

Since the 'Castle' class were the only ships built to my design, I may perhaps be excused for giving this class more space than their humble role deserves – and writing in the first person.

In 1975 it was clear that the new international rules on Exclusive Economic Zones would need a considerable increase in the size of the RN Fishery Protection Squadron, The first step was to charter the *Jura*, belonging to the independent Scottish Department of Fisheries. She was found reasonably satisfactory and five (later seven) generally similar vessels of the 'Island' class were ordered. The following year, following another reorganisation, I found myself heading the main surface-ship design section. Our main task was to be the detail design of the Type 43 destroyer but she was still in concept and it would be at least a year before we could start. It was decided that we should design the second-generation OPV while we were waiting. This was seen very much as a training exercise; it had been 18 years since I had worked on ship design and the rest of the section had even less experience.

[32] The whole section on FPBs owes much to the memories of J T Revans passed in a private letter to the author in July 2001. Geoff Hudson has also helped considerably.

[33] The author's very first job was to try, unsuccessfully, to design suitable stiffening.

[34] This trial flap was made by the shipwrights at *Hornet*, the Coastal Forces base. Dr Gawn (AEW) was concerned about the dangers of porpoising, but this did not occur.

[35] It took about 20 years for me to convince people that a flap would help at least some frigates. Eventually, trials on *Avenger* gave an improvement of about 1.5kts (Chapter 7).

[36] Nineteen were ordered, including *Dark Scout*, but *Dark Horseman* was cancelled in November 1957 after launch. *Dark Scout* was of all aluminium construction.

[37] One of the best propellers tried was a slightly modified E-boat propeller.

[38] Mainly because a re-arming German Navy was taking over the Baltic approaches.

[39] J T Revans & Cdr A A C Gentry, 'The "Brave" Class Fast Patrol Boats', *Trans RINA* (1960), p367.

[40] There were even thoughts of a stern paddle wheel.

[41] At 50kts the whole back of the propeller is covered in a cavitation bubble, making it a slightly easier design problem than 40-45kts with only partial cavitation. Even so, it was a great achievement by Vospers and Rader.

[42] Revans had to be 'borrowed' from his new job to get the settings right.

[43] I did a boarding in about that sea state.

[44] We also looked at hovercraft, airships and hydrofoils, the latter leading to the purchase of *Speedy*.

[45] A very effective commander in Director of Operational Requirements Sea helped greatly.

[46] See Chapter 12.

[47] A Chinook landed on during the Falklands War.

Offshore protection differed in many respects from 'hot' war: 100 per cent 'kill' was not necessary, and we had only to catch enough to frighten other lawbreakers. The 16kt speed of the 'Islands' was criticised but there were very few trawlers in European waters which could exceed 12kts. Even so, a little more speed would be welcome. Fishing was virtually impossible above Sea State 5 (4m wave height) and there was little point in boarding a suspect in worse seas.[43]

There were some preliminary studies for a slightly better 'Island'. I maintained that it was uneconomic to devote effort and incur first-of-class costs for a 'slight' improvement. Unless a case could be made for a considerable improvement we should buy more 'Islands'.[44] The argument centred on the need for a helicopter deck – the case for an embarked helicopter was soon dismissed as the Lynx cost more than the intended cost of the ship and its hangar would preclude the fitting of a landing deck large enough for bigger helicopters. There did seem a case for a big deck so that the larger Sea King and Merlin could land and refuel in rescue operations and this case was soon accepted in Whitehall, including the Treasury.[45]

Jura and the 'Islands' were already being criticised for excessive motions and I had a literature survey carried out on the effect of motions on human behaviour.[46] The 'Islands' were much the same size and similar in form to the wartime 'Flower' class corvettes. I compared the many subjective accounts of life in the 'Flowers' (205ft), with the wartime 'Castles' (252ft) and the 'Rivers' (301ft) and tentatively decided on 80m (262ft) as acceptable with a form based on First World War Admiralty 'S' class destroyers. In parallel with this, Dr Adrian Lloyd was using a new computer simulation to compare these Great War ships and others with my new form at various lengths. As a result

of his work I decided that I could reduce the length to 75m.

This length was greater than needed from space considerations but had important advantages. The flight deck was big enough for a Merlin helicopter[47] and pitch and heave motions were much reduced. Because there was space to spare, I was able to arrange living and working spaces close to amidships where the motion was least; in particular the bridge was almost amidships.

This approach was developed in discussion with the Captain Fishery Protection, the Scottish marine superintendent and a progressive trawler owner – including a trip to sea in *Cygnet* – and it was rough. The new ship was to have the same engines as the 'Islands' but they were arranged in separate engine rooms as a precaution against flooding. The extra length brought the speed up to 19kts. A MACK with a large crow's nest gave her a distinctive appearance carried over into the Type 24 frigate studies. We hoped to sell 'Castles' in the export market and produced sketches and a model showing various heavy armament fits (see Chapter 7). There were no supporting calculations but I think they were feasible though quite costly. ASWE did an interesting study on the gun for the RN vessels. The main requirement was a first-round kill at 6000 yards against a terrorist launch. The Centurion tank 105mm came out best and also, at £100,000, the cheapest. However, the Staff decided it could be improved and added 90° elevation and power loading which brought the price up to £6 million – so they got the 40mm/60 cal. Bofors.

My sketch design was widely circulated through industry, who were invited to do better or quote for my design. We had an elaborate marking frame against which submissions were judged as a result of which we chose my

Leeds Castle, a bigger offshore patrol vessel that could accept a Sea King helicopter (indeed, a Chinook has been landed on a 'Castle'). Note the knuckle and high freeboard, with the bridge well aft. (*MoD*)

design to be built by Hall Russell. To our great surprise, no one challenged this choice.

In early 1982 I was able to observe helicopter landing trials in *Leeds Castle*. These were held off the Eddystone with waves just over 4m but quite short. The test pilot was very interesting: the limiting factor was roll angle instead of vertical velocity as in a frigate. He cleared the ship for operation up to Sea State 5. I spent much of the afternoon in the crow's nest with Adrian Lloyd whose advice had influenced the hull form considerably. The bow shape with considerable flare and a knuckle was mine and I drew his attention to the way in which the spray sheets were thrown clear and, even in these quite severe seas, the fore deck was dry. He countered my argument by saying that it was only my heavy flare which generated the spray and if I had taken his advice there would be no spray – I still think I was right.

The design displacement was 1350 tons but we had calculated an extra deep of 1500 tons with some voids filled with oil. When the Falkland War broke out, they filled everything and they sailed at 2050 tons, serving as dispatch vessels.[48] I had given them enormous bilge keels (see photo on page 178) and during the trials we had difficulty in getting them to roll enough to test the stabiliser fins. During the war both ships lost their fins due to fatigue failure of the shafts and no one noticed the difference. Reports from sea after the war were very enthusiastic.[49] I suspect from measured motions that the COs on the bridge, near amidships, exaggerated their good behaviour.

The Hydrofoil *Speedy*

The RN had displayed interest in hydrofoils since the early 1920s but all projects had been unsuccessful.[50] By 1978 Boeing had published papers on the use of hydrofoils in the fishery-protection role and the US Coastguard were operating the Grumman *Flagstaff*. OPV studies showed that there was merit in hydrofoils in the role if they did not cost too much – implying an adaptation of an existing craft. The UK were also involved in a NATO group studying ASW hydrofoils using towed array (700-1300 tons). Put together, there was a good case for purchasing such a craft as a demonstrator. The Boeing 'Jetfoil' was the only craft available within the timescale which, for financial reasons, was very tight.[51] The next year *Speedy*, with the author on board, was able to run speed trials in Puget Sound at 43kts.[52] Boeings delivered her as a bare hull and machinery and she was fitted out by Vosper Thornycroft as sub-contractor to Boeing. On completion, she commenced a lengthy trials programme, which was curtailed by the Nott Defence Review. The author's summing-up was: 'She achieved all we promised and most of what we hoped for.'

The Second Generation MCMV

Round about 1960 a committee was set up to consider the next generation of MCM craft. The team was led by the Admiralty Research Laboratory, Teddington, and was to be a very wide-ranging study. When the team came to AEW, Haslar, they were clearly expecting a very conventional approach, but had a surprise.[53] Our choice was a catamaran, chosen to provide a wide working deck with plenty of space for additional equipment. First choice for propulsion was two very large air propellers (helicopter rotors on end) above the sweep deck to shield the airborne noise. Big outboard motors would be fitted for cruising in safe waters. Our second choice was still a catamaran but with a steam reciprocating engine driving a paddle wheel between the hulls. This was based on noise trials with a Dockyard steam paddle tug dating from about 1890 which proved very quiet at important frequencies. Other establishments came up with equally far out – but promising – ideas.

There was a debate central to the whole programme as to whether the 'vessels' should be combined hunter/sweeper or whether two types were needed. Eventually the decision came down in favour of the combined vessel, mostly on manpower grounds, though direct cost also favoured the combined vessel. The runner-up was a bottom-crawling, submarine 'tank'.

The Development of the 'Hunt' Class
Even the decision that the next MCMV would be a conventional combined hunter/sweeper left many choices free. One in particular caused a great deal of debate – should the hull be laminated wood or glass reinforced plastic (GRP)?[54] Full-scale test sections of both forms of construction were made and tested by underwater explosions. Initially neither did well – one GRP section was said to look like Shredded Wheat after the bang. With experience, both types were made to perform well, though by that time there was so much plastic glue in the 'wood' version that it was described as Wood Reinforced Plastic!

[48] Displacements from memory.

[49] D K Brown, 'Service experience with the "Castle" class', *The Naval Architect* (Sept 1983), p255. Also subsequent correspondence.

[50] D K Brown, 'Historic Hydrofoils of the RN', *High Speed Surface Craft* (April 1961).

[51] Grumman could not meet our very tight timescale and at that time Rodriguez did not have a craft big enough.

[52] She was accepted with the speed reading 50 mph in a specially lightened condition.

[53] At that date AEW had a quite unjustified reputation for being old-fashioned – just as we led the world in topics such as noise-reduced propellers, submarine control etc.

[54] Note that 'Fibreglass' is one company's trade name and best avoided.

Speedy, a Boeing Jetfoil, seen after completion in the UK. The author carried out preliminary trials in Puget Sound during which 50mph was reached.
(*D K Brown collection*)

55 D Henton, 'Glass Reinforced Plastics in the Royal Navy', *Trans RINA* (1967).

56 We cut out many sections for examination. The bulkheads and deck were such good insulators that they were barely warm on the side remote from the fire.

57 I think it was sold and became a houseboat.

58 R H Dixon, B W Ramsay & P J Usher. 'Design and Build of the GRP Hull of HMS *Wilton*', RINA Symposium on *GRP Ship Construction*, London 1972. The other papers in this volume are relevant.

There were still many options[55] – what sort of glass fibre and which resin? Sandwich construction, framed or monocoque? At that time GRP was seen as a bad fire risk but by the right choice of material this was completely changed. *Ledbury* had an oil fire which burnt at about 800°C for 3 hours with comparatively slight damage to the structure.[56] The other material problem was water absorption which was also overcome after numerous and prolonged tests.

The first GRP structure tried consisted of a sandwich with two GRP skins enclosing a core of small GRP 'boxes', and it failed under severe shock. Better sandwiches have been tried but the problem is that after an explosion or fire there is no way of checking if the joint from skin to core is still sound. The decision was made to use a single skin with frames and this has been adopted in all three generations of RN MCMVs. Initially, there was a tendency for the frames to tear away from the skin under explosive loading and the 'Hunt' class frames are bolted to the skin. More recent resins have obviated the need for this complication in the *Sandown*s. The alternative of a thick monocoque has been used successfully but it seems to have no advantage over the well proven British design. In the mid-1980s a GRP hull was designed in MoD and built by the Halmatic company using a single skin stiffened by longitudinal corrugations instead of frames. It proved cheap to build and did well in both static strength test and in explosions, but the idea was too late for the *Sandown* class.[57]

Wilton[58]

It was then decided to build a prototype vessel to prove this new material under service conditions. The prototype was to be an exact replica of a 'Ton' class. The *Derriton* was scrapped and all her machinery, equipment, etc was to be transferred to the new vessel, *Wilton*. She was to complete as the world's largest 'plastic' ship. The main hull had a surface area of 10,000ft², with another 15,000ft² of decks and bulkheads and a GRP superstructure, a total of 130 tons of GRP using 900,000ft² of glass cloth. (*Wilton*'s life expectancy has been quoted as 60 years and she is halfway there. She should be preserved as the world's first plastic ship.)

Though GRP is strong in tension it lacks stiffness and such structures can be prone to buckle. Experience from earlier tests had shown how this could be allowed for in the design. This led to a very lightly stressed structure – maximum stress about 1 ton/in². Vosper Thornycroft paid great attention to the training of the workforce and to their safety. The solvent Styrene is both a fire and health hazard and levels had to be carefully controlled and monitored. (A few people could not tolerate it at all.) Glass fibres can cause dermatitis, but with the care taken actual problems have been very rare.

There were no serious difficulties in building *Wilton* and her long service life has been relatively trouble-free. There were early problems with corrosion of underwater fittings and with painting but these were soon overcome with more suitable materials. She was, however, accident

Wilton, the first GRP warship. After a long career, she is now a floating club house. (*MoD*)

The 'Hunt' class *Atherstone*. Strict controls on magnetic signature meant that there was little weight growth during the building and consequently the ships are virtually indistinguishable one from the other. (*Vosper*)

prone, with two collisions and a small fire in early years. One collision removed her bow but her mould had not been destroyed and a new section was moulded and glued in place, demonstrating that GRP is easy to repair. GRP is damaged by most paint removers so a barrier coat of epoxy polyamide was applied over the GRP before normal paints were applied.

GRP construction is not cheap – at the time *Wilton* was built (completed 1973) it cost about £5500 per ton compared with £1500 for a steel hull, equating to about £0.5 million in a ship. However, this was the prototype and the cost was halved during the 'Hunt' programme.

The Learning Curve

It is well known that the unit cost of the later units of a run of similar artefacts will reduce considerably as a result of learning by both management and workforce, including the introduction of short cuts, and also due to the wider distribution of fixed costs such as tooling. This has been quantified as 'Caquot's Law' – the direct production cost of a mass-produced article varies in inverse proportion to the fourth root of the number of units in the production run.

This rule applied very well to mass-produced Second World War merchant ships of the 'Liberty', 'Victory' and the 'T2' tanker classes. It is also followed closely by the Vosper-built ships of the 'Hunt' class in which the man hours required for the eleventh vessel were little more than half that required for the first ship. Nuclear submarines

built at Barrow and *Leander*s built at Yarrows show significant reductions in cost, though at a slower rate.[59]

Note that savings from the learning curve occur only if there is a run of ships from the same builder and hence one cannot normally have these savings as well as those from competition; it is one or the other unless the total order is large enough to split into two equal and numerous parts. Benefits from learning are not automatic but require a determined effort from management and workforce to 'learn'.

The 'Hunt' class

The 'Hunts' were to be combined sweepers and hunters. As a sweeper, they towed an updated Oropesa sweep for moored mines, and influence sweeps for magnetic and acoustic mines. This implied some dozen bits of 'iron-mongery' – floats, diverters, generators, monitors, etc – all with wires and cables needing big winches and reels on board. At sweeping speed the propellers had to generate several tons of towing force to pull all this gear. The large, slow-running propellers were as quiet as possible but the flow in the towing condition was very different – and more difficult – from that in the free-running or hunting mode.

As hunters they would locate a mine with the hull-mounted Type 193M sonar. If a suspect object was detected, the ship would circle round it the better to identify it (the shadow was often useful). If it was a likely mine, a remote-controlled micro submarine (the French PAP 104) would be sent down for a closer look with closed-

[59] Caquot gives an exponent of 0.25; Barrow SSN 0.32; Yarrow's *Leander*s 0.13. The two latter figures are a rough guide only: the SSN were not identical and the *Leander*s were not from a single large order. The twelfth *Sandown* took about 55 per cent of the man-hours of the first.

[60] A J Harris, 'The "Hunt" Class Mine Counter Measures Vessels', *Trans RINA* (1980), p485.

[61] In preparing for the 1991 Gulf War extra guns were fitted. However, on arrival, they found that the use of weapons by ships without linked operations rooms was forbidden!

[62] D K Brown, 'Damn the Mines!', *USNI Proceedings* (March 1992). The author was in *Dulverton*.

[63] They supported the USN vessels as well as the five 'Hunts'.

[64] C M Plumb & D K Brown, 'Hovercraft in Mine Countermeasures', *High Speed Surface Craft Conference*, Brighton 1980.

Right: Hovercraft are almost immune from mine explosions, as demonstrated by this trial against an elderly SRN-3 craft (just visible, bottom right). After the plume fell she was re-boarded and her engines, radar and radio still worked. (*BHC*)

Below: An impression of the SRN-4 cross-channel ferry as an MCMV. She could carry all the kit of a 'Hunt' class and operate at least to the same speeds – but transit would be at 65kts. (*D K Brown collection*)

circuit television. If it was a probable mine the PAP could drop a demolition charge and, once the PAP was safely out of the way, the charge – and mine – could be exploded.

Weight was strictly controlled to keep the pressure signature low and an early weight-reduction programme took 70 tons off the early design figure, though a small part of the 'saving' proved impracticable in build.[60] All forms of magnetic material were limited but some degaussing was still needed. The main engines and the pulse generator were low-magnetic 9-cylinder Deltics and there were three Foden generators. The engines and generators were mounted on four rafts suspended from hull brackets above the waterline. The rafts were a very clever item of GRP design by Slingsby, the glider builders. Under ultra quiet conditions the propellers were turned by hydraulic motors working off the auxiliary engine. A bow thruster (another special, quiet design) and two big rudders gave excellent manoeuvrability.

A full scale mock-up was built at Woolston and, once

it had been approved by designers and operators, very few changes were permitted. A machinery unit was assembled on shore and tested. The design was produced in association with Vosper Thornycroft, who prepared the 7000 drawings (+ 4000 equipment drawings). Thirteen ships were completed between 1978 and 1988, two by Yarrows, the rest by VT. The first, *Brecon*, cost £24 million but the last required only half the man-hours, the effect on cost being concealed by inflation. There were problems but all were overcome. Since the hull was non-conducting an elaborate electrical earthing system was needed – as was a lightning conductor! Electronic spaces in GRP were transparent to radio frequencies and needed screening. The gun was intended for peacetime patrol work and would be removed in war to reduce magnetic signature.[61]

When *Brecon* went to sea there were numerous com plaints of seasickness; model tests and computer simulations were rechecked but no explanation was found. There were no such complaints from the second ship, nor from *Brecon*'s second crew when she recommissioned. A naval doctor found the explanation – *Brecon*'s first crew had all complained of sickness on their previous ships!

By the end of the Gulf War in 1991 the minehunting system was fairly old but worked very well. The five British 'Hunts' dealt with the sophisticated mines leaving the numerous moored mines to our allies.[62] There is a story which deserves to be better known – when the allied fleet returned to Kuwait City led by a US battleship and overwhelmingly USN, the American admiral signalled to the five little 'Hunts': 'You've led us in war, now lead us into harbour in peace.'

A Forward Support Unit was installed in a number of containers which could be taken to a convenient location for a particular operation. During the 1991 War the FSU containers were carried in the LSL *Sir Galahad*.[63] A Vosper hovercraft was purchased and adapted to carry spare acoustic sweeps from the FSU to craft at sea but was scrapped under the Nott Review before the scheme could be tried.

MCM Hovercraft, MCM(H)[64]

The Inter-Service Hovercraft Unit was set up in 1961, only two years after the historic first crossing of the Channel by SRN-1. By the mid-1970s attention was centred on the role of hovercraft in MCM. When the author took over in 1976 most aspects had been proved in full-scale trials and outline drawings were available for an MCM(H) based closely on the commercial cross-channel car ferries, the SRN-4. This craft could carry and operate all the 'Hunt' class sweeps, up to the same speed and in the same sea states at least.

The SRN-4 hovercraft in commercial form met the noise target and was close to the magnetic signature (it would have been fully met with small changes). The pressure signature was low but unusual – there was even a possibility of using it to clear pressure mines. The noise target was met while turning – some 10 per cent of the time – unlike the 'Hunts'. All these signature levels were inherent

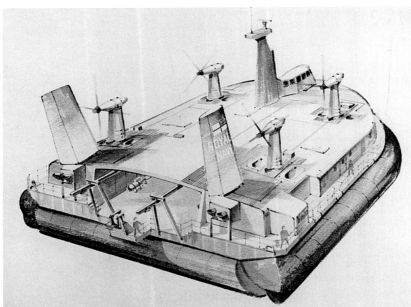

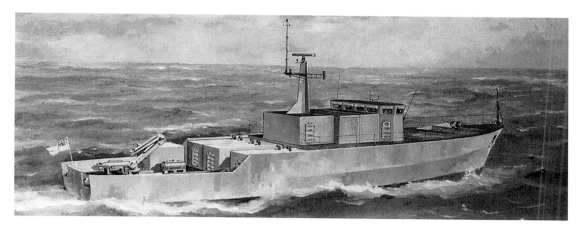

Left and below: The Utility Minehunter aimed at one-third the cost of a 'Hunt' class. The diesel generators, operations room and sonars were in containers. The author considers this the design of which he is the most proud.
(*Artist's impression and profile MoD*)

[65] On a long voyage frequent refuelling would be needed, reducing the transit speed to a mere 45kts, or three times that of a 'Hunt'.

in the air cushion and did not need expensive equipment or noise mounting, and there was no need for frequent monitoring. Mine explosions were tried against the ageing SRN-3, which withstood seven 1100lb charges with the last just clear of the skirt. When she re-emerged from the spray she was still hovering and the commercial radar and radio were still working.

The pylon-mounted propellers of the SRN-4 gave her exceptional manoeuvrability and track keeping – better than a 'Hunt' in severe wind and waves. It was proved that a hovercraft could use a Type 193M sonar at least as well as a 'Hunt', though the MCM(H) would normally use twin towed, side scan sonars to locate mines. The hovercraft could deploy at 70kts.[65] In war, a hovercraft unit could operate from any beach using a containerised support unit (though the noise made them unwelcome neighbours in peacetime). The craft would have had a built-in jacking system for maintenance.

Costing a hovercraft unit proved difficult; they were much cheaper to build than 'Hunts' but more expensive to run. Life costing over 20 years is not easy and we tried various approaches, all of which showed a clear cost advantage for the hovercraft. (We also costed USN style helicopters but they were incredibly expensive.) From the Director General (Daniel) downwards, Ship Department was enthusiastic but the Staff and sonar teams were opposed. The argument was fought without publicity but it was prolonged and bitter. It is one of the author's major professional regrets that the RN does not have an MCM Hovercraft unit. I was sent to support sales drives in Teheran, Kuala Lumpur and Bangkok but, without RN purchases, customers were not convinced.

A very good case was put forward by the Hydrographer for a HM-5 side-wall hovercraft to be used as a survey vessel in the Thames estuary, but this was another victim of Nott.

ERMISS, the Explosion Resistant Multi-Influence Sweep System

There was increasing concern that future mines would be camouflaged (disguised as rocks) or even buried beneath

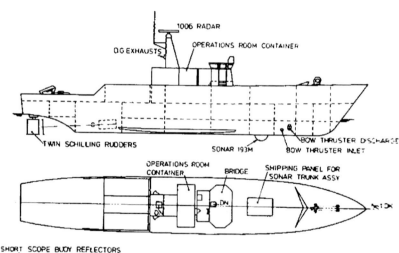

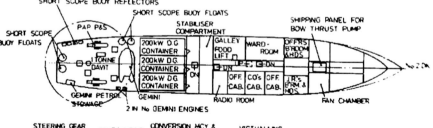

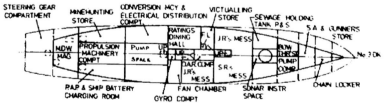

66 H W Groning, 'A New Concept in Mine Countermeasures', *International Defence Review* (1979).

67 Most of the other national team leaders were brilliant and likeable; three reached the top of their profession. The social life was splendid.

68 I received the best compliment of my career. Daniel said, 'Not a bit what I wanted but I rather like it.'

69 The Saudi version had a light sweep.

70 I particularly liked the British Hovercraft Corporation comment that they could not meet the endurance at 12kts as requested but could meet it at 50kts.

71 A Bunney, 'The Application of GRP to Ship Construction', *RINA Junior* (1986).

72 A special alloy with very low magnetic properties.

73 I am not a great believer in these matrix solutions. They are easy to manipulate so as to come to the pre-conceived answer or, if they do not, are ditched. It is well worth while going through the motions as it may expose one's own prejudices but throw away the answer. D K Brown, 'HMS *Sandown* – the third generation', *Warship Technology 8* (RINA 1989).

74 The author was initially unhappy with this but was eventually convinced by the old paper comparing the 'Hams' and 'Tons' mentioned earlier.

75 A remark somewhat weakened by a comment from the technical director's daughter: 'My daddy designed that ship and he doesn't know anything about computers.'

76 N Friedman, *Naval Weapon Systems* (Annapolis 1989), p450.

the seabed, making hunting very difficult indeed. ERMISS was seen as a possible solution; originally devised in the USA it was backed by other nations in NATO – France, UK, Netherlands and Germany (NATO PG 14). The principle was entirely different from other forms of MCMV in that the vessel should pass through a minefield exploding mines underneath itself without serious damage.[66]

The vessel consisted of an inflatable, peripheral rubber tube like an inflatable dinghy but much bigger and self-propelled (up to 18,000 tons was contemplated). This supported a raft clear of the water in the form of an egg box. Each cell was sealed at the bottom with a flexible diaphragm and filled with water to a carefully tuned depth. The air space between the raft and the sea was slightly pressurised and, though this provided some lift, ERMISS was not a hovercraft. It was hoped that variations in air pressure would tune the signature. Noise and magnetic generators would be installed so that ERMISS could represent a wide range of likely targets.

A preliminary full-scale test of a section of the inflatable structure showed that it could resist the explosion of a mine underneath. Negotiations to set up the project were lengthy, and when the author took over ERMISS was given a 5 per cent chance of success, but there was nothing else in sight that could do the job and the UK contribution was small in the development phase. It was an interesting task and very instructive on the problems and rewards of an international project.[67] Progress was made and when the author in turn handed over the project he was able to tell his successor that the chance of success had risen to 10 per cent. The test section failed in the final explosion and the project was abandoned. (In the author's view it could have been made to work but only at great expense and other ways of dealing with the problems were in sight.)

The Utility Minehunter (UMH)

Towards the end of the 1970s, Jack Daniel (DG Ships) realised that, though the 'Hunts' were very capable vessels, their cost meant that the RN could never afford enough of them. He suggested building some cheap MCMVs which would complement the 'Hunts', doing the easier tasks whilst the 'Hunts' tackled the more difficult aspects. John Coates, then Chief Naval Architect, chaired two exciting meetings during which we developed Daniel's ideas in brain-storming fashion (the author was head of forward design). It was soon apparent that a cheap sweeper was not possible as the towing pull was so great that powerful engines and hence a big hull was needed. However,

a cheap hunter seemed possible.

Our principle was the well-known engineering rule 'If in doubt, leave it out'. Fairly soon, we devised a scheme in which simple, bare GRP hulls would be built in a single yard not engaged in the 'Hunt' class programme. There would be three diesel generators, each in a standard ISO container, fitted out in a factory, on the upper deck. The operations room and annex were also containerised and assembled and tested in a factory. The sonar gear could be fitted in a box that was non-standard but could be accepted by ordinary container handling gear. Putting these items together was well within the capability of a big yacht builder – we even proposed to give them a pre-cut wiring harness. The equipment would be the well-tried Type 193M sonar and PAP submarine for disposal. Putting everything on the upper deck led to stability problems and she ended much fatter than the much-touted 'fat frigate'.

Our operational research mathematician, Ian Smith, had examined the original basis for the 'Hunt' class requirements and found the very stringent signature levels derived from the need to sweep close up to an invasion beach. Such operations were now unlikely and levels were relaxed a little with some limitation on minimum operating depth of water. This enabled us to use commercial equipment for some purposes. Our target was one-third the cost of a 'Hunt' and probably could have been achieved. The preliminary report was accepted by Daniel and passed to the staff.[68]

Needless to say it was 'improved' in Whitehall, with a new and very expensive sonar, a new gun and so on. The cheap minehunter was dead and *Sandown* was conceived. The UMH was and remains the author's favourite design and it made a lot of sense at the time. In the twenty-first century when the RN is cutting down on MCMV numbers, *Sandown*, a most capable ship, makes sense.

The Sandown Class

Though the new vessels were inspired by the utility minehunter, there was little in common except they were hunters with no sweeping gear.[69] Possible contenders were a new design, a single role 'Hunt', the Tripartite MCMV, or a hovercraft. Possible builders were invited to comment on the draft Staff Target at an early stage.[70] It was decided to go ahead with a new design led by Vosper Thornycroft, directed by Bernard Ramsay in Ship Department.

There was another review of the material and design of the hull structure, shown in the table.[71]

Structure	Cost	Weight	Shock	Fire	Magnetic	Life
Laminated Wood	Medium	Low	Poor	Poor	Excellent	Poor
Non Mag Steel	V High	High	Excellent	Good	Good	Good
Aluminium	High	Medium	Good	Poor	Good	Medium
Unstiffened Thick GRP	High	V High	Good	Excellent	Excellent	Good
GRP/Foam Sandwich	Low	Low	Medium	Poor	Excellent	Medium
Stiffened GRP	Medium	Medium	Good	Excellent	Excellent	Good

Matrices such as these are very sensitive to input changes. At a meeting with the German Navy they used much the same headings to reject GRP and chose non-magnetic steel.[72] They had a lot of experience with the steel and saw first cost as low whereas, lacking experience in GRP, they thought it expensive, while the British view was the opposite.

The signature levels for a hunter are less stringent than for a sweeper – towing a sweep the ship goes over the mine first! – but were still severe. Six different materials including various form of GRP, wood, steel, reinforced cement etc were considered under six headings such as first cost, ease of maintenance, durability, fire resistance etc. A single skin GRP structure much as the 'Hunts' was the clear winner.[73] Some improvements were possible due to new materials and techniques. For example, compliant resins meant that it was no longer necessary to bolt the frames to the skin.

Very high standards of manoeuvrability were required, which could most easily be met by twin Voith-Schneider cycloidal propellers. Commercial versions had high levels of both mechanical and hydrodynamic noise, but a lengthy programme involving MoD research establishments and the manufacturer brought the signature to an acceptable level. Bow thrusters were also fitted and a computer ship control system was installed to operate the complex propulsion/manoeuvring equipment. Accommodation was grouped amidships in the low-motion area and also to protect the crew from the explosion of contact mines. This led to a freeboard forward which was much less in relation to the length than in the 'Tons' and 'Hunts'.[74] The Type 2093 sonar was a new variable depth set. They mounted the new 30mm gun.

The first of class was ordered in 1985 and launched in April 1988. Vospers had devised a novel scheme of outfitting sections of GRP structure before assembly, but despite this they were expensive ships, very much the same as the 'Hunts', mainly due to the high cost of the sonar. At the launch of *Sandown* the managing director (Peter Usher) boasted that she was not only their first computer designed ship but also the first in which all the production scheduling – the arrival of each item in the assembly shop just before it was needed – was also computerised.[75] It is understood that they have proved very successful in service. Twelve have been ordered, as well as three for Saudi Arabia, while Spain is building a modified version. The mine threat remains serious.

EDATS (Extra Deep Armed Team Sweep)

During the early 1970s NATO became aware of the Soviet 'Cluster Bay' mines.[76] These were moored close to the bottom and on detecting a submarine would fire a rocket-propelled charge at it. A special sweep was devised which would follow the bottom contours and use explosive cutters to cut the moorings of such mines. Since the mine was only activated by submarines, quite simple sweepers could be used.

The principle was proved on chartered trawlers in 1978, and in 1980 the twelve 'River' class ships were ordered. They were designed and built by Richards (Lowestoft), based on an oil rig support vessel with considerable input from Ship Dept. In peacetime they have been used as RNR training vessels.

Sandown was originally seen as much cheaper than a 'Hunt', but the class acquired more and more advanced equipment and ended up at about the same cost, although for a much more capable hunter. Here the name ship uses her Voith Schneider propulsors to turn at rest. (*Mike Lennon*)

11 Helicopter Carriers, Amphibious Forces and other Projects

SINCE THE SECOND WORLD WAR there have been a number of ships built (and many more designed) for 'auxiliary', but very important, roles. The main types are replenishment ships to support a task force, and amphibious warfare vessels to land a military force and support it when ashore. Many of these ships are complex and expensive, but they are essential to the success of an operation and hence must have some capacity for self-defence. There is always room for debate on the scale of this self-defence leading into the debate as to whether the ships should be RN or Royal Fleet Auxiliary (RFA) manned, which can have surprising consequences, as will be seen in specific examples later in this chapter.

Cheap Helicopter Carriers

The success of wartime escort carriers and MAC ships encouraged the concept of cheap aircraft carriers or, latterly, helicopter carriers. Early studies were based on the Seamew ASW aircraft, but this proved too small for effective operations against modern submarines. This shows the nub of the problem: an effective aircraft is much bigger – and more expensive – than a wartime Swordfish.

	Swordfish	*Seamew*	*Merlin helicopter*
Weight (kg)	4200	7270	14,200
Length (m)	10.9	12.5	22.9
Width, folded (m)	5.2	16.7 (unfolded)	6.0
Aircraft crew	2-3	2	6
Maintenance crew	2	?	13

Conduct of operations requires that aircrews be briefed in a capable operations room 'linked' to other ships and aircraft. The numerous aircraft, their trained crews and full electronic fit are a major investment that requires protection whatever the cost of the hull, demanding at least a point defence system (including an AIO), signature reduction, subdivision, shock resistance, firefighting, etc; all of these are costly – one has almost defined a CVS.

There are roles in which cheap helicopter carriers are useful, but such roles must be tightly defined to avoid creeping growth and, conversely, to correct any impression that a full aircraft carrier can be obtained on the cheap. The ship with its supplies and aircraft becomes a high-value unit and was seen to require vertically-launched Sea Wolf, full AIO and communications and some signature reduction. Whitehall would not believe the cost estimates. One approach is to combine roles – to carry several helicopters on a replenishment ship. *Fort Victoria* (see below) can carry four Merlin helicopters in a hangar at the after end, with a sizeable flight deck. While this is a worthwhile solution it has problems, as the vertical motions at the stern of a long ship are severe and airflow over the deck is not good.

About 1980 there was a considerable number of studies into ships which combined the role of replenishment ship and helicopter carrier in different proportions. The simplest variants had a box hangar forward and a big deck with three landing spots aft. This arrangement is only suitable for an aircraft complement of up to about six, above which movement in the hangar becomes too difficult.[1] If more numerous aircraft are needed a conventional carrier style with an island superstructure and flight deck with about five spots and hangar below is required. Two lifts are essential since one may be disabled by accident or damage and lifts to raise a Merlin are not cheap. This configuration would make an alternative deck for V/STOL aircraft to land, refuel and for some limited re-arming. It could not have full maintenance facilities without escalating to the size and cost of a CVS.

There was prolonged discussion about whether these ships should be RN or RFA manned, a discussion that raised some very interesting points. Operation of the ship required far fewer men as an RFA, but since their pay was higher, they had much longer leaves and had bigger and more attractive living quarters, the overall cost seemed little different. The RFA authorities were insistent that it be powered by commercial diesels citing the need for special training as ruling out gas turbines. The RN were equally insistent that it be powered by gas turbines citing the need for special training as ruling out diesels. Once again, there was little difference in the cost – really big diesels do not come cheap. Originally the RN manning would have had a ship CO of Commander rank but when it was decided that the air group needed a Captain it was inevitable that the ship CO would be upgraded. On the standard scale of complement this brought a considerable increase – stewards, a dentist, some instructor officers (meteorologists)!

One major problem applied to both configurations: flight operations made it virtually impossible to have any replenishment rigs on the port side and probably no more than two to starboard. It was not easy in the 'carrier' configuration to keep the hangar deck high enough to prevent flooding after damage (and inevitable capsize as in the case of the ferry *Herald of Free Enterprise* in 1987) and the solution added to the size of the ship.

[1] See Chapter 4 where similar conclusions were reached in early studies leading to *Invincible*.

Two designs for a cheap helicopter carrier with some replenishment capability. The version with a hangar forward (*above*) is suitable for only up to about six aircraft, beyond which moving within the hangar becomes too difficult. For more aircraft the 'through deck' carrier configuration (*left*) becomes almost inevitable. Neither of these designs was built, but some of the thinking went into *Ocean*. (*D K Brown collection*)

[2] Anon, 'RFA *Argus*, a new air training ship for the RN', *Warship Technology* (May 1987).

[3] It is said that one has been fitted with an outboard motor and is in use as a cattle ferry on Belfast Loch.

[4] H W J Chislett, 'Replenishment at Sea', *Trans RINA* (1972), p321. Respectively, the collier *Muriel* with *Trafalgar*; tanker *Petroleum* with *Victorious*.

[5] The ship was *Wanderer*. See R Whinney, *The U Boat Peril* (London 1986).

[6] Vice-Admiral D B Fisher, 'The Fleet Train in the Pacific War', *Trans INA* (1953), p212. This paper was originally issued in 1948 and withdrawn at official request! Published 1953 without discussion.

[7] G Jones, *Under Three Flags* (London 1973).

Argus served as the mercantile *Contender Bezant* in the Falklands and was later purchased and given a major conversion to the helicopter carrier configuration seen here. (*Mike Lennon*)

The conclusion had to be that the two roles were not compatible. However, much of the thinking was to read across to *Ocean* (LPH). The design of a helicopter carrier to support amphibious operations proved worthwhile. It would be part of a force containing merchant ships whose signatures would obscure those of the LPH and, since opposed landings are not envisaged, self-protection could be reduced. There is a risk in this, since the LPH is vital to the success of such an operation and its loss would be a disaster.

Argus

During the Falklands War the container ship *Contender Bezant* (built 1981 near Venice) was requisitioned as a helicopter carrier but reverted after the war (see later section). She arrived in the Falklands area in June 1982 and could carry nine helicopters (including some Chinooks) and four Harriers. Her configuration with twin funnels and two large gantry cranes made aircraft operation difficult.

However, there was still interest in this ship as a replacement for the air training ship *Engadine* and in March 1984 a contract was placed with Harland & Wolff to purchase and convert her at a price of £63 million; she was renamed *Argus*.[2] There were many problems, some unforeseen, such as the presence of asbestos and lead-based paint. Without

cargo her stability was excessive, and this was cured in two ingenious ways. The new superstructure, seven decks high, was built of heavy plate (8-10mm), easier to fabricate, weighing 800 tons – the new mast alone weighed 26 tons. In addition, the hatch covers were inverted and the shallow trays so formed were filled with concrete to a total of 1800 tons. Hatch covers in the way of the two 18-ton capacity lifts (weight 55 tons) were removed.[3]

Argus has a full naval communication fit (Link 11 and 14). She has accommodation for 253 RFA, RN and air group personnel. She can carry out RAS with 3500 tons of fuel plus 1000 m^3 of AVCAT. The original machinery has been retained, modified to run on naval-quality dieso. The main and auxiliary engine rooms have been separated by a bulkhead improving subdivision, and the shaft tunnel has been separated from the engine-room. At a full load displacement of 28,081 tons, she was the largest ship in naval service.

She can carry helicopters and transport, but not operate, Harriers; a typical load is twelve Harriers and six Sea Kings. *Argus* has proved invaluable as headquarters or hospital ship for various intervention forces but there is no such thing as a cheap helicopter carrier. Plans to convert her sister, *Contender Argent*, were abandoned, to be replaced many years later by *Ocean*.

'Arapaho' and *Reliant*

During the 1970s the USN tried to develop a container-ised kit ('Arapaho') for fitting to a merchant ship in 3 days and to support four Sea Kings for 15 days. Progress was slow due to lack of funds and the project was recast in 1980. This scheme was followed with interest by the RN and when an urgent requirement came forward in 1982 for a helicopter ship, arrangements were made to lease the US kit. Negotiations were complete early in 1983 but the gear was not yet ready.

However, by May, some eighteen containers and sixty-nine modules forming the hangar and flight deck arrived. Fifty-five more containers had to be fitted out in the UK providing accommodation, water and sewage plant, stores, etc. These were fitted by the end of September and, after two months setting to work, trials began in December 1983. The ship chosen was the *Astronomer*, which had served as an aircraft transport during the Falklands War, now renamed *Reliant*.

She served satisfactorily for several years but the con-cept of a rapid-fit kit built in advance and installed in an emergency was seen to be impractical. Ships varied too much and the kit would have to be designed to fit a par-ticular class, while the ships would need advance prepa-ration. As demonstrated during the Falklands War, quick conversions of container ships as transports can be most valuable but they can never equate to a true helicopter carrier.

Replenishment at Sea

The RN carried out trials in 1902 of replenishing at sea with coal and in 1906 with oil.[4] Though both trials were said to be successful there was little further development. There is no record of refuelling at sea in the First World War and between the wars there was little interest since the British Empire had numerous fuelling depots world-

Fort Grange, a replenishment ship for dry stores displacing 22,750 tons, launched in 1976. The ship can operate up to four Sea King helicopters, although normally only one is embarked. (*Mike Lennon*)

During the Falklands War the mercantile *Astronomer* was employed as a temporary helicopter carrier, with a hangar made from containers. Later she was purchased, becoming *Reliant*, and was used for trials with the US 'Arapaho' system for conversion to helicopter carrier. In this May 1986 view the ship has a Harrier on deck. (*Mike Lennon*)

wide. In the early years of the Second World War it became apparent that few escorts could cross the Atlantic with-out refuelling and a tanker sailed with each convoy fitted to refuel escorts from astern, though there were experi-ments in the beam method by 1943.[5] The full nature of the problem became apparent in the Pacific.[6] Compared with the USN the RN Fleet Train was slow, unreliable and expensive in manpower. Following the war a major effort was made to catch up.

Many trials were carried out, mostly involving *Bulawayo* (the ex-German *Nordmark*).[7] The first task was to develop a self-rendering winch that would pay out as the supports on the two ships moved towards each other due to rolling and other motions in a seaway and then take up the slack as the ships moved the other way. The behaviour of two (or more) ships in close company is complicated, and can be hazardous (as with the sinking of the minesweeper *Fit-tleton* by *Mermaid* in 1976). With the two ships abeam there is an overall force pushing the ships together and a turning moment pushing the bows apart. This is safe but there is a transitional case when the smaller ship is coming up from astern in which the bows are sucked together.

8 ADM 1/29139, October 1958, originally Top Secret (PRO).

9 Each battalion comprised 1050 men, 16 tanks (Centurion), 8 self-propelled guns and 60 '3-ton equivalents'.

Model tests and cautious trials established safe procedures.

By about 1970 quick and efficient procedures were established and the hardware was available. To ensure that all concerned keep in practice, about 55 per cent of fuel burnt by the RN is taken on at sea. The normal method of refuelling is the jackstay rig alongside, though astern refuelling is possible if both beam stations are occupied. A jackstay rig can also be used to transfer solid stores up to 4 tons in weight, though increasingly helicopters are used for stores transfer (VERTREP).

Replenishment Ships: AOR Fort Victoria

The concept was originally known, informally, as the 'one stop ship', an apt description as it was intended to supply fuel, dry stores and ammunition in a single replenishment operation. There were an exceptionally large number of constraints, many of which were not obvious. It had to be able to come alongside at most naval fuel depots to fill its tanks, and the length of the jetty fixed the maximum length of the AOR. It was to be RFA manned which, by agreement, meant that it had to abide by merchant ship rules as far as possible. Both the seamen's union and the Department of Transport accepted that there would be exceptions, and though they were helpful each exemption required negotiation and justification. Merchant ship rules forbade accommodation over fuel tanks or ammunition stowage but with a large crew and a ship almost full of fuel and ammunition this was not practicable. With such a cargo firefighting capability had to be available at a moment's notice so that naval practice of a permanently-filled fire main was needed, which meant expensive bronze piping instead of steel – and so it went on. Boat stowage to tanker standards took up upper deck space that was in great demand.

It was soon clear that this would be a most valuable ship whose loss would jeopardise an operation, so on came vertically-launched Sea Wolf, an operations room, Link communications etc, and up went the cost. The first estimate came as a shock to Staff and ministers, and drew the usual parrot-cry of 'gold plating'. After a long interval a design competition was held, which ended in much higher prices being quoted. This, too, was disbelieved and a further competition was held, which was won by Harland & Wolff. Eventually, *Fort Victoria* was completed very much in accord with the Ship Department (Brown/Andrews) sketch design, years late and much over budget.

Amphibious Forces

In January 1958 the Chiefs of Staff invited the Admiralty to examine the technical problems of replacing the ageing amphibious force and the following month a study group was set up.[8] The force to be lifted was two assault battalions with supporting arms.[9] The study group reported in October 1958 having considered three groups of design.

Bow loading, beaching LST.

Stern loading, non-beaching LST.

LSD.

USN designs were considered but rejected as bigger and more complex than were needed and hence too expensive.

The draught forward of the beaching LST was governed by the ability of wheeled vehicles to 'wade', some 5-6ft depending on type (it was assumed that the Centurion tanks would be Duplex Drive, capable of swimming). This limit affected the draught aft, depending on the beach slope selected. UK planners wanted to be able to land on beaches with a slope of $1/120$, which meant a shallow draught, small propellers, and a hull form which was resistful and a poor seaboat. US plans called for a $1/50$ slope, which made for a more seaworthy vessel at the expense of severe limits on the number of beaches that could be used.

Two studies were prepared for a beaching LST, one with four Deltics (6000shp) and the other with two G6 gas turbines (10,000shp). Speeds above 17kts were not examined as the cost would be high and top speed would only be usable in calm weather. Each vessel carried half a battalion.

There would be few limitations on the form of non-beaching stern loaders and speeds from 18 to 24kts were examined using a version of the *Whitby* class Y 100 steam machinery for the fastest version. Such vessels did have a major, unsolved problem. Vehicles would be transferred to an LCM using the stern ramp and it was clear that this operation could only be carried out at sea in very calm weather and, even then, it would be slow, taking 5 hours.

The bigger LSD study was based on the USN LSD-28 (*Thomaston*) but omitting some of the more expensive items of equipment. It could carry a full battalion. This ship was to develop into the *Fearless*, discussed later. The dock could accept nine LCM or three LCM and one LCU. The smaller LSD could carry two-thirds of a battalion and six LCM. Model tests in both head and following seas were recommended for the beaching LST and the LSD. (The very wide transom of the LSD posed the risk of broaching in a following sea.)

Fort George, a very capable 32,500-ton replenishment ship with fuel, stores and ammunition capability. Three large helicopters are usually carried, but five can be handled if needed. (*Mike Lennon*)

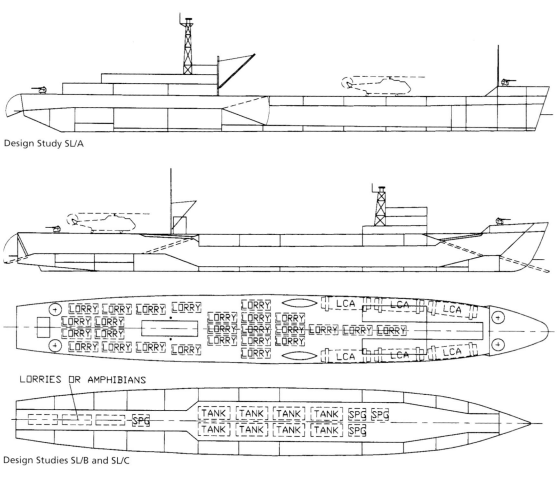

Design Study SL/A

LORRIES OR AMPHIBIANS

Design Studies SL/B and SL/C

1958 Landing Ship Tank Designs. In 1958 five LST designs were produced. All could carry a tank and vehicle load of 676 tons. The 'SL' series were stern loading non-beaching LSTs; the 'BL' series bow loading and beaching LSTs. Design SL/A was powered by Y100 steam turbines producing 20,000shp, which gave a speed of 23kts at deep displacement. SL/B, powered by two gas turbines producing 10,000shp with a speed of 19kts at deep displacement, was identical in appearance to SL/C driven by four Deltic diesels producing 6000shp, with a speed of 16kts at deep displacement. BL/C and BL/D were identical in appearance. BL/C was powered by four Deltic diesels, speed being 14kts at deep displacement. BL/D had two gas turbines giving a speed of 16kts at deep displacement. Note the differences in hull design and bridge design. (*Drawings by John Roberts from originals in PRO ADM 1/29139*)

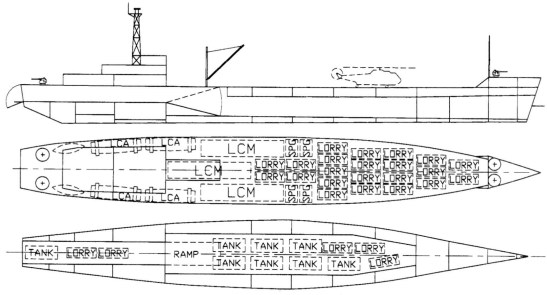

Design Studies BL/C and BL/D

10 No records have been found of this craft.

11 For a time, the category 'Assault Ship' was not thought 'politically correct' and they had a range of titles.

12 Based on a design study by Sir Rowland Baker.

13 ADM 167/157 (PRO).

The estimated costs are of interest.

	Cost (£ million)
Beaching LST	2.75-3.0 + 6 LCA @ £15,000 each
Stern LST	3.-3.5 + 4 LCA @ £15,000 and 3 LCM @ £50,000 each
LSD	5.0-8.0

For comparison the following figures were quoted at 1958 prices:

	Cost (£1000)
Repeat LCT 8	600
LCT 9[10]	900
LCM 7	35
LCM 8	60
Repeat LST 3	2500
US LPD	$ 30 million

A model of the *Fearless* class LSD under test at Haslar in confused seas. Waves within the dock were an additional problem that required extensive testing to resolve. (*D K Brown collection*)

Assault Ships[11] *Fearless and Intrepid*

The wartime Landing Ships Dock, built in the USA,[12] proved of great value in support of amphibious operations and, following the 1958 studies discussed above, it was decided to design and build two similar vessels. These were loosely based on the USS *Raleigh*, whose plans were made available, and a constructor, Peter Lover, went to sea in *Raleigh* as a Constructor Commander.

The sketch design was agreed in 1960.[13] They were intended to carry troops, tanks and other vehicles and land them using their own minor landing craft and, to a limited extent, helicopters. They were also to act as a Brigade Headquarters Ship. They were to carry four LCA(2) in davits, each transporting 35 troops. The LCM 9 was to carry two Centurion tanks or four 3-ton vehicles and stores up to 100 tons. (In 1960 it was thought that there would be no tanks bigger than Centurion but trucks might grow.) The LCM (later LCU) were carried in a dock at the after end of the ship; hence small size was desirable in the LCM. This made a very difficult design problem, and they were never able to carry the full design load, though they were to prove very valuable in the Falklands War. It was intended that the full number of vehicles and men would be landed in five trips by each craft.

When ballasting down, the well deck would be awash in about 30 minutes when it would take a further 15 minutes to flood the dock using four steam pumps. It was immediately apparent that waves in the dock would be a major problem and numerous model experiments were run at Haslar to reduce the problem. In an emergency, it was thought that the ships could make 16kts with the dock flooded.

They have a large helicopter deck but no hangar. Two landing spots were provided but one was obstructed when the full number of vehicles was stowed. They were

intended to operate with Wessex helicopters but it was noted that the wheel loading on the deck for vehicles was greater, allowing a margin for bigger helicopters in future. They had accommodation for 400 troops (700 on short crossings) and could carry 15 tanks, six self-propelled guns and up to 50 vehicles (3-ton). Their armament has always been light: originally four Sea Cat mountings and two 40mm, but *Fearless* had two Phalanx CIWS in 2001.

Particulars

Displacement, deep (tonnes)	11,540
Dimensions (ft)	523 (oa) x 80 x 20 (deep)
shp/speed (kts)	22,000/20
Fuel, endurance @	2040, 5000 @ 20kts
	6 months out of dock
Complement	450

The estimated cost in 1960 was £8.5 million.

They were ordered and laid down in 1962 as part of an expansion of amphibious forces, completing in 1965-7. They proved invaluable in the Falklands War and in numerous confrontations elsewhere.

LPH Ocean

The primary role of this ship is to carry, operate and maintain a squadron of twelve Sea King or Merlin helicopters in support of the amphibious force and to accommodate a Royal Marine commando of 500 men (800 overload)

with their vehicles. Up to six Lynx helicopters can also be carried; Chinooks can be operated from the flight deck (though not hangared) and Sea Harriers can be transported and flown off lightly-loaded.[14]

An invitation to tender for the design and build was issued in February 1992 and a contract was placed with VSEL in May 1993.[15] The hull, main machinery and many non-military equipments were to be built by Kvaener Govan (formerly Fairfield) on the Clyde. She was launched on 11 October 1995, incurring some damage, but after repairs and some further outfitting she sailed under her own power to Barrow in November 1996. She was named *Ocean* by the Queen at Barrow on 20 February 1998 when military equipment had been installed.

Ocean uses a mixture of naval and merchant ship standards. The hull form is that of *Invincible* but slightly beamier. Subdivision is to RN standards[16] with no fore and aft access below the hangar deck and there are five fire zones and three NBCD citadels. She is longitudinally framed to Lloyd's rules except for the lower decks and fore and aft ends generally.[17] The steel is of good commercial standard, ductile at low temperatures. The above-water form is mainly of flat surfaces, both to ease fabrication and to minimise radar reflection.

She has the largest hangar ever fitted in a Royal Navy ship – 111.3m x 21m and 6.2m minimum headroom. There are two 16.75m x 9.75m lifts and two fire barriers. The flight deck has six helicopter spots with parking space for six

[14] Anon, 'HMS *Ocean* – A new helicopter carrier', *Warship Technology*, RINA (March 1998).

[15] The losing tender by Swan Hunter was said to be £71 million higher; as a result of this failure the firm went into receivership.

[16] Three compartment flooding.

[17] The big side openings for her landing craft required special design and approval.

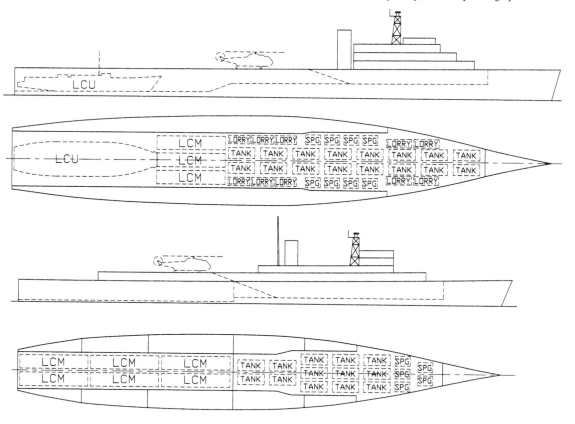

1958 Landing Ship Dock. Studies DL/A (top) and DL/B were eventually to lead to *Fearless* and *Intrepid*. Both were powered by two Y100 steam turbines producing 20,000shp. Deep displacement speeds were 20kts (DL/A) and 22kts (DL/B). Deep displacements were 11,500 tons (DL/A) and 8000 tons (DL/B). (*Drawing by John Roberts from originals in PRO ADM 1/29139*)

[18] The davits can also handle the Dutch LCA Mk 2.

[19] The Army representative said he would like swivelling ramps if they did not cost too much. To my surprise, the ramp manufacturer said that factor of safety on their standard ramp was such that they could accept tanks with very minor changes.

[20] Before the second meeting I had a design study with a large scale drawing of the 650ft ship of 11,500 tons which I unrolled towards the end of the meeting. The dialogue was what I had predicted:
Royal Marine colonel: 'That's not what we want.'
Brown: 'But it is what you asked for.'
The army colonel dryly remarked that the fjord where it was proposed to disembark was not 650ft wide – you will have problems!
The meeting adjourned.

Ocean at Marchwood in January 1999. Her hull form is closely based on *Invincible*. (Mike Lennon)

Lynx. A runway 130m long is available. The vehicle deck is on 4 deck and is 47.5m x 23.25m with a 4.0m headroom. There is a side ramp and a stern ramp for access. Armament comprises three Phalanx CIWS and four twin 30mm. There is a very capable command and control system based on ADAWS 200. Four LCVPs Mark V are carried in davits. Designed and built by Vosper Thornycroft, these can carry 35 Marines and their equipment at 15kts.[18] There is also a Pacific 22 RIB as rescue boat.

There are two separated engine-rooms each with a 6750kW Pielstick reversing engine driving through a reduction gearbox.

Sir Lancelot Class LSL

These ships were designed in the 1950s under the direction of the Department of Transport as agents for the War Office and, on completion, they were operated by commercial companies under charter. They had a helicopter deck and could carry 16 main battle tanks, 34 other vehicles and 534 troops. They were built to commercial standards and were not intended for use in opposed landings. They were, however, intended to land troops and vehicles (with Mexiflotes) on suitable beaches in the event that ports were destroyed. Since they were regarded as merchant ships, the rules said that if they grounded they had to be docked for inspection and hence beaching was only practised once, just before a planned docking. They were taken over by the RFA in 1980.

The Big Landing Ship Logistic

By 1980 it was clear that the 'Sir' class would need a major update or replacement. A meeting was held in an attempt to clarify requirements. The Army merely wanted a Ro-Ro ship with decks and ramps strong enough to take reinforcements of main battle tanks[19] across the North Sea in a time of rising tension, but the Royal Marines and Navy had a much more elaborate requirement – to loiter off northern Norway for several weeks and then land marines and heavy vehicles.

It was envisaged that the ship should be RFA manned with the usual condition that merchant ship rules should be followed as far as possible. The large number of troops made them into 'passenger ships' requiring lifeboats in addition to the landing craft. This translated into a very large vessel, 650ft long and 11,500 tons. The project went no further.[20]

Sir Galahad

Following the loss of the first *Sir Galahad* in the Falklands war a replacement was designed and built by Swan Hunter. She is a most versatile ship, carrying fifteen Challenger tanks and other vehicles, together with Mexiflotes and 400-500 troops. Alternatively, she can operate up to six Merlin helicopters, stowed in the tank deck with two large lifts to the upper deck with two spots. During the 1991 Gulf War she served as an MCMV depot ship for five 'Hunt' class and three USN minehunters using the con-

The LSL *Sir Galahad* acting as a support ship for five 'Hunts', *Hecate*, and three USN MCMVs in the Gulf in 1991.
(*D K Brown collection*)

tainerised Forward Support Unit.[21] She was able to embark the containers in 20 hours using her own crane and could have disembarked them more quickly had the amphibious landing gone ahead.

LPD[22] *Albion and Bulwark*

The two new LPD are direct replacements for the aged *Fearless* and *Intrepid*. Indeed, the new design team has paid several tributes to their predecessors, including that greatest homage: copying. In particular, the difficult dock design was very closely based on the earlier ships.

In the early 1980s there was a general review of the RN amphibious force, as a result of which it was decided in 1985 to go ahead with two new LPD. Three one-year design studies were funded but failed to produce a satisfactory response. Downs and Ellis[23] give the reasons as: firstly, the Ministry was unable to make an input into competitive studies; secondly, splitting design resources between three contenders working on a short timescale meant insufficient depth of study.[24] A new study was initiated in 1990 with a single contractor who was forbidden to take part in the design and build stage.[25] This ended with a cost estimate some 30 per cent over the planned budget. Yet another study was set up and in 1994 tenders were invited for the detailed design and build. VSEL was the only tenderer and their quoted price was much in excess of budget. After lengthy discussion of cost-saving measures an acceptable price was agreed.[26]

The payload was almost exactly the same as the earlier ships – 305 troops (405 overload), 31 'high' vehicles or tanks, 36 light vehicles and 30 tons of cargo. The dock could take four LCU Mark 10[27] (one USN LCAC hovercraft could be accommodated) and four LCP Mark 5 are carried in davits. There is a side ramp on the starboard side in addition to the stern ramp, and internal ramps connect the vehicle deck to both the dock and the helicopter deck. The flight deck has two spots for Merlin or Sea King and a third stowed, or could accept one Chinook. There is no hangar but some helicopter support facilities are available. Particular attention has been paid to access for fully-equipped troops to assembly areas and on to the deck or dock. Overhead rails are installed to move munitions and heavy stores.

The development of the hull form proved difficult, as most of the weight was forward and the after end was empty. Numerous model tests and computational fluid dynamics eventually reduced the power by no less than 34 per cent compared with the original design. Subdivision is to SOLAS 1990 (roughly two compartment flooding) but firefighting is to RN standards. Watertight wing compartments alongside the vehicle deck aid survivability.[28]

The hull structure is generally to Lloyd's rules for fast cargo ships but with higher standards of watertight subdivision and scantlings increased to those suitable for a draught some 2m greater than the actual design draught, for increased strength. External plates are of steel that is tough at low temperatures. Some changes were made to

[21] Her Master was most enthusiastic over his ship's capability but still outlined his ideas for an even better Mark II.

[22] LPD is supposed to stand for 'Landing Platform Dock', a nonsensical title. In the USN equivalent, P stands for Personnel, a rational interpretation.

[23] This section is based (with permission) on a symposium paper by D S Downs and M J Ellis, 'The Royal Navy's New Building Assault ships *Albion* and *Bulwark*', given at RINA Warship '97; and also the article 'HMS *Albion*' in *Warship Technology* (May 2001).

[24] The author would strongly endorse these views.

[25] A very strange approach excluding design teams with experience.

[26] It is interesting that one cost saving measure was to increase the size of the ship, making outfit easier. Often advocated, this seems to be the first time it was tried in the UK.

[27] The LCU Mark 10 is a drive-through craft with a ramp at each end, speeding dock operation. It can carry a Challenger II tank.

[28] Good. Baker got this right in the Second World War, unlike modern Ro-Ro ships.

The LPD *Bulwark* after launching at Barrow. (*BAE Systems*)

increase resistance to shock from explosions. Fatigue life was set at 10^8 wave encounters (30 years).

Diesel-electric propulsion was chosen in the light of the wide speed range and manoeuvrability needed. This system requires an engine room complement of about 60, one third of that of *Fearless*. A bow thruster is fitted. Overall complement is 325, compared with 550 in *Fearless*.

A very elaborate control and communication system is supplied, since the army commander will be based on the ship during the early phases of an operation as well as the naval task force commander.

Particulars

Displacement, deep (tonnes)	18,500 (*c*21,500 docked down)
Dimensions (m)	176 x 28.9 x 6.1
Power and Speed	Two x 6MW; 18kts
Armament	Two Goalkeeper CIWS, two 20mm
Radar	Type 996, two Type 1007

Albion is running trials in early 2003.

Landing Ship Dock (Auxiliary)(formerly Alternative Landing Ship Logistic (ALSL))

The Strategic Defence Review of July 1998 envisaged a considerable increase in the RN's amphibious capability. At much the same time *Sir Bedivere* showed that the SLEP

of these aged LSLs was not cost effective. A review of requirements led to the ALSL, which could transport troops, their vehicles and other equipment and deliver them in an assault role. They would also be able to provide logistic support to troops already ashore, take part in humanitarian operations and work as troopships.[29]

A contract was placed in December 2000 with Swan Hunter to design and build two ALSL and two more were ordered from BAE Govan in November 2001.[30] The new ships will be much bigger than the 'Sirs' which they replace, with a deep displacement of 16,000 tons and a length of 176m. They will have diesel-electric propulsion driving a pair of azimuthing thrusters giving a speed of 18kts, similar to that of the rest of the amphibious force. There will also be a bow thruster. Stability will be to warship standards which a study has revealed, unsurprisingly, also satisfies SOLAS 90. The steel is chosen to permit limited operation in ice. They will be fitted 'for but not with' light AA guns. The superstructure will be forward without a hangar but with a large flight deck behind – probably one spot for helicopters up to Chinooks or Ospreys in size and a parking space. There will be a dock for one LCU or two LCVP. They will normally carry 350 troops (twice that in overload), and have 2½ times the vehicle capacity of their predecessors. There is a stern ramp and and side ramp well forward. These ships will not beach but disembark their cargo using Mexiflotes which they themselves carry. A particular feature of

[29] UK details ALSL design. *Warship Technology*, RINA July 2000.

[30] Replacing *Sir Geraint* and *Sir Percivale*. They will be named *Lyme Bay* and *Largs Bay*. The second pair will be named *Mounts Bay* and *Cardigan Bay*. The design is based on the Dutch *Rotterdam*.

Challenger, a seabed operations vessel designed to identify and recover military artefacts from deep water. She fell victim to defence cuts before she could demonstrate her value. (*Mike Lennon*)

these ships, developed from *Ocean* and *Albion*, is wide troop gangways from berth to assembly area to deck or dock.

The first ship, *Largs Bay*, was launched in February 2003 and is due to enter service in July 2004. The first Govan ship will be launched in October 2003. The cost is £95 million each.

The Seabed Operations Vessel *Challenger*

This ship had a number of difficult roles, all posing problems of ship and equipment design. She was required to search the seabed using hull-mounted sonar in shallow water and a towed, unmanned submersible in deeper water. She was to inspect items found on the seabed, and carry out work using a pressurised diving bell or a submersible with diver lockout facilities, and recover objects. The 'objects' could include RN or NATO ordnance lost in exercises, or Soviet devices lost or deliberately placed.

The number of options considered was very large, including two ships, conversions, multi-hull, etc but after consideration a monohull was chosen. She was positioned using two Voith-Schneider units aft and three bow thrusters forward, computer controlled. Her position was determined from satellite systems. A diving bell was operated through a moonpool amidships and an unmanned submersible over the stern. She was designed to RN damaged stability standards to reduce the chance of her sinking. A particular problem would arise if she sank while a diver was in the decompression chamber. A pressure tight tube was arranged to take any such cases to a hyperbaric lifeboat. A RINA paper[31] discusses the problems which were overcome in much more detail than is possible here. All these features were expensive and she cost as much as a frigate.

Particulars

Displacement (tonnes)	6500 standard
Dimensions (m)	127 x 18 x 10.85 (Depth)
Machinery	Five Ruston 16RKCZ driving 3.3kV generators, two 6RKCZ harbour diesels.
Crew	186[32]

She was completed in 1984 but soon fell victim to defence cuts and was sold. When last heard of (2001), she was mining the seabed for diamonds off Africa.

Icebreakers

In the mid-1950s it was decided to increase the RN presence in the Falklands Islands dependencies. It was hoped to build an icebreaker and the USN generously made the drawings of the 'Wind' class available. British engines were selected which made the ship much longer. The cost rose and the project was abandoned, the former netlayer *Protector* being chosen instead with a minimum of changes. A few years later another design study was progressed in more detail but it, too, foundered on cost. She would have been called *Terra Nova*; her substitute was *Endurance* of Falklands fame.

[31] P J R Symons and J A Sadden, 'The Design of the Seabed Operations Vessel', *Trans RINA* (1982), p41.

[32] There was the usual debate as to whether they should be RN or RFA. A naval crew was selected on the basis of security.

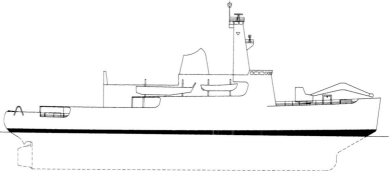

Several attempts were made to design and build an icebreaker to replace the ex-netlayer *Protector* for Antarctic work but all failed on cost grounds. This is Design Study I for a vessel to be called *Terra Nova*. This impressive icebreaker/oceanographic survey ship made use of Canadian, American and Scandinavian experience in the design. Deep displacement was approximately 7000 tons with dimensions 278ft x 64ft. Machinery suggested was four Ruston AO engines developing 15,000bhp; ASR1 diesels were also considered. It was cancelled as an economy measure in 1967, her replacement being the purchased Polar Ship *Endurance* (ex-*Anita Dan*). (*Drawing by John Roberts from original in PRO DEFE 24/90*)

12 Naval Architecture

[1] D K Brown, 'Defining a Warship', *Naval Engineers Journal*, ASNE (March 1986). The last two sentences above were framed and hung on the wall of Preliminary Design in Washington – signed by the author.

[2] Intact stability has been explained in the author's previous books, in great detail in *Warrior to Dreadnought*, p207, and also in *The Grand Fleet*, p199.

[3] See *Warrior to Dreadnought*, p207.

UNTIL RECENTLY British warships were designed within the Admiralty or Ministry of Defence. Ship Department and its predecessors, DNC Department, E-in-C, etc, operated with a small design section, which would draw on the expertise of a considerable number of specialist sections. Initially, these dealt with the traditional naval architecture subjects of Stability, Speed, Seaworthiness and Strength while the E-in-C and DEE had their own specialist groups, such as Gearing, or Batteries. Following the merger of the old RCNC with the RNES, some were merged – Materials (Steels to paints), Stealth, Fire, Battleworthiness and others.

In earlier years these specialists would respond to queries from design sections and reply from their own experience or, where necessary, task the relevant research establishment – AEW, NCRE, AEL, AML etc. This interface was valuable, as it was not uncommon for a busy design section to ask the wrong question, and even more common for them to fail to understand or apply the reply. Increasingly, the role of the specialist sections changed to the setting of standards, first in the 'General Hull Specification' and later in 'Naval Engineering Standards'. Once these standards were soundly based, the specialist sections were given authority to monitor compliance, though there was always a procedure to grant exemptions or make changes where necessary.

These standards were derived from hard and often painful experience, and modified in the light of new technology and changes in the availability of materials.

Such standards must change from time to time, and it is as proper for the designer to challenge them as it is foolish for him to ignore the accumulated wisdom contained in them.[1]

Stability

Intact Ship

The principles of stability for an undamaged ship were understood by about 1870, and by the end of the century mechanical aids were available which made the calculations merely tedious.[2] Stability after damage was much more difficult and, though the principles were well understood by the early twentieth century, only simple comparative calculations were possible before modern computers became available. Only these basic principles will be outlined in this book.

There were two major developments in the post-war years: firstly the criteria of acceptable stability were more clearly defined; secondly, later the introduction of powerful computers enabled much more realistic calculations to be carried out.

Even the word 'Stability' is used with several different meanings. The proper meaning to a naval architect is that stability is a measure of the force needed to heel a ship through a small angle – a ship is stable if a fairly large force is needed to heel it. A ship may also be said to be stable if it can be heeled to a large angle without capsizing. This second meaning is an extension of the first meaning but it is not the same. Finally, a ship is sometimes said to be stable if it rolls gently. This meaning is almost the opposite of the first two usages and should be avoided.[3]

For any floating body the buoyancy associated with the underwater volume will always be equal to the weight – displacement (Archimedes' Principle). Both weight and buoyancy forces are vertical and when the ship is upright they are in the same line, balancing exactly (upper small sketch in diagram opposite).

As the ship heels the shape of the underwater volume changes and the position of the centre of buoyancy through which the force acts will move. Initially, the buoyancy force will move towards the more deeply immersed side and the pair of forces (Weight and Buoyancy) will act as a couple tending to bring the ship upright. As the deck edge goes under on one side and the bilge comes out on the other, the outward movement of the buoyancy force will slow down, stop and then reverse.

The distance between the forces of weight and buoyancy is known as the 'righting lever', represented by 'GZ'. Values of GZ are plotted against angle of heel in the curves

Curve of righting levers (GZ).
(*W J Jurens*)

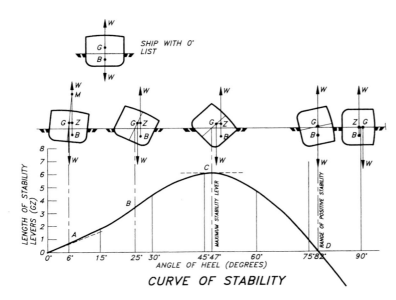

CURVE OF STABILITY

of righting levers, usually abbreviated to 'GZ curve'. The key parameters are the value of the maximum GZ and the angle at which it occurs. Initially, the range of stability up to the angle at which GZ becomes zero was thought to be important but later it was recognised that this was unrealistic. The angle at which large openings such as boiler room inlets went under, the 'down flooding angle', was a more realistic limit.

The GZ curve and associated calculations can only be an approximation to reality because, for one thing, it assumes the water surface is flat and horizontal – no waves. However, over a century's experience has shown that it is a good approximation.[4]

Stability after Damage

This case is much more complicated than that for an intact ship. For a start, there are numerous types of damage: small holes (splinters, cannon shell) over a considerable length, one big hole (contact torpedo – 30ft x 15ft), or splits from a non-contact explosion. In any of these cases flooding could spread through damaged bulkheads or systems such as ventilation that were not fully tight. Early welded structures with unsuitable materials and poor procedures were more likely to serious failure under explosive loading than riveted structures, but by the end of the Second World War these problems had been overcome and welded structures were seen as far stronger.

The intact portion of a damaged ship would be unsymmetrical and the ship would have large angles of both heel and trim. This lack of symmetry meant that many of the short cuts that made calculations feasible for the intact ship could not be used, and the complexity of direct calculation for a damaged ship made it almost impossible.[5] It was customary to consider only flooding amidships so that trim could be neglected, and usually only two compartments flooded. This ignored the loss of stability when trim brought the quarterdeck under water, a contributory cause of numerous losses. A few examples of severe flooding were included in the Ship's Book.[6]

There were few cases of extensive flooding to study. If the ship sank, it would not usually be possible to record the true extent of flooding. Even for ships that survived, repair was the first consideration and detailed records were rare.[7] However, by the end of the Second World War there were a considerable number of well founded guidelines of 'Do's and Don'ts'.

Post-war Criteria

In the early post-war years there were no formal stability criteria, but the subject was taken very seriously, each case being considered on its merits. Senior constructor officers had experience of war, many had served at sea in uniform, and they knew all too well that damage in war is frequent. They also recognised that sinking from loss of stability following damage in ships of destroyer or frigate size was fairly rare, particularly among the more modern ships, showing that pre-war judgement was not far out.

Almost alone amongst major navies the RN had lost no undamaged warships from poor stability and bad weather.

Some cases were re-examined. The author re-worked both stability and strength calculations for *Kelly* after damage. Probability theory was badly taught (and it still is) but began to influence thinking, particularly on the extent of damage and the spacing of bulkheads. The Type 82 design team (led by Eric Tupper) saw the need for more rigorous standards and adopted the US 'Sarchin and Goldberg' criteria. The Type 21 frigate was designed by contract and it was essential to have formal standards in the contract.

Stability Standards

It was decided to introduce the USN standards[8] that derived from the investigations into the loss of three USN destroyers in the typhoon of December 1944.[9] Technically, this tragedy went far to justifying the conventional GZ curve. The three ships which were lost had the poorest characteristics; the next poorest were in grave danger, whilst those which had good GZ curves were not in serious danger, though even in some of these the motions caused numerous injuries.

The USN inquiry placed the blame primarily on the admiral for requiring a course and speed inappropriate for small ships in such a storm. The direct cause of loss was a combination of wind pressure that forced the destroyers over to a large angle together with rolling in waves through large angles either side of the steady wind heel. This combination brought the boiler room intakes into the water and flooding began. To make matters worse, the main switchboard was below the intakes and shorted, causing loss of steering.

The new rules required a calculation of the wind force on exposed topsides to be equated to the righting force represented by the GZ curve with enough margin to allow for rolling. This wind-loading criterion was most demand-

[4] The Great Pacific Typhoon of 1944 which caused the loss of three USN destroyers and the subsequent investigations showed the value of the traditional GZ curve whilst leading to better methods of using the information. See C R Calhoun, *Typhoon – The Other Enemy* (Annapolis 1981).

[5] The author did carry out calculations with trim for the 'Tribal' class (Chapter 5). Even for this very simple ship it took 3 months, but did show the need for a extra bulkhead and more freeboard aft.

[6] This was a compendium of important instructions carried on board and is not to be confused with the Ship's Cover, held in the design section.

[7] During the post-war target trials it was usually forbidden to sink the ship, as its scrap steel was needed quickly.

[8] T H Sarchin and L L Goldberg, 'Stability and Buoyancy Criteria for USN Surface Ships', *Trans SNAME* (1962).

[9] D K Brown, 'The Great Pacific Typhoon', *The Naval Architect* (Sept 1985); and C R Calhoun, *Typhoon – The Other Enemy* (Annapolis 1981).

An extract from a Ship's Book showing the effect of flooding the engine room and boiler room of a *Whitby*. This limited damage reduces stability by about a third.
(*PRO ADM 239/431*)

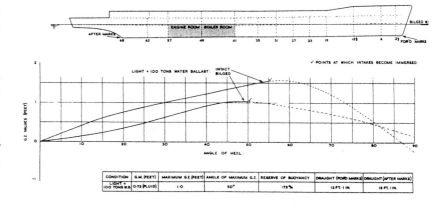

**STABILITY CURVES:
ENGINE ROOM AND BOILER ROOM BILGED**

Incident I

CONDITION	G.M. (FEET)	MAXIMUM G.Z. (FEET)	ANGLE OF MAXIMUM G.Z.	RESERVE OF BUOYANCY	DRAUGHT (FOR'D MARKS)	DRAUGHT (AFTER MARKS)
LIGHT + 100 TONS W.B.	0·72 (FLUID)	1·0	50°	173%	12 FT. 1 IN.	15 FT. 1 IN.

The wartime destroyer *Kelly* in dock after being torpedoed. Recalculations of her strength and stability after surviving such massive damage were fed into the post-war 'Tribal' class design. (*D K Brown collection*)

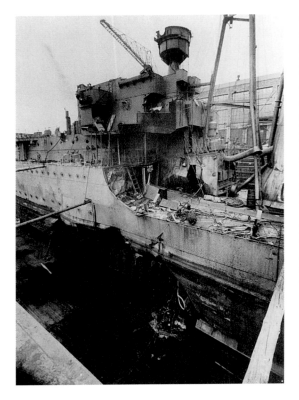

ing and many older ships in service failed to meet it. There were other rules concerning movement of weights and personnel.

It is essential to realise that stability standards are minimum values below which a ship in service must not fall. The standards are not just design aims, and must still be met after many years in service. A growth margin is included in the design for this reason.[10]

After the Falklands War Ship Department was asked to devise a simpler presentation of stability data for ships. They had a Stability Statement giving the results of the latest inclining, curves of stability to work out new conditions and a number of worked examples showing the effects of damage. Advice was taken from inside and outside the Ministry but it was concluded that there would only be a minor change – stability, particularly after damage, is not simple. The only change was to add an expiry date to the Stability Statement after which a new inclining was needed (see Appendix 4).

Power and Speed

For many years after the Second World War, the traditional Froude methods of estimating power and speed and selecting a hull form continued to give good service.[11] A provisional form would be selected from the Iso-K books, which summarised the results of all model tests ever carried out at AEW since 1872.[12] Almost always some changes were needed to suit the new design, such as a gen-

eral increase in beam, lengthening the cut-up, or local changes to accommodate the weapon stowages. It is important to realise that there is no one ideal form (see photograph on page 17). The form suits the role. A model would then be made in wax and tested at Haslar, which would then be modified to reduce its resistance. Such modifications depended on the powers of observation, and experience of the experimenter in charge, who would look for waves or turbulence generated by the model.[13] Typically, one would expect a reduction of about 5 per cent as a result with the saving in fuel, more than paying for the cost of testing. The most useful data for early nuclear submarines came from a Royal Aircraft Establishment report of 1923 on airship form. (see Chapter 9).

The diameter, pitch and rotational speed of the propeller would be selected from the tabulated data of tests carried out in the late 1930s with large, 20in diameter, models. Even when advanced design methods were introduced for quietness, this data proved very useful in providing a starting point. Other model tests measured the interaction between hull and propeller – the flow round the hull upset the inflow to the propeller, whilst the suction of the propeller altered the flow round the aft end of the hull.

Tabulated and plotted data were incorporated in computer databases. In general, only the more recent forms, suitable for modern roles, were fed into the database, but the old data was available if needed and it was easy to create a trend curve appropriate to a particular vessel.

Ship tanks are very versatile and there were many tests and trials of which only a few proved useful. One of the most valuable was that of transom flaps, based on the success in the 'Gay' class but neglected for many years, since on resistance alone the slight benefit at top speed was offset by a penalty at lower speeds. Eventually it was shown that there was an improvement in propeller performance at all speeds, leading to an increase in speed of 1.5kts when tried on a Type 21 (*Avenger*). It was shown by model tests and a full-scale trial that the introduction of long chain molecules (polyethylene oxide) at about 30 parts per million would reduce viscous resistance by about 30 per cent. Air lubrication was tried, but without success. (Propeller development is covered under Stealth in Chapter 13.)

For most of the period AEW had a dedicated trials section who would fit the required instrumentation,[14] carry out the trial and pass the data back for analysis. Model testing is not exact and a correction based on previous ship-model correlation remains essential.

Seakeeping

'There are three things too wonderful for me ...
The Way of a Ship in the midst of the Sea' –
Proverbs

By the end of the war it was recognised that the next generation of escorts – 1945 sloop merging into the *Whitby*

10 Knowledge that there is a margin for growth may encourage its profligate use.

11 Confirmed by towing trials with *Penelope*, discussed under Stealth in the next chapter.

12 Had the Germans invaded in 1940, DNC gave the highest priority to getting these books to Canada.

13 The experimenter would usually be a senior draughtsman (PTO II), often with four years in the Dockyard Technical College behind him, regarded as pass degree standard.

14 Accurate thrust and torque meters (not easy), rev counters etc. The trials section also had a deep knowledge of cheap and comfortable hotels near trials sites which would serve meals at odd hours.

Coventry off the Falklands: hit by three bombs flooding five main compartments, she could not survive. The calculation of the effects of massive, asymmetric flooding could not be handled in design without a capable computer. (*D K Brown collection*)

– would need be able to maintain speed in rough weather in pursuit of fast submarines. The final configuration of the *Whitby* class was proposed by Neville G Holt, drawing on his experience as a yachtsman and sea-time as Constructor Captain during the war, and developed by R W L Gawn at AEW.[15] It featured fine waterlines forward, a high freeboard forward (carried aft), and a reduced moment of inertia by concentrating weights (armament, engines) close to amidships. This design soon won a high reputation throughout NATO for seakeeping and even with more recent theoretical understanding of seakeeping has proved hard to beat.[16]

Modern understanding of the motions of a ship is based on 'strip theory' in which the forces acting on transverse slices of the ship in a random sea are integrated along the length.[17] The general conclusions have been verified by trials on ships, notably one in which a *Leander* (*Hermione*) and a 'Tribal' (*Ghurka*) were driven at high speed (22kts) through very severe seas.[18] It was found that theory estimated pitch and heave quite accurately; occurrence of green seas over the deck was less well forecast, as the interaction between ship and wave was not properly represented (this has since been improved but is still a problem). It took many more years before rolling behaviour could be computed accurately.[19]

The well-established theory has made it possible to show the effect of varying the dimensions on ship motions. Pitch and heave are dominated by length, but longer ships are more highly stressed and there is a practical limit to length. Freeboard is roughly dependent on length – at the end of the war freeboard was taken as $1.1\sqrt{L}$ ft. In later ships $1.3\sqrt{L}$ has been used as a guideline. Slamming is a complex problem but the starting point is adequate draught.

Perhaps the biggest problem in seakeeping is to decide what levels of motion are desirable and how much it is worth paying for improvement: neither is easy. Helicopter operation is of major importance in ASW and for

No 1 ship tank at Haslar, built in 1887 but with a new carriage installed in 1960. All British surface warship hull forms for both world wars and up to the early 1990s were developed and tested here. It was drained in November 1993 and is now an office. (*D K Brown collection*)

frigates is usually limited by the vertical velocity at the landing spot; but in the smaller *Leeds Castle* it was found that landing was limited by roll angle. This illustrates a general point, that limits are almost always multiple – eliminate one problem and the next is not far behind. If vertical velocity is eliminated (a rock such as Rockall!), helicopter operation would be limited by wind speed, a point often neglected by over-enthusiasts for SWATH. Helicopter operation from frigates can be improved by making the ships longer or by moving the helicopter deck closer to amidships where motions are less.

Reduced operational capability in bad weather is largely due to human failings. Seasickness (and probably poor decision-making) is mainly associated with vertical acceleration exceeding 0.8m/sec^2 in the frequency range 0.15 – 0.3 Hz, though other aspects, even smell, can con-

[15] Known as 'Dickie' Gawn – but not to his face.

[16] Naval architects distinguish between 'seakeeping', the motions of a vessel in rough seas, and 'seaworthiness', which brings in practical factors such as the watertightness of doors and hatches, the strength of structure exposed to the impact of green seas, safe access, etc. Both are important.

[17] Much of this chapter is based on a state-of-the-art survey: D K Brown and E C Tupper, 'The Naval Architecture of Surface Warships', *Trans RINA* (1988). For those wishing to dig deeper into the technology, there is a lengthy discussion with 63 references to key papers. Only a few of the more easily understood of these references are repeated here. The authors received the Institution's Silver Medal for this paper.

[18] R N Andrew and A R J M Lloyd, 'Full Scale Comparative Measurement of the Behaviour of Two Frigates in Severe Head Seas', *Trans RINA* (1981).

[19] William Froude established the basic theory in 1860 but it is still difficult to solve the equations for real cases. See D C Stredulinsky, N G Pegg and L E Gilroy, 'Motion and Wave Prediction and Measurements on HMCS *Nipigon*', *Trans RINA* (2000), p248 for an up-to-date comparison of estimates and measurements.

[20] The author at sea in *Cygnet* in rough weather felt fine until his stopwatch revealed motions at 0.18 Hz when he knew he should feel ill!

[21] D K Brown and P D Marshall, 'Small Warships in the RN and the Fishery Protection Task', *RINA Symposium* (March 1978). See also: D K Brown, 'Service Experience with the Castle Class', *Naval Architect* (Sept 1983). Our ideas worked!

[22] The 'Castles' had very deep bilge keels and fins. During the Falklands War both ships lost their fins and no one even noticed. See: K Monk, 'A Warship Roll Criterion', *Trans RINA* (1987).

[23] D K Brown, 'The value of reducing ship motions', *Naval Engineers Journal*, ASNE Washington (March 1985).

[24] The author's views are manifest in the photo of the 'Castle' (see page 178).

[25] D K Brown, 'Fast Warships and their Crews', RINA *Small Craft* (1984), pt 6. This generated much controversy among the Light Coastal Forces Association but Captain Peter Dickens gave me general support.

[26] This whole section is derived from: Dr D W Chalmers, *Design of Ships' Structures* (London 1993). This was originally written as an internal manual and it was my job to approve it for use. It was hard going but worth it. Dr Chalmers also revised the draft of this passage.

[27] W J M Rankine, *Shipbuilding – Theoretical and Practical* (London 1866).

tribute.[20] This was used in the design of the 'Castle' class, where the vertical acceleration was kept to an acceptable level in sea states averaged over the year.[21] Manual tasks are governed by transverse acceleration levels (Roll acceleration), and these can be controlled by large bilge keels or active fin systems.[22] More costly solutions lie in the SWATH or hydrofoil, the 'cost' often lying in limitations in other aspects, such as training, as well as financial.

A simple approach to the value of improved seakeeping has been published.[23] Annual Navy Estimates show that the cost of keeping one frigate at sea for a day is about £100,000 and all or part of this sum is wasted if capability is reduced by motions. This can be used to demonstrate the value of considerably longer frigates. Though this approach is crude, no one has come up with a better one.

Secondary factors in hull form individually have only a slight effect on motions, but the cumulative effect of getting them all right is significant. Flare and knuckles can affect wetness but their precise value is a matter for heated argument.[24] The effect of motions on the crew of fast attack craft is very severe.[25] Hydrofoils should be much more successful in the role.

The dimensions and form of a ship have to satisfy the requirements of both powering and seakeeping. Luckily it is very nearly true to say that seakeeping dominates the fore end and powering the aft end form.

Strength[26]

The concept of the structure of a ship acting as a hollow girder resisting the uneven forces of weight and buoyancy goes back at least as far as the beginning of the nineteenth century. Traditional, frame-built wooden ships were lacking in rigidity and liable to flex, leading to rapid decay from rot. Sir Robert Seppings (1811) introduced a system of diagonal framing that greatly improved rigidity and made it possible to build much bigger ships. Lang and Edye (Admiralty naval architects) adapted Seppings' work for the structure of Brunel's *Great Western*.

Overall, weight and buoyancy must be equal in any floating body but this conceals large differences at points along the ship. Local differences in weight and buoyancy lead to vertical forces in the structure (shearing force) and to bending along the length (bending moment). This approach was set out in principle by Rankine in 1866,[27]

Seakeeping – what it is all about. A Mark III Lynx on the flight deck of a destroyer in severe weather. Manhandling weapons in these conditions is very difficult and hazardous. (*Westland*)

and made into a usable design method by Reed and his assistant White.[28] Further refinements were introduced following Biles' experiments with *Wolf* after the loss of *Cobra*.[29]

In the years leading up to the Second World War, and for some time after, strength calculations were based on two situations. The ship was considered at rest, head-on to waves of the same length (L) as the ship and with a height of L/20. In the first case the ship was supported with a wave crest at each end reducing support amidships (Sagging). The other case was with a crest amidships and the ends drooping (Hogging). When the ship was sagging the bottom was in tension and the upper deck was compressed. In hogging the opposite was the case and the deck was in tension and the bottom compressed.

It was then possible to design structure to resist these loads. Tension loads were easy to deal with since all that was required was to keep the stress below a figure found safe from experience for that material.[30] Compressive loads were more difficult: there was no way of calculating the buckling strength of a panel of plating with stiffeners. An approximation was to consider a single stiffener with an appropriate width of plating as a strut. With experience, this worked quite well though the solutions were probably conservative (that is, heavier than necessary).

It was recognised that this whole approach was a crude representation of reality and, in particular, very long waves with a height of L/20 were rare. For this reason, nominal stresses in long ships were accepted at much higher values than in smaller vessels (for example, 9.8 t/in² deck in *Hood*

compared with 5-6 t/in² for a frigate). Since the overall approach was comparative, with previous successful ships as the basis, there was a proper reluctance to make significant changes. This conservative approach was largely justified by wartime experience when, despite the use of high speed in bad weather, there were no serious structural failures in undamaged ships, though minor leaks were too frequent. Many ships broke in half after underwater damage.

A major objective of the post-war Ship Target Trials programme was to understand the behaviour of structures under explosive loading, and hence to design ships better able to resist such attack. Preliminary analysis by E W Gardner indicated that thin plating with numerous, closely-spaced longitudinals was the way to go.[31] This also led to a lighter structure, and memories of pre-war limitation treaties still saw virtue in light weight *per se* while it was still believed that cost was directly proportional to weight rather than to complexity of systems.

In service, this type of structure proved expensive to build, prone to minor damage, and easily corroded. The *Leander*s, and even more the 'Tribals', walked back a little, with slightly fewer longitudinals and thicker plating – enthusiastic young men are often right, but overdo it. More thought was being given to fatigue strength where a metal exposed repeatedly to alternating stresses well below the maximum permissible level will eventually fail. Fatigue cracks in riveted structures would usually (not always) stop at the first seam. K J Rawson in his design of the 'Tribal' structure took the line that cracking of ordinary

The 'Tribal' *Gurkha* during a comparative trial with the *Leander* class *Hermione* in 1978. This trial verified most of the computer estimates of the time as regards motions. However, it did show that the effect of slamming meant that stress quite well forward of amidships was higher than expected from earlier theories. (*D K Brown collection*)

[28] E J Reed, 'On the Unequal Distribution of Weight and Support in Ships and its effect in Still Water, Waves', *Phil Trans Royal Society* (London 1866).

[29] D K Brown, *Warrior to Dreadnought*, p185

[30] Stress is load per unit area. It is not the same as strain, extension per unit length.

[31] D K Brown, *A Century of Naval Construction*, p203.

The hull forms of early post-war frigates were based on W J Holt's experience as a yachtsman, developed by model tests by Gawn at AEW, Haslar. They proved hard to beat, even with modern theory. This pair of model and ship photos (*Leander* herself above) shows that model performance does accurately represent that of the full-size vessel – only the size of the spray droplets is different. (*D K Brown collection*)

steel, assembled under shipyard conditions, was inevitable but, by keeping the stresses low, such cracks would not spread. He was proved right: examination of a 'Tribal' near the end of a long life showed numerous small cracks, none of which had spread.

Ken Rawson also introduced the use of an American method, credited to Schade, of calculating the overall strength of a 'grillage', a panel of plate with stiffeners running in both directions. Schade's method was only approximate and soon superseded by more accurate calculations, but it was a big advance on anything that had gone before – junior constructors were made to analyse old failures using the new method to prove its value.

Another advance in the 'Tribals' was their flush upper deck. Stresses in a hull increase considerably at a discontinuity – to break a strong stick, it helps to cut a notch. Several wartime classes, like the *Southampton*s and the previous 'Tribals', had suffered cracking at the break of forecastle, and the *Daring*s had a massive reinforcement in this area, as did the *Blackwood*s. Rawson was able to show that the weight of such reinforcement was greater than that of extending the forecastle deck to the stern.

Several leading academics were pointing out that the behaviour of a ship in waves was dynamic and that the old static approach should be dropped. This seemed possible, since the development of seakeeping theory combined with the use of big computers had led to the 'Strip

Theory'. The hydrodynamic forces on each longitudinal section (strip) of the ship could be integrated as it passed through representative sea states. This was a valid approach and was used successfully for moderate sea states, but it was hard to apply and mistakes were easy to make. It was possible to consider the flexibility of the hull, important in slamming loads. However, it was not possible fully to represent the above water part of the ship, and the calculation failed as the deck went under.

Another number-crunching computer program was 'Finite Element Analysis'. This split the structure into a very large number of elements and calculated the interactions between them when the structure is loaded. This tool is essential for heavily loaded or complicated structures, but input of data is a lengthy task, not to be undertaken unless it is needed.[32]

As mentioned above, comparative trials had been carried out in severe sea states between a *Leander* and a 'Tribal' class frigate, to assess the effect of hull shape on wave loading.[33] The structural aspects of the trial were later reported by Clarke[34] and in particular the effect of slamming. The 'Tribal' class were designed with closely-spaced transverse frames forward which it was hoped would resist slamming loads. Unfortunately, it was not then known that the peak slamming pressures occurred further aft in the hull form adopted, and some further stiffening was needed. The maximum stress amidships was in fair agreement with theory but did not decrease as rapidly towards the bow as expected. A number of ships have been fitted with recorders to measure how often different levels of strain were exceeded during years at sea. This enabled a reasonable prediction to be made of the maximum stress likely to be reached in a 20-25 year life.

This data provided a sound basis for a simple design method not very different from the old Rankine method. This time the wave height to be used for all ships is 8m regardless of the size of the ship.[35] It has been calculated that there is a 1.5 per cent chance of exceeding this loading in 10^7 wave encounters – roughly 22 years service with 30 per cent of the time in 'average' North Atlantic weather.

Structural design had come to be seen as 'easy' and new management systems encouraged progress charts to be ticked as complete under 'structure' without real checking. There were a number of problems, some potentially serious: the Type 21 and Batch I and III Type 42s needed stiffening, clearly visible in photos. However, this was not confined to the RN. The French *Tourville*, the Soviet *Sovremennyy*[36] and the US FFG-7 classes all show signs of stiffening in service. An Information Exchange Project (IEP) was set up between the UK, USA, Australia and Canada on structural design. The first meeting was embarrassing as we each confessed our structural sins. More careful quality control has, it is hoped, largely eliminated such problems in design, though fabrication remains a problem.

Most of these problems arose from discontinuities or sharp corners, which multiply the stress locally.[37] Prob-

[32] There is a risk that it takes so long that the answer comes too late to be used.

[33] R N Andrew and A R J M Lloyd, 'Full Scale Comparative Measurement of the Behaviour of Two Frigates In Severe Head Seas', *Trans RINA* (1981).

[34] J D Clarke, 'Measurement of Hull Stresses in Two Frigates during a Severe Weather Trial', *Trans RINA* (1982), pp63-83.

[35] J D Clarke, 'Wave Loading in Warships', in C S Smith and J D Clarke (eds), *Advances in Marine Structures* (Dunfermline 1986).

[36] At the 1993 Merseyside Review, the Russian destroyer *Gremyaschiy* showed a newly-fitted, riveted doubler at the break of forecastle.

[33] R N Andrew and A R J M Lloyd, 'Full Scale Comparative Measurement of the Behaviour of Two Frigates In Severe Head Seas', *Trans RINA* (1981).

[34] J D Clarke, 'Measurement of Hull Stresses in Two Frigates during a Severe Weather Trial', *Trans RINA* (1982), pp63-83.

[35] J D Clarke, 'Wave Loading in Warships', in C S Smith and J D Clarke (eds), *Advances in Marine Structures* (Dunfermline 1986).

[36] At the 1993 Merseyside Review, the Russian destroyer *Gremyaschiy* showed a newly-fitted, riveted doubler at the break of forecastle.

[37] Years ago, one Chief, inspecting structural drawings, would start flapping his arms saying 'I'm a stress. How do I get from A to B?' A modern structural designer commended this approach but would have said strain rather than stress. The RN College lecture notes drew attention to this problem from at least 1913.

lems at the break of forecastle have already been mentioned, but there are similar problems at the end of superstructure blocks. Such blocks are often made short in the hope that they will not carry load, a hope which is often misplaced. A rigid superstructure will not flex with the hull and may tear away from the deck at the ends. The best solution is to arrange the superstructure ends on main transverse bulkheads that will accept the load and distribute it, but this is not always possible or is forgotten.

As a means of eliminating the superstructure-end stresses an approach which was actively pursued by the IEP team was the use of GRP superstructures. Because this material is much less stiff than steel it cannot impose strains on the deck. Tests have gone well and most problems overcome. The problems of GRP design had been overcome in the design of the 'Hunt' class (see Chapter 10).

This account has been confined to the overall strength of the ship, but there are many other problems which, though of detail, are important and difficult. Perhaps the most important of these is bulkhead design to resist underwater explosions without leaking round the boundary. It is probably too much to say that this problem has been solved but it has been greatly reduced. There are also problems of wave impact, of vibration and many others.

Structural design is not easy, but common sense guided by theory, together with a good eye for discontinuities and sharp corners, will work wonders and should give warships 25 years of relatively trouble-free life.

The Canadian frigate *Margaree* in heavy seas. This class was designed by (Sir) Rowland Baker, who believed that it was inevitable that green seas would come on board and fitted a turtleback forecastle to get rid of water quickly. No evidence was found to support his view and turtlebacks were not repeated. (*D K Brown collection*)

Above: Edinburgh, a Batch III Type 42, showing the strengthening along the deck edge.
(*Mike Lennon*)

Right: The large test frame at NCRE, Rosyth, with a prototype GRP minesweeper hull inside. Note the size of the men.
(*D K Brown collection*)

[38] The external loading section of the British Pressure Vessel Standard (BS5500) is based on RN submarine design practice <u>not</u> the other way round.

[39] Many submarine COs would take their boat some 10 per cent below the nominal diving depth to give confidence. This practice was well known and allowed for in the design and in the recommended operational depth.

Submarine Pressure Hull Design

Submarine hulls have to resist water pressure at the maximum depth to which the submarine may descend, with a very small factor of safety, usually 1.5.[38] This factor has to take into account inaccuracies in the theory, imperfections in building, etc, as well as allowing for accidental excursions below the intended depth. Normal engineering practice with a low factor of safety would involve a proof test to about 1.2-1.3 times design pressure, but the risk to a submarine is thought too great.[39]

Prior to the war, the only guide to strength for British designers was the 'boiler formula' – Stress = Pressure x Radius/ Plating thickness. This was used in comparison with figures for submarines that had inadvertently dived well past their operational depth. This simple formula is surprisingly accurate for plating strength (yield between frames) and is insensitive to errors in shape, but assumes the frames are strong enough. Since there was no way of calculating frame strength, these were selected in very conservative – heavy – fashion.

The diagram opposite shows the possible modes of failure for a pressure hull. Overall collapse due to instability involving a whole compartment is more dangerous, harder to estimate and very sensitive to errors in shape – out of circularity – and is usually associated with inadequate frames. Early theoretical work was used in the *Porpoise* class, which used a few deep frames at intervals with smaller frames between. The *Oberon*s had an improved design, with special T-bars of uniform size. The aim was to ensure that frame yield would not occur until twice the design pressure, even with the maximum shape error. This led to study of fabrication methods to ensure minimum practical out-of-circularity.

There is also a failure mode in which the plating between frames buckles in a large number of nodes. This is unlikely under static loading but can occur under explosive attack.

Few submarines are truly cylindrical, and even these have end bulkheads that pose a problem both in themselves and in their intersection with the cylindrical hull, with these problems acerbated by penetrations for torpedo tubes, etc. Many SSN have conical sections increasing the difficulties of calculation.

Much of the development work involved tests on large structural models. These had to be very carefully made, simulating to scale the out of circularity of real submarines. It was not possible to represent weld characteristics exactly but it was believed that any errors were on the safe side.

Fatigue failures occur when a structure is loaded alternately in compression and tension. Since a submarine hull is always in compression it might be thought that fatigue could be forgotten; but this is not so – the contraction of welds as they cool leads to locked-in tensile stresses which, when compressed, can lead to fatigue failure, particularly at changes in hull diameter and at penetrations. All these problems have been explored and solutions found, largely by S B (Bill) Kendrick and his staff at NCRE (USN designers use his work too).

A submarine model under test at Haslar. This later method of measuring forces and moments used the Planar motion Mechanism, seen here on the back of the carriage of No 2 ship tank. The model could be oscillated 'bow up – bow down' while readings were taken which could be fed into computer simulations of manoeuvres. (*MoD*)

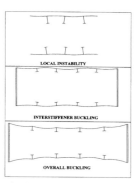

The diagram shows three ways in which a submarine pressure hull can collapse under pressure. Buckling between stiffeners is the easiest to calculate and the only one that could be designed for until after the war. Overall collapse was solved by work at NCRE leading to hulls which were both lighter and stronger. Local instability is unlikely under normal loading but common after explosive attack.

Left: A wartime X-craft midget demonstrates local instability with dimples in the plating between frames, caused in this case by an underwater explosion. (*MoD*)

13 Other Technologies

[1] I prefer the term 'battleworthy', parallel to 'seaworthy', and also a term used by the RAF of aircraft. More recently, a third sub-title has been added: 'recoverability' – the ability to repair damage.

[2] E P Lover, 'Cavitation Tunnel Testing for the RN', Newcastle University Conference 1979; and D K Brown, 'Stealth and *Savage*', *Warship* 32 (1984).

[3] This is similar to the wingtip vortices from aircraft, and to the vortex formed when bath water is running away.

[4] More detail is given on these tests and the way in which trials were carried out using windows in the bottom in D K Brown, 'Stealth and *Savage*', *Warship* 32 (1984).

[5] Theory predicted failure of one very thin design, so it was made and tried, and it did break!

MUCH OF THIS CHAPTER is devoted to the defence of the ship, not only from the enemy but also from corrosion and marine life forms. The defence of a ship against enemy attack forms a multi-layered system. It begins with pre-emptive strikes against enemy bases, followed by destruction of launching vehicles (aircraft, submarines) before they can launch, and then either destruction of incoming weapons or decoying them away from the target. It is impossible to make a ship invisible to the wide range of sensors available but reducing signatures makes the enemy's task more difficult and enhances the effectiveness of decoys. Some missiles will always get through, calling for passive defence measures. In the RN Survivability is divided into:

Susceptibility – The avoidance of weapons using stealth, decoys and hard kill.
Vulnerability – Resistance to damage and damage control.[1]

Stealth [2]

The introduction of the acoustic mine and, later, of the acoustic torpedo by the US in 1943, placed a new emphasis on making ships quieter, further emphasised as passive sonars were developed. The main noise sources are:

Speed	Source	Frequency	Notes
Low	Machinery	Low	Easily identified
Medium	Propeller cavitation	High	Broad band
High	Flow turbulence	High	Broad band

Machinery Noise
Machinery noise will usually occur at discrete frequencies, corresponding to rotational speed or reciprocating rate, and this makes it easy to identify ship types and classes. The first step is to balance rotating machines so that noise at the rate of shaft rotation is much reduced, and the machine is then clad with absorbent material or placed in an insulating box. The machine and its box are further supported on flexible mounts to isolate them from the hull and hence the sea. It may prove easier to mount several machines on a 'raft' which is then itself flexibly mounted. Great care is needed to ensure that there are no 'shorts' conducting sound direct to the sea, as for example through cooling water pipes (not forgetting the cooling water itself). Inspection forms a major element in the cost of noise reduction.

The machinery spaces can also be screened by a cloud of air bubbles emitted from ducts round the hull ('Masker'). Successful trials of bubble screening were carried out in 1917, but were not followed up in the mistaken view that noise reduction was unnecessary in ships using active sonar (asdic).

Propeller Cavitation
The boiling point of water falls as pressure is reduced and at very low pressures water will boil at normal sea water temperatures. A propeller blade generates thrust from pressure on the face (rear side) and from suction on the back (forward side), and this suction can cause the water to boil or 'cavitate' – a word coined by Sir Charles Parsons when the phenomenon proved troublesome in *Turbinia*. In Second World War destroyers cavitation would lead to a loss of thrust and efficiency from the mid-20kts upward with a reduction in top speed of about 1kt. The bubbles of water vapour so formed would collapse with violence (up to 100 tons/in^2) and dig deep pits in the hard bronze propeller – up to 0.5in deep in a few hours at full speed. It came as a surprise to find that cavitation led to noise at speeds as low as 8kts from a wartime propeller in good condition and lower still if damaged. However, around 1950 scientists at Portland put glass windows in the bottom of the frigate *Helmsdale* and there was cavitation clear to see. At the tip of the blade water will spill over from the pressure side to the suction side, causing a vortex that has very low pressure at the centre, also causing cavitation and hence noise.[3]

At first it was thought that reducing the rotational speed (rpm) and increasing the blade area would increase the speed at which cavitation started. Nine sets of model propellers for the *Diamond* were tested at AEW Haslar of which two were tried full scale on the ship, while seven models and six full scale tests were tried for *Savage*.[4] No improvement was obtained.

The next step was to build on the theoretical work of Dr Lerbs at Haslar. The radial distribution of thrust over the propeller was reduced towards the tip to decrease the strength of the vortex. Each section was pitched to allow the water to flow onto the blade at very small angles of incidence and the thin blade sections were curved (cambered) to generate thrust. There were many problems, not the least of them being the 3 weeks of tiresome arithmetic to carry out the design (and 5 months for a skilled craftsman to make the model). The theory was incomplete and empirical corrections ('fudge factors') had to be devised. The strength of these complex, thin blades was uncertain until John Conolly devised a new approach, and proved it with full-scale strain measurements on a propeller working in the sea – very difficult with the equipment of the day.[5]

Eventually, a Lerbs propeller was made and tried (Set J). It was very promising with a 0.75kt improvement in quiet speed, but the thrust produced was not what was intended and it was about 5 per cent down in efficiency. It had a blade area 1.1 times the area of a circle of the same diameter, the blades overlapping considerably.[6] Fourteen models were tested, making variations on pitch, camber and blade area, and five were tried full-size on *Savage*. By the time the author joined, the team were fairly confident of how to deal with cavitation on the back and face of the blade. Theory suggested that the problem of tip vortex cavitation could be reduced by increasing the number of blades, so five-, seven-, nine- and eleven-bladed models were tried. The law of diminishing returns set in with eleven blades but five blades gave considerable benefit over three on the model. This gain was not fully repeated at full scale, but the reduction in vibration with five blades made it worthwhile, and most surface warships since have had five blades.[7] (In single-screw ships the flow pattern is usually better suited to four blades.)

By 1957 some fourteen models designed by Arthur Honnor were tested, leading to a five-bladed propeller for *Whitby*. Trials were very successful: quiet speed was nearly double that of wartime propellers, efficiency was at least as good and vibration was negligible.[8] This became the first production design, but the same approach was used for other classes and soon all the RN surface fleet had quiet propellers – 10 years ahead of any other navy. There were teething troubles but these were overcome. Viewing trials became part of the 'first of class programme' for each new class.

Once there was confidence in reading across from model to ship the designers started making *ad hoc* changes to the model – 'Joe, file a bit off where the bubbles start' – and transfer the optimum shape to full scale. In the

In a viewing trial the propeller was observed through glass windows in the bottom of the ship. These were usually under the steering gear, and the position was cramped and very uncomfortable, particularly if the ship was pitching. The propeller was made to appear stationary by using stroboscopic lighting.
(*D K Brown collection*)

author's view, this was real engineering, taking the best available theory as far as it would go, building on this from scientific testing, then empirical corrections based on tests and trials, file a bit off and another successful design is complete.

Much of this development read across to submarines even though the problem was different (*Scotsman* was the main trials ship in the early days). At depth, the sea pressure is too great for cavitation, but the changes in flow as each propeller blade passes through wake shadows behind fins, etc generate low frequency pressure pulses at 'blade rate' (rpm x number of blades), which can be heard at long distances. The understanding of design theory from the *Savage* series has enabled this, too, to be moderated, usually with a larger number of blades, heavily skewed (see Chapter 9 for the pump jet).

Air bubble screening was originally seen as an alternative to quiet propellers. The first attempt was called 'Nightshirt' and consisted of a spider's web of small pipes ahead of the propeller from which air could be blown. It caused a considerable drop in efficiency, about 1.5kts loss of speed, and usually vibrated itself apart very quickly. The second version, 'Agouti', was far more successful. Air was passed down the propeller shaft and out through ducts cut in the leading edge of the blades into the sea through a series of small holes. This had no effect on efficiency and was effective in reducing noise, particularly at higher speeds when cavitation could not be prevented. The mechanical complexity, particularly with controllable-pitch propellers was considerable!

For some time 'Agouti' and quiet propellers were seen as rivals, but the trials in *Penelope* in 1970 showed they were complementary and both were needed. A modern noise-reduced propeller (Type 23 'Duke' class) is displayed in the National Maritime Museum.

The Type 14 *Hardy* burning after an Exocet hit during weapon trials. She was also hit by a Sea Skua ASM, a Mark VIII torpedo, and numerous shells, before being sunk by AS mortar projectiles. The amount of damage she withstood before sinking was remarkable, but she was out of action after the first hit. (*D K Brown collection*)

[6] Some people thought its success was solely due to its area and a conventional propeller of the same area was made, tried and failed.

[7] As far as I know, the different effect of number of blades in model and ship has not been explained, but I devised a large empirical correction to allow for it which is still in use.

[8] I was trials officer and was taken down for a cup of cocoa in the stokers' mess – it was the first time that a cup would stand on a mess table without vibrating off!

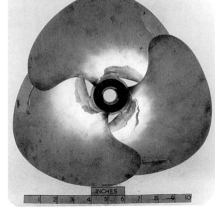

Top right: Savage Set J.
(*D K Brown collection*)

Above: A selection of propeller models tested during the early development of quiet propellers. The three-bladed model in the centre is *Savage* Set R, the first success. The five-bladed model, centre left, is typical of surface ship designs for many years.
(*D K Brown collection*)

Right: The larger, No 2 cavitation tunnel at Haslar enabled more realistic tests to be carried out. This destroyer model, seen from below, has a typical wartime propeller on the port (lower) shaft and a more modern 'quiet' design on the starboard shaft. The newer design has only very faint traces of cavitation compared with the older model.
(*D K Brown collection*)

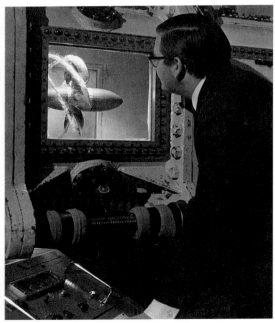

Flow Noise and the Penelope Trial

At speeds above about 20kts the main noise source is turbulence in the water flow over the hull itself. To investigate this noise source the frigate *Penelope* was towed behind the *Scylla* at speeds of up to 22.9kts during 1970.[9] *Penelope*'s machinery was shut down (with the exception of one small generator, elaborately mounted, on the quarterdeck to work the steering) and her propellers were removed. The towrope was 6000ft long, but stretched a further 25 per cent under load, so that *Scylla*'s noise and flow would not interfere.[10]

The noise levels recorded from *Penelope* represent the lowest-possible level for a conventional surface ship and the most recent ships are nearly there. Resistance meas-

A conventional cavitation test on a five-bladed propeller driven from behind. The flow is from right to left along the shaft axis and uniform over the propeller swept disk. Though not entirely realistic, such tests are fairly quick to set up, enabling development to advance rapidly.
(*D K Brown collection*)

urements were also taken in confirmation of William Froude's trials with *Greyhound* in 1872. Finally, a very detailed survey was made of the flow through the propeller position, measuring both velocity and direction of the flow at each point.

Above Water Signatures

Much can be done to reduce the radar signature of a

[9] H J S Canham, 'Resistance, propulsion and wake tests with *Penelope*', *Trans RINA* (1975).

[10] Those most involved were given a 1ft length of the rope – mine is still in use as a doorstop as I write.

Left: Penelope was used for a number of propeller trials and, as shown here, was towed at 23kts by *Scylla* to measure the noise generated by the flow over the hull.
(*D K Brown collection*)

Below: Much was learnt from post-war ship target trials, particularly with respect to underwater explosions breaking the back of the ship, as seen here with *Scorpion*.
(*D K Brown collection*)

11 It is said that one specification read that 'all right angles must be more than 93° or less than 87°'.

12 P Sims and J S Webster, 'Tumblehome Warships', *Trans SNAME 1977*.

13 D K Brown, 'The Battleworthy Frigate'. NECI, Newcastle 1990. This paper was used as lecture notes for naval constructors at University College, London until 2000.

14 Old damage control school motto.

15 Most of those that were not damaged had only just arrived when the fighting stopped.

16 It has been said that a point defence missile system is intended to defend a point that would not need defending if the system were not there.

17 G A Ransome, 'RN accidents and losses since 1945', *Warship Supplement* 91, 92 and 93 (1987-88), World Ship Society.

18 There was very considerable scatter in examples considered; figures quoted are 50 per cent probability.

19 Damage extent varies roughly with the square root of the charge size.

ship by shaping the above water parts. Re-entrant corners must be avoided[11] and the hull sides sloped. If the sides are sloped outwards to the deck edge (flare), as in the Type 23 class, stability will be improved if the ship sinks deeper in the water. Sloping the other way (tumblehome) has a very bad effect on stability.[12] Further reduction can be obtained by using radar absorbent material.

Infra-red signatures can be reduced by cooling the hot exhaust gases and by the use of low-emissivity paint. Neither of these measures will make 4000 tons of hot steel invisible but the reduction of the signatures makes decoys much more effective. (See 'Hunt' class, in Chapter 10, for magnetic and pressure signatures.)

Battleworthiness[13]

'To float, to move, to fight.'[14]

Admiral of the Fleet Lord Chatfield said that 'Ships are built to fight, and must be able to take blows as well as to deliver them'. In each of the opening years of the Second World War there were almost as many incidents of damage to destroyers as there were such ships in commission, while in the Falklands War 60 per cent of frigates were damaged.[15] Even in peacetime warships are more prone to accidental damage than are merchant ships.

The first line is active defence, *ie* pre-emptive strikes on enemy bases, destroying the attacking vehicle before it can launch or killing the missile in flight. It has often been argued that the consequence of a hit from a modern weapon is so serious that all funds should go to active defence. However, some weapons will always get through, and attention must be paid to passive defence, minimising the effect of a hit; but the balance between active and passive defence is not easy to draw and nor is the balance between defence and other functions.[16]

The threat can be divided into three headings – accident, terrorism and enemy attack. Accident covers fire and explosion (98 major incidents), collision (125) and groundings (50) – figures in brackets are RN incidents from 1945 to 1984.[17] Terrorist attacks have been few, but the potential threat remains, as shown by the attack on the USS *Cole* in Yemen in 2000. There is a bewildering array of weapons which can be used against warships, but their effects can be considered under six headings: – Fire, Flood, Structural collapse, Shock, Blast, Impact (splinters etc).

Non-contact underwater explosions such as those from ground mines and torpedoes cause violent and rapid flexing of the hull, which leads to buckling and collapse of the hull girder, the most common cause of loss amongst Second World War destroyers. There is no certain protection but some things can help. Discontinuities in primary structure, such as a break of forecastle, must be avoided. Overall design stresses should be kept low, mainly by increasing the depth, keel to deck. Shaft glands at bulk-

heads should be flexible, allowing considerable relative movement between shaft and structure. The lethal radius of these weapons is fairly small and the measures outlined make the enemy's task more difficult. Contact torpedoes and mines still pose a threat (as in the 1991 Gulf War) – a Second World War torpedo will, typically,[18] make a hole 30ft long by 15ft high, rendering structure non-watertight over double that distance.[19]

The shock from such explosions will cause violent movements of equipment, which may break. Cast iron should be avoided, as should overhanging (cantilevered) weights. Flexible mounts have been devised which attenuate the shock considerably. These have been very successful and shock damage has been rare – this immunity leads to proposals to abolish shock protection, the very factor that made such damage rare! One ship of each new class is subjected to high shock loads to confirm the effectiveness of the treatment.

Underwater weapons will almost certainly cause flooding which can sink the ship (usually by capsize) or immobilise it by flooding machinery spaces. A typical RN frigate should survive with any three compartments flooded, four with a little luck (in the Falklands War *Coventry* had five compartments flooded and stood no chance). The machinery spaces can also be attacked by air-flight weapons and a good defence is provided by the so-called unit system, introduced to the RN in the 'E' class cruisers of the First World War. The simplest style for a steam ship is alternating spaces – boiler-room, engine-room, boiler-room, engine-room – arranged so that either boiler-room can work either engine-room, so if one space of each kind survives the ship can move. COGOG ships can be given similar capability. An early computer study gave the following results.

Arrangement	% probability of loss of mobility from one hit
One unit, 2 spaces (boiler-room, engine-room)	50
Two adjacent compartments each with a complete power plant (COGOG)	25
Two widely-spaced units	10

Great care is needed to ensure that units are truly independent and do not rely on a common auxiliary system. The next generation of all-electric ships should be even better, with multiple generators, widely spaced, driving separated motors, perhaps podded outside the hull.

The unit system has been extended to the philosophy of 'zones', up to five in a frigate, each independent for power, ventilation (preventing the spread of smoke), chilled water, cooking, toilets, etc. Complete implementation is very difficult as, in the limit, each equipment should be duplicated within a zone to allow for maintenance, but even partial implementation is a big step forward. Ideally, the crew should live in the zone in which they fight, obviating the need to open doors and hatches when going to Action Stations.

Blast and splinters from air-flight missiles can destroy large areas of topside structure and the vital equipment within. Protection by armour is not possible – a Falklands-type Exocet (a small missile) could probably penetrate 12in of armour.[20] One can limit the effects, but the main protection is to concentrate components of a system, duplicate them and separate the alternates. Some protection to main cable runs may be worth while. If this is incorporated with the structure it need not cost too much and could reduce the number of splinters hitting the cables by 99 per cent.

At the end of the Second World War flooding was the only one of these effects for which calculation was possible, and even this, without a computer, was very approximate. Damaged stability calculations are now available at the click of a mouse, and far more accurate. Other effects were considered subjectively in the light of full-scale trials with obsolete ships, often modified to try new ideas. Trials had to be abandoned when the dangers of asbestos were recognised. A very few were held, but they had to be at least 200 miles from shore and access was only possible in full air-fed suits. A trial known as HULVUL was possible using the first asbestos-free frigate in 1988.[21] There were over 100 separate trials, starting with a burning helicopter on the flight deck. A later trial had half the boiler room structure replaced with a replica of the Type 23 structure for a big underwater explosion. Lessons from the Falklands War are discussed in the next section.

In the meantime, computer simulation advanced rapidly. By the mid-1980s the effects of blast and splinters could be reproduced fairly accurately and it was possible to study whipping and shock. Fire was still not properly represented but progress was being made. The aim is to be able to write a specification somewhat on the lines of – after one hit anywhere with a 500kg warhead the ship is to have x% chance of retaining y% of her fighting capability.[22]

The outstanding problem is that ships are lost from quite simple faults, so computer assessments must go into very great detail. By the time that level of detail is available for a new ship it is probably too late to make changes. The approach would seem to be a two-stage one. The first stage would be a very crude analysis of major features, such as bulkhead spacing. This would be followed when the design is complete by a very detailed study. Few alterations would be possible in the current design but lessons could be read for the next generation.

The real problem in damage limitation is to decide what the object is. It cannot be to build an 'unsinkable ship'.[23] The author has suggested that the aim is to make the enemy's task as difficult as possible and ships must not be disabled by a trivial attack. Ultimately, the responsibility lies with the designer – can he sleep at night when his creation is sunk, knowing he has done his best?

Lessons of the Falklands War

It is tempting to say, and nearly true, that there were no new lessons. Many old lessons were re-learnt and minor improvements in procedures (both ashore and afloat) and in equipment were made. The official Action Grid had over 180 entries but most of these were either trivial, or in some cases pious aspirations, unlikely to lead anywhere. Contemporary accounts in the press were usually wrong.[24] Constructor Commander Rod Puddock was with the Task Force both to advise on emergency repairs and to record damage and other lessons.[25] (Note that this author does not always agree with the official lesson. It is hoped that personal views will be kept clearly separate.)

Submarine threat. Following the sinking of the cruiser *General Belgrano* by HMS *Conqueror* no major Argentine surface warship left harbour. The SSN acted as the 'Grand Fleet', ruling the sea; the uncertainty of their whereabouts formed an important part of the deterrent. The one operational Argentine diesel-electric submarine caused much AS activity but was not located.

AEW. The lack of airborne early-warning was the most serious deficiency, eventually reduced by fitting Searchwater radar to eight Sea King helicopters. The lack of AEW caused much wasteful patrolling by Sea Harriers.

Gunfire support. Destroyers and frigates fired some 8000 rounds of 4.5in ammunition during the whole war in support of ground troops and, additionally, some elderly Sea Slug missiles were fired at coast defence batteries – a frightening thought. It is claimed that these bombardments played an important part in the collapse of Argentine morale. Certainly the range and accuracy were most impressive. For example, on D-Day, *Ardent* fired on Goose Green airfield at a range of 22,000 yards, destroying a Pucara with her first 20 rounds and going on to fire another 130 rounds during the day. On the other hand, in 1916 during preparation for the Somme battle, British guns were firing 10,000 rounds *per hour* on a very small area.

Close-range AA guns. Only one Argentine aircraft was shot down by light AA guns, though Argentine AA on shore was more effective. The official lesson was that the fleet needed more and better light AA, and much has been done to implement this approach by fitting CIWS such as Phalanx and Goalkeeper. On the other hand, it seems valid to argue that light AA was ineffective against mostly obsolescent Argentine aircraft and would be useless against modern aircraft and missiles.

Fire. In the Second World War fire following bomb attack was quite uncommon but in the Falklands serious fires were all too frequent. Almost all serious fires involved oil fuel – 'dieso' – which had a flash point only slightly lower

[20] The use of ceramic or composite armour is often proposed. For the same level of protection Kevlar would weigh about a quarter that of steel, but cost 15-20 times as much.

[21] There was a lot of opposition from sailors at that time to having 'their' ship blown up. I could not understand this, as I would far prefer 'my' ship to go in a useful trial than be scrapped. However, we took great care to keep the real name secret but *Navy News* revealed it was *Naiad*.

[22] 'Procuring for Survivability' RINA Conference. D Manley, *Warship 2001*. This approach has been further developed in recent years.

[23] At least two 'unsinkable' ships lie on the bottom – *Titanic, Bismarck*.

[24] For an excellent account of the war at sea see J D Brown, *The Royal Navy and the Falklands War* (London 1987). This book is particularly good on the assembly of the force and operational aspects not covered here. Technical aspects are covered in the Defence Committee report *Implementing the Lessons of the Falklands Campaign*, HMSO May 1987. The principal Ship Dept witness was the Chief Naval Architect, Keith Foulger, whose clear and comprehensive evidence comes through in the report.

[25] He received the OBE for his services to the Task Force. A summary of his report appeared in *JNE*.

than that of wartime oil (dieso 56°C, FFO 66°). Stowage was probably safer and firefighting certainly better.

Aluminium in structural form does not burn but does soften at about 550°C (when life is extinct and all equipments ruined) and melts at 650°. By way of comparison, steel melts at about 1500°, and ship fires typically reach 900°. Aluminium is a very much better conductor of heat than is steel. Foam mattresses could have burnt, but there is little evidence that they were involved in most fires. Following major furnishing fires at the Manchester Woolworth's and at Summerland (Isle of Man) in the mid-1960s, replacement materials had been sought. These had only been found with great difficulty – at that time industry was not interested in fire-resistant foam – and the first order was about to be placed. There was a small amount of PVC-covered electric cable in older ships which could give off toxic fumes in a fire. Newer insulating materials were not absolutely free of fumes but the risk was small. Transmission of fire through a bulkhead gland was virtually impossible and there is no evidence that it occurred. Direct transmission through the steel bulkhead was possible if cooling by hose was not used.

Sheffield's fire was started by burning fuel from an Exocet in a ready-use fuel tank. The tank was high in the ship so that fuel would be available in the event of loss of electric power, while its shape helped to settle out any impurities. These were worthy objects, but fuel must be stowed low down both for protection and because it is easier to blanket a low tank with foam if a fire does start.

The biggest problem was smoke: in wartime fore and aft access for small ships had been on the open upper deck, but the new ships had covered access on 2 deck and not all the bulkhead openings were smoke-tight. None were tight on the Type 21 frigates, which had a single ventilation system for the whole ship. Improved firefighting arrangements are covered later.

Linings obstructed access to the ship's side for leak stopping, and a considerable reduction in their extent was made at the expense of increased housekeeping work. There was a prolonged and rational debate over the extent of linings in the Type 23, which led to a much lesser extent than in earlier ships. Some materials (unbacked Formica) fractured into sharp fragments on impact.[26]

Exocet. The effect of Exocet was no surprise. The RN had seen film and results of French tests before it purchased

[26] They had been tested but against high-velocity bullets which did not cause fragmentation.

Shock tests were carried out against one ship of each new class, usually just before the first refit so that any defects could be made good. This trial is with *Invincible* (not an Argentinian propaganda picture!). (*D K Brown collection*)

Sheffield burning. As with almost all Falklands War fires, fuel was the major material burning.
(*D K Brown collection*)

this missile. Two of the RN's earliest Exocets were fired into the frigate *Undaunted* in 1978, making the missile's potential very clear.

Machinery. The Defence Committee particularly praised the reliability of warship machinery, dismissing unofficial reports that said there were few engines functioning fully on return. *Invincible* carried out a routine engine change at sea in sheltered waters after fighting stopped. Time between routine changes of Olympus had increased from the original figure of 3000 hours to 4500 hours. Six frigates had engine changes on return, of which four were routine. Two steam frigates were unable to develop full power due to action damage.

Committees. There were a number of effective committees covering different aspects of vulnerability before the war but they lacked cohesion. In particular, naval committees concentrated on training and technical committees on material. While there is no evidence that this lack of co-ordination caused any serious problems, improvement was clearly possible and desirable. A joint Vulnerability Policy Committee was set up (the author was its first chairman with a naval deputy) co-ordinating the work of several working parties.

Miscellaneous. There were many minor points: for example, there was a perceived need for many more welding sets and operators skilled in their use.

Self Protection. Everyone got used to carrying anti-flash gear, gas mask case,[27] life jacket, immersion suit helmet, etc.[28] Heating was turned down to encourage men to wear warm clothing, a protection against flash and of value if they had to swim. *Hermes* was able to operate in the war zone almost fully closed down,[29] but this was not possible with the much smaller complement of *Invincible*.

Contaminated fuel. Some problems were caused by biological contamination in the fuel tanks when fuel was purchased from untried refineries.

Perhaps the biggest lesson to be re-learnt was that serious damage is almost inevitable in war. Sixteen of the twenty-one destroyers and frigates that reached the Falklands were hit; those that were not were late arrivals.[30] During the early years of the Second World War there were almost as many incidents of damage to destroyers each year as ships in commission. An earlier Defence Committee report (1983) said: 'Fire precautions and damage control are not appropriate matters on which to cut corners; the resulting economies are false if they contribute to loss of lives or ships.' In response, the MoD pointed out that in a cost limited ship some compromise was inevitable.

Fire

The major fires during the Falklands War excited considerable attention from the media, though the accounts were almost always wrong.[31] With one exception the fires were associated with oil fuel and, though foam-filled furniture may have been involved, it was not the origin of the fires. There was an interesting exchange of views with the Home Office a little later over the fire hazards of domestic furniture. Their concern was to adopt materials which would not be ignited by a dropped cigarette; the ship designers' was to choose materials which would not give off toxic or corrosive fumes when in a fire. This led to very different choices, but it would seem that both were right. A frigate carries some 700 tonnes of fuel (dieso), 45 tonnes of ammunition, and about 100 tonnes of other combustible material (personal effects, furnishings, paper, etc), this last category being very widely distributed and with a big superficial area, increasing smoke generation. The first step is to keep the fuel low down, as this not only provides some protection but also if a fire starts it is easier to put a foam blanket over it.

Personal effects such as uniforms and civilian clothes present a problem. The best solution seems to be fire-resistant stowage. Private additions need not be forbidden but they do need control, particularly sleeping bags. An inspection team visiting a frigate found a highly-flammable bean-bag in the wardroom! Office paper should be reduced with computer recording. There is no insulation for cables (30 tonnes) which is completely fire-resistant but current ships have the best available – and the older ships were not bad.

Fires will always start, even by accident, and the first step is rapid action by a well-trained crew, a topic outside the scope of this book. The next step is to confine the fire and smoke to a limited area. Modern frigates are divided into five zones each with their own firefighting system. It is essential that the zone boundaries (bulkheads) prevent the spread of flames and smoke. Proper testing both on completion and in service is necessary but expensive.

Materials should be selected that give off the smallest amount of fumes when in a fire.[32] Speed is of the essence in firefighting and automatic systems have been developed which extinguish the initial flame in fractions of a second. The ban on fluorocarbons was a setback, as these were used in all machinery spaces for firefighting, but recent work with water mist (not sprinklers) has shown great promise. Good access for firefighters is needed and

[31] Aluminium in bulk does not burn.

[32] Small quantities of ordinary wood are acceptable, but 'fire-resistant' wood is not, because of the fumes given off when in a fire.

The frigate complex at Devonport where frigates can be refitted under cover. This has obvious advantages in terms of speed and efficiency. (*D K Brown collection*)

33 Yield strength is the maximum
stress at which elongation is
directly proportional to load. UTS
(Ultimate Tensile Strength) is the
stress at failure in tension.

34 Tests showed that B quality
could stop a fast running crack at -
40°C at a stress of 12 tons/in². A
quality was similar.

35 K Hall *et al*, 'Materials For RN
Submarines', *RINA Symposium*
(1993).

36 Proof stress is that
corresponding to 0.2 per cent
extension equivalent to yield
strength in metals where the yield
point is not well defined.

escape routes should have luminous markers that can be seen in smoke. Small breathing apparatus sets (ELSA) are now available which provide air during escape.

Firefighting needs good communications and visibility requires thermal imaging cameras. More recent accidental fires give confidence that the fire hazard has been greatly reduced since the Falklands War.

Materials

Surface Ship Steels

By the early 1950s development was complete of two steels for the main structure of surface warships. 'A' quality had a yield strength and ultimate tensile strength (UTS) very similar to commercial mild steel but it was made to higher standards, in particular, it retained toughness to -30°C.[33] It has been used extensively in post-war RN ships, but by 1980s commercial steels were available meeting the same

standards. 'B' quality had higher yield and UTS replacing D, DW and S quality steels. It has been used to a limited extent in warship structures where tensile stresses are high. More often the likely failure mode is buckling, where high tensile strength is of little value. In general, high tensile strength steels have a fatigue life at best no better than mild steel and often worse.

	A	B
Yield Stress (tons/in²)	16	20
UTS (tons/in²)	28·3	31-38
Elongation (%)	22	17

In earlier welded ships it was usual to use a number of riveted seams intended to stop any cracks which might start in the plates. Both A and B quality were 'tough', even at low temperatures, which means they will not allow a crack to extend, and where ordinary mild steel was used it was common to run occasional strakes of A quality to stop cracks without the need for riveting.[34]

Submarine Steels, etc[35]

Starting with *Explorer* and *Excalibur*, a new carbon manganese molybdenum steel, UXW, was introduced. A very similar steel was used for the *Porpoise* class, but thicker plating was needed and the composition was altered, which led to welding problems. To alleviate this difficulty, the steel was used in the normalised and tempered condition with a drop in yield strength.

The later *Porpoise*s and the *Oberon*s had QT28 with a minimum proof stress of 28 tons/in², which was used in the quenched and tempered state.[36] For *Dreadnought* and early SSNs a stronger steel, QT35, was introduced. Despite lengthy development testing and care in manufacture this steel was prone to cracking, as manufacturing methods were not up to the standard of cleanliness required. The USN had similar problems with early HY80 but were quicker to find a solution, and US-made improved HY80 was used for the SSBN and a few SSN. A British equivalent, Q1(N), was developed and introduced in *Superb*; with a yield strength of 25.6 tons/in², it was used up to and including the *Trafalgar*s. Q2(N) with a yield strength of 45 tons/in² has been developed. Care is needed to ensure that the weld strength matches the plate strength – in general, diving depth will increase in direct proportion to yield strength.

Typical Yield Strength (or Proof Strength)

	tons/in²
Mild steel	15.8
S	18.4
UXW	25
QT28	27.8
QT35	35.9
HY80	35.6
Q1(N)	35.6
Q2(N)	44.6

A 'Castle' class OPV in dock. The underwater paint is an early self-polishing co-polymer with a very long life. It was blue – a marked contrast to the usual red. Note the large bilge keels and the knuckle. (*D K Brown collection*)

There are many materials which are stronger than Q2(N) but, so far, fabrication problems and the difficulty in working penetrations for hatches and torpedo tubes have prevented their use. The table below compares theoretical collapse depths for a mythical submarine in different materials.

	Metres
HY80	1000
HY130	1600
Titanium	3000
GRP	3500
Carbon RP	6000

Seawater Systems

There are numerous cooling water systems in a nuclear submarine containing seawater at the pressure corresponding to depth, the largest being the main turbine condensers. Failure of any of these systems could lead to the loss of the submarine; indeed, such a failure is believed to have caused the loss of USS *Thresher*. Materials used must be corrosion resistant, erosion resistant and strong enough to resist diving pressure. Such materials were – are – not easy to come by, and there were worrying problems for a time. At the end of the war, the few piping systems were of mild steel or gunmetal. Later diesel boats tried copper-nickel-iron and then cupro-nickel. Early nuclear boats used 70/30 cupro-nickel. Castings were aluminium bronze and later nickel-aluminium-bronze. This latter material has a very complicated micro-structure and great care was needed in manufacture and in welding to get a satisfactory and lasting result. It did have the virtue of the so-called 'leak before break' effect, giving warning of impending failure.

This brief note on submarine materials is only illustrative: there were many other materials, each with its own problems. Building and running a submarine fleet is demanding.

Painting and Preparation

Developments in paint and in preparation for painting have made an enormous, and largely unrecognised, contribution to reducing the cost of running a navy. Paint can do many things whose relative importance will vary from one part of the ship to another; paint will always play a major part in preventing corrosion and, when appropriate, will provide a non-slip surface, easy to clean and easy to maintain with an attractive appearance. Under water, paint should prevent the growth of biological fouling and, above water, it can help to reduce radar and infra-red signatures.

These benefits do not come cheap: it has been estimated that the cost of preparation and painting may amount to 2-3 per cent of the building cost – upwards of £3 million – but well worth it. Much of the cost is due to interference with other work that must be stopped when the nastier paints are being sprayed.

In the Beginning

At the end of the Second World War most paints were simple, oil-based types, cheap and easy to apply but offering poor protection. Under water, the hull was coated with an anti-fouling paint called Pocoptic, based on an American formulation and good for its day. Even so, frictional resistance went up by 0.25 per cent per day out of dock (double that in tropical waters – 90 per cent in 6 months). This was soon replaced by 161P, developed by the Central Dockyard Laboratory (CDL) and made in Portsmouth Dockyard; this roughly halved the rate of fouling. The significance of this improvement is made clear in a paper dealing with a proposed modernisation of *Majestic*.[37] The extra displacement would reduce her speed by 0.5kt with a clean bottom but, 6 months out of dock, the modernised ship would be a whole knot faster due to improved anti-fouling paint.

Preparation

It is much easier to prevent rust forming than to remove it afterwards. From about 1960 plate was grit-blasted as soon as it arrived in the yard and given a very thin coat of tough primer that would not interfere with welding. When this coat was damaged it would be touched up at once. Some of the more advanced coatings required a further blast to shiny bare metal immediately before application. Proper preparation has made an enormous difference to the life of a ship. *Hermes* was the only ship in the Falklands task force painted to Second World War standards, and the only one noticeably rusty on her return.[38]

Topsides

An old-fashioned First Lieutenant would paint ship at every opportunity, and long life was not seen as important – after 10 years up to 80 coats of paint were found on the exterior of *Leander*s, weighing 45 tons.[39] It was found that the mismatch of 'touch-up' patches was due more to differences in gloss than to shades. Considerable improvements have been made.

Decks

The dominating requirements for decks are that they should be non-slip and easy to clean, and these are contradictory. For much of the period the helicopter deck had a very rough finish on which the tyres would grip. This was hard to clean and the rest of the upper deck was grit blasted, covered with a zinc metal spray that was then covered in a glossy epoxy paint. Abrasive tread strips were then stuck to give grip. This complicated system protected the metal of the deck and was generally safe but the tread strips soon came to look untidy. This system was developed in Australia and came to the RN via the Inter-Naval Corrosion Conference, a most useful group of five navies who met every 3 years to pool their experience.[40] Latterly, an epoxy paint has been introduced which is suitable for both the upper deck and helicopter deck. It took some time to persuade shipyards and Dockyards that a fully weatherproof tent was needed for the application.

37 ADM 167/133 (PRO).

38 The author worked on her as an apprentice in the 1940s.

39 The hydrofoil *Speedy* was weight-critical and could not take off at over 117 tons. On commissioning, the builders gave the captain a 1-pint tin of touch-up paint and told him it was to last at least one commission.

40 The social life was splendid.

Illustrious arriving off the Falklands in 1982 to relieve the *Invincible* (background). Such was the hurry to dispatch the new carrier that she was sent out without anti-fouling, allowing a valuable quantification of the effects of fouling.
(D K Brown collection)

Machinery Space Bilges

This was, and perhaps still is, the most difficult area of all. In the older steam ships, the machinery spaces were warm and moist, with much of the bilge area almost inaccessible. Corrosion was rapid: *Rothesay* was found to have fourteen longitudinals on one side and nine on the other so badly corroded as to be virtually useless – it was lucky she did not break in half. Initially, a paint based on chlorinated rubber was used, the best available, but not up to the severe conditions. The introduction of the gas turbine made matters worse, for the synthetic lubricating oil they used proved to be the world's best paint-stripper. From about 1960, the bilges were zinc-metal sprayed, but it was some time before application problems were solved and the sprayed surface was often damaged during machinery installation.

Eventually, Central Dockyard Laboratory (CDL) developed a very hard epoxy to cover the zinc and this proved excellent, though it is so hard that touching-up damaged areas is almost impossible.

Outer Bottom

The first line of defence is 'Impressed Current Cathodic Protection' (ICCP), in which a carefully monitored electrical potential is applied to the hull, preventing electrical action between the hull and the seawater. The current requirements would be enormous if the hull were bare metal so it is coated with coal tar epoxy paint chosen because it is resistant to the high current density round the electrodes. Early *Leanders* did not have ICPP and after 6 years there would be extensive pitting up to 8mm deep. The later ships were protected and after the same time in service showed no more than occasional 0.5mm pits.

The earlier anti-fouling paints used copper oxide as the toxin. As this leached out it left a rough surface. If it dried out, as when the ship docked, a new coat had to be applied. Each coat added roughness due to ripples in application and dirt inclusions. During the 1970s International Paints introduced a 'Self Polishing Anti-Fouling' which was very long lasting, did not suffer from drying out, and actually got smoother in service. Trials supported these claims, but worries over health took a long while to resolve. It seems that the original coat may last half the life of the ship, while the increase of resistance is negligible.[41] The saving in fuel and reduction of dockings has saved very large sums of money. The toxin used in the original version is harmful to marine life and was phased out in 2002, being replaced by a less effective copper compound. The long-term solution probably lies in a 'non-stick' paint.

Each coat of painting adds to roughness, as there will be paint ripples and overspray; dirt inclusions while docking adds 25 micron on average. A rule of thumb is that 10 microns of roughness adds 1 per cent to frictional resistance, which allowing for wave making, etc means 0.5 per cent on the fuel bill. R L Townsin details roughness measurements on a Type 42 destroyer: after blast cleaning and

[41] A token 1/16 per cent per day is allowed for mechanical damage to the paint.

priming average roughness was 55 microns,[42] with three coats of anti-corrosive 135 microns, and as completed 180 microns.[43] Roughness and fouling add about £80,000 to the annual fuel bill of a frigate – £4 million for the Navy as a whole. Early in the post-war years a typical warship would complete with an average roughness of some 300 microns and deteriorate in service. More recently, greater care and improved equipment has brought this down to about 100 microns and self-polishing paints really do get smoother in service.

Fouling

The underwater form of a ship offers a happy home to many marine organisms, loosely grouped as 'fouling'. The main components are: diatom slime, slippery to the touch but with an equivalent roughness of some 600 microns, due in part to the grit which it picks up; then there are vegetable growths – grass – and zoological growth such as barnacles.

At the end of the Falklands War, *Illustrious* was sent out without any anti-fouling paint. After 5 months afloat in the River Tyne (then lethal to most living organisms) and a further 9 months in the South Atlantic the frictional resistance was about 2½ times that of a clean ship, corresponding to a 3kt loss of speed.[44] After the bottom was cleaned, shaft power was reduced by 80 per cent at lower speeds and 56 per cent at full speed, restoring the design performance.

Submarine Paints

Until the 1960s the external, anti-corrosion paint was an oil-based paint, ACC 655, with a high lead content, which was then replaced by coal tar epoxy with a life of 10 years. There was a problem in finding a satisfactory anti-fouling that would retain a black colour. Until the 1970s pocoptic black was used, which had cuprous oxide as the toxin but heavily diluted with carbon black. The later 317E had black cuprous sulphate and oxide and was also used as the boot topping in surface ships.[45] Self-polishing anti-fouling paints were treated with caution, as there were fears that submarines could be tracked using residue from the paint.

Conclusions

The reduction of serious corrosion has largely obviated the need for plating to be replaced during the life of the ship, resulting in a great reduction in docking time and cost. The fuel saving from anti-fouling has also been very considerable, and these savings have made possible a considerable reduction in the size and number of Dockyards. Day-to-day maintenance has been eased. Many of these savings are due to the work of the chemists at the Central Dockyard Laboratory at Portsmouth, both in developing special paints and in producing a 'consumers' guide' to commercial materials. The closure of CDL[46] may well be a false economy. This is all too brief an account omitting many lesser but difficult problems.[47]

A junior rates bunk space in a Type 22 frigate – a far cry from the hammocks of the Second World War era. (*D K Brown collection*)

Lifesaving Gear

Very soon after the Second World War the Admiralty set up a committee under Admiral Talbot to review the causes of death of RN personnel during the conflict. They concluded that well over half the deaths occurred after men had left the ship, either in the water or on unprotected life rafts.[48] A standing RN Lifesaving Committee was set up, with membership from seamen, constructors and doctors. Initially there was some debate as to whether to go for inflatable gear or something akin to the old cork jackets with inherent buoyancy, but the decision came down for inflatables. The RAF had considerable experience of inflatable gear and their advice was freely given.

Survivors must be able to board a life raft easily; once inside they must be protected from cold wind and spray or hot sun, and insulated by a double skin from the cold seawater. The 'passenger' space should be virtually airtight so as to preserve a high humidity, preventing evaporation from wet clothing, and conserving body warmth (or keeping cool in the tropics). The raft should carry food and water for several days, be difficult to capsize and easy to right if it does, and be conspicuous. The buoyancy should be subdivided to reduce the effect of a puncture and there should be a repair kit. Regular checks are essential but the effort needed should be as small as possible. None of these requirements is as easy as it sounds.[49]

By about 1950 a 20-man raft had been designed, tested

42 One millionth of a metre.

43 R L Townsin *et al*, 'Speed, Power and Roughness', *Trans RINA* (1980).

44 M Barret, '*Illustrious* – Effects of no anti-Fouling paint', *Naval Architect* (March 1985).

45 94MM was used briefly on SSNs but was soon abandoned because of its high mercuric chloride content.

46 Founded about 1840.

47 The author was responsible for painting for many years.

48 One of the most horrifying documents I have read. No department was responsible for lifesaving equipment; the inflatable lifebelt had been condemned as unsafe on trials in August 1939 but remained in production throughout the war. In Arctic waters a survivor on a Carley float would live for about an hour, and in temperate waters for several hours.

49 This author was on the Lifesaving Committee in the mid-1970s.

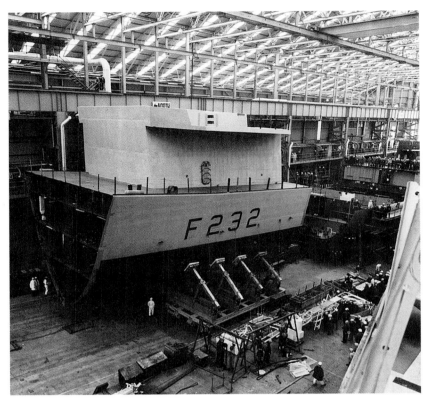

A large section of the Type 23 *Lancaster* ready for assembly in Yarrow's module hall. Note the original pendant number, later changed because 'Form 232' was used to report groundings, collisions and similar embarrassing accidents. (*Yarrow*)

50 Overload capacity 27. There was also an 8-man raft for small craft.

51 For some reason supporters of round versus oval rafts waged war with religious fervour.

52 Dr John Coates RCNC, who has contributed to this and other sections, received the OBE for his work in testing lifesaving gear.

53 When the Indian frigate *Khukri* was sunk during the Indo-Pakistan war of 1971, most of her lifesaving gear was destroyed. I was told this by one of the few survivors, who had an Olympic medal for swimming.

54 This suggests that damage exercises had not been realistic.

55 There can be problems from sub-contractors. The gas release on one unit proved unreliable. The actual manufacturer was horrified to learn that his unit was used in lifesaving. It was intended for pub soda siphons where if it failed first time a thump would ensure it worked next time.

and some had been issued.[50] It was oval in shape and had double buoyancy tubes made from three-ply rubberised cotton.[51] It had inflatable hoops that supported the tent and helped in righting a capsized raft. It had entry in the form of a sleeve, which could be closed by frozen hands. The stowage had a hydraulic release that would ensure that they floated clear of a sinking ship. There was also a survival pack with food and water. By the early 1970s better, artificial materials were available and a new circular 24-man raft was introduced.

The problem with the wartime lifebelt was that it would not keep the head of an unconscious man out of water – rather the opposite. A new jacket was designed using two-ply cotton; it proved able to keep an unconscious man's head out of water, on a target price of £5. It was thought that a man jumping off a high place might break his neck – leaping into the sea from a carrier flight deck disproved this.[52] Special jackets were developed which would keep a heavily-armed Marine afloat and another for those on hazardous duties who might be unconscious when they hit the water.

An immersion suit was developed by 1950 but was not generally issued until the late 1970s. Space on the upper deck for all this gear was hard to find, and it had to be dispersed so that a single hit would not destroy it all.[53] During the Falklands War it was found that manholes were too small for a well-fed sailor carrying full survival gear.[54] On the other hand, the relatively light casualties on the war-

ships that sank suggest that the lifesaving gear was effective. Since that war ELSA, a shortlife breathing apparatus, has been issued to make possible escape from toxic fumes.

Careful maintenance and regular inspection are essential – yachtsmen beware.[55]

Habitability[56]

When the war ended in 1945 the ratings' mess decks aboard RN ships would have seemed quite familiar to Nelson's men. A 'mess' consisted of a bare wooden table with long benches either side; in the deckhead over there were hooks from which hammocks could be slung. The design standard for most ships was $20ft^2$ per man for junior rates and $25ft^2$ for senior rates. Wartime additions of equipment like radar had reduced the space available while at the same time increasing the complement; actual space per man was about $15\text{-}17ft^2$ for juniors and $17\text{-}19ft^2$ for seniors – this for all purposes. Food was cooked centrally and carried a considerable distance to the ill-ventilated messes. Drastic changes were needed, particularly when conscription ended and volunteers had to be attracted and retained.

Trials in the early 1950s of cafeteria eating,[57] close to the galley and separate from living spaces, showed real advantages without dramatic increase in space requirements,[58] while at the same time food quality was improved and wastage much reduced. Parallel trials of bunks were also successful. In the mid-1950s the *Leanders*, 'Tribals' and 'Counties' were designed with cafeterias, bunks, seating for all,[59] and some increase in overall space per man – $21ft^2$ for juniors and 25 for senior rates, of which $4ft^2$ was allocated to the dining hall. Older ships in refit were, as far as was possible, brought up to these standards. Experience showed that, though these standards were a big step forward, there was need for more. There was too little distinction between Chief Petty Officers and POs, the use of 'my' bunk as a settee was very unpopular, and storage spaces were inadequate when civilian clothes were allowed. Messing areas were generally unattractive in appearance. There was an interim improvement in 1966, mainly affecting the *Leanders*.

These problems were fully tackled in the '1970 Standards' for accommodation; it helped when experience showed that space in the dining hall could be slightly reduced. Space per man was increased to $24ft^2$ for junior rates, $29ft^2$ for POs and $35ft^2$ for CPOs, while seats were provided for all, clear of the sleeping area. Fleet Chiefs ($52ft^2$) were to have single cabins, Chiefs 2-, 4- or 6-berth and POs 6-berth. A new range of furniture was designed, and a firm of consultants produced a range of decor schemes. Washplaces were replaced by bathrooms with showers and stainless steel basins, and were completely lined. Laundries and drying rooms were added.[60] All these improvements took up space and added to the 'hotel' electrical load, but they were essential if young men were to be attracted and retained in the navy. Officers' accom-

A *Sandown* class GRP minehunter under construction by Vosper Thornycroft. (*Vosper Thornycroft*)

modation had been fairly spacious but unattractive and junior officers usually shared. By 1970 all (except those under training) had single-berth cabins with new-design furniture. Galleys were now all-electric, and great attention was paid to convenience and to hygiene.[61] Simple air flow had given place to full air-conditioning, working well in later ships.

There were many who thought these standards were too luxurious for a fighting ship (even a few ratings thought this and would have preferred more pay and austere living). This view came to the fore after the Falklands War when some blamed accommodation standards for contributing to fire and making damage control difficult. This was argued out in the final design of the Type 23 frigates and only a few changes were made. British ships are very similar in space per man to the average for NATO (slightly below) and the standard is broadly similar. During the 1980s there were few complaints.

The length and hence overall size of a frigate is governed by the upper deck length that is required for weapons and sensors, with allowance for physical and electronic clearances. Typically, this will leave space for about 100 men at current standards. Additional men are expensive – £80,000 per man to build, much more than the capital cost of a London hotel room. Big increases might mean larger engines, as well as a general increase in ship size. There is keen pressure to reduce complement but damage control is very dependent on skilled manpower and compromise is needed, though it is a difficult balance to get right.

Ventilation

There were at least two major investigations into ventilation between the wars, which showed the need for considerable improvement, but at the time of the first money was too short for much to be done and the later one was too close to the outbreak of war. During the war things could only get worse: many heat-generating equipments were installed, with more men in less space, while the ships were closed down for long periods. Operations took place in extreme conditions in the Arctic and in the Tropics. It was clear that something had to be done.[62]

Before the war most manned spaces had a fan supply of fresh air and natural exhaust, whilst smelly compartments had forced extraction and natural supply, usually from neighbouring compartments. If properly designed, installed and maintained, this system could work quite well in moderate climates, but all too often these conditions were not met. During the war air-conditioning was introduced for operations spaces, and for submarines.[63]

It was clear that electronic devices would increase in number and power which, with thermionic valves, meant a very great generation of heat. The threat of nuclear war and fall out meant that ships would have to close down very quickly and remain closed down for long periods in conditions from the Arctic to the Tropics.

[56] H D Ware, 'Habitability of Surface Warships', *Trans RINA* (1986). This was written when Harry Ware was on my staff. He liked to be referred to as the last Chief Draughtsman, a historic title later changed to PTO (1).

[57] The *Majestics* were intended to have cafeteria messing at the end of the war, and there was plenty of experience in US-built ships such as escort carriers.

[58] There was a near-mutiny in *Vanguard* when she introduced a cafeteria, but this seem to have been due to teething troubles.

[59] This involved using lower bunks as seats.

[60] *Warrior* (1860) had a laundry!

[61] Galley floors were among the very few areas of complaint in the 1980s.

[62] A J Sims, 'The Habitability of Naval Ships under Wartime Conditions', *Trans INA* (1945); N G Holt and F E Clemitson, 'Notes on the Behaviour of HM Ships during the War', *Trans INA* (1949). The discussions of these two papers are particularly valuable.

[63] One submarine, without air conditioning, made a routine report of air temperature and humidity in the boat – the reply said that the conditions reported would not support human life.

Design Parameters.[64]

Climate	Max T° C	Sea T°	Internal T°	Relative Humidity %
Extreme Tropics	34.5	32	29.5	50
Arctic	-29	-2	18	30 (min)

In the mid-1950s the decision was made to install full air-conditioning in the 'Tribal' class frigates.[65] There were teething troubles but the scheme was generally successful and has been adopted in all later ships. One lesson was the need for standby units. It was also found that air-conditioning machinery takes up space and weight, and consumes a considerable amount of electric power, much of which appears as waste heat. Warships have a particular problem in that passageways are very congested and hence designers are driven to small trunks with air at high velocity, which can be noisy.[66]

The units supply a mixture of fresh and recirculated air that is filtered and either heated or cooled before being distributed. There are two main conditions: Cruise, in which fresh air is drawn directly, while in the Action state air is drawn through NBC filters.

The 'heat load' within a compartment is made up of heat from men, machinery (including the air conditioning machinery), boundaries – sun and sea – and the fresh air. Air conditioning has made a great difference to life at sea and, though expensive, must be seen as essential.[67]

Welding and Modular Construction

In 1945 it was generally accepted that future warships should be welded and that this should be associated with pre-fabrication of units under cover in the shop. The units should be as large as possible within the limits of the yard's craneage. Serious cracking in welded structures[68] led to the introduction of riveted 'crack-arresters', usually at the upper deck edge and at the turn of bilge. These crack-arresters were gradually omitted as better steel and improved procedures became available. During the war there had been extensive use of lap welds but, in future, all welds would be butted, which implied more accurate cutting to shape. Cutting was by flame cutters controlled at first by optical scanning of drawings and later by direct computer input. This had an important side benefit: the smoother hull had less resistance and endurance went up by some 5 per cent.

The first post-war frigates were designed so that radar offices and similar spaces could be built separately, fitted out and tested ashore before being inserted into the ship, but this feature was not used as far as is known. Steady development followed; wider plates meant fewer welds, as did a reduction in the number of longitudinals. Design and planning meant more welds could be made in the 'down-hand' position with the welder above his work. There was increasing use of machine welding, which produced welds more quickly and of better quality. Modernisation of shipyards enabled bigger units to be handled, though they were still quite small, at between 10 and 30 tons.

By the late 1970s it was realised that outfit work was very expensive, particularly on the slip. Easton quotes the following cost ratios (about 1980):[69]

Prefabrication shop (structure)	1
Unit Assembly	5
Work on berth	10
Afloat	20

The idea grew of fabricating very much larger sections that could be fitted out through their open ends or with the deck off[70] before being joined to form the ship.[71] Construction would begin of structural units weighing 40-60 tons. Some limited outfitting would take place before they were joined into modules of up to 400 tons that were fitted out prior to being moved to the slip.

Slightly earlier, there had been an alternative approach, also referred to as 'Modular Construction'. The idea here was that weapon systems could be installed in a box or boxes, tested ashore and dropped into the ship where there would be power supplies, chilled water, etc arranged to connect. There were at least three schemes: the USN went for very large boxes in their SSES system, which would hold a complete system; Germany developed and used the MEKO system, with boxes of about normal container size; the British scheme, 'Cellularity', used much smaller boxes grouped in 'cells' that could be enlarged. A full-scale mock up of a large cell was built at Portsmouth and showed great promise.[72]

[64] H D Ware, 'Habitability of Surface Warships', *Trans RINA* (1986).

[65] The design owes a great debt to Reg White, then a leading draughtsman (retired as chief).

[66] Typical early installations are described in R N Newton, *Practical Construction of Warships* (3rd edition, London 1960).

[67] H D Ware, 'Habitability of Surface Warships', *Trans RINA* (1986).

[68] An example was the carrier *Vengeance* during Operation 'Rusty' in December 1948, an exercise in the Arctic to test the effects of extreme cold weather, in which a crack ran right across the flight deck and down the sides.

[69] R W S Easton [Managing Director, Yarrows], 'Modern Warships, Design and Construction', Council of Engineering Institute, Glasgow 1983.

[70] Fabricating the deck separately had other major advantages. With it upside down, all the pipe and cable runs could be installed easily.

[71] Bath Iron Works (Maine) were the pioneers in this approach.

[72] P J Gates, 'Cellularity: An Advanced Weapon Electronics Integration Technique', *Trans RINA* (1985).

It was claimed that these modular schemes made mid-life modernisation simple and cheap.[73] However, power supplies and so forth were very different for different weapon fits and changes were still difficult. It was eventually decided that mid-life modernisation was uneconomic and only limited updates would be undertaken. This was probably the right decision for the wrong reasons. The Type 42 modernisation was said to cost more than a new ship, but examination of the figures showed that one of the biggest items was Dockyard overheads charged on weapon systems which they did not touch!

Yarrows alone invested some £3 million in computer aided design but, as the managing director pointed out, investment in people is even more important. At all levels a better-educated workforce was needed – and achieved. Computer design reaches into production; pipe and cable systems can be planned. Some 12,000 cables in a Type 23 can be cut to length before installation. There are also about 12,000 key drawings defining a Type 23.

Also, round about 1980 new cutting and welding methods were introduced. The plates and frames were cut very accurately, saving a great deal of time on rectification and setting up. Plasma welding, under water, virtually eliminated weld distortion (the so-called Starved Horse effect leading to corrugated side plating). Computer controlled planning ensured that each item required in the assembly area arrived just before it was needed. The importance of this cannot be overemphasised: a Type 23 has some 6 million 'parts', all of which must be in the right place at the right time.[74] All these measures reduced building cost very considerably[75] – also making mid-life modernisation almost impossible.

Vosper Thornycroft were able to adapt much of this modular approach for GRP construction in the *Sandown* class. Some 10,000 drawings were produced using CAD, which ensure that every part fits. Much of the GRP lay-up uses preimpregnated glass cloth fed into the mould by machine, with hand press down. Units weighed up to 20 tons and were fitted out before being inserted into the hull.[76]

Conclusions

Many of the topics here may seem remote from the usual image of warship design, but they all matter. It is the duty of the naval architect to get them all right or, where they conflict, to reach the best compromise. His ship must have the best hull form, itself a compromise, the right steel, in a structure which will withstand the pressure of the sea and the attack of the enemy over a long life and protected from corrosion. The naval architect must also remember that men live in the ship and as well as good food and reasonable comfort they should be proud of the appearance of their ship. A warship is the representative of its country and, as such, should have an awesome beauty, frightening to the wrongdoer. Get it all right and the designer too may be proud of 'his' ship.

A modern warship-builder: Yarrow's shipyard on the Clyde, where many frigates have been built. (*Yarrow*)

[73] Many of the claims in technical journals were greatly exaggerated. It was implied that an AS frigate could become an AA ship in a few days.

[74] D K Brown, 'The Duke Class Frigates examined', *Warship Technology*, Part 1 in No 8, Part 2 in No 9 (1989).

[75] A substantial amount of the savings attributed to competition in the 1980-90 era was actually due to improved building methods.

[76] D K Brown, 'Sandown', *Warship Technology*, Part 8 (1989).

14 In Conclusion

The Royal Navy's Task

For half a century after the end of the Second World War there was a clear threat from the Soviet Union. At sea the perceived threat came first from the powerful cruisers of the *Sverdlov* class, which had an important effect on RN planning – for example, the 5in cruiser destroyer was seen as a *Sverdlov* killer (as was the battleship *Vanguard*). At the same time there was an enormous build-up of the Soviet submarine force. The Korean War was seen (perhaps wrongly) as demonstrating Soviet will for conquest.

The Admiralty dreamt of restoring something like pre-war glory and only slowly realised that the economy would not support a large navy. The protection of the remains of the Commonwealth – 'East of Suez' – was important while there were a number of small but troublesome confrontations. The Korean War led to fairly large frigate programmes and a very large programme of minesweepers. Gradually, the primary task was seen as protection of convoys bringing US troops across the Atlantic to reinforce the central and northern fronts. The Soviet naval air force, based on the Kola Peninsula, was seen as an increasing threat and the carrier CVA-01 was designed to counter this threat by pre-emptive strikes.

With the demise of the fleet carrier force the RN's role became even more concentrated on escort work. More recently the Falklands War, the 1991 Gulf War, and Afghanistan have all shown the value and flexibility of sea power, which is much less dependent on land bases and minimises problems of overflight of neutral or hostile territory. This has led (2002) to a new amphibious force and the promise of new carriers equipped with the Joint Strike Fighter.

Constraints

Shortage of money was and is the most obvious constraint, and funds for the navy have never been abundant. However, naval manpower has affected the size of the fleet and the design of ships, leading in particular to dramatic improvements in living conditions to help attract and retain personnel. There are other limiting factors, perhaps the capability of British industry being the main one. One may instance the introduction of the gas turbine, in which British aviation firms were world leaders, replacing steam turbines whose supporting industry was dwindling. Competition may have been effective in keeping prices down but, in 2002, almost all major warship building is in the hands of BAE Systems.

Missiles began to dominate – *Norfolk* firing an Exocet. (*D K Brown collection*)

Technology

In ship technology (hull and machinery) the UK has led in many areas, and been well up in others.[1] It is suggested that much of this success was due to the close links between the design team and research establishments working in hydrodynamics and structures. By far the greatest British achievements have been in the field of noise reduction, so that RN surface ships and submarines have been the quietest, a full generation ahead of their rivals. From about 1960, 10 years before other navies, AEW Haslar was able to design propellers with about double the quiet speed of earlier designs, and much quieter even above that speed when cavitation has begun. Air bubble screening was developed at AUWE, Portland, with 'Agouti' adding to the performance of quiet propellers, whilst 'Masker' screened machinery noise. Pumpjets from ARL Teddington further reduced submarine propulsor noise. AEL, West Drayton, and NCRE, Dunfermline and Rosyth, did wonders in reducing machinery noise.

Questionnaires on seakeeping among NATO navies consistently show British ships as leaders.[2] Submarine pressure hull design has been led by NCRE, whilst Ship Department with help from ARL developed the first full computer aided ship design system. The E-in-C led the way on gas turbine propulsion in NATO. New materials – GRP, steels, paints – have made ships stronger and reduced the maintenance load. It is notable that many of these advances may be attributed to a single individual and, where possible, these have been named in this book.[3]

One of the greatest post-war US naval architects, Dr Reuven Leopold, summarised his doctrinal thesis in a paper on innovation. His two examples of successful innovation were both British – gas turbines and fin stabilisers.[4] He even gave a lecture in Ship Department, Bath, on this theme and was rather surprised that his British audience were not sure that the decisions taken were right and, even if they were right, that they had not been taken for the wrong reasons. NATO Committees formed a very competitive environment: to address one's colleagues on the theme 'First Again' was very gratifying.

The Ships

These have been described and, at least in part, appraised in earlier chapters, and here one can only draw a few general conclusions. The first group of frigates were outstanding. The *Whitby*s and their derivatives were truly great, whilst the diesel-engined ships were inevitable given the state of the UK turbine industry – and some are still giving good service. The *Blackwood*s were uncomfortable but had almost the AS capability of a *Whitby* at half the cost. They would have been better and probably cheaper with simpler structure making them a little bigger. They were first-rate in ASW, second-rate only because they had little capability for any other role. Had war come, they would have been better appreciated.

The 'Tribals' were an attempt at a second-rate, multi-role ship and failed to do anything very well and were unduly costly,[5] though they introduced several technical developments. The *Leander*s were so good that it was difficult to design a better ship at a comparable price. Attempts at a cheap frigate failed because the only long range ASW sensor was a big hull mounted sonar making the ship and its services itself big and expensive. Towed

Good seakeeping is vital to modern surface warships and the *Leander*s (this is *Diomede*) were the best for their size in NATO – at least prior to the 'Dukes'. (*D K Brown collection*)

[1] The author has been associated with several of these advances but only as part of a team.

[2] Canada's *St Laurent* is another favourite, but she was designed by Rowland Baker, a British constructor.

[3] Apologies for any omissions or errors.

[4] Dr R Leopold, 'Innovation Adoption in Naval Ship Design', *Naval Engineers Journal* (December 1977).

[5] I cannot understand why the 'Tribals' were more expensive than the *Leander*s.

[6] It is claimed that Sea Slug was no worse than the early models of Terrier and that it should have been developed rather than replaced.

[7] P J Usher and A L Dorey, 'A Family of Warships', *Trans RINA* (1982). This paper by two senior directors of Vosper-Thornycroft was taken very seriously. Their claim that a larger ship would be cheaper to build was examined by DNC cost estimators, who concluded that there would be little difference in cost. I argued, unsuccessfully, that if there was no difference in cost the larger ship should be chosen for improved seakeeping and easier maintenance.

Right: Hardy, of the Type 14 *Blackwood* class. They were a reasonably successful attempt at a cheap frigate. (*Crown Copyright*)

Below: Coniston, lead ship of the successful 'Ton' class. (*D K Brown collection*)

Bottom: Norfolk, lead ship of the numerous Type 23 'Duke' class. (*Mike Lennon*)

array sonar made cheap and effective frigates possible, as for example the 'Duke' class.

The 'County' class had an excellent hull with novel and successful machinery but was let down by the failure of Sea Slug to live up to expectations.[6] *Bristol* would have been more capable and cheaper but lost its role with the cancellation of the carriers. The Type 42 proved a valuable type of ship but was too small. The Type 22 was the true *Leander* replacement and a success.

Carriers exemplify the saying 'Big is Beautiful'. Contractors for the new carriers under development have found that increasing the size actually reduces the cost, due to easier installation and maintenance. Many people both in the Admiralty and in industry had been saying this for years but no one listened.[7] The *Invincible*s were another success.

At the other end of the scale, MCM vessels starting with the 'Ton' and 'Ham' classes have been very successful. GRP construction has been developed in partnership with Vosper-Thornycroft through *Wilton*, the 'Hunt' class to the *Sandown*s, and their capability has been proved in several operations.

The principal attributes of an attack submarine are speed, diving depth and silence. British submarines are constrained in cost, and many good designs have been dropped for that reason, but they are the quietest. *Valiant* started from scratch and hence is the author's personal choice for all-time greatness, but *Swiftsure* and *Trafalgar* still improved on that good start. Comparisons of designs between different navies with differing roles and constraints are difficult but one such exercise is summarised in Appendix 5.

It is hoped that the reader will now be convinced that most of the decisions made by the Naval Staff and Ship Department were correct, or at least inevitable. Technically, there has been a willingness to innovate shown by novel designs such as the *Whitby, Invincible,* quiet submarines and the GRP minehunters. New ideas continue to flow, illustrated by the trimaran *Triton* and the WR-21 gas turbine, possibly combined with all-electric propulsion (see below).

The Royal Navy may not be the first-rate power seen at the end of the Second World War but the quality and flexibility of the fleet is being demonstrated in no uncertain terms. At the time of writing (mid-2002) the future appears bright, though the time taken to get new designs into service remains a matter for concern.

A Glimpse of the Future

At the time of writing, the future is very bright with two big aircraft carriers, a new class of nuclear submarines, six destroyers (six more to come) and numerous amphibious force ships planned, with steel work started on some. Let us hope these ships materialise. Brief notes follow.

The early studies for the two new carriers are outlined in Appendix 6. These are being developed by two competing consortia (led by BAE and Thales) and the final version may differ. Both team have increased size in order to reduce cost and it seems that the new ships will displace about 50,000 tons.

The Daring class Destroyer (Type 45)
The Type 45 destroyer programme is being led by BAE Systems and six have been ordered, with a promise of six more to come (2002).[8] Much of the Horizon project work,

[8] Names announced are *Daring, Dauntless, Diamond, Dragon, Defender* and *Duncan.*

An impression of the Type 45 destroyer to be built by BAE Systems and Vosper Thornycroft.
(*BAE Systems*)

[9] The technology is very much that tried in the RM60 engines for *Grey Goose*.

[10] 'IEP for *Daring* Class', *Warship Technology* (May 2001).

[11] Names announced are *Astute*, *Ambush*, *Artful*.

including the weapon system, can be incorporated so that a fairly short timescale is hoped for – just as well considering the age of the Type 42.

Armament includes a Sylver vertical launch system with Aster 15/30 missiles (PAAMS), a Mk VIII Mod 1 gun and two smaller guns. Aster 15 is a close-range weapon and Aster 30 longer range; both are highly manoeuvrable. There will be a British Sampson multi-function radar and the S1850 search radar, hull and towed array sonars. Batch II ships will have enhanced land-attack capability.

Accommodation is provided for a crew of 235, of which 187 are the basic complement and the remainder a training margin. Space per man is up by an average of 39 per cent with single-berth cabins for officers, single or double for senior rates and six-berth for junior rates. The bow and much of the superstructure will be built in a new Vosper-Thornycroft yard in Portsmouth Dockyard, with the rest being divided between BAE yards on the Clyde (Yarrows) and at Barrow. 01 will be assembled on the Clyde, later ships at Barrow.

Basic details are:

> 7350 tonnes, deep. 162.4m x 21.2m. Endurance 7000 miles at 18kts.

The follow-on class, known as the Future Surface Combatant, is being studied – it may be an enhanced *Daring* but might be a trimaran.

The WR-21 Gas Turbine

The Northrop Grumman/Rolls Royce WR-21 gas turbine has been selected for the Type 45 destroyer and may be used in the new carriers. This 25MW engine has been developed by Rolls-Royce under a USN project, now joined by the UK and France; development costs up to the beginning of 2001 has been stated as £300 million. Northrop Grumman has a 50 per cent work share, Rolls-Royce 40 per cent and DCN 10 per cent. It has an exhaust recuperator, an intercooler and variable area inlet nozzles

to the power turbine using units based on RB211 and Trent aircraft engines.[9] This gives it a flat fuel consumption curve and its fuel consumption averages 27-30 per cent less than conventional gas turbines. Because of the improvement at low power it is possible to do away with cruising engines, saving space and maintenance and simplifying gearboxes. It is designed to fit the same base as the widely used LM-2500 engine.

A prototype completed a 500-hour test at DERA, Pyestock, in 1997 and an engine to full production standards was due for a 3150-hour trial at Indret (France) late in 2001. The WR-21 will power an integrated electric propulsion system serving both ship propulsion and services. Podded propulsion has been used in several recent cruise liners but is probably seen as unproven at the power of a Type 45.

The first six ship sets were ordered early in 2001 at a cost of £84 million.[10] They will each deliver 21.5MW and there will be two engines in the forward machinery space, together with two 2MW diesel generators. The after machinery space is separated by one compartment and will contain two advanced induction motors of 20MW with supporting services. The system has been developed over a decade by the USN at Philadelphia.

Astute class attack submarines

BAE Systems were awarded a £1.9 billion contract for the design and build of three *Astute* class in March 1997.[11] Originally described as 'Improved *Trafalgars*' they have the PWR 2 reactor from *Vanguard*, implying an increase in pressure hull diameter, and have six tubes instead of the five in *Trafalgar*. They have an updated tactical weapon system, a 50 per cent increase in weapon load, reduced complement and are even quieter. They will displace about 7200 tons, partly to reduce building costs. Fabrication of *Astute* began in September 1999 but the programme has been delayed and she is not expected to enter service until late 2006. Originally a second batch of two was planned but this may be increased to three at a cost of £1.7 billion as this would save the cost of a *Trafalgar* refuelling.

An impression of *Astute*. (BAE Systems)

Future Attack Submarine (FASM)[12]

Studies have begun into attack submarines to follow the *Astute*s. It is almost certain to be nuclear powered but alternatives are considered – seven out of ten current options are nuclear powered. Targets include a 10 per cent reduction in first cost and 30 per cent reduction in through life costs compared with the *Astute*.

Amphibious Warfare Ships

Both the LPDs (*Albion* and *Bulwark*), and the Alternative Landing Ship Logistic are covered in detail in Chapter 11.

Electric Propulsion

There have been a number of developments in electric propulsion which are truly revolutionary. The weight of a generator or motor is expected to be about one-tenth of that of current machines, whilst reduction in the size of the bulky rectifier is likely to be even greater. The main generators will supply auxiliary power for all purposes and it should be possible to adopt a degree of separation and redundancy which will greatly reduce vulnerability to enemy attack.

The Trimaran Triton

Trimarans have been in use in the Pacific for all of recorded history and the idea was picked up by Nigel Irons in his record-breaking vessel *Ilan Voyager*.[13] Professor D R Pattison RCNC and his assistant J W Zhang at University College London developed the idea in a series of design studies for much larger ships, including a range of warships from patrol vessels to aircraft carriers, as well as ferries.

The obvious advantage of this configuration is a reduction in the power required at high speed by about 20 per cent, but there are many others. Pitch and heave in head seas will be about the same as in a conventional ship of the same length but less than in such a ship with the same payload. The outriggers govern stability, allowing heavy weights to be carried high up, whilst the broad deck amidships allows a convenient landing deck for helicopters and for their hangars. The outriggers give some protection against torpedoes and sea-skimming missiles and can help to reduce the ship's signatures.

The Ministry of Defence began to show official interest, as did Vosper-Thornycroft, and model tests were carried out in the Haslar ship tanks together with structural

12 'Affordability is the future for FASM', *Warship Technology* (May 1999).

13 Ilan stands for 'Incredibly Long And Narrow'.

The trimaran demonstrator *Triton*. (*Vosper Thornycroft*)

investigations at Rosyth. The loading and hence the stresses in the cross structure were the main area of uncertainty. It would be easy to overdo it and build a heavy (and costly) structure which would nullify the advantages, whilst an underestimate would be catastrophic. Damage stability calculations were more complex but presented no serious problems. These investigations confirmed the advantages and gave a very good guide to the structural design.

The characteristics of the trimaran made it seem very suitable for the future frigate programme to follow the Type 45, but it was thought unwise to commit a major part of the navy to a concept which had not gone to sea. It was decided to build a demonstrator to prove the basic approach. There followed a lengthy period of negotiations and studies leading to a design which was big enough and fast enough to prove the concept yet simple enough to be affordable. The contract was awarded to Vosper-Thornycroft at the end of July 1998 at a cost of £13 million. Cutting of steel began in January 1999 with construction in four 250-ton blocks. *Triton* was launched 97 per cent complete – on time – on 6 May 2000. Preliminary trials were in July 2000 and she was accepted at the end of August.

Particulars

Length, overall	98.7m, side hulls 34.2m
Beam, overall	22.5m (main hull 8.0m, side hulls 1m)
Depth	9.0m
Design draught	3.37m
Displacement	1200 tons (design)
Maximum speed	20kts
Range	3000nm (20 days)
Crew	12 (plus up to 12 trials staff)

The main hull is of round bilge form with gently rising buttocks to a small transom stern. The side hulls are multichine outboard with a plane inboard face for ease of construction. The structure may be seen as simplified warship style with fairly thin steel plating and longitudinal framing, though it is not designed to warship shock standards. It complies with Det Norske Veritas's High Speed and Light Craft rules. There are nine watertight bulkheads to satisfy damage stability requirements and contribute to transverse strength in way of the cross deck. Since the wetted surface area of a trimaran is greater than that of a monohull, it is important to reduce fouling as much as possible. She has been coated with Hempel's SP-EED biocide free, silicone-based anti-fouling paint with a very low friction, non-stick surface. It is hoped that this paint will have a life of 15-20 years.

There is a flight deck that can accept a Lynx helicopter, and up to eight containers can be carried with trials equipment. There is a work boat with crane to starboard of the superstructure. *Triton* is a diesel-electric ship with two Paxman generators giving 2085kW. The main shaft is driven by a 3.5MW motor with a single fixed pitch propeller and the fixed side hull thrusters are of 350kW, each which give a speed of 12kts. The cabins are single or twin pre-fitted modules complete with a 'wet' (toilet) space. Variations in geometry, such as with two side hulls, one behind the other, on either side, have been tested.

It is understood that Phase I trials have been completed very satisfactorily. These have confirmed her performance, handling and general operation. In particular, seakeeping will be studied in increasingly severe sea states, which will include monitoring of the stresses in the hull. These trials are being run in partnership with the US Navy Sea Systems command, who provided the Trials Instrumentation System (TIS) – it has been said that this cost more than the ship! She will also carry out trials with an unmanned air vehicle.

Early in 2002 the main electric motor will be changed to a permanent magnet machine leading into Phase 2 trials up to March 2004. Details are not finalised but will probably include integrated technology masts, 8MW and 1.25MW gas turbines, composite shafts and electric rudders. In later years she will be used for trials by MoD and may be chartered by others concerned. In 2003 she was fitted with a propeller made of carbon-reinforced plastic.

In the author's personal view, all design is a compromise and if one aspect is enhanced, there is usually a price to pay elsewhere. However, in the development of the trimaran it seemed that virtually everything improved at the cost of a small increase in structural weight and complexity.

Appendices

Appendix 1

Purchasing power of the pound 1945–1985.

Date		Date	
1945	15.47	1966	7.62
1946		1967	7.36
1947	15.32	1968	7.18
1948	14.82	1969	6.78
1949	14.17	1970	6.47
1950	13.70	1971	5.99
1951	13.19	1972	5.55
1952	11.70	1973	5.17
1953	11.22	1974	4.65
1954	11.08	1975	3.95
1955	10.65	1976	3.23
1956	10.13	1977	2.81
1957	9.73	1978	2.58
1958	9.39	1979	2.38
1959	9.21	1980	2.06
1960	9.24	1981	1.85
1961	9.06	1982	1.68
1962	8.67	1983	1.61
1963	8.45	1984	1.55
1964	8.29	1985	1.49
1965	7.94		

Appendix 2

Reynold's Number

The behaviour of the flow over a body moving through a viscous liquid such as water is governed by the 'Reynold's Number' defined as:

Length x Velocity/ (Kinematic Viscosity of the liquid)
Reynold's Number governs the viscous resistance which, per unit area, is highest at low Reynold's Number and hence small changes of Reynold's Number have the greatest effect at low Reynold's Number. At very low values of Reynold's Number the flow is 'laminar' – very smooth. Laminar flow is unlikely to occur to any great extent on a ship but may occur on a model, making it difficult to scale the result to full size. At higher values the flow is 'turbulent', full of eddies.

In scaling viscous resistance from model to ship it is usually sufficient to use an overall value of Reynold's Number based on ship length. However, in the case of a submerged submarine the resistances of the appendages – bridge fin, rudder, hydroplanes, flooding holes etc – form a major part of the overall resistance. Strictly, each should be scaled independently using its own value of Reynold's Number based on chord length or as appropriate. This approach was lengthy and difficult with the methods available until about the 1960s. It was probably first applied as *Dreadnought* was completing, when there were several 'rival' estimates of her speed.

Reynold's Number also governs the scaling of viscous flow over a propeller, and hence cavitation effects, where it is even more difficult to define the appropriate length. Early studies used diameter, but this gave misleading results. Clearly something related to chord length was needed but which chord? For quite sound reasons the chord at 0.7 radius was regarded as typical though the author in some fairly successful approximations used a mean value, dividing the area of the face of the blade by the radius of the propeller. The next problem with a propeller is the choice of the appropriate velocity over a blade that is rotating as well as moving forward. It is possible to combine rotational velocity with forward motion but the former varies with radius. Again the magical 0.7 radius seems to work as a mean.[1] The problem is still not over, as the action of the propeller increases the speed of the water ahead of it and, strictly, this effect should be included. It was and, in the author's opinion, still is too difficult and any errors are reduced by an appropriate 'fudge factor'.

Reynold's Number is a convenient shorthand telling fellow engineers that viscous effects predominate and scaling from model to ship needs care and experience.

[1] For most propellers, half the total water flow through the propeller disk takes place outside 0.7 radius.

Appendix 3

[2] J L Hannah, 'Merchant Vessel Conversions: The Falklands Campaign', *Trans RINA* (1985). John Hannah ran the Bath Support Group – callers were surprised when told his home phone number was Faulkland xyz. (Faulklands is a small village, just outside Bath, NOT the islands.)

[3] *The Task Force Portfolio*, 2 vols, Liskeard (anon 1981).

[4] Dr David Chalmers RCNC, who has been most helpful in the writing of several sections of this book, designed ten decks and received the OBE for his work.

Merchant Vessel Conversions:
The Falklands Campaign 1982[2]

Contingency plans had been made and, when activated following the Argentine attack, worked well. A Naval Staff Advisory Group in Whitehall was in direct contact with the Commanders-in-Chief, while a Bath Support Group brought together the technical departments – Ship Department, Weapons, Stores, Dockyards, etc. There was plenty to do: the Falklands were 8000 miles away and many ships were needed to support a fleet so far from home. Ships Taken Up From Trade (STUFT) comprised 5 troopships, 3 troopship support, 1 hospital ship, 4 aircraft ferries, 2 repair ships, 1 MCMV mother ship, 5 trawler minesweepers, 24 tankers, 5 cargo, 3 solid stores, 3 ammunition, 2 despatch ships and 4 tugs.[3]

Twenty-five flight decks[4] and nine VERTREP decks were fitted and most vessels needed communications and water plant. They transported 8000 men, 18 Harriers, 12 Chinooks, 32 Wessex, 13 Sea King, 216 Land Rovers, 110,000 tons of freight and 400,000 tons fuel, and carried out 1200 RAS operations – and much more. By far the greater part of the work was done in the Royal Dockyards (ironically, many of those working at Portsmouth had already received their redundancy notices). The majority of the vessels were in hand for less than a week, none more than 2 weeks; the work was often preceded by 2 to 3 days of preparation. It was common for a constructor to join a ship at its last port before arriving in the UK and chalk out the flight deck arrangements *en route* in the light of the steel available at the conversion yard.

One of the first – and biggest – conversions was that of *Canberra* to a troopship with two flight decks. It was decided to requisition her on Saturday 3 April 1982 and by Monday Vosper Ship Repairers had completed the drawings, approved by the PNO (Stephen Hunter) and the steel was ordered. Work started in advance of the ship's arrival on Wednesday, 7 April and during the next 2½ days two flight decks were installed and communications and

RAS arrangements fitted. Vosper put in 500 man-weeks of work, but a few men sailed with her to complete the work. The two flight decks weighed 150 tons and were high in the ship, adding to top weight, but partially offset by the removal of 95 tons of water from the swimming pool – it proved a good rule of thumb that the weight of a flight deck was equal to that of water in a pool. With 2200 troops on board, *Canberra*'s displacement had increased from 40,500 to 43,000 tons.

The flight decks of the early ships were designed without much regard to weight and were very heavy. That of the *Norland* was designed to save weight, but the extra labour involved was surprising and the remaining decks were designed for easy construction.

John Hannah has listed (see footnote 2) seven main problem areas which affected most conversions and these will be considered in turn.

Endurance. Many of the STUFT were cross-channel ships of limited endurance. Most had to be fitted to RAS and, as the normal refuelling point was low down, piping had to be installed up to the RAS connection. Tankers were vital, supplying up to 180,000 tons per month, resulting in a supply chain holding 400,000 tons. Pre-war plans existed for the conversion of BP 'River' class tankers to supply over the stern. The optimistic estimate for conversion was one day – during the war it was actually completed in 4 hours. Where possible, ballast tanks were converted to fuel stowage.

Fresh water was an even greater problem: a merchant seaman expects about 50 gallons per day; an RN sailor makes do on 25 gallons. Aircraft are even more demanding, since if stowed on deck they must be washed frequently in fresh water to remove salt deposits that would attack their alloy structure. It was decided to fit reverse osmosis plants, as they were easy to install and operate and made less demand on support services. However, there were only two UK firms making these plants, and they were not held in stock. Manufacture took 5 days and nights and installation 2 to 3 days – very often final installation and trials was on passage, with the company's engineers retrieved from Gibraltar or Ascension.

Habitability. Liners such as *Canberra*, with peacetime passenger accommodation for 1750, had to carry 2200 troops. Camp beds made up the difference, whilst bathrooms and feeding arrangements were sufficient. Container ships, used as aircraft transports, were more difficult. Their peacetime complement of about 40 was augmented by 150. Containers and Portacabins had to be installed as accommodation.

Stability. Warships are designed to float with no more than moderate heel with three or four main compartments flooded and still withstand moderate weather. Merchant ships were designed to very much lower damage standards, set by international agreement through IMO:

St Helena with her Falklands War helicopter deck lined by the crew as the ship left Portsmouth in June 1982. (*Mike Lennon*)

cargo ships would generally sink if any main compartment abaft the fore peak was flooded; passenger liners were intended to float with two main compartments flooded, though with a freeboard of only 3in.[5] There was also a concession that some ships on short sea routes might only need a one-compartment standard, a concession that the author considers was granted too easily, particularly for ro-ro ships – remember *Herald of Free Enterprise.*[6] The UK Department of Transport was rigorous in enforcing these rules, but some foreign-flagged ships had to be rejected as failing even these modest standards. Weight growth since completion and top weight added for the war made these problems even worse.

Everything possible was done to improve matters. One ship had two extra bulkheads fitted,[7] some had solid ballast added, while limitations on the use of fuel were imposed on most. Care was taken to select the best ships (what were the others like?). Hannah concludes: 'the use, of merchant vessels in an emergency, especially for the carriage of troops or vital equipment, is *potentially very hazardous*' (Hannah's italics).[8]

Firefighting. Merchant ship firefighting rules were strict and, in general, additional firefighting arrangements were needed only to cope with the carriage of petrol and ammunition. The loss of *Atlantic Conveyor* shows the dangers inherent in the carriage of flammable materials.

Aviation arrangements. A flight deck for a Sea King is 15m x 10m, with an area clear of obstructions two to three times that size, and weighs about 70 tons. The deck of a ro-ro ferry is usually strong enough and the only work is clearing obstructions such as bulwarks. Liners often had light aluminium superstructures, not strong enough to support such a deck. Poor *Queen Elizabeth II* had to have much of her superstructure removed.

On big container ships, such as *Astronomer*, it was possible to arrange makeshift aircraft shelters from containers. There were many details needed for aircraft operation – lights, holding down clamps, firefighting, non-skid paint, battery charging, etc – all of which was time-consuming to fit. After the war, *Astronomer* was purchased as RFA *Reliant* and given the USN 'Arapaho' containerised helicopter operating system. It was not a great success and the conclusion was that improvisation to suit individual ships was preferable.

Communications. A basic naval fit was needed. Usually, there was insufficient room in the wireless office and space had to be found nearby. A travelling team of MoD officers installed the gear and RFA radio officers were appointed to operate it.

Self Defence. Initially, weapons were not fitted but as the war developed, light anti-aircraft guns (old 20mm Oerlikons) were installed if possible. Barrels were scarce and some ships had mountings only, getting the barrels as they approached the war zone from ships going home.

Five trawlers were fitted out as minesweepers at Portland. During the war they were mainly employed as small transports, but at the end they cleared 20 mines.[9]

It was a shoestring operation but worked well thanks to the resources, men and stores, in the Royal Dockyards, now no longer there. Many people contributed, but it is proper to pay tribute to the late John Hannah, OBE, RCNC who masterminded the programme.

[5] These standards have been raised considerably for <u>new ships</u> in SOLAS 90. Cargo ships must float with one compartment flooded and both they and liners are to have greater reserve after flooding.

[6] As a student in the 1940s I was taught that this concession was exceptional and liners should be two-compartment standard. I was horrified to discover how conditions had deteriorated.

[7] The constructor in charge of this one rang me over Sunday lunch to say she was not safe to leave the estuary.

[8] As a result of these studies I was asked to join the Department of Transport committee drawing lessons from the *Herald of Free Enterprise* tragedy. This eventually led to some retrospective improvements in ro-ro ships, particularly after the *Scandinavian Star* and *Estonia* tragedies.

[9] They were known as the 'Ellas', as four had names ending in -ella (like *Northella*).

The oilfield support vessel *Stena Seaspread* in the Falklands where she served as a repair ship. An early Type 22 and an *Oberon* class submarine are alongside. (*D K Brown collection*)

Appendix 4

The Inclining Experiment

In principle, the inclining experiment is very simple, but in the real world few things are simple and almost everything can go wrong to give seriously misleading results. A weight (w) is moved across the deck through a distance (l) and the heel (θ) produced is measured. Then -

$$W.gm.\theta = w.l$$

Where W is the displacement and gm the metacentric height, both at the time of the experiment. Since the position of the metacentre can be calculated from the geometry of the ship, the position of the centre of gravity can be deduced.

The RN College notes had a series of 'Do's and Don'ts', all based on painful experience:

- Make sure the ship is afloat. Many shipyard basins were shallow and if the bottom was soft mud the ship could move but not to the correct extent.
- Ensure the ship is upright and close to the design trim.[10]
- Check the water density fore, aft and amidships. It was not uncommon on riverside berths to have salt water fore and aft and 'fresh' water from a sewer amidships.
- Measuring the draughts is difficult unless the water was dead calm. If the surface is moving more than about 6in, give up. Check amidships – if there are no draft marks, measure down from deck edge.

There would be four equal lots of ballast, two on either side. One lot would be moved across and the angle measured using a very long pendulum (actually, two as a check). Then the second lot would be moved and the new angle measured. If this was not twice the first, you had a problem. One and then the other would be moved back and then the other two lots were moved across. While this was going on, all people on board had to remain still in marked positions. In the bigger shipyards the ballast would be cast-iron blocks with their weight cut in to them, but in small yards there might just be four skips of scrap with their alleged weight chalked on the side.[11]

At this point, the displacement and metacentric height as inclined was known and the real problems began. One had to estimate the weights (and their position) on board which would come off before completion – workers, their toolboxes, temporary wiring, etc and the ballast. Then one estimated the weights to go on to complete – stores, fuel, crew and effects. Most errors probably lay in this part.

An inclining experiment was a very good experience for a young assistant, with a management task followed by scrambling round the ship learning where every thing went.[12] Then there was a lengthy calculation, which was prone to error. In the author's first job he had an inclining about every 2 weeks and it had to be complete and written up before the next one. Years later, when checking such experiments the author was assured that with the aid of a computer programme the work could not be carried out in less than 3 months![13]

Appendix 5

Comparisons

It is always difficult to compare one design with another, particularly when they use different codes of practice and have different roles. During 1987-8 British and US forward design groups produced frigate studies to the same requirements and these studies were made public.[14]

In the first phase both teams worked to the same armament (127mm gun, anti-ship missiles, CIWS and a helicopter). They both had a sustained speed of 27kts and an endurance of 5000 miles at 19kts. The UK ship came out at 4548 tons, the US at 5832 tons (full load). The major differences lay in protection, complement[15] and machinery. In order to study difference in 'ship' design, the US vessel was redesigned to UK standards in these three aspects.

The revised ships compare:

	US	UK
Length (m)	133	125
Dspt Full (tons)	5578	4548
Internal Vol (m³)	18,672	18,740 inc. superstructure

One of the bigger differences was in structure. The US came out at 1174 tons and the UK 926 tons, a difference of 247 tons.[16] Some of this was due to the US concept of 'vital spaces' thought so important that they should be able to operate even if the rest of the zone (see Chapter 13) is disabled. The UK view is that major damage in a zone would inevitably disable the vital space. The US ship has a much larger double bottom.

USN rules on damaged stability are much more explicit regarding the treatment of heel and trim, though the author believes this difference is reduced in interpretation. USN rules would forbid the low quarterdeck adopted in many RN ships (good!). The medium-speed diesel generators used in the USN are 141 tons heavier than the high speed units used in the UK. There are many other differences, including the compound effect by which the bigger ship needs more fuel and attracts bigger margins and grows even more. Finally, this author noted that the Limeys are thirsty, requiring 6 tons of beer and 13 tons more fresh water.

The study's authors also attempt to estimate cost differences. Taking the UK ship built in UK as a base line 100, they suggest the same ship built in the USA would cost 108, while the US variant would cost 124 (the original US ship would cost 122 due to simpler machinery). It is a fascinating paper.

[10] My first inclining was of an 'Eddy' class tanker with considerable heel and heavy trim trim. There was no way to bring the ship to a design condition, but it was possible to calculate the actual position of the metacentre – a lengthy and tedious calculation but it made a foot difference in GM.

[11] It was usual to throw a bucket of whitewash over the scrap after weighing to prevent additions or removals.

[12] I still remember with pleasure visiting the bullion room of the Royal Yacht to estimate the weight of gold and silver on board!

[13] In the early years there was an almost religious feel to an inclining, and the answer (GM) was expected to be accurate to about 1/100ft, a ridiculous pseudo accuracy. Inclining the trials vessel *Decibel* in poor weather I reported the GM as 'about 32ft'. Luckily I had an understanding ADNC and after a tough examination he accepted my view that it did not matter if it was 33ft or even 31ft.

[14] L D Ferreiro (US) & M H Stonehouse (UK), 'A Comparative Study of US and UK Frigate Design', *Trans SNAME* Vol 99 (1991) and *Trans RINA* (1994). (Note only the RINA version has the discussion at both venues.)

[15] US 24 officers, 190 PO & CPO, 76 JR; RN 25 officers, 69 PO & CPO, 110 JR.

[16] Some discussers (including this author) thought that the figure given was not typical of US practice. See p29 of ref 1, RINA.

Appendix 6

The Future Aircraft Carrier

In 1997 the Ministry allowed two constructors to publish in outline some of the concept studies leading towards the design of future aircraft carriers for the RN.[16] Possible ship designs have to be considered in the light of the aircraft that will be carried, and it was envisaged that about 20 fixed-wing Harrier replacement aircraft and 10 ASW (probably helicopters) would be carried, though studies looked at both fewer and more aircraft. The most likely fixed-wing plane was the US Joint Strike Fighter (JSF), a programme, to which the UK made a significant contribution. V/STOL JSF are about twice the weight of a Harrier and more demanding in fuel and weapon arrangements. Alternatives considered included a conventional take-off (catapult) and landing (CTOL) aircraft such as the F-18 or a navalised Eurofighter Typhoon, and short take-off but arrested recovery (STOBAR). The helicopters were assumed to be Merlins, though Chinooks could be accepted.

It soon became clear that the prime mover should be the WR-21 gas turbine, and studies quickly showed that these should drive through electric generators, convert-ers, and rectifiers to propulsion motors. Four such engines would give a speed of about 30kts. Initial studies were based on conventional equipments, but developments, sponsored by MoD, in permanent magnet motors have shown great promise, as have parallel work on rectifiers. This combination offers the possibility of turbines and generators in the island, eliminating uptakes and down-takes passing through – and obstructing – the hangar. The main generators will also power ship's services, a scheme known as Integrated Full Electric Propulsion (1997 studies).

One option considered was to give the *Invincible*s a major update (SLEP), but the risk of running a ship for 60 years did not seem worthwhile. A container ship could be converted, but the capability would be poor compared with a new build and the cost saving would not be great.

Options to be considered were:

Type	Number of aircraft
STOVL	15, 20, 26, 40
CTOL	26, 40
STOBAR	26
SLEP	20
STUFT	20

[16] J F P Eddison and J P Groom, 'Innovation in the CV(F) – an aircraft carrier for the 21st century', *Warship 97*, RINA 1997.

The BAE Systems study for the future carrier CV(F). The Ministry of Defence eventually awarded the development contract jointly to BAE and the competing consortium led by Thales. (*BAE Systems*)

Funds would be enough for three small ships or two of the larger variant. Design study contracts were placed for a ship of about 40,000 tons. It is hoped that *Ocean* will fill the gap when one carrier is under refit.

These studies incorporate a very large number of innovations that would normally be seen as risky, but most have been proven on full-scale test rigs.

WR-21 Turbines
Integrated Full Electric propulsion
Structural radar-absorbent material
The JSF
Combat system
Complement reduction
Vulnerability and signature reduction
CTOL catapult and arrester gear

It is hoped to order the first ship in 2004 to complete about six years later.

Some representative studies:

Ship style	Invincible	STOVL	CTOL	LPH
Fixed wing	6 Harrier	16 JSF	20 F-18	12 JSF
Helicopter	9 Sea King	4 Merlin	3 S3A, 3 Merlin	4 Merlin
Displacement	21,581 tons	26,212 tons	38,794 tons	21,653 tons

In November 1999 two consortia[17] were awarded £30 million contracts for six studies – large (40 aircraft) and small (30 aircraft) versions of STOVL, STOBAR and CTOL designs. Delay in a decision on the final phase of the Joint Strike Fighter led to these contracts running on into the risk-reduction phase. A key date is in late 2003 when the style of the CV(F) must be decided in order to meet in service dates of 2012 and 2015. The decision will be affected by the choice of AEW aircraft, and the conventional E-2C Tracker has not been ruled out.

As this book is being prepared for publication, the Ministry has revealed the results of the 'competition'. The Thales design (sub-contracted to BMT Defence Services, Bath) was preferred but BAE Systems will be given overall responsibility for the programme as prime contractor with Thales as partner – and the Ministry accepting 10 per cent of the risk.

The ships will displace about 60,000 tons and carry up to 48 aircraft, mainly the Lockheed Martin F-35 Future Joint Combat Aircraft (formerly the Joint Strike Fighter). They will have two widely-separated islands on the starboard side and podded propulsors.

It is hoped to place a £2.8 billion order for detailed design, build and initial support in early 2004 for completion in 2012 and 2015 – I hope I live to see them! Sections will be built by BAE Systems (Clyde), Vosper-Thornycroft (Portsmouth), Swan Hunter (Tyne) and Babcock (Rosyth). It is expected that assembly will be at Rosyth.

[17] Thales – Lockheed Martin, Raytheon, and BMT; CVF – BAE Systems, Rolls Royce, and Harland & Wolff.

Bibliography

Basic particulars
Robert Gardiner (ed), *Conway's All the World's Fighting Ships 1947-1995* (London 1995).

The Early Years
Norman Friedman, *The Post War Naval Revolution* (London 1986).

Naval Policy
Eric Grove, *Vanguard to Trident* (London 1987)
Desmond Wettern, *The Decline of British Sea Power* (London 1982)

The Cold War
Norman Friedman, *The Fifty Year War* (London 2000)
David Miller, *The Cold War* (London 1998)

Weapons
Norman Friedman, *World Naval Weapon Systems* (Annapolis 1991). (1991/1992 edition mainly used)

Aviation
Norman Friedman, *British Carrier Aviation* (London 1988)

Previous history
David K Brown, *Nelson to Vanguard. Warship Development 1923-1945* (London 2000)
David K Brown, *A Century of Naval Construction* (London 1983)
George Moore, *Building for Victory* (Gravesend 2003). For warship building programmes for the Royal Navy 1939-45.

Papers etc
Transactions of the Royal Institution of Naval Architects, as referenced

Glossary and Abbreviations

Initials etc used only once are explained on the page
and will not usually appear in the Glossary.

£M	Million pounds sterling
AA	Anti-Aircraft
AD	Aircraft Direction
ADAWS	Action Data Automation Weapon System
AEA	Atomic Energy Authority
AEL	Admiralty Engineering Laboratory (West Drayton)
AEW	Admiralty Experiment Works (Haslar)
AIO	Action Information Organisation
ALSL	Auxiliary Landing Ship Logistic
AML	Admiralty Materials Laboratory (Holton Heath)
AOR	Replenishment ship (ammunition, dry stores, oil)
ARL	Admiralty Research Laboratory (Teddington)
ASDIC	Submarine detection equipment (later Sonar)
ASNE	American Society of Naval Engineers
ASR I	Admiralty Standard Range (diesel) 1
ASW, A/S, AS	Anti-Submarine Warfare, Anti-Submarine
ASWE	Admiralty Surface Weapons Establishment (Portsdown)
AUWE	Admiralty Underwater Weapons Establishment (Portland)
AVCAT	Aviation fuel (jet)
AVGAS	Aviation fuel (petrol)
B	Beam
BAE	British Aerospace, later BAE SYSTEMS (Marine)
BIBS	Built In Breathing System (submarine escape)
Bidder	A/S torpedo Mark 30
Blue Slug	Surface-to-surface version of Sea Slug
BS	British Standard
CASD	Computer Aided Ship Design (see GODDESS, CONDES)
CCH	Command Cruiser
CDL	Central Dockyard Laboratory (Portsmouth)
CF299	Sea Dart surface-to-air missile
CFD	Computational Fluid Dynamics
CL	Light Cruiser (guns 6in or less)
C_M	Midships Section Coefficient (Mid Sec Area/BxT)
CMS	Coastal Mine Sweeper
CO_2	Carbon Dioxide
COGOG	Combined Gas or Gas (machinery)
CONDES	Concept Design CASD system
COSAG	Combined Steam and Gas (machinery)
CP	Controllable Pitch (propellers)
C_P	Prismatic Coefficient (Immersed Volume/Lx Mid Sec Area)
CRBF	Close Range Blind Fire (director)
CVA	Fleet Aircraft Carrier (Attack)
CVS	Small Aircraft Carrier
C_W	Waterplane Area Coefficient (Waterplane Area/LxB)
DN Plans	Director Naval Plans
DA	Probably development of six-barrel Bofors
DCNS	Deputy Chief of Naval Staff
DEE	Director of Electrical Engineering
DERA	Defence Evaluation and Research Agency
DEPC	Defence Equipment Procurement Committee
DGS, Ship Dept	Director General Ships, Head of Ship Department,. Foxhill, Bath
DGW	Director General Weapons, Ensleigh, Bath
DH.110	Sea Vixen all-weather fighter
DNC	Director of Naval Construction
Dounreay	Nuclear Test Establishment, Scotland (HMS *Vulcan*)
DP	Dual Purpose (AA/surface weapon)
DPT	Originally Dreadnought Project Team (or its Director), later Director Polaris Technical
DSMP	Director Submarine Projects
DTSD	Director Tactical and Staff Duties (issues Staff Targets and Requirements)
EC	Escort Cruiser
EDATS	Extra Deep Armed Towed Sweep
E-in-C	Engineer-in-Chief
ELSA	Emergency Life Support Apparatus
EPC	Equipment Procurement Committee
EW	Electronic Warfare
FAA	Fleet Air Arm
FADE	Fleet Aircraft Direction Escort
FFWP	Future Fleet Working Party. To reconsider the shape of the fleet after cancellation of CVA-01
FPB	Fast Patrol Boat
FPS	Fly Plane System; fire control system (valves)
FRC	Fleet Requirements Committee
FSA	A/S Frigate, First Rate
FSB	A/S Frigate, Second Rate
FSU	Forward Support Unit (containerised support for MCMV)
GODDESS	Government Defence Design System for Ships, CASD
GRP	Glass Reinforced Plastic. (Fibreglass is a trade name and should not be used)

GW	Guided weapon	Match	A/S system in which a small helicopter drops a torpedo on target set by ship's sonar
GZ	Righting Lever (of stability)		
HA	High Angle		
Haslar	Site of Admiralty ship tanks, AEW	MCDP	Medium Calibre Dual Purpose (gun)
HDML	Harbour Defence Motor Launch	MCM(H)	Mine Counter Measure (hovercraft)
HDWS	High Definition Warning Surface (radar)	MCMV	Mine Counter Measure Vessel
		MEO	Marine Engineer Officer
HILO	High-Low, mix of first and second rate ships	Mexiflote	Powered raft - ship to shore for landings
HTP	High Test Peroxide (H$_2$O$_2$)	MoD	Ministry of Defence
HULVUL	Hull Vulnerability Trials using *Naiad*.	Mopsy	Short-range missile
'Hunt'	Second World War escort destroyer; later an MCMV class	MTB	Motor Torpedo Boat
		N.113	Scimitar fighter aircraft
HY80, HY100	High Yield steel (US): 80,000 or 100,000 lbs/in^2 yield strength	N.139	Unknown (AEW?)
		NA.39	Buccaneer strike aircraft
ICCP	Impressed Current Cathodic Protection; an electrical means of preventing corrosion of the hull.	NAB	Nickel Aluminium Bronze
		NATO	North Atlantic Treaty Organisation
		NBCD	Nuclear, Biological, Chemical Defence
IEP	Information Exchange Project (between navies). *Also*:	NC	Non Cemented (armour)
		NCRE	Naval Construction Research Establishment
IEP	Integrated Electric Propulsion	NDB	Nuclear Depth Bomb
Ikara	Rocket-launched A/S torpedo developed in Australia	NMM	National Maritime Museum
		NPC	Naval Policy Committee
IMO	International Maritime Organisation (merchant ship safety rules)	NQ1	High Tensile Steel
		NST, NSR	Naval Staff Target, Naval Staff Requirement
IMS	Inshore Mine Sweeper		
INA	Institution of Naval Architects (Royal from 1960)	OMEC	One Man Escape Chamber
		OPV	Offshore Patrol Vessel
ISO	International Standards Organisation	OR	Operational Requirement
JNE	Journal of Naval Engineering	ORC	Operational Requirements Committee
JSF	Joint Strike Fighter	P.1127	Kestrel
Kestrel	Hawker P.1127, ancestor of Harrier	P.1154	Supersonic VSTOL fighter project
Komet	Soviet anti-ship missile	P.177	Saunders Roe rocket/jet fighter
KVA	Kilo Volt Amps (electric power)	PAAMS	Principal Anti-Aircraft Missile System
L	Length	PAP	A French remote-controlled mine disposal system
LA	Low Angle		
LCA	Landing Craft Assault	PNO	Principal Naval Overseer
LCAC	Landing Craft Air Cushion (hovercraft)	Polaris	Submarine-launched ballistic missile
		PRO	Public Record Office (Kew)
LCM	Landing Craft Mechanised	psi	Pounds per square inch (pressure, stress)
LCP	Landing Craft Personnel		
LCT	Landing Craft Tank	PTO	Professional and Technology Officer, 1-4 (corresponds to Chief, Senior, Leading Draughtsman and similar grades)
LCU	Landing Craft Utility		
LCVP	Landing Craft Vehicle and Personnel		
Limbo	Prototype of A/S mortar Mark X		
Link	Automated transfer of data between operations rooms of a group of ships. Link 11 is the definitive NATO equipment.	PVC	Poly Vinyl Chloride
		PWR1 & 2	Pressurised Water Reactors
		QR	Quintuple Revolving (torpedo tubes)
LPD	Landing Ship Dock (P stands for Personnel in USN, Platform in RN)	QT28, QT35	Quenched and Tempered Steel, 28 or 35 tons/in^2 yield
LPH	Landing Ship Helicopter (P as above)	RAE	Royal Aircraft Establishment (Farnborough)
LRS	Long Range System (fire control)		
LSD	Landing Ship Dock (originally Assault Ship)	RAS	Replenishment At Sea
		RCNC	Royal Corps of Naval Constructors
LSL	Landing Ship Logistic	REA	Radar Echoing Area
LST	Landing Ship Tank	RFA	Royal Fleet Auxiliary

RINA	Royal Institution of Naval Architects (From 1960)
RNES	Royal Naval Engineering Service (civilian electrical & mechanical engineers later merged with RCNC)
RNPL	RN Physiological Laboratory
RRA	Rolls Royce and Associates
Ruler	Anti-torpedo weapon
S.55	Helicopter that developed into the Wessex
SCC	Ship Characteristics Committee
SCOSE	Standing Committee On Submarine Escape
Sea Cat	Close-range AA missile
Sea Dart	Surface-to-air missile
Sea Slug	Surface-to-air missile
Sea Wolf	Close-range surface-to-air missile
shp	Shaft horse power
SLEP	Ship Life Extension Programme
SOLAS	Safety Of Life At Sea Convention setting out safety rules for merchant ships
Sonar	Submarine location sensor
Squid	A/S mortar
SRN	Saunders Roe hovercraft
SS(B)N	Ballistic Missile Nuclear Submarine
SSN	Nuclear Submarine
STAAG	Stabilised Tachymetric AA Gun (twin 40mm Bofors)
STD	Simple Tachymetric Director
STUFT	Ships Taken Up From Trade
SWATH	Small Waterplane Twin Hull
SWDCG	Ship and Weapon Design Co-ordination Group
T	Draught
Tartar	USN surface-to-air missile
TIR	Target Indication Radar
TNT	TriNitroToluene (high explosive)
TIU	Target Indication Unit (gunnery)
Trident	Submarine-launched ballistic missile
UMH	Utility Mine Hunter
USN	United States Navy
UTS	Ultimate Tensile Stress
UXW	High tensile steel
V-T	Vosper-Thornycroft shipbuiilders
VERTREP	Vertical Replenishment using helicopter
VSEL	Vickers Shipbuilders and Engineers Ltd
VSTOL	Vertical/Short Take Off and Landing
YARD	Yarrow-Admiralty Research Dept, for machinery (the initials are still used, but neither the Admiralty nor Yarrows are involved)

Index

C

D

E